GALLERY OF
Best
COVER LETTERS

SECOND EDITION

DAVID F. NOBLE

JIST Works
America's Career Publisher

Gallery of Best Cover Letters, *Second Edition*
A Collection of Quality Cover Letters by Professional Resume Writers

© 2004 by David F. Noble

Published by JIST Works, an imprint of JIST Publishing, Inc.
8902 Otis Avenue
Indianapolis, IN 46216-1033
Phone: 800-648-JIST   Fax: 800-JIST-FAX   E-mail: info@jist.com

Visit our Web site at **www.jist.com** for information on JIST, free job search tips, book chapters, and ordering instructions for our many products! For free information on 14,000 job titles, visit **www.careeroink.com**.

Other books by David F. Noble:

Gallery of Best Resumes
Gallery of Best Resumes for People Without a Four-Year Degree
Professional Resumes for Executives, Managers, and Other Administrators
Professional Resumes for Accounting, Tax, Finance, and Law

Quantity discounts are available for JIST books. Please call our Sales Department at 1-800-648-5478 for a free catalog and more information.

Acquisitions and Development Editor: Lori Cates Hand
Production Editor: Stephanie Koutek
Proofreaders: Jeanne Clark, Deb Kincaid
Interior Designer: Debbie Berman
Page Layout: Trudy Coler
Cover Designer: designLab, Seattle
Indexer: Virginia Noble

Printed in the United States of America.

08 07 06 05   9 8 7 6 5 4 3

Library of Congress Cataloging-in-Publication Data

Noble, David F. (David Franklin), 1935-

Gallery of best cover letters : a collection of quality cover letters by

professional resume writers / by David F. Noble.-- 2nd ed.

    p. cm.

Includes bibliographical references and index.

ISBN 1-56370-990-2 (softcover)

1. Cover letters. I. Title.

HF5383.N618 2004

650.14'2--dc22

2004000677

ISBN 1-56370-990-2

Contents

Why a Gallery of Best Cover Letters?

Why Cover Letters by Professional Resume Writers?

How This Book Is Organized

This useful "idea book" of best cover letters has three parts: Best Cover Letter Tips; a Gallery of 310 cover letters; and an Exhibit of 23 resumes, together with tips for improving resumes. These cover letters and resumes were written by 79 professional writers. With this book, you not only have a treasury of quality cover letters and resumes, but will also learn how to view them as superior models for your own cover letters and resumes.

Who This Book Is For

This book is for *job searchers* who are applying for new positions, *career changers* who are looking for professional roles with other employers, *job changers* who are proactively climbing the corporate ladder, *graduate students* who are applying for higher levels of employment, and *new university graduates* who are seeking entry-level positions. The book is also for experienced workers who are scaling down their work, military personnel who are returning to civilian life, and women who are returning to the workforce after raising children. Because of the wealth and variety of quality cover letters in this new Gallery, this book is for *any job searcher* who wants examples of top-quality documents to create an outstanding cover letter for himself or herself.

What This Book Can Do for You

This collection of professionally written cover letters shows you how to present yourself effectively through a cover letter to a prospective employer so that you can be more competitive as a job applicant.

Part 1: Best Cover Letter Tips

Best Cover Letter Tips at a Glance

A quality resume can make a great impression but can be ruined quickly by a poorly written cover letter. This section shows you how to eliminate common errors in cover letters. It amounts to a *crash writing course* that you won't find in any other job search book. After you read the following sections, you will be better able to write and polish any letters you create for your job search.

This Gallery has 34 categories of professional cover letters for a wide variety of occupations. Regardless of your career or occupation, you should check out all the letters throughout the Gallery for design tips, ways to express ideas, and impressive formats. At the bottom of each cover letter are comments that call your attention to noteworthy features or solutions to problems.

Part 3: Best Resume Tips

Best Resume Tips at a Glance

Dedication

In memory of my mother,
Christena Brightwell Noble,
the *letter writer*

Acknowledgments

This second edition of *Gallery of Best Cover Letters* was possible because of all the cover letter and resume submissions of the writers featured in this book. For their names, see the List of Contributors at the back of the book. When I compiled the first *Gallery* (*Gallery of Best Resumes,* JIST Works, Inc., 1994), I first became acquainted with professional resume writers only as names on a mailing list from the Professional Association of Résumé Writers, which I had joined. After the publication of that first *Gallery* and during the preparation of its sequels (*Gallery of Best Resumes for Two-Year Degree Graduates,* JIST, 1996; *Professional Resumes for Executives, Managers, and Other Administrators,* JIST, 1998; and *Professional Resumes for Tax and Accounting Occupations,* CCH Incorporated and JIST, 1999), I joined a second organization—the National Résumé Writers' Association (NRWA)—and met many of the writers at annual meetings of their respective organizations.

For the third edition of the *Gallery of Best Resumes,* this second edition of the *Gallery of Best Cover Letters,* and the upcoming third edition of the *Gallery of Best Resumes for People Without a Four-Year Degree* (all published by JIST in 2004), I rejoined the Professional Association of Résumé Writers & Career Coaches and the National Résumé Writers' Association and joined for the first time Career Masters Institute. During work on these new editions, I learned of a fourth organization, the Professional Résumé Writing and Research Association, and received submissions from members of this group as well. In these new editions I am happy to showcase the latest work of members of all four of these professional organizations.

Originally, this cover letter book was possible also because of Mike Farr and Bob Grilliot of JIST Works. When I wrote the *Gallery of Best Resumes,* a *Gallery of Best Cover Letters* was the first title I thought of next, but other titles intervened. Bob Grilliot was the one who expressed a market need for the first edition of this book on cover letters, and Mike Farr approved it. I am grateful to him again for showing interest in this second edition.

Many thanks to Lori Cates Hand for her guidance at JIST throughout the project. Special thanks are directed again to my wife, Ginny, who managed and performed at home all of the many tasks that were necessary to create yet another *Gallery.*

Introduction

Like the earlier *Gallery* books in this series, *Gallery of Best Cover Letters* is a collection of quality cover letters from professional resume writers, each with individual views about cover letter writing. Unlike many cover letter books whose selections "look the same," this book contains cover letters that look different because they are *real* cover letters prepared by different professionals for actual job searchers throughout the country. (Certain information in the cover letters and companion resumes has been fictionalized by the writers to protect, where necessary, each client's privacy.) Even when several cover letters from the same writer appear in the book, most of these letters are different because the writer has customized each letter according to the background information and career goals of the client for whom the related resume was prepared.

With one exception, all of the 310 cover letters in this second edition are new. This means that they are the latest examples of cover letters for contemporary job seekers. If you want to know what kinds of cover letters are helping job searchers find positions in today's job market under current economic conditions, this new edition will give you answers. A number of the captions at the bottom of each cover letter page indicate how a particular applicant was successful in focusing a job search, securing an interview, or eventually getting the targeted job. And unlike the first edition of this book, this second edition includes several text (.txt) versions of cover letters for online distribution.

Why a Gallery of Best Cover Letters?

One reason is that error-free cover letters are more difficult to write than most people imagine. When you put together a resume, you can work with just phrases, clauses, and lists. The common writing dangers are misspellings, errors with capital letters, wordy phrases, and faulty parallelism (for example, not having certain words in a series or list grammatically parallel). When you write a cover letter, however, you are somewhat obligated to write sentences that hang together in several paragraphs in a meaningful sequence. To write sentences and paragraphs is to enter a minefield of all of the potential errors and stylistic weaknesses that an individual with good communication skills can make. And many people who try to write a cover letter do make such errors—often unknowingly.

This *Gallery of Best Cover Letters* shows you, example by example, how to create cover letters that are free of errors and writing weaknesses that could ruin your chances for an interview. By studying the sentences and paragraphs in these letters, you can compare your writing with what you see and find new ways to express what you want to say to win that interview.

Another reason for having a *Gallery of Best Cover Letters* is that many of the cover letters in cover letter books on bookstore shelves are—there's no other way to say it truthfully—models of bad writing. Often they exhibit not just a stylistic weakness here and there, but grammatical errors that would sabotage your job search if you used those passages verbatim in your own cover letters. To browse through the letters in this book is to walk through a minefield free of mines.

Why Cover Letters by Professional Resume Writers?

Instead of assuming that "one cover letter style fits all," the writers featured in this book believe that a client's past experiences and next job target should determine the type, design, and content of each resume and its related cover letter. The writers interacted with clients to fashion resumes that seemed best for each client's situation at the time and to create one or more cover letters for the job(s) the clients were seeking.

This book features resumes from writers who share several important qualities: good listening skills, a sense of what details are appropriate for a particular resume and its cover letter, and flexibility in selecting and arranging the resume's sections and the cover letter's paragraphs. By "hearing between" a client's statements, the perceptive resume writer can detect what kind of job the client really wants. The writer then chooses the information that will best represent the client for the job being sought. Finally, the writer decides on the best arrangement of the information for that job. With this book, you can learn from these professional writers how to shape and improve your own job search documents. You can create such documents yourself, or, if you want, you can contact a professional writer who, for a fee, might create a custom resume and cover letter for you. See the Appendix, "List of Contributors," for contact information for the professional writers whose works are featured in this book.

Almost all of the writers of the cover letters in this *Gallery* are members of the Professional Association of Résumé Writers & Career Coaches (PARW/CC), the National Résumé Writers' Association (NRWA), Career Masters Institute, or the Professional Résumé Writing and Research Association. Many of the writers are certified. For example, those who have CPRW certification, for Certified Professional Résumé Writer (again, see the Appendix, "List of Contributors"), received this designation from PARW after they studied specified course materials and demonstrated proficiency in an examination. Those who have NCRW certification, for National Certified Résumé Writer, received this designation from NRWA after a different course of study and a different examination. A few contributors are not currently members of any organization but are past members of one or more professional organizations.

How This Book Is Organized

Part 1, "Best Cover Letter Tips," contains a discussion of some myths about cover letters, plus strategies for writing cover letters and tips for polishing them. Some of the advice offered here applies also to writing resumes.

Part 2 is the Gallery itself, containing 310 cover letters, which are grouped according to 34 occupational categories (for these, see the Table of Contents). Within each category, the cover letters are arranged alphabetically by occupational title. Note that the occupational title is that of the *target position* the applicant is seeking, not the applicant's current or recent title. In resumes, job titles have to do with the individual's present and past positions. Cover letters, however, are concerned with a target position. You should keep this fundamental difference in mind as you use this book. (If the target position is not stated clearly in a cover letter, the applicant's current or most recent job was used to determine the occupational category of that letter.)

Even though most of the cover letters were written with a target position in mind, you can learn much by reading any or all of them. That is, to get the most from this book about writing cover letters, you should look at all of the cover letters in this collection and not just at those related to your particular profession or position of interest. All of the cover letters form a hunting ground for ideas that may prove useful to you for developing your own cover letters.

In the *Gallery of Best Cover Letters*, you will notice a few letters displayed in .txt format. This format is appropriate for the electronic submission of letters or resumes, which many employers now encourage because of timeliness and expediency in processing. Any of the letters in this book can be prepared for electronic transfer. If you intend to apply online for positions, be sure you follow the submission guidelines posted by the employer. If they are not clearly explained, phone or e-mail the company to inquire. You don't want to be disqualified for a job that suits you well because you did not follow the steps for successful submission.

Part 3 presents some resume-writing strategies, design and layout tips, and resume-writing style tips for making resumes visually impressive. These tips contain references to resumes in an Exhibit of 23 resumes at the end of Part 3. These references are to resumes that illustrate a strategy or a tip, but the references are not exhaustive. If you browse through this Exhibit, you may see other resumes that exhibit the same strategy or tip.

Even though the Exhibit contains only 23 resumes, it offers a wide range of resumes with features you can use in creating and improving your own resumes. Notice the plural. An important premise of an active job search is that you will not have just one "perfect" resume for all potential employers, but different versions of your resume for different interviews. The Exhibit of resumes, like the Gallery of cover letters, is therefore not a showroom where you say, "I'll take that one." It is a valuable resource of design ideas, expressions, and organizational patterns that can help make your own resume a "best resume" for your next interview.

The Appendix is the "List of Contributors," which contains the names, addresses, phone numbers, and other information of 79 professional resume writers from Australia, Canada, and the United States who contributed cover letters and resumes for this book. The list is arranged alphabetically by country, state or province, and city. Although most of these resume writers work with local clients, many of the writers work with clients by phone, e-mail, and the World Wide Web.

You can use the Occupation Index to look up cover letters by the job being sought. This index, however, should not replace careful examination of all of the cover letters. Many cover letters for some other occupation may have features that are adaptable to your own occupation. Limiting your search to the Occupational Index may cause you to miss some valuable examples.

Who This Book Is For

Anyone who wants ideas for creating or improving a cover letter can benefit from this book. It is especially useful for active job seekers—those who understand the difference between active and passive job searching. A *passive* job seeker waits until jobs are advertised and then mails copies of the same resume, along with a standard cover letter, to a number of ads. An *active* job seeker believes that both the resume and the cover letter should be modified for a specific job target *after* having talked in person or by phone to a prospective interviewer *before* a job is announced. To schedule such an interview is to penetrate the "hidden job market." Active job seekers can find in the Exhibit's focused resumes a wealth of strategies for targeting a resume for a particular interview. The section "How to Use the Gallery" at the beginning of Part 2 shows you how to use the Gallery for improving your cover letters.

What This Book Can Do for You

Besides providing you with a treasury of quality cover letters and companion resumes whose features you can use in your own letters and resumes, this book can help transform your thinking about these job search documents. If you think that there is one "best" way to create a cover letter or resume, this book will help you learn how to design resumes and cover letters that are *best for you* as you try to get an interview with a particular person for a specific job.

1

P·A·R·T

Best
Cover Letter
Tips

Best Cover Letter Tips at a Glance

Best Cover Letter Tips

In an active job search, your cover letter and resume should complement one another. Both are tailored to a particular reader you have contacted or to a specific job target. To help you create the "best" cover letters for your resumes, this part of the book debunks some common myths about cover letters and presents tips for polishing the letters you write.

Myths About Cover Letters

1. **Resumes and cover letters are two separate documents that have little relation to each other.** Your resume and cover letter should work together in presenting you effectively to a prospective employer. The cover letter should draw attention to the most important information in the resume, the information you want the reader to be certain to see.

2. **The main purpose of the cover letter is to establish a friendly rapport with the reader.** Resumes show that you *can* do the work required. The main purpose of cover letters is to express that you *want* to do the work required. But it doesn't hurt to display enthusiasm in your resumes and refer to your abilities in your cover letters. The cover letter should demonstrate qualities and worker traits you want the prospective employee to see, such as good communication skills, motivation, clear thinking, good sense, thoughtfulness, interest in others, neatness, and so on.

3. **You can use the same cover letter for each reader of your resume.** Modify your cover letter for each reader so that it sounds fresh rather than canned. Chances are that in an active job search, you have already talked with the person who will interview you. Your cover letter should reflect that conversation and build on it.

4. **In a cover letter, you should mention any negative things about your life experience, work experience, health, or education in order to prepare the reader in advance of an interview.** This is not the purpose of the cover letter. You might bring up these topics in the first or second interview, but only after the interviewer has shown interest in you or offered you a job. Even then, if you feel that you must mention something negative about your past, present it in a positive way, perhaps by saying how that experience has strengthened your resolve to work hard at any new job.

5. **A resume is more important than its cover letter.** In a way, the cover letter can be more important. The cover letter is usually the first document a prospective employer sees. The first impression is often the most important one. If your cover letter has an embarrassing error in it, the chances are good that the reader may not bother to read your resume or may read it with less interest.

6. **An error in a cover letter is not important.** The cost of a cover letter might be as much as a third of a million dollars—even more—if you figure the amount of income and benefits you don't receive over, say, a 10-year period for a job you don't get because of the error that got you screened out.

7. **To make certain that your cover letter has no errors, all you need to do is proofread it or ask a friend to "proof" it.** Trying to proofread your own cover letter is risky, even if you are good at grammar and writing. Once a document is printed, it has an aura about it that may make it seem better written than it is. For this reason, you are likely to miss typos or other kinds of errors.

    Relying on someone else is risky, too. If your friend is not good at grammar and writing, that person may not see any mistakes, either. Try to find a proofreader, a professional editor, an English teacher, a professional writer, or an experienced secretary who can point out any errors you may have missed.

8. **After someone has proofread your letter, you can make a few changes to it and not have it looked at again.** More errors creep into a document this way than you would think possible. The reason is that such changes are often done hastily, and haste can waste an error-free document. If you make *any* change to a document, ask someone to proofread it a final time just to make sure that you haven't introduced an error during the last stage of composition.

9. **It doesn't take long to write a cover letter.** You should allow plenty of time to write and revise…and revise…a cover letter to get it just right for a particular reader. Most people think that writing is 90 percent of the task of creating a cover letter, and revision is 10 percent. It's really the other way around: writing is closer to 10 percent of the task, and revision is 90 percent. That is true if you really care about the cover letter and want it to work hard for you.

10. **It doesn't take long to print the cover letter.** To get the output of a printer looking just right, you may need to print the letter a number of times. Watch for extra spaces between words and sentences; unwanted spaces are usually easier to see in the printed letter than on-screen (if you are using word processing). Fix any problems with vertical alignment between the date at the top of the letter and the complimentary close (an expression such as "Sincerely yours") if the date and the closing are not flush with the left margin but are tabbed to the center or the right side of the page. Finally, be sure that you leave enough vertical space for your signature between the complimentary close and your typed name.

Tips for Writing Cover Letters

To write well, you need to know why you are writing, the reader(s) to whom you are writing, what you want to say, how you want to organize what you say, and how you want to say it. Similarly, to write a good cover letter, you should know clearly its purpose, audience, content, organization, and style. The following tips, or strategies, should help you consider these aspects of cover letter writing. Consider using some of these strategies to ensure that your letters are impressive, even outstanding—and thus get the attention you deserve.

Purpose Strategies

1. **Make it clear in your letter that you really want the job.** See Cover Letters 15, 16, and 161. An employer doesn't want to know that you just want a job. An employer wants to know that you *really* want a particular job. If you display a ho-hum attitude in a letter, the chances are that you will receive a ho-hum response, which usually means rejection.

2. **Consider putting a subject line near the beginning of the letter to indicate the target position you are seeking.** See Cover Letters 5, 12, 44, 77, 90, 104, 106, 109, 112, 119, 121, 129, 139, 166, 168, 173, 178, 241, 242, 262, 267, 279, 296, 299, 300, 305, and 307.

Audience Strategies

3. **Make certain that the letter is addressed to a specific person and that you use this person's name in the salutation.** Avoid using such general salutations as Dear Sir or Madam, To Whom It May Concern, Dear Administrator, Dear Prospective Employer, or Dear Committee. (To ensure anonymity, however, some of the resume writers who have provided sample cover letters for this book have used general salutations. In the actual letters, these would be replaced with specific names.) In an active job search, you should do everything possible to send your cover letter and resume to a particular individual, preferably someone you've already talked with in person or by phone and with whom you have arranged an interview. If you have not been able to make a personal contact, at least do everything possible to find out the name of the person who will read your letter and resume. Then address the letter to that person.

4. **Don't let your opening statement or one in your first paragraph give the reader a chance to think "No" and read no further.**

   Example: "I am hoping that you are looking for a new auditor."

   The reader can think "I'm not" and stop reading.

   Example: "If you think your auditor should be as good at building team work as he is at building reports, we should talk." (See Cover Letter 21.)

   The reader can't disagree with this reasoning and will probably read further.

5. **Play down experience that may threaten a prospective employer.** A senior applicant with much experience may have more skills, expertise, and administrative savvy than the hiring employer. Should the employer feel threatened by this disparity, it may be better to tone down some skills and expertise than to display all of one's strengths without restraint.

6. **Target your cover letter by researching the prospective company and showing in the letter that you know important information about that company.** See Cover Letters 25, 36, 253, 278, and 298. Complimenting the employer in the first sentence is a nice touch in Cover Letter 56.

7. **For individuals leaving the military, avoid using military terms that may be unfamiliar to civilians.** Feel free, however, to play up military responsibilities and achievements that a potential employer will understand and appreciate. See Cover Letter 197.

8. **If you don't want your present employer to know about your job search, explain clearly the need for confidentiality.** See Cover Letters 205 and 239.

9. **Toward the end of the cover letter, consider repeating the recipient's name to convey friendliness and to provide a personal touch.** See Cover Letters 47, 52, 119, 169, and 222.

Content Strategies

10. **If you are replying to an ad without a person's name and have no way to learn it, consider omitting the salutation and varying the subject line.** See Cover Letters 6 and 167.

11. **When you are short on professional work experience to qualify for a position, consider related voluntary experiences or an internship that may help you qualify.** See Cover Letters 280 and 290.

12. **If you are responding to a job that has been posted on an online database, include the reference number, if one has been provided.** See Cover Letters 55 and 65.

13. **Numbers that quantify accomplishments in dollar amounts or percentages are impressive.** See Cover Letters 1, 72, 79, 134, 160, 178, 181, 192, 209, 226, 237, 240, 257, and 264. Numbers in the opening sentence can be especially eye-catching. See Cover Letter 137.

14. **If you speak two or more languages fluently, say so in your cover letter.** Being bilingual is an important asset in today's job market. See Cover Letters 29, 212, and 288.

15. **Be sure to mention how your real-world experience in an unrelated field has helped qualify you for the current job target.** See Cover Letters 41, 49, 272, 285, and 304. Likewise, if you are returning to a field, explain how your intervening job or additional education is relevant. See Cover Letters 150, 151, and 154.

16. **If you are responding to an ad placed in a newspaper, be sure to include the date of the ad.** See Cover Letters 93, 168, 214, 221, 263, and 302.

17. **If you have been downsized and don't want to mention it in your cover letter, consider including the information but "downsizing" its impact by focusing instead on your strengths, abilities, and experiences.** See Cover Letter 182.

18. **Speak positively about a return to the workplace from retirement.** See Cover Letter 175.

Resume Connections

19. **If the intended reader of your resume suggested that you send it, or if you have recently spoken with the person, say this in the first sentence of the cover letter.** Indicating that the resume was requested helps to get

your resume past any "gatekeeper"—the person who opens the mail and makes preliminary routing decisions—and into the hands of the appropriate reader. See Cover Letters 58, 117, 199, 207, and 266.

20. **Similarly, if a third party has suggested that you submit your resume to the reader, mention that at or near the beginning of your cover letter.** See Cover Letters 14, 37, 86, 110, 157, 185, 194, 208, 212, 231, 253, 269, 274, and 286. Even mentioning the third party in the middle or near the end of the letter may be beneficial. See Cover Letter 82.

21. **Put in your letter important information for which there is no room in the resume.** See Cover Letter 47, which describes the honor of being selected by National Geographic to participate in a summer institute. See also Cover Letter 110, which mentions the winning of a contest. In Cover Letter 157, a candidate for a position in criminal investigation links his survival skills to growing up in a tough neighborhood.

22. **Think of the cover letter as a hook for the resume.** A cover letter is not an end in itself but a means for getting the reader to read the resume. The letter might refer specifically to the most important part of the resume—the part that you want the reader to see for sure. See Cover Letter 24, which contains a boxed sentence referring to examples that are highlighted with borders in the resume. See also Cover Letter 102, which summarizes in a paragraph the candidate's experience with one company and thus echoes the corresponding information in the accompanying resume.

23. **Create a .txt or .pdf version of your cover letter and resume so that you can customize them as needed and e-mail them in response to online ads or post them to online job databases.** See Cover Letters 3, 26, 102, 259, 271, and 303.

Testimonials

24. **Consider using one or more testimonials in a cover letter.** A testimonial is a quotation from a former or current boss, a coworker, or someone else who knows the quality of your work or the strength of your character. Testimonials can be effective in setting your letter or resume apart from other "stock" submissions. If you use testimonials in your cover letters or resumes, be sure to get permission from the sources. See Cover Letters 1, 30, 82, 125, and 162. As a variation, Cover Letter 119 contains comments derived from a behavioral assessment the candidate completed.

Anecdotes

25. **If you have an impressive success story to tell about previous work experience, consider telling the story in your cover letter.** See Cover Letter 33. Similarly, Cover Letter 273 contains a humorous but fictitious story that illustrates the value of the candidate's expertise.

Follow-Up Plans

26. **At the end of the letter, consider keeping control of the follow-up by indicating that you will phone later.** See Cover Letters 11, 25, 27, 36, 76, 77, 94, 109, 112, 127, 138, 171, 181, 184, 191, 192, 213, 230, 233, 241, 264, 268, 274, 282, 286, 298, 300, and 301.

27. **If you think that calling the prospective employer seems pushy, you can soften the tone of the statement about calling by asking permission.** See, for example, Cover Letters 24, 63, 243, and 244.

Organization Strategies

28. **Consider presenting important information in two corresponding columns: the employer's needs (or requirements) and your qualifications.** See Cover Letters 38, 58, 80, 81, 130, 142, 169, 187, 212, 261, 262, and 287. Resume 270 encloses this information to create an attractive chart.

29. **Try a change in format for a change of pace.** See Cover Letters 90, 125, and 264.

Style Strategies

Tone

30. **Try not to sound desperate, even a little bit.** The following examples may seem extreme, but try to avoid using any similar statements in your letter:

    "I'll take anything you have to offer."

    "It makes no difference what kind of job you have."

    "I can start immediately."

    "I am available for employment right away."

    "When's the first paycheck?"

31. **It's okay to be enthusiastic in a cover letter.** See Cover Letters 22, 212, and 242.

32. **Consider beginning or ending the letter with a quotation that sets the tone and provides insight for understanding your work, character, attitude, outlook, or whatever else you want to convey.** See Cover Letters 7, 41, 51, 301, and 302.

Persuasiveness

33. **Consider making your cover letter not only informative but also persuasive.** See Cover Letters 17, 21, 46, 161, 196, 243, 244, and 256.

34. **Strive to make your cover letter hard to ignore.** Your task is easier, of course, if you are a great catch for any company. See Cover Letters 21, 100, 170, 177, 196, 227, and 243.

35. **To grab attention, try making your first sentence a bold assertion or question.** See Cover Letters 1, 17, 21, 33, 77, 100, 120, 243, and 254. Cover Letter 293 begins with an excerpt from the mission statement of the Boys & Girls Clubs of America.

Font and Text Enhancement

36. **Consider using a combination of bullets and boldfacing to call attention to information you think the reader must see.** See Cover Letters 15, 32, 57, 65, 67, 79, 82, 84, 86, 100, 125, 128, 144, 162, 173, 178, 210, 213, 228, 242, 250, 262, 265, 268, 274, 284, 301, and 305. It's hard to keep your eyes away from information that is bulleted and bold.

37. **For a change, consider putting key points in italic.** See Cover Letters 1, 73, 211, 234, and 237.

38. **Consider using decorative bullets that relate to the kind of job you are seeking.** See the airplane bullets in Cover Letter 22.

39. **To catch the reader's attention, consider inserting a graphic that relates to the job you are seeking or that echoes a graphic appearing in your resume.** See Cover Letter 89. To add a bit of humor, a cartoon character is used in Cover Letter 212. A whimsical cartoon is included at the bottom of Cover Letter 236.

40. **To help the reader see your area of expertise, put a banner at the top of your letter.** See Cover Letters 136, 137, 276, and 299. Cover Letter 196 contains a banner in a shaded, shadowed box. Think of other ways to make information visually stand out. A catchy statement at the beginning of Cover Letter 177 helps to ensure that this letter will be read. Cover Letter 217 begins with three words in boldface, and Cover Letter 256 offers an intriguing statement both centered and underscored. Cover Letter 232 uses a box and a second color (not shown) to explain what the candidate can do for the employer. Finally, a simulated classified ad is used in Cover Letter 180.

Language

41. **Try to make each paragraph fresh and free of well-worn expressions commonly found in cover letters.** See, for example, Cover Letters 46 and 170.

Tips for Polishing Cover Letters

You might spend several days working on your resume, getting it "just right" and free of errors. But if you send it with a cover letter that is written quickly and contains even one conspicuous error, all of your good effort may be wasted.

You can prevent this kind of tragedy by polishing your cover letter so that it is free of all errors. The following tips can help you avoid or eliminate common errors in cover letters. By becoming aware of these kinds of errors and knowing how to fix them, you can be more confident about the cover letters you send with your resumes.

Word-Processing Tips

1. **Adjust the margins for a short letter.** If your cover letter is 300 words or longer, use left, right, top, and bottom margins of one inch. If the letter is shorter, you should increase the width of the margins. How much to increase them is a matter of personal taste. One way to take care of the width of the top and bottom margins is to center a shorter letter vertically on the page. A maximum width for a short cover letter of 100 words or fewer might be two-inch left and right margins. As the number of words increases by 50 words, you might decrease the width of the left and right margins by two-tenths of an inch.

2. **If you write your letter with word-processing or desktop-publishing software, use left justification to ensure that the lines of text are readable and have fixed spacing between words.** The letter will have a "ragged" look along the right margin, but the words will be evenly spaced horizontally. Be wary of using full justification in an attempt to give a letter a printed look. You can make your letter look worse by giving it some extra-wide spaces between words. Resume writers who are experienced with certain typesetting procedures—such as "kerning," "tracking," and hyphenating words at the end of some lines—can sometimes use full justification effectively for variety in their documents. Note that if you use kerning and tight tracking to fit more words on a line, extra-narrow spaces can look unappealing as well.

Using Pronouns Correctly

3. **Use *I* and *My* sparingly.** When most of the sentences in a cover letter begin with *I* or *My*, the writer may appear self-absorbed, self-centered, or egotistical. If the reader is turned off by this kind of impression (even if it's false), you could be screened out as someone who is not a team player without ever having an interview. Of course, you will need to use these first-person pronouns some of the time because most of the information you put in your cover letter will be personal. As a compromise, try to avoid using *I* and *My* at the beginnings of most of the sentences and paragraphs.

    One strategy is to make some of your sentences "you-centered," where "you" means the reader. Sentences that begin with "You" or "Your" are friendlier than those that always begin with "I" and "My." Avoid referring to yourself in the third person, as in "this writer" or "this applicant." You avoid using "I," but the temperature of the letter drops considerably. Avoid also passive verbs (see upcoming Tip 8). They may help you avoid "I" at the beginning of a sentence, but the tempo of your letter slows down, and your language becomes indirect.

4. **Refer to a business, company, corporation, or organization as "it" rather than "they."** Members of the Board may be referred to as "they," but a company is a singular subject that requires a singular verb. Note this example:

New Products, Inc., was established in 1980. It grossed more than a million dollars in sales during its first year.

5.   **If you start a sentence with *This*, be sure that what *This* refers to is clear.** If the reference is not clear, insert some word or phrase to clarify what *This* means. Compare the following examples:

> My revised application for the new position will arrive by noon on Friday. *This* should be acceptable to you.
>
> My revised application for the new position will arrive by noon on Friday. *This revision* should be acceptable to you.

In the first example, a reader of the second sentence won't know what *This* refers to. Friday? Noon on Friday? The position? The revised application for the new position? The insertion of *revision* after *This* in the second sentence of the second example, however, tells the reader that *This* refers to the revised application.

6.   **Use *as follows* after a singular subject.** Literally, *as follows* means *as it follows,* so the phrase is illogical after a plural subject. Compare the following lines:

Incorrect:	My plans for the day of the interview are as follows:
Fixed:	My plans for the day of the interview are these:
Correct:	My plan for the day of the interview is as follows:
Better:	Here is my plan for the day of the interview:

In the second set, the improved version avoids a hidden reference problem—the possible association of the silent "it" with *interview.* Whenever you want to use *as follows,* check to see whether the subject that precedes *as follows* is plural. If it is, don't use this phrase.

Using Verb Forms Correctly

7.   **Make certain that subjects and verbs agree in number.** Plural subjects require plural forms of verbs. Singular subjects require singular verb forms. Most writers know these things, but problems arise when subject and verb agreement gets tricky. Compare the following lines:

Incorrect:	My education and experience has prepared me…
Correct:	My education and experience have prepared me…

Incorrect:	Making plans plus scheduling conferences were…
Correct:	Making plans plus scheduling conferences was…

In the first set, *education* and *experience* are two things (you can have one without the other) and require a plural verb. A hasty writer might lump them together and use a singular verb. When you reread what you have written, look out for this kind of improper agreement between a plural subject and a singular verb.

In the second set, *making plans* is the subject. It is singular, so the verb must be singular. The misleading part of this sentence is the phrase *plus scheduling conferences*. It may seem to make the subject plural, but it doesn't. Phrases that begin with such words as *plus, together with, in addition to, along with,* and *as well as* usually don't make a singular subject plural.

8. **Whenever possible, use active forms of verbs rather than passive forms.** Compare these lines:

Passive:	My report will be sent by my assistant tomorrow.
Active:	My assistant will send my report tomorrow.
Passive:	Your interest is appreciated.
Active:	I appreciate your interest.
Passive:	Your letter was received yesterday.
Active:	I received your letter yesterday.

Sentences with passive verbs are usually longer and clumsier than sentences with active verbs. They often leave out the crucial information of who is performing the action of the verb. Spot passive verbs by looking for some form of the verb *to be* (such as *be, will be, have been, is, was,* and *were*) used with another verb.

A tradeoff in using active verbs is the frequent introduction of the pronouns *I* and *My*. To solve one problem, you might create another (see Tip 3 in this list). The task then becomes one of finding an active verb to replace the passive verb, as in the following:

Active:	Your letter arrived yesterday.

9. **Be sure that present and past participles are grammatically parallel in a list.** See Tip 51 in Part 3. What is true about parallel forms in resumes is true also in cover letters. Present participles are action words that end in *-ing*, such as *creating, testing,* and *implementing.* Past participles are action words that usually end in *-ed*, such as *created, tested,* and *implemented.* These types of words are called *verbals* because they are derived from verbs but are not strong enough to function as verbs in a sentence. When you use a string of verbals, control them by keeping them parallel.

10. **Use split infinitives only when *not* splitting them is misleading or awkward.** An *infinitive* is a verb preceded by the preposition *to,* as in *to create, to test,* and *to implement.* You split an infinitive when you insert an adverb between the preposition and the verb, as in *to quickly create, to repeatedly test,* and *to slowly implement.* About 50 years ago, split infinitives were considered grammatical errors; these days, however, opinion about them has changed. Many grammar handbooks now recommend that you split your infinitives to avoid awkward or misleading sentences. Compare the following lines:

Split infinitive:	I plan to periodically send updated reports on my progress in school.
Misleading:	I plan periodically to send updated reports on my progress in school.
Misleading:	I plan to send periodically updated reports on my progress in school.

The first example is clear enough, but the second and third examples may be misleading. If you are uncomfortable with split infinitives, one solution is to move *periodically* further into the sentence:

I plan to send updated reports periodically on my progress in school.

Most handbooks that allow split infinitives also recommend that they not be split by more than one word, as in *to quickly and easily write.* A gold medal for splitting an infinitive should go to Lowell Schmalz, an Archie Bunker prototype in "The Man Who Knew Coolidge" by Sinclair Lewis. Schmalz, who thought that Coolidge was one of America's greatest presidents, split an infinitive this way: "*to instantly and without the least loss of time or effort find....*"[1]

Using Punctuation Correctly

11. **Punctuate a compound sentence with a comma.** A compound sentence is one that contains two main clauses joined by one of seven conjunctions (*and, but, or, nor, for, yet,* and *so*). A comma is customarily put before the conjunction if the sentence isn't unusually short. Here is an example of a compound sentence punctuated correctly:

I plan to arrive at O'Hare at 9:35 a.m. on Thursday, and my trip by cab to your office should take no longer than 40 minutes.

The comma is important because it signals that a new grammatical subject (*trip,* the subject of the second main clause) is about to be expressed. If you use this kind of comma consistently, the reader will rely on your punctuation and be on the lookout for the next subject in a compound sentence.

---

[1] Sinclair Lewis, "The Man Who Knew Coolidge," *The Man Who Knew Coolidge* (New York: Books for Libraries Press, 1956), p. 29.

12. **Be certain not to put a comma between compound verbs.** When a sentence has two verbs joined by the conjunction *and,* these verbs are called *compound verbs.* Usually, they should not be separated by a comma before the conjunction. Note the following examples:

> I *started* the letter last night *and finished* it this morning.
>
> I *am sending* my resume separately *and would like* you to keep the information confidential.

Both examples are simple sentences containing compound verbs. Therefore, no comma appears before *and.* In either case, a comma would send a wrong signal that a new subject in another main clause is coming, but no such subject exists.

Note: In a sentence with a series of three or more verbs, use commas between the verbs. The comma before the last verb is called the *serial comma.* The serial comma is optional; many writers of business documents and newspaper articles omit this comma. For more information on using the serial comma, see resume writing style Tip 66 in Part 3.

---

13. **Avoid using *as well as* for *and* in a series.** Compare the following lines:

Incorrect:	Your company is impressive because it has offices in Canada, Mexico, as well as the United States.
Correct:	Your company is impressive because it has offices in Canada and Mexico, as well as in the United States.

Usually, what is considered exceptional precedes *as well as,* and what is considered customary follows it. Note this example:

> Your company is impressive because its managerial openings are filled by women as well as men.

14. **Put a comma after the year when it appears after the month and day.** Similarly, put a comma after the state when it appears after the city. Compare the following pairs of lines:

Incorrect:	On January 1, 1998 I was promoted to senior analyst.
Correct:	On January 1, 1998, I was promoted to senior analyst.
Incorrect:	I worked in Chicago, Illinois before moving to Dallas.
Correct:	I worked in Chicago, Illinois, before moving to Dallas.

15. **Put a comma after an opening dependent clause.** Compare the following lines:

Incorrect:	If you have any questions you may contact me by phone or fax.
Correct:	If you have any questions, you may contact me by phone or fax.

Actually, many fiction and nonfiction writers don't use this kind of comma. The comma is useful, though, because it signals where the main clause begins. If you glance at the example with the comma, you can tell where the main clause is without even reading the opening clause. For a step up in clarity and readability, use this comma. It can give the reader a "feel" for a sentence even before he or she begins to read the words.

16. **Use semicolons when they are needed.** See resume writing style Tip 67 in Part 3 for the use of semicolons between items in a series. Semicolons are used also to separate main clauses when the second clause starts with a *conjunctive adverb* such as *however, moreover,* and *therefore.* Compare the following lines:

Incorrect:	Your position in sales looks interesting, however, I would like more information about it.
Correct:	Your position in sales looks interesting; however, I would like more information about it.

The first example is incorrect because the comma before *however* is a *comma splice,* which is a comma that joins two sentences. It's like putting a comma instead of a period at the end of the first sentence and then starting the second sentence. A comma may be a small punctuation mark, but a comma splice is a huge grammatical mistake. What are your chances for getting hired if your cover letter tells your reader that you don't recognize where a sentence ends, especially if a requirement for the job is good communication skills? Yes, you could be screened out because of one little comma!

Another use of the semicolon is to separate items of a series when an item has internal punctuation. Compare these sentences:

Incorrect:	The committee consisted of a manager, three salespersons, and Beverley, who was hired yesterday.
Correct:	The committee consisted of a manager; three salespersons; and Beverley, who was hired yesterday.

In the first sentence, commas separate the three items of the series, but visually the comma after Beverley can be confusing. Does it signify another series item to follow? In the revision, semicolons separating the series items make the items plain. There is no way to think that the comma after Beverley precedes another series item to follow.

17. **Avoid putting a colon after a verb or a preposition to introduce information.** The reason is that the colon interrupts a continuing clause. Compare the following lines:

Incorrect:	My interests in your company *are:* its reputation, the review of salary after six months, and your personal desire to hire handicapped persons.
Correct:	My interests in your company *are these:* its reputation, the review of salary after six months, and your personal desire to hire handicapped persons.
Incorrect:	In my interview with you, I would like *to:* learn how your company was started, get your reaction to my updated portfolio, and discuss your department's plans to move to a new building.
Correct:	In my interview with you, I would like to discuss *these issues:* how your company was started, what you think of my updated portfolio, and when your department may move to a new building.

Although some people may say that it is okay to put a colon after a verb such as *include* if the list of information is long, it is better to be consistent and avoid colons after verbs altogether.

18. **Understand colons clearly.** People often associate colons with semicolons because their names sound alike, but colons and semicolons have nothing to do with each other. Colons are the opposite of dashes. Dashes look backward (see resume writing style Tip 68 in Part 3), whereas colons usually look forward to information about to be delivered, as in the following sentence:

Three items are on the table: a book, a pen, and a lamp.

One common use of the colon does look backward, however. Here are two examples:

My experience with computers is limited: I have had only one course on programming, and I don't own a computer.

I must make a decision by Monday: That is the deadline for renewing the lease for my apartment.

In each example, what follows the colon explains what was said before the colon. Using a colon this way in a cover letter can impress a knowledgeable reader who is looking for evidence of writing skills.

19. **Use slashes correctly.** Information about slashes is sometimes hard to find because *slash* often is listed in grammar reference books under a different name, such as *virgule* or *solidus*. If you are not familiar with these terms, your hunt for advice on slashes may lead to nothing.

At least know that one important meaning of a slash is *or*. For this reason, you often see a slash in an expression such as *ON/OFF.* This usage means that a condition or state, like that of electricity activated by a switch, is either ON or OFF but never ON and OFF at the same time. As you see in resume writing style Tip 64 in Part 3, this condition may be one in which a change means going from the current state to the opposite (or alternate) state. If the current state is ON and there is a change, the next state will be OFF, and vice versa. With this understanding, you can recognize the logic behind the following examples:

Incorrect:	ON-OFF switch (on and off at the same time!)
Correct:	ON/OFF switch (on or off at any time)
Incorrect:	his-her clothes (unisex clothes, worn by both sexes)
Correct:	his/her clothes (each sex had different clothes)

20.   **Think twice about using *and/or*.** This stilted expression is commonly misunderstood to mean *two* alternatives, but it literally means *three*. Look at the following example:

> If you don't hear from me by Friday, please phone and/or fax me the information on Monday.

What is the person at the other end to do? The sentence really states three alternatives: just phone, just fax, or phone *and* fax the information by Monday. For better clarity, use the connectives *and* or *or* whenever possible.

21.   **Use punctuation correctly with quotation marks.** A common misconception is that commas and periods should be placed outside closing quotation marks, but the opposite is true. Compare the following lines:

Incorrect:	Your company certainly has the "leading edge", which means that its razor blades are the best on the market.
Correct:	Your company certainly has the "leading edge," which means that its razor blades are the best on the market.
Incorrect:	In the engineering department, my classmates referred to me as "the guru in pigtails". I was the youngest expert in programming languages on campus.
Correct:	In the engineering department, my classmates referred to me as "the guru in pigtails." I was the youngest expert in programming languages on campus.

Note this exception: Unlike commas and periods, colons and semicolons go *outside* double quotation marks.

Using Words Correctly

22. **Avoid using lofty language in your cover letter.** A real turn-off in a cover letter is the use of elevated diction (high-sounding words and phrases) as an attempt to seem important. Note the following examples, along with their straight-talk translations:

Elevated:	My background has afforded me experience in...
Better:	In my previous jobs, I...
Elevated:	Prior to that term of employment...
Better:	Before I worked at...
Elevated:	I am someone with a results-driven profit orientation.
Better:	I want to make your company more profitable.
Elevated:	I hope to utilize my qualifications...
Better:	I want to use my skills...

In letter writing, the shortest distance between the writer and the reader is the most direct idea.

23. **Check your sentences for an excessive use of compounds joined by *and*.** A cheap way to make your letters longer is repeatedly to join words with *and*. Note the following wordy sentence:

> Because of my background and preparation for work and advancement with your company and new enterprise, I have a concern and commitment to implement and put into effect my skills and abilities for new solutions and achievements above and beyond your dreams and expectations. [44 words]

Just one inflated sentence such as that would drive a reader to say, "No way!" The writer of the inflated sentence has said only this:

> Because of my background and skills, I can contribute to your new venture. [13 words]

If, during rereading, you eliminate the wordiness caused by this common writing weakness, an employer is more likely to read your letter completely.

24. **Avoid using abstract nouns excessively.** Look again at the inflated sentence in the preceding tip, but this time with the abstract nouns in italic:

> Because of my *background* and *preparation* for *work* and *advancement* with your company and new *enterprise*, I have a *concern* and *commitment* to implement and put into *effect* my skills and *abilities* for new *solutions* and *achievements* above and beyond your *dreams* and *expectations*.

Try picturing in your mind any of the words in italic. You can't because they are *abstract nouns,* which means that they are ideas and not images of things you can see, taste, hear, smell, or touch. One certain way to turn off the reader is to load your cover letter with abstract nouns. The following sentence, containing some images, has a better chance of capturing the reader's attention:

Having created seven multimedia tutorials with my videocamera and Gateway Pentium computer, I now want to create some breakthrough adult-learning packages so that your company, New Century Instructional Technologies, will exceed $50,000,000 in contracts by 2005.

Compare this sentence with the one loaded with abstract nouns. The one with images is obviously the better attention grabber.

25. **Avoid wordy expressions in your cover letters.** Note the following examples and the shorter alternatives that follow them in parentheses:

> at the location of (at)
> for the reason that (because)
> in a short time (soon)
> in a timely manner (on time)
> in spite of everything to the contrary (nevertheless)
> in the event of (if)
> in proximity to (near)
> now and then (occasionally)
> on a daily basis (daily)
> on a regular basis (regularly)
> on account of (because)
> one day from now (tomorrow)
> would you be so kind as to (please)

Trim the fat wherever you can, and your reader will appreciate your cover letter's leanness.

26. **At the end of your cover letter, don't make a statement that the reader can use to reject you.** For example, suppose that you close your letter with this statement:

> If you wish to discuss this matter further, please call me at (555) 555-5555.

This statement gives the reader a chance to think, "I don't wish it, so I don't have to call." Here is another example:

> If you know of the right opportunity for me, please call me at (555) 555-5555.

The reader may think, "I don't know of any such opportunity. How would I know what is right for you?" Avoid questions that prompt yes-or-no answers, such as, "Do you want to discuss this matter further?" If you ask this kind of question, you give the reader a chance to say no. Instead, make a closing statement that indicates your optimism about a positive response from the reader. Such a statement might begin with one of the following phrases:

> I am confident that...
> I look forward to...

In this way, you invite the reader to say yes to further considering your candidacy for the job.

2
P·A·R·T

The Gallery of Best Cover Letters

The Gallery
at a Glance

How to Use the Gallery

You can learn much from the Gallery just by browsing through it. To make the best use of this resource, however, read the following suggestions before you begin.

Look at the cover letters in the category that contains your field, related fields, or target occupation. Use the Occupation Index to help you find cover letters for certain fields. Notice what kinds of cover letters other people have used to find similar jobs. Always remember, though, that your cover letter should not be "canned." It should not look just like someone else's cover letter, but should reflect your own background, unique experiences, knowledge, areas of expertise, skills, motivation, and goals.

Use the Gallery primarily as an "idea book." Even if you don't find a cover letter for your specific position or job target, be sure to look at all the letters for ideas you can borrow or adapt. You may be able to find portions of a letter (the right word, a phrase, a strong sentence, maybe even a well-worded paragraph) that you can use in your own letter but modify with information that applies to your own situation or target field.

Compare some of the beginning paragraphs of the letters. Notice which ones capture your attention almost immediately. In your comparison, notice paragraph length, sentence length, clarity of thought, and the kinds of words that grab your attention. Are some statements better than others from your point of view? Do some paragraphs fit your situation better than others?

Compare some of the closing paragraphs of the letters. What trends do you notice? What differences? What endings are more effective than others? What are the different ways to say thank you? What are the best ways to ask for an interview? How are follow-up plans expressed? Which closing paragraphs seem to match your situation best? Continue to note differences in length, the kinds of words and phrases used, and the effectiveness of the content. Jot down any ideas that might be true for you.

If you find this kind of comparative study useful, compare the middle paragraphs across the letters of the Gallery. See how the person introduces herself or himself. Look for a paragraph that seems to be a short profile of an individual. Notice paragraphs devoted to experience, areas of expertise, qualifications, or skills. How does the person express motivation, enthusiasm, or interest in the target position? Which letters use bullets? Which letters seem more convincing than others? How are they more persuasive? Which letters have a better chance of securing an interview?

As you review the middle paragraphs, notice which words and phrases seem to be more convincing than other typical words or phrases. Look for words that you might use to put a certain "spin" on your own cover letter as you pitch it toward a particular interviewer or job target.

After comparing letters, examine the paragraphs of several letters to determine the design or arrangement of each one. For example, the first paragraph of a letter might indicate the individual's job goal, the second paragraph might say something about the person's background, the third paragraph might indicate qualifications, and the last paragraph might express interest in an interview. This letter would then have a Goal-Background-Qualifications-Interview design or pattern. If you review the letters in the Gallery this way, you will soon detect some common cover letter designs—the purpose of doing this is to discover which designs are more effective than others—all so that you can make your cover letter the most effective letter it can be.

By developing a sense of cover letter design, you will know better how to select and emphasize the most important information about yourself for the job you want to get.

Try comparing the cover letters also for their visual impact. Look for horizontal and vertical lines, borders, boxes, bullets, white space, and graphics. Which cover letters have more visual impact at first glance, and which ones make no initial impression? Do some of the letters seem more inviting to read than others? Which ones are less appealing because they have too much information, or too little? Which ones seem to have the right balance of information and white space? If visual impact is important, you will want to send a letter through the regular mail on fine paper or as an e-mail file attachment that can be read in Microsoft Word and printed from it without a loss of your letter's formatting. If sending a letter online quickly is more important than the letter's appearance, you may want to send your letter as a text (.txt) file with a minimum of formatting or copy and paste it directly into an e-mail message.

After comparing the visual design features, choose the design ideas that might improve your own cover letter. Be selective here and don't try to work every design possibility into your letter. Generally, "less is more" in cover letter writing, especially when you integrate design features with content.

The Gallery contains sample cover letters that were prepared by professional resume writers to accompany resumes. (Some representative resumes are included in Part 3 of this book.) In most cases, the names, addresses, and facts have been changed to ensure the confidentiality of the original sender and receiver of the letter. For each letter, however, the essential substance of the original remains intact.

Use the Gallery of cover letters as a reference whenever you need to write a cover letter for your resume. As you examine the Gallery, consider the following questions:

1. **Does the writer show a genuine interest in the reader?** One way to tell is to count the number of times the pronouns *you* and *your* appear in the letter. Then count the number of times the pronouns *I, me,* and *my* occur in the letter. Although this method is simplistic, it nevertheless helps you see where the writer's interests lie. When you write a cover letter, make your first paragraph *you*-centered rather than *I*-centered.

2. **Where does the cover letter mention the resume specifically?** The purpose of a cover letter is to call attention to the resume. If the letter fails to mention the resume, the letter has not fulfilled its purpose. Besides mentioning the resume, the cover letter might direct the reader's attention to one or more parts of the resume, increasing the chances that the reader will see the most important part(s). It is not a good idea, however, to put a lot of resume facts in the cover letter. Let each document do its own job. The job of the cover letter is to point to the resume.

3. **Where and how does the letter express interest in an interview?** The immediate purpose of a cover letter is to call attention to the resume, but the *ultimate* purpose of both the cover letter and the resume is to help you get an interview with the person who can hire you. If the letter doesn't display your interest in getting an interview, the letter has not fulfilled its ultimate purpose.

4. **How decisive is the person's language?** This question is closely related to the preceding question. Is interest in an interview expressed directly or indirectly? Does the person specifically request an interview on a date when the writer will be in the reader's vicinity, or does the person only hint at a desire to "meet" the reader some day? Some of the letters in this book are more proactive and assertive than others in asking for an interview. When you write your own cover letters, be sure to be direct and convincing in expressing your interest for an interview.

5. **How does the person display self-confidence?** As you look through the Gallery, notice the cover letters in which the phrase "I am confident that..." (or a similar expression) appears. Self-confidence is a sign of management ability and essential job-worthiness. Many of the letters display self-confidence or self-assertiveness in various ways.

6. **Does the letter indicate whether the person is a team player?** From an employer's point of view, an employee who is self-assertive but not a team player can spell T-R-O-U-B-L-E. As you look at the cover letters in the Gallery, notice how the letters mention the word *team.*

7. **How does the letter make the person stand out?** Do some letters present the person more vividly than other letters? If so, what does the trick? The middle paragraphs or the opening and closing paragraphs? The paragraphs or the bulleted lists? Use what you learn here to help you write effective cover letters.

8. **How familiar is the person with the reader?** In a passive job search, the reader will most likely be a total stranger. In an active job search, the chances are good that the writer will have had at least one conversation with the reader by phone or in person. In that case, the letter can refer to any previous communication.

After you have examined the cover letters in the Gallery, you will be better able to write an attention-getting letter—one that leads the reader to your resume and to scheduling an interview with you.

An important note about style and consistency: The 310 cover letters and 23 resumes in this book represent 79 unique styles of writing—the exact number of professional resume writers who contributed to this book. For this reason, you may notice a number of differences in capitalization. To showcase important details, many of the writers prefer to capitalize job titles and other key terms that usually appear in lowercase. Furthermore, the use of jargon may vary considerably—again, reflecting the choices of individual writers and thus making each letter and resume truly "one of a kind."

Variations in the use (or *non*use) of hyphens may be noticeable. With the proliferation of industry jargon, hyphens seem like moving targets, and "rules" of hyphenation vary considerably from one handbook to another. In computer-related fields, some terms are evolving faster than the species. Thanks to America Online, the term *on-line* is more often shown as *online,* but both forms are acceptable. And electronic mail comes in many varieties: *email, e-mail, Email, and E-Mail.* But the computer world is not the only one that has variety: both *healthcare* and *health care* appear in the cover letters and companion resumes in this book.

Although an attempt has been made to reduce some of the inconsistencies in capitalization and hyphenation, differences are still evident. Keep in mind that the consistent use of capitalization and hyphenation *within* a cover letter or resume is more important than adherence to any set of external conventions.

Note: To ensure the privacy of their clients, the professional resume writers whose work appears in this book have *fictionalized* the information about their clients. Omitting an address or salutation in a cover letter is another way of protecting a client's privacy. For this reason, some of the letters in this book include generic salutations such as "Dear Hiring Manager" or "Dear Sir/Madam." In an actual letter, such a salutation should be replaced with the name of an individual who works at the company to which you are applying.

Note: In some of the comments below the cover letters, the views of the resume writers themselves appear in quotation marks.

555-555-5555
jmf@email.com
5555 Kraft Lane, Knoxville, TN 55555

MARK FISHER, MBA, CPA

February 4, 2004

Barry Fox, President
National Bank
5555 George Street
Lincoln, NE 55555

Dear Mr. Fox:

"Your hard work positions our organization well for 2003."

General Manager

When was the last time you hired a **Senior Management Executive** who was able to hit the ground running and *generate expense reductions quickly*? Please allow me to introduce myself. As a Certified Public Accountant with extensive financial and auditing experience, I approach every situation from the perspective of operational efficiency.

Producing results requires leadership. Achieving fast results demands a new perspective, an ability to embrace and implement change, and buy-in from everyone involved. Results-driven highlights include ...

- Listening to front-line employees and responding to their concerns and suggestions. *Recommended that senior management eliminate customer online disconnect ability, yielding a $5 million annual savings.*

- Developing the incentive plan for sales reps that *drove market penetration to 35% on customer loyalty product sales.*

"During his tenure, Mark demonstrated a strong ability to drive for results for his team."

Director, Consumer Ops

- Being *hand selected* by senior management for the Capstone Leadership Program, *a privilege afforded to the top 5 to 10% of* employees.

Controlling costs and reducing expenses are critical to an organization's profitability and viability. If you are looking for a results-driven leader holding a CPA and MBA who can *produce positive results quickly,* perhaps we should meet to discuss your needs and how I might help. I look forward to speaking with you.

Sincerely,

Mark Fisher

Enclosure

1

Certified Public Accountant. *Cindy Kraft, Valrico, Florida*

The first paragraph introduces the applicant, the second indicates bulleted achievements quantified in dollars and percentages, and the third proposes a meeting. Two testimonials sell the applicant.

PAUL KEENE, CPA, CMA

October 24, 2004

Hiring Agent, Title
Company Name
Address

Dear Hiring Manager:

As an accomplished financial professional with a solid background in both GAAP and managerial accounting, as well as experience as a controller, I believe I offer expertise that would be of benefit to your company. With a proven record in building solid financial infrastructures, improving accounting and reporting procedures, and providing sound financial analysis, I would like to explore the possibility of putting my talents to work for you.

As you can see from my enclosed résumé, I was brought into my current position to integrate and upgrade the financial operations of four affiliated companies. For this challenging task, I successfully introduced a new financial reporting system, brought the books of all four companies into compliance with GAAP standards, instituted new procedures that standardized and improved operational reporting, and established new systems that simplified asset accounting. In addition, as a certified management accountant trained to use the EVA™ metric system, I am frequently called upon to provide the expert financial analysis that drives successful corporate decision making.

Equally skilled in closing the financial books and conducting analysis of financial results, I consider myself a team player willing and able to tackle any challenge in the financial arena. However, my true passion lies in cost analysis and the identification of cost-saving opportunities. Related to this, I pride myself on my ability to develop clear, cohesive financial reports that provide the basis and justification for change and improvement initiatives. Knowledgeable and forward thinking, I have proven to be a respected and valued financial leader in the past. With a record of success behind me, I am confident that I will be an asset to you as well.

I will be relocating to your area shortly and hope to find a rewarding position that provides the same diverse, fast-paced challenge that I currently enjoy. Therefore, I would be pleased to have the opportunity to meet with you to discuss your needs and how I might be able to meet them. Feel free to contact me at the address and phone number listed below. I look forward to speaking with you soon.

Thank you for your consideration.

Sincerely,

Paul Keene, CPA, CMA

Enclosure

5 SIDNEY ROAD • BRIARCLIFF, NEW YORK 10001 • (333) 333-3333
pkeene@aol.com

Controller. *Carol A. Altomare, Three Bridges, New Jersey*

A cover letter for a resume should direct attention to the resume. The second paragraph mentions the resume and directs the reader's eyes to it and the notable accounting achievements it contains.

Re: Senior Tax Consultant

I have:

~ 10+ years tax and consulting experience working with industry leaders Penney Waterhouse, Delloise & Tooshe, and Motorcola.

~ Level 3 CGA, a Master's degree in Accountancy, and a Master's degree in Taxation.

~ Strong technical tax skills that include transfer pricing, corporate tax, sales and use tax, customs duties, excise taxes, VAT, tax research, international tax legislation, and tax reviews for contingent liabilities.

~ Gained a reputation for client service, commitment, knowledge, and creativity.

In my most recent position as Senior Associate with Penney Waterhouse, I specialized in transfer pricing issues and planning for corporate clients both in Canada and the U.S. In addition to demonstrating the strong tax research and analysis skills required of the position, I demonstrated the critical ability to understand and gain comfort with the financial systems of large corporate clients - a skill necessary for completing the financial analyses for complex transfer pricing reports.

Throughout my career, I have developed the ability to thoroughly understand a company's business and industry, analyze data, identify material tax issues, and provide sound recommendations to the simplest and most complex tax issues.

I would welcome the chance to meet in person to learn more of this position and to see if my expertise meets your needs. Please feel free to review my attached resume and contact me at (555) 666-2222 to arrange an interview.

Thank you for your consideration.

Sincerely,
Julia Gaither

Senior Associate Tax Consultant. *Ross Macpherson, Whitby, Ontario, Canada*

This cover letter is in .txt (text) format for e-mailing. The letter begins with bullets so that the first 10 to 15 lines in the reader's e-mail window capture attention and display the applicant's qualifications.

William DeCoons, CPA

555 Seneca Ave., Waldwick, NJ 55555, (555) 555-5555 x555, wdecoons@aol.com

December 14, 2004

Mr. Robert B. Mishkoff
Mishkoff/Work Executive Search, Inc.
555 Madison Ave., Ste. 400
New York, NY 10022

Dear Mr. Mishkoff,

As an active partner in a CPA accounting firm who has developed the firm's consulting business, I am seeking to focus <u>all</u> my energies into management consulting.

My background includes 18 years of experience in accounting, auditing, finance and consulting. I am skilled in performing diverse financial analysis and developing business plans for various public- and private-sector enterprises and high-income individuals.

For each challenge, I have exceeded expectations and produced excellent results. Most notably, I

- Developed a business plan for a client that would expand his business while protecting his assets.
- Developed a consulting niche with municipal clientele that will net more than $100,000 in annual fees.
- Prepared a "Full Accounting of a Trust" by utilizing accounting software that would provide the format required by the New York State courts.
- Grew my private practice to more than $110,000 in revenues.

My goal is to join a progressive management consulting firm where I can help create value through innovative financing. I think and act "outside the box," and a company that values profitable problem solving will value me, for that is what I do best.

I prefer to stay in the metropolitan New York City area and anticipate an annual compensation package in excess of $100,000.

I look forward to speaking with you regarding any current search assignments appropriate for a candidate with my qualifications. Thank you in advance for your consideration.

Sincerely,

William DeCoons, CPA

Enclosure

4

Certified Public Accountant. *Igor Shpudejko, Mahwah, New Jersey*

This CPA wanted to transition to full-time management consulting. After doing some consulting, he discovered that he liked to find problems and fix them. The letter is addressed to a recruiter.

Brooke Cummings

0000 Rock Cove • Parker, CO 80134
555.555.5555 • brooke@earthlink.com

November 7, 2004

Janis Dodge
Senior Vice President—Chief Financial Officer
New Era Mortgage Corporation
12345 Beverly Boulevard, Suite 100
Los Angeles, CA 92612

Re: Vice President—Controller

Dear Ms. Dodge,

Accounting can be a powerful resource to an organization. It is up to the controller to educate the organization on how to effectively use accounting resources to improve productivity and profitability.

I was delighted when Jane Doe informed me of the Vice President—Controller position at New Era Mortgage Corporation. I am currently the Controller at Colorado Funding, a mortgage lender in Lone Star, CO. My financial management expertise, leadership skills, and extensive experiences are an excellent fit with your position, and I am very interested in relocating to the area to be closer to family and friends.

As a top performer with 20+ years of experience in accounting, I have the knowledge and expertise it takes to bring about positive change. My enclosed resume highlights my contributions and accomplishments in the areas of general accounting, financial statements, audits, cash management, budgeting, profit performance, strategic planning, and regulatory compliance. I take great pride in my work and my abilities. I have made great strides in being recognized as a key player on the management team. My accomplishments will speak for themselves.

My success is due to a passion for quality and excellence, tenacity, and a willingness to confront and conquer tough challenges. I have exceptional organizational skills and a keen eye for detail. My strengths lie in building quality financial processes that meet and exceed expectations. I believe gaining a thorough understanding of all aspects of the business is required to financially guide the organization.

You will find that I am very skilled at developing sound action plans, as well as administering and following through on those plans. I strive to build and maintain a principle-centered environment that preserves the organization's core values while stimulating growth and profitability.

I am eager to begin contributing to the bottom line of New Era Mortgage Corporation. I welcome the opportunity to explore my potential with you.

Thank you for your consideration; I look forward to speaking with you soon.

Sincerely,

Brooke Cummings

Enclosure: Resume

5

Controller. *Roberta F. Gamza, Louisville, Colorado*

This letter names the source of a referral. The reference to the resume summarizes the applicant's areas of accomplishments, and the letter shows strongly that she can do the job and wants it.

KALLEN G. CASEY, CPA
000 GUST COURT ◆ **COLUMBIA, MISSOURI 55555**
RESIDENCE: 555-555-5555 ◆ **WIRELESS: 555-555-5555**

CORPORATE TAX CONSULTANT

LETTER OF INTRODUCTION

I am relocating to the Chicago area and am exploring new career opportunities as a **senior corporate tax consultant** and/or **business development strategist** in tax consulting. My goal is to affiliate with either a "Big Four" accounting and tax consulting firm or a major corporate entity where I can lead and/or co-manage a tax division. Tax consultants will be integral strategists in the profitable growth of complex corporate entities in today's environment. If you have need for a senior corporate tax consultant with expertise in new business development, we should meet.

Throughout my career, I have developed…

- ✓ Expertise in corporate tax and compliance to enhance shareholder value through heightened profitability.

- ✓ Comprehensive tax solutions that impact corporate tax rates and reduce federal, state and local liabilities in an increasingly complex tax environment.

- ✓ Talent for new business development and relationship building with corporate executives, facilitating partnerships and opportunities never before attempted.

As Co-Chair of the Mid-America Tax Conference and frequent speaker on multistate tax matters, I am recognized nationally for my expertise in corporate tax solutions. I have been instrumental in the origination of a highly profitable business development program for tax consulting achieved through motivational leadership blended with sound corporate tax and strategic thinking. My challenge was to expand and strengthen the firm's presence through the introduction of new business initiatives to win competitive positioning and accelerate revenue growth. I spearheaded the implementation of such a program through the company nationwide. Throughout my career, I have brought absolute value to the firm's current and long-term business objectives.

With strong communication and presentation skills, I thrive in fast-paced, high-visibility environments that require innovative leadership and decisive action. I have the ability to capture the attention of a variety of audiences.

My résumé is enclosed for your review. If you are looking for a senior corporate tax specialist who will make an immediate and positive impact on your revenue streams, I would welcome a personal interview to discuss how my qualifications would benefit your firm. Thank you for your consideration.

Sincerely,

Kallen G. Casey

Enclosure

6

Senior Corporate Tax Consultant. *Gina Taylor, Kansas City, Missouri*

This applicant was moving to a new city. The writer highlights the individual's abilities as a business development strategist and his strengths in developing new revenue streams. He received two offers.

KATY SNOW

000 East Street • Charlottetown, NC 20000
(555) 555-5555

January 19, 2004

Mr. James Cathcart
Speedway Enterprises
5555 Racing Boulevard, Suite 555
Charlottetown, NC 55555

Dear Mr. Cathcart:

It is a long way we've come from those early race cars run in 1948 to the dynamic cars we have today, from the first NASCAR race in Daytona to the intricately engineered tracks of the present. Truly the exciting history of NASCAR is even more eventful today.

Those early days have disappeared, like the physician who made house calls, but they will never be forgotten. And neither will I forget my early years growing up in California, where my mother worked for an exhaust manifold manufacturer, Edelbrock, and my husband raced motorcycles. We attended NASCAR races at Riverside and Ontario Speedways in the early '70s.

Over the years, though, I built not race cars, but a career in accounting and finance, moving across the country (no longer by motorcycle but by car), eventually settling in Charlottetown in 1990. During this period I assumed responsible positions as a controller, operations manager, or finance manager, with wide-ranging challenges, from accounting and finance to operations, information and systems integration, and human resources.

With each opportunity came new challenges. With each advancement and move, I went through the same experience—a desire to grow and build value within each organization I joined. Along the way, I became even more enchanted with NASCAR events, frequently traveling on weekends to races in Charlotte, Bristol, Martinsville, and Atlanta. And two years ago, I took "NASCAR 101" (my name) at Central Community College to learn more about racing, its advertising and promotion strategies, and pre- and post-race driver activities. I even toured Lowe's Motor Speedway. The class, presented by NASCAR TV commentator Tony Raines, was enlightening, engaging, and exhilarating.

Over the last few years, I've been preparing myself for the next step: to apply these skills to an organization within the NASCAR industry. My children are grown, and, with fewer familial obligations, my life has changed. Now I would like to join a winning NASCAR team. During this period of change, I view my situation much as Napoleon did when asked how he intended to combat seemingly insurmountable circumstances. His reply: "Circumstances? . . . I *make* circumstances."

If you are interested and have a need for someone with my skills, a desire to work hard, and enthusiasm for NASCAR, then give me the green flag. To quote William D. Smith, Vice President of the Jewel Tea Company back in 1948 (and it still makes sense today): "Take your job seriously—but don't take yourself too seriously. Believe that HOW you work is more important than WHERE you work [unless it's NASCAR] . . . To keep young you must play and you must have fun; make your job and your life a game—and play the game to win."

If you need a capable, devoted, and hardworking professional, I may be able to help. Can we talk?

Sincerely,

Katy Snow

7

Controller. *Doug Morrison, Charlotte, North Carolina*

Having always worked in accounting and finance, this applicant wanted to combine her skills with her avocation—being an avid, lifelong NASCAR fan—and change her work environment completely.

Margaret V. Baxter

000 Anoka Drive   555-555-5555
Waterford, Michigan 55555   mbaxter@network.net

Dear Practice Manager:

My previous five-year-long position as a Medical Receptionist/Biller was the best job of my life! I enjoyed the patients and my coworkers. I loved the challenges it presented and that each day was different. My most recent job took me away from the medical field, and I have really missed it. That's why I am contacting you—to learn about employment opportunities for an experienced, effective, and, most important, motivated receptionist/biller/administrative support provider. My resume describes my experience.

When you review my resume, I hope you will notice that, although I have been working with engineers and automobiles instead of patients and charts, the same skills are important. For example, in my current position I must be highly accurate when working with vehicle part numbers. That isn't much different from coding patient charts with the precise ICD-9 numbers. Among my responsibilities is keeping track of vehicles, keys, and projects. That ability to multitask is equally valuable in a medical office. Also, people are people, and I believe I possess strong communication and interpersonal skills.

Bottom line, I am eager to get back into the medical field to share my enthusiasm and commitment to patients. I am confident that I would be an enhancement to your practice. I am prepared to work hard to get back up to speed with the billing side of the office as quickly as I can. I hope you will give me a call to arrange an interview. Thank you for your time and attention.

Sincerely,

Margaret V. Baxter

Enclosure

8

Medical Receptionist/Biller. *Janet L. Beckstrom, Flint, Michigan*

This applicant wanted to move from a position that was too analytical and had little interaction with people and to return to a position in a field she truly enjoyed (medical office administration).

DEBORAH GRABER

9999 Oakridge Circle
Souderton, PA 00000
(555) 555-5555
dgraber@dotresume.com

Date

Name
Company
Address
City, State ZIP

Dear Name:

Are you looking for an experienced office manager?

For the past 15 years, I have been a successful manager and office coordinator. My supervisors describe me as an asset to the company—a team player who can be counted on to get the job done. It is these personal qualities, as well as my experience, that I would bring to XYZ Company. Some highlights of my experience include the following:

- A track record of promotions, excellent performance evaluations, and customer service awards.

- Skills in bookkeeping and finance—balancing receipts, analyzing sales trends and labor costs, computing payroll figures, and processing accounts payable.

- A proven ability to manage—supervising, scheduling, and training employees; solving difficult problems; and troubleshooting computers.

A copy of my résumé is enclosed for your review. I would welcome the opportunity to discuss career prospects with XYZ Company. Thank you for your consideration, and I look forward to hearing from you soon.

Sincerely,

Deborah Graber

Enclosure

9

Office Coordinator. *Jan Holliday, Harleysville, Pennsylvania*

This manager-coordinator wanted to move from a retail environment to a corporate setting. The letter focuses on transferable skills, which are indicated especially in the second and third bulleted statements.

CATHERINE A. HINES
000 Baywood Drive
Inglewood, CA 99999
(444) 444-4444
catherinehines@resume.com

March 11, 2004

Ms. Maria Lopez
Workforce Development Council
917 134th Street, SW, Suite B-3
Inglewood, WA 99999

Dear Ms. Lopez:

Please consider my résumé for the opening that you have listed on the Workforce Development Council Web site for an Administrative Assistant.

As indicated on my résumé, I possess extensive experience in administrative support and office management. Additionally, my prior experience as an Administrative Assistant at the WDC before my transfer to the Benson Career Transition Center should prove beneficial since I'd be able to hit the ground running and would require very little, if any, training. For this reason, I believe that I would be a great candidate for the current opening.

I welcome the opportunity to discuss how my knowledge, skills and abilities may meet the WDC's needs. Please feel free to contact me at the phone number above to schedule a mutually convenient interview time.

I look forward to hearing from you soon.

Sincerely,

CATHERINE A. HINES

10

Administrative Assistant. *Diana Ramirez, Seatac, Washington*

In this straightforward letter, the first paragraph identifies the target position, the second directs attention to the resume, the third speaks of an interview, and the fourth demonstrates interest.

Nancy M. Larson

0000 East 55th Street ◆ Tucson, AZ 55555
555-555-5555 ◆ nmlarson@earthlink.net

February 12, 2004

Name/Title
Company
Address
City, State ZIP

Dear _____:

As an experienced Executive Assistant and Office Manager who has successfully supported senior-level management personnel over an 18-year career, I have developed the skills and acquired the knowledge to ensure the highest level of competence, time management, confidentiality, and effective operations. My ongoing objective is to make the job of the boss easier, and I have consistently been successful in doing just that. It is this ability, plus a commitment to quality, that I believe would bring added value to you and your organization.

As a highly competent Executive Assistant, my team and individual performance has been praised by past employers based on

- Loyalty and service

- Detailed research and information for the completion of special projects

- Proficient computer and office service skills

- Time management and excellent prioritizing and organizational strengths

- Extensive experience scheduling and coordinating activities and collaboration with other internal and external customers at all levels of management

I have enclosed a résumé for your review that will enable you to obtain a more in-depth idea of the scope and breadth of my experience. However, since it is difficult to get one's personality on paper, I would welcome the opportunity to meet and discuss how my strengths and abilities would be of benefit to you. I will call next week to schedule a meeting at a mutually convenient time. Thank you for reviewing the materials, and I look forward to speaking with you.

Sincerely,

Nancy M. Larson

Enclosure

11

Executive Assistant/Office Manager. *Kay Bourne, Tucson, Arizona*

The applicant had no degree, so it was important to sell the applicant's skills and experience. The bulleted items, indicating topics of past-employer praise, function as testimonials.

Eileen K. Terzo
0000 Kathleen Court
Manhasset, New York 55555
555.555.5555

February 21, 2004

Ms. Nancy Joos, Executive Vice President
Hill Street Kennel
45 Main Street
Dix Hills, New York 11801

Re: Administrative Assistant Supervisor

Dear Ms. Joos:

I am writing to inquire about an Administrative Assistant Supervisor position within Hill Street Kennel. I offer five years of administrative experience in servicing a Fortune 500 company. Competent and knowledgeable in the administrative field, I am positive my skill set will be of benefit to your company.

At ADP, Inc., I manage the entire order process for all outside sales representatives. I communicate daily with clients to ensure that all deliverables have been met, and I prepare reports, spreadsheets and documentation for client service representatives and district managers. In addition, I currently supervise all the temporary employees in my department, wherein I delegate projects, prepare their schedules and evaluate their performance.

I am presently seeking to join a company that offers opportunity for growth and advancement. I have followed your company for the last few years and have been impressed by your dedication to service and excellence. I bring to Hill Street Kennel strong leadership competencies, solid judgment and decision-making abilities.

If you are interested in a self-motivated and highly competent candidate, we should speak. I am available for an interview at your convenience. I appreciate your time and look forward to speaking with you.

Sincerely,

Eileen K. Terzo

Enclosure

12

Administrative Assistant Supervisor. *Deanna Verbouwens, Hicksville, New York*

The opening paragraph of this "cold-call" cover letter to a corporation indicates the applicant's qualifications for filling a position if one is available. The third tells why she wants to join this company.

Susan E. Williams

0000 Indianwood Road
Clarkston, Michigan 55555

555-555-3333
sueew@network.net

Date

Name
Company
Address
City, State ZIP

Dear Director of Employment:

A BBA degree, 20+ years of experience in the banking industry, and a background in administrative support—that's what I have to offer your organization. After a rewarding career at Michigan National Bank, I find myself in the position of seeking new career opportunities. My resume is enclosed for your review.

My career at the bank encompassed diverse areas that required skills valuable to any industry. For example:

- ❖ Thorough understanding of administrative/office operations
- ❖ Event-planning and management experience
- ❖ Customer-focused attitude
- ❖ Attention to detail and strong organizational skills
- ❖ Ability to oversee multiple responsibilities simultaneously
- ❖ Computer fluency

In combination with my financial responsibilities, I took a personal interest in every client. There were cases that necessitated my intervention to arbitrate differences between feuding beneficiaries. Sometimes I was called upon to schedule doctor appointments or arrange for home repair on a client's behalf. But serving the client (or the client's estate, as the case may be) was always my top priority.

Thank you for taking the time to review my credentials. I hope you feel a personal meeting would be beneficial; I am available at your convenience. If you have any questions—or when you are ready to schedule an interview—please give me a call at 555-555-3333.

Sincerely,

Susan E. Williams

Enclosure

13

Administrative Assistant. *Janet L. Beckstrom, Flint, Michigan*

This applicant was downsized by a bank after 30 years. The writer prepared this general cover letter. The applicant was hired as an Administrative Assistant for a large medical center.

GERI SAYA

8 ROLLING HILL ROAD • FARMINGTON, NJ 22222 • (333) 444-5555

November 25, 2004

Name, Title
Company Name
Address

Dear Hiring Manager:

As a hardworking individual with excellent interpersonal skills and a demonstrated commitment to helping others, I would like to explore the possibility of putting my skills and experience to work for you as a receptionist/customer assistant. I learned of your opening through a friend, Cindy Walters. She indicated that she thought I would provide a good match for your needs.

As you can see from my enclosed résumé, during my career I held a variety of administrative positions, nearly all within American Telephone, where I established a reputation for efficiency, accuracy and exceptional service to internal and external customers. A receptionist for the company's School of Business for six years, I redefined the role to encompass customer service responsibilities. In addition to greeting and directing visitors to the facility, I took an active role in addressing problems and finding appropriate solutions, doing whatever was necessary to ensure smooth operation of this 30-classroom facility.

Customer service is a field particularly suited to my strengths as I enjoy helping people, am quick on my feet, and deal effectively with difficult people. I consider myself a team player who is enthusiastic about helping out in any way I can. In addition, I am organized and well equipped to handle the demands of multiple projects. In the past, I have proven to be a valued employee. I am confident that I will be an asset to you as well.

I would be pleased to have the opportunity to discuss future employment and look forward to speaking with you. Feel free to contact me at the address and phone number listed above.

Thank you for your consideration.

Sincerely,

Geri Saya

Enclosure

14

Receptionist/Customer Assistant. *Carol A. Altomare, Three Bridges, New Jersey*

The opening paragraph names a referral, and the second indicates the applicant's excellent customer-service skills. The third expresses her enthusiasm; and the fourth, her interest in an interview.

PURDEEP MEHTA

000 Elizabeth Street
Augusta, Ontario A1A 1A1
555-555-5555

February 17, 2004

Joseph Camarra
Director of Administration
Fieldway Automotive Partners
440 Torris Boulevard
Augusta, Ontario
B2C 3D4

Dear Mr. Camarra,

I understand you are looking for a "Girl Friday"—someone to take control of the critical administrative and customer service functions at your location in Pinehurst, Ontario. If you're looking for a motivated and hardworking professional with an above-average performance record, outstanding interpersonal skills, and a "get it done" attitude, I think you've found the best person for the job.

Over the past few years, while working for Group Six Security, I have routinely met with your company's representatives. From this contact, I have gained an understanding of the work that you do and an appreciation for your need for strong administrative support. In my current role with TGO Consulting, I do just that: managing all critical administration for the company and supporting the activities of 30 consultants and project managers.

I invite you to review my attached résumé, which details the skills and experience I offer. Highlights include

- ✓ **Strong communications and interpersonal skills**—personable and friendly, with the ability to work well with colleagues, superiors, clients, and vendors
- ✓ **Extensive administrative and office support skills**—includes invoices, billing, scheduling, A/P and A/R, file management, and data entry
- ✓ **Outstanding customer service**—award-winning performance providing friendly and effective customer service in both corporate and retail environments
- ✓ **Self-motivated and hardworking**—personally love challenges, extremely quick learner, and motivated to exceed expectations

I believe that my strong skills and solid work ethic would make a significant contribution to your team, and I would welcome the opportunity to meet in person to discuss this position and why I believe I am the strongest candidate you will see.

Thank you for your consideration, and I look forward to speaking with you soon.

Sincerely,

Purdeep Mehta
Encl.

15

Administrative Support Position. *Ross Macpherson, Whitby, Ontario, Canada*

The applicant had heard about an unposted job through contacts in the industry. This cover letter was a bid for that position. Bullets point to her skills and traits. The entire letter displays confidence.

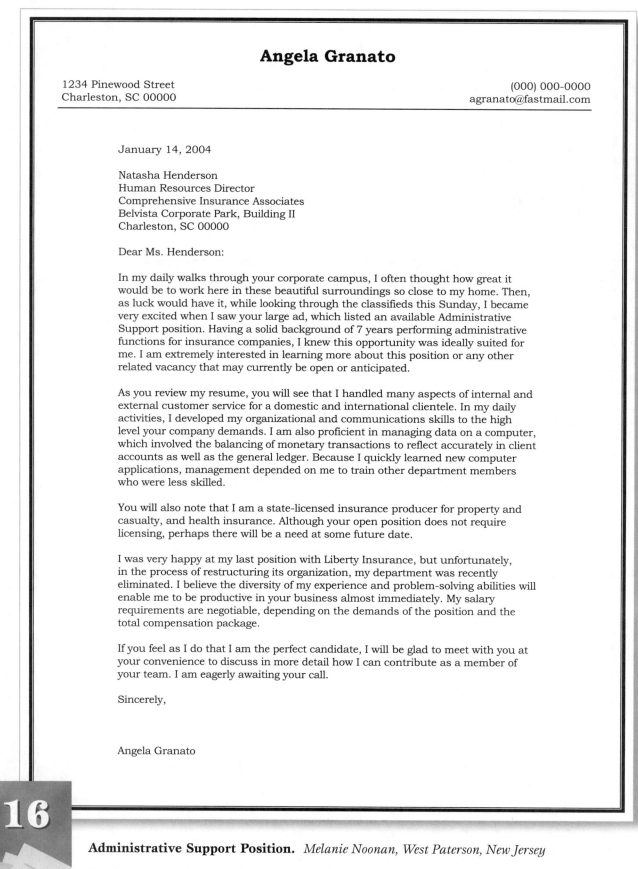

Angela Granato

1234 Pinewood Street   (000) 000-0000
Charleston, SC 00000   agranato@fastmail.com

January 14, 2004

Natasha Henderson
Human Resources Director
Comprehensive Insurance Associates
Belvista Corporate Park, Building II
Charleston, SC 00000

Dear Ms. Henderson:

In my daily walks through your corporate campus, I often thought how great it
would be to work here in these beautiful surroundings so close to my home. Then,
as luck would have it, while looking through the classifieds this Sunday, I became
very excited when I saw your large ad, which listed an available Administrative
Support position. Having a solid background of 7 years performing administrative
functions for insurance companies, I knew this opportunity was ideally suited for
me. I am extremely interested in learning more about this position or any other
related vacancy that may currently be open or anticipated.

As you review my resume, you will see that I handled many aspects of internal and
external customer service for a domestic and international clientele. In my daily
activities, I developed my organizational and communications skills to the high
level your company demands. I am also proficient in managing data on a computer,
which involved the balancing of monetary transactions to reflect accurately in client
accounts as well as the general ledger. Because I quickly learned new computer
applications, management depended on me to train other department members
who were less skilled.

You will also note that I am a state-licensed insurance producer for property and
casualty, and health insurance. Although your open position does not require
licensing, perhaps there will be a need at some future date.

I was very happy at my last position with Liberty Insurance, but unfortunately,
in the process of restructuring its organization, my department was recently
eliminated. I believe the diversity of my experience and problem-solving abilities will
enable me to be productive in your business almost immediately. My salary
requirements are negotiable, depending on the demands of the position and the
total compensation package.

If you feel as I do that I am the perfect candidate, I will be glad to meet with you at
your convenience to discuss in more detail how I can contribute as a member of
your team. I am eagerly awaiting your call.

Sincerely,

Angela Granato

16

Administrative Support Position. *Melanie Noonan, West Paterson, New Jersey*

The first paragraph makes known the applicant's extreme interest in the advertised position. The
letter then indicates her experience, licensing, and reason for applying. See Resume 3 (page
365).

D

One Concentric Circle
Nobleton, Virginia 12345
June 1, 2004

Dear Sir or Madam:

How does one make an office run smoothly, like a well-oiled machine?

- By understanding its components and their interrelationships, for example, the different kinds of equipment necessary to run a modern office, how they are used, and how they interact and interface.

- By understanding not only modern equipment, such as computers, scanners, and fax machines, but also older kinds of equipment, such as typewriters. By understanding not only when to use computers, but also when typewriters work faster and better and when the human hand works faster and better than the typewriter.

- By understanding not only the machinery, but the people who use it. By understanding how they feel about the technology they use. By understanding the conditions under which they use them best.

I have been making things run smoothly at Brite Industries for more than ten years. I understand machines, and I like machines. But it's my understanding of people that has made possible the kinds of success documented in the attached résumé, detailing my progressively responsible administrative career at Brite and elsewhere. Many listen. I listen and acknowledge. It's one thing to be heard, but another to know you're being heard. I think, and then determine better and faster ways of doing things. When something goes wrong, I discover the misunderstanding that caused the problem and clarify it.

This is how I saved $100,000 and increased productivity 40% at Brite. This is how I upgraded five positions, significantly improving morale. This is how I anticipated a question from our president, ensuring it was answered *before* it was asked. This is how I recommended, for an incident center, a new location that was subsequently approved by management, saving both time and money. This is how I significantly reduced absenteeism through informal and formal counseling to departmental staff.

And this is how I can help you. Please take a look at the attached document. I am confident that, on reviewing it, you will agree I have the potential to become a worthy member of your team. Kindly phone to set a convenient time to meet, so that we could discuss how I might best serve your organization.

Sincerely yours,

Anna Marie Di Magenta

P.S. Please call me at (777) 654-3210.

17

Office Equipment Support Position. *Howard Earle Halpern, Toronto, Ontario, Canada*

Cover letters that resemble other cover letters can be boring. This letter is different in *offering* the reader original ideas to be helpful in the selection process, instead of *asking* for something.

BRENDA BELLOWS

000 Morris Street • Bronx, NY 00000
Home: (555) 555-5555   Brenda456@mail.com   Mobile: (555) 555-5555

November 13, 2004

Name
Title
Employer
Address
City, State ZIP

Dear Mr. or Ms. Name:

A high-performing marketing organization staffed with individuals demonstrating a successful track record is an essential part of your company's continued growth.

I believe you will agree that my qualifications, highlighted in the enclosed resume, confirm that I have the creativity, marketing savvy and management experience that can contribute to your company's success.

Specifically, what do I offer?

- Fashion, beauty, fragrance and cosmetics industry background
- Developing marketing programs, promotions and events
- Coordinating national print and broadcast advertising
- Leading the creation and production of marketing materials
- Nurturing strategic partnerships with clients and trade publications
- Managing and delivering multiple projects/budgets in deadline-driven environments

Examples of my accomplishments:

- Restructured entire co-op advertising program at Estée Lauder, improving budget controls, tracking system and forecasting
- Orchestrated successful marketing programs for an outdoor advertising association, including the annual award show and gallery that increased participation 50% each year
- Initiated sales/marketing tool that contributed to new business development at a start-up media company
- Saved more than $100,000 just in production/tagging costs through effective negotiation skills

I welcome the opportunity to meet with you and discuss the value I would add to your team as a Marketing Coordinator.

Sincerely,

Brenda Bellows

18

Marketing Coordinator. *Louise Garver, Enfield, Connecticut*

With print, broadcast, and outdoor advertising experience, this applicant wanted to move to the next level in marketing. This letter enabled her to win interviews that led to an excellent offer.

MARK GREENE

November 30, 2004

Hiring Agent, Title
Company Name
Address

Dear Hiring Manager:

As a highly motivated, goal-oriented sales and marketing professional with a proven ability to contribute to company growth and profitability, I believe I offer expertise that will be of benefit to your company. With an extensive background in sales, marketing, client relations, and management, I would like to consider putting my skills and experience to work for you as your next [position title].

As you can see from my enclosed résumé, my background encompasses creative experience as a still-life stylist for an advertising production company, as well as the more diverse role of studio manager for a commercial still-life photography studio. As a manager, I held responsibility for building client contacts, developing effective marketing strategies, and closing sales. While directing a staff of assistants and stylists in designing and executing projects, I successfully grew the business from a single cosmetic account to a dozen retail and catalog clients, including well-known companies such as Clinique, Revlon, Lord & Taylor, and Bloomingdale's.

Among my strengths, I have excellent relationship-building skills that have served me well in establishing valuable contacts throughout client organizations. In addition, I possess strong interpersonal and organizational skills and pride myself on the attention to detail I bring to each project. I am also a skilled multitasker and thrive in fast-paced, team-oriented environments.

In the past, the combination of my creative instincts, marketing and sales expertise—and management skills—along with my disciplined approach to project execution, have allowed me to make significant contributions to bottom-line revenues. With a solid track record behind me, I am confident I can do the same for you.

I welcome the opportunity to meet with you to discuss your needs and how I might be able to meet them. Please feel free to contact me at the address and phone numbers listed below.

Thank you for your consideration.

Sincerely,

Mark Greene

Enclosure

19

Photographer/Still-Life Stylist. *Carol A. Altomare, Three Bridges, New Jersey*

This applicant wanted a job more focused on sales and marketing. The letter refers, in turn, to his expertise, background, experience, strengths, significant contributions, and interest in an interview.

Frederick Charleston

55 NE Resnold Drive • Vancouver, Washington 99999

email: fc333@hotmail.com

555-555-5555

December 1, 2004

Attention: Hiring Professional
Ginger's Airline Products
555 NW Pioneer Street
Vancouver, WA 99999

Dear Hiring Professional:

Enclosed is my résumé for your review. As you will note, the United States Navy has provided me 19.5 years of experience in aviation. I am experienced in all aspects of aviation maintenance—proficient in providing maintenance on a variety of aircraft and able to effectively manage and train a maintenance crew, provide quality assurance, and maintain aircrafts at 100% for readiness and safety.

My management skills are well proven, and I enjoy working with each individual. If a particular position and individual are not working out, I take the time to review the individual's personality, looking for strengths and then using that person in a more suitable position. I find that taking strengths and fitting them to requirements result in much higher production with less manpower turnover.

The position you have available appears to be one that closely matches my skills. I would like the opportunity to meet with you personally to see where my strengths and your company requirements may blend. Please call me at the number provided to set up an interview.

Thank you for your time.

Sincerely,

Frederick Charleston

20

Aircraft Maintenance Manager. *Rosie Bixel, Portland, Oregon*

Employers want to hear at least two statements from an applicant: "I can" and "I want to." The first two paragraphs deliver "I can" information; the last paragraph indicates the applicant's interest.

CONFIDENTIAL   *Ready to relocate to the Clovis area*

Charles Henry Kraft

0000 Sledgeway Street — Anchorage, Alaska 55555
☏ 907.555.5555 (Cell) — apmaster@whiz.att.net

Thursday, February 26, 2004

Mr. Joe North
Director of Maintenance
TopLine Airlines, Inc.
555 Northridge Parkway
Suite 555
Clovis, New Mexico 55555

Dear Mr. North:

I want to make it easy for TopLine Airlines to add me to your team as your newest aircraft
maintenance supervisor.

As a first step, I thought you deserved to see more than the usual tired lists of jobs held and
training completed. In their place you'll find a half dozen examples of maintenance teams
motivated, productivity boosted, liability reduced—in short, problems solved. And, while a
résumé format tailored to your needs is good at documenting results, it cannot tell you *how* I
contribute to our leadership's peace of mind.

Therefore, as you read, I hope the following ideas stand out:

> I am only as good as the last job I signed off—conditions in the remote parts of Alaska leave
> little room for maintenance errors.

> I am only as good as my last quarter's MX statistics. If I don't spot and correct trends, we'll
> lose time and money.

> I am only as good as the teams I attract, recruit, train, and retain. Our labor market is among
> the tightest in the nation.

I'm employed now and my company likes my work. However, I want to relocate to be closer to
my family. That's why I am testing the waters with this confidential application.

When it comes to something as important as finding TopLine Airlines's next aircraft maintenance
supervisor, words on paper are no substitute for people speaking with people. So let me suggest a
next step. I'd like to get on your calendar in a few days so that we can explore how I might serve
your special maintenance needs.

Sincerely,

Charles Henry Kraft

Encl.: Résumé

CONFIDENTIAL

21

Aircraft Maintenance Supervisor. *Don Orlando, Montgomery, Alabama*

This writer is a master at avoiding clichés and whatever else is trite, timeworn, and customary.
Study this and his other cover letters in this book for his fresh ideas.

ALICIA DWYER

47 Bedford Road, Carindale, QLD 4444
(b) (07) 7777 7777 • (h) (07) 5555 5555
aliciad@powerup.net

27 March 2004

Stewart McAdam
Vestal Airlines
Level 62, Riverview Place
Park Road
BRISBANE QLD 4444

Dear Mr. McAdam:

Fasten your seatbelt…as I navigate you through the career profile of a highly accomplished, dynamic professional, who just so happens to have a great sense of humour and your vital prerequisite: a passion for people and for life.

Throughout my career, working predominantly within the *airline industry*, I have demonstrated an exceptional record of accomplishment, continuously setting myself high standards and achieving *outstanding quantifiable results.*

My attached résumé emphasises numerous achievements and expounds upon my proven record of excellence within human resource management; my proactive formulation of benchmark interview and recruitment procedures; and my outstanding leadership, communication and interpersonal expertise.

I submit the following highlights for your perusal:

> ✈ Spearheaded development of high-volume recruitment and selection procedures and personally conducted more than 2,000 interviews. Accountable for annual wages expenditure in excess of $15 million.

> ✈ Directed and motivated more than 400 management and staff, consistently employing dynamic leadership and team-building skills in combination with excellent coaching and training expertise. Facilitated delivery of Corporate Culture Program to 16,000 staff over two-year period.

> ✈ Key ability to build strong, respectful business and corporate relations across all levels of management. Achieved minimal customer disruption and maximum level of efficiency in servicing corporate clientele during 10-month pilot dispute.

> ✈ Excellent educational qualifications and accreditations, including Graduate Diploma of Counselling, Accredited "Target Selection" Certificate, Accredited OH&S Certificate, International Interpersonal Management Skills and Certificate IV Workplace Training and Assessment.

What is more challenging to put down on paper is my genuine love of people—my love of drawing out the very best that is within and motivating individuals to achieve results beyond their personal expectations.

I am proud to state that during my 11 years in the aviation industry, I have seen individuals, without exception, work harder than they have ever worked before and rise to levels above those to which they would normally aspire.

Vestal Airlines enjoys an excellent reputation throughout the industry. I am eager to share my expertise within your organisation as a vital catalyst for growth and the achievement of personal and corporate excellence. So…

…before we reach cruising altitude, I invite you to read the attached. No, not safety instructions, although it could be just as lifesaving …

Yours sincerely,

Alicia Dwyer
Enc.

22

Airline Position. *Beverley Neil, Victoria Point West, Queensland, Australia*

This applicant's experience was in the aviation industry but not related specifically to airlines, which was her target. The writer devised this letter to show how the experience was relevant. The applicant got an interview.

Marjorie Sims

0000 First Avenue
Pittsburgh, PA 99999
(555) 555-5555
msims@dotresume.com

Date

Name
Company
Address
City, State ZIP

Dear Name:

The ability to work well with people from diverse backgrounds, represent my organization in a positive light, and "get things done" through effective leadership and collaboration are my strongest attributes. Some recent accomplishments include the following:

- Selected by superiors to serve as manager, group representative, and role model
- Received excellent evaluations for management and organizational skills
- Valued by colleagues as advisor in the areas of training and instructional design
- Coordinated a major event, which was acclaimed as outstanding

Having just completed a master's degree in administration, I am ready to transition my teaching experience to a corporate position as an education director / trainer. I am confident that I can utilize my management and interpersonal skills to meet any challenge.

My résumé is enclosed for your consideration. I would appreciate the opportunity to meet in person to discuss how my experience and education can benefit your organization.

Thank you for taking the time to review my qualifications. I look forward to your response.

Sincerely,

Marjorie Sims

Enclosure

23

Corporate Education Director/Trainer. *Jan Holliday, Harleysville, Pennsylvania*

This applicant was a teacher who wanted to transition to an education position in corporate administration. The letter highlights her people skills and relevant management experience.

JOHN HARMAN
1111 Greenberry Court
Montgomery, Alabama 00000
jharman2@capitol.net
☎ [334] 555-5555 (Home) — [334] 555-6666 (Cell)

Friday, January 20, 2004

Ms. Sandy Reisman
Industrial Training Program Developer & Technical Writer
Alabama Industrial Development Training
One Technology Court
Montgomery, Alabama 00000

Dear Ms. Reisman:

As soon as I saw your announcement for a Training Program Developer and Technical Writer, I thought my experience in manufacturing in Alabama might make me a perfect match for you. Said another way, I wish I had the benefit of AIDT-trained employees in my plants. Thinking about AIDT's immediate future, I wanted to meet your needs, our employers' needs, and the needs of people seeking to enter the workforce. I have covered the details in the attached résumé.

My résumé documents function, performance, and results—not just lists of job titles and responsibilities. There are 15 examples of payoffs I've gotten for employers just like the ones AIDT serves. The six training examples are highlighted with borders. As you read, I hope this central idea stands out: All my job titles have a manufacturing aspect. However, I was always evaluated on how well I recruited, trained, and retained my workforce. I was measured on productivity. Even so, there is essential information no résumé can transmit well.

I think of myself as a trainer with a subject matter expert's point of view. That's always been necessary because my bosses didn't grade my work based on lesson plans, test question ease indexes, or strict compliance with standardized terminology in writing objectives and samples of behavior. They demanded what your customers demand: increased productivity, reduced costs, and lowered liability. So I did much more than skills training. For me, skills without a solid work ethic didn't count for much. All my "students" got both the skills and attitude to underwrite their success in the workplace.

I know you'll soon make a decision about whom to interview. Nevertheless, I would like to hear about AIDT's "needs analysis" in your own words. If I am fortunate enough to be hired, that's the best way I know to be productive right from the start. May I call in a few days to explore opportunities for a meeting?

Sincerely,

John Harman

Encl.: Résumé

24

Training Program Developer and Technical Writer. *Don Orlando, Montgomery, Alabama*

To make this letter different from the average letter, the writer placed "CONFIDENTIAL" in a header and a footer, used a graphic for "phone," and put a border around the sentence about borders.

Nancy T. Ditillio

000 Raven's Way ▪ Martinsburg, WV 21775 ▪ 555-000-0732 ▪ nditillio@hotmail.com

October 4, 2004

AB&C Group
Robert Vance, Human Resources
One Executive Way
Ranson, WV 25438

Dear Mr. Vance:

Finding and retaining good employees are reported to be two of the biggest challenges faced today by businesses large and small. Retention data suggests that employees target and remain faithful to companies that are committed to their personal and professional development.

A recent visit to the AB&C Group Web site confirmed for me that yours is a company dedicated to employee development and training. Your acknowledgement in the *Wall Street Journal,* the Ranson Learning Center, and the Elaine Looney Achievement Center are testimonies to your commitment. I share in that commitment and have a proven record of achievement to that end. For these reasons, it is with great interest and enthusiasm that I am submitting my resume for consideration in filling your current opening for a **Director of Corporate Training.**

With more than 18 years in the education, employment, and training arena, I am confident I have much to offer:

- ► **Experience designing, developing, and delivering training.** I have written curricula covering everything from life skills and career management to computer software applications and the Internet. I have trained college students, corporate professionals, customer service representatives, professional peers, and factory workers, to name a few.

- ► **A proven record of delivering projects on time,** best exemplified by my experience in successfully writing and coordinating the submission of numerous federal grants.

- ► **Strong platform skills** and ongoing recognition as a high-energy, entertaining, and motivational trainer and workshop facilitator.

- ► **Supervisory and leadership experience,** whether serving on a board of directors for a community organization or coaching and mentoring individuals to define and take charge of their own success.

- ► **Creativity** and an innate ability to identify areas in need of improvement and the vision to develop and implement successful action plans.

Since this correspondence can only provide you with a brief overview of my skills and accomplishments, I would welcome the opportunity to talk with you about AB&C Group and your vision for developing your corporate training programs. I will phone early next week to follow up on this correspondence and explore the possibility of scheduling some time with you. I look forward to talking with you then.

Sincerely,

Nancy T. Ditillio

25

Director of Corporate Training. *Norine Dagliano, Hagerstown, Maryland*

This letter was a response to a newspaper ad. Bulleted items incorporate both the actual requirements listed in the ad and the candidate's experience that matches each requirement.

MARIANNE M. CLARK
0000 Berkeley Lane
Frederick, MD 21701
marck@aol.com
301.555.5555 (home)
301.000.0000 (cell)

Dear Hiring Manager:

Could you use a high-energy, creative salon professional
who appreciates the vital link between well-trained,
motivated personnel and increased company profits? If so,
I would enjoy speaking with you to discuss how my skills
and experience might strengthen your organization.

With more than 20 years in the cosmetology industry, I
recently made a short-term move from "behind the chair"
to a training and management position at Hair Club for
Men. As has always been my nature, I met this new challenge
head-on. I am proud to say that, through expert training
and motivational team building, my contributions have proven
instrumental in positioning the Falls Church, Virginia, center
as a leader in the corporation for sales and service.

I discovered that I not only love personnel training but also
am good at it! My current manager credits me with being
"an integral part of changing the way the < HCM > seasoned
stylist thinks when it comes to what is best for the client."

I feel I have taken advantage of all that my current position
has to offer and am ready to push my career to the next level
as a full-time Trainer or Manager. I am very open to a
geographic move and amenable to travel.

My resume is pasted below. I have also attached, for your
convenience, a copy in Word 2000 format. This will provide you
with some additional information about my background.

Please phone or email me at the address or numbers printed
above. I look forward to talking with you!

Sincerely,
Marianne M. Clark

26

Trainer/Manager. *Norine Dagliano, Hagerstown, Maryland*

This electronic cover letter in .txt (text) format was used by the candidate for online posting and
for sending the letter with an electronic resume by e-mail to a hiring manager (in that case
including an actual name).

AEVAH B. JONES

0000 Summers Court ● Anywhere, Michigan 55555 ● (555) 222-2222
aevah@email.com

December 8, 2004

Tomas Smith, Director
ABC Incorporated
555 Main Street
Anywhere, Michigan 55555

Dear Mr. Smith,

As a successful and established recruiting professional, I bring more than eight years of experience and knowledge in locating highly qualified candidates pursuing mid-management to executive-level positions for various employers in diverse industries. I have the drive for developing business relationships and enjoy working one-on-one with employers and candidates. I find networking is key to professional and personal growth.

Through my efforts and success as a recruiter, I have received two prestigious awards from my last employer and have built a reputation for providing genuine leadership and working effectively with others. My talents and expertise in creative sourcing, networking, interviewing techniques and presentations have allowed me to make significant contributions to my employers, as noted in my résumé.

Since I have been very successful in recruiting and enjoy the everyday challenges of my profession, I have decided to launch my career as an independent recruiter. I would appreciate the opportunity to speak with you personally to provide more details on my background and the expertise I can offer your firm.

Your time and consideration in reviewing my credentials are appreciated. I will contact you next week to see if we can schedule a day that we can meet to answer any questions you may have regarding my qualifications. I look forward to speaking with you soon.

Sincerely,

Aevah Jones

Enclosure

27

Independent Recruiter. *Maria E. Hebda, Trenton, Michigan*

The letter indicates in four paragraphs the applicant's experience and motivation, awards and areas of expertise, new direction and interest in an interview, and plans for following up the letter.

James Howard

0000 Tracer Downs ♦ Perry, GA 00000 ♦ (H) 000-000-0000 ♦ (C) 000-000-0000

(Date)

Mr. (Ms.) _____
(Company)
(Address 1)
(Address 2)

Dear Mr. _____

(Insert 2-line paragraph about how you heard of the position and why you are applying for it. For example: "If the information in the *Times Courier* is still accurate, you are currently seeking to fill the position of Customer Service Manager. This letter is to introduce myself as a candidate for just such a position.")

I am an experienced and highly qualified management professional. My areas of expertise lie in operations management, facilities management, transportation and embarkation, inventory and logistics, purchasing and procurement, personnel and human resources, materials management, public and motivational speaking, written and oral communications, information gathering, data analysis, team coordination, and budget administration. I accepted my current position with the Air Logistics Center at Robins AFB, GA, in an attempt to gain meaningful employment within the infrastructure of civil service. Because opportunities for advancement from this position are quite limited, I am seeking a position within the community at large where my wealth of knowledge and expertise can be fully utilized to the benefit of both my employer and myself.

The enclosed résumé briefly outlines my experience and accomplishments. If my qualifications appear to meet your current needs, I would be happy to discuss my background in a meeting with you. Please feel free to contact me at the above telephone number.

Sincerely,

James Howard

Enclosure

28

Customer Service Manager. *Lea J. Clark, Macon, Georgia*

This letter, based on a template, is in progress. Some information is not yet supplied. The first paragraph still has directions for the paragraph. In effect, you are looking over the writer's shoulder.

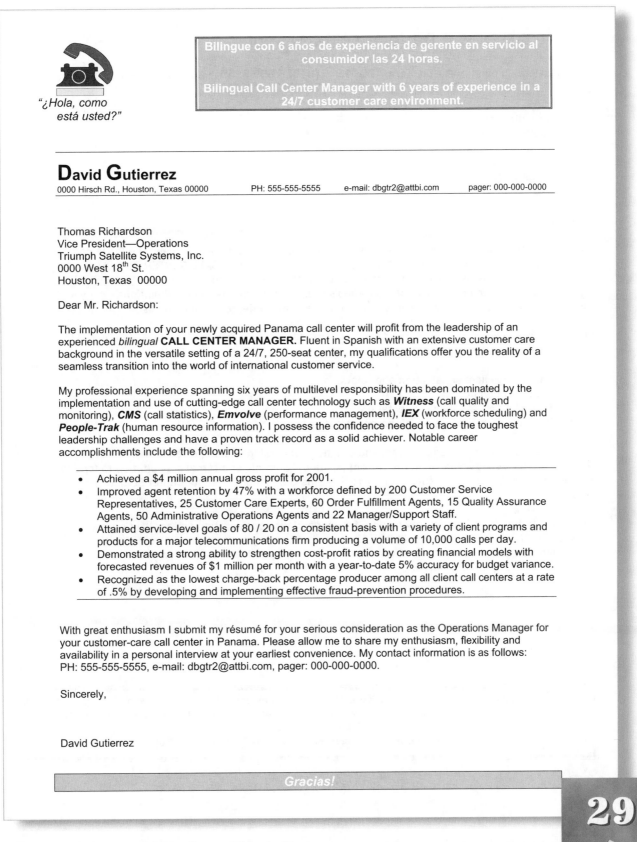

"¿Hola, como está usted?"

Bilingue con 6 años de experiencia de gerente en servicio al consumidor las 24 horas.

Bilingual Call Center Manager with 6 years of experience in a 24/7 customer care environment.

David Gutierrez

0000 Hirsch Rd., Houston, Texas 00000   PH: 555-555-5555   e-mail: dbgtr2@attbi.com   pager: 000-000-0000

Thomas Richardson
Vice President—Operations
Triumph Satellite Systems, Inc.
0000 West 18th St.
Houston, Texas 00000

Dear Mr. Richardson:

The implementation of your newly acquired Panama call center will profit from the leadership of an experienced *bilingual* **CALL CENTER MANAGER.** Fluent in Spanish with an extensive customer care background in the versatile setting of a 24/7, 250-seat center, my qualifications offer you the reality of a seamless transition into the world of international customer service.

My professional experience spanning six years of multilevel responsibility has been dominated by the implementation and use of cutting-edge call center technology such as **Witness** (call quality and monitoring), **CMS** (call statistics), **Emvolve** (performance management), **IEX** (workforce scheduling) and **People-Trak** (human resource information). I possess the confidence needed to face the toughest leadership challenges and have a proven track record as a solid achiever. Notable career accomplishments include the following:

- Achieved a $4 million annual gross profit for 2001.
- Improved agent retention by 47% with a workforce defined by 200 Customer Service Representatives, 25 Customer Care Experts, 60 Order Fulfillment Agents, 15 Quality Assurance Agents, 50 Administrative Operations Agents and 22 Manager/Support Staff.
- Attained service-level goals of 80 / 20 on a consistent basis with a variety of client programs and products for a major telecommunications firm producing a volume of 10,000 calls per day.
- Demonstrated a strong ability to strengthen cost-profit ratios by creating financial models with forecasted revenues of $1 million per month with a year-to-date 5% accuracy for budget variance.
- Recognized as the lowest charge-back percentage producer among all client call centers at a rate of .5% by developing and implementing effective fraud-prevention procedures.

With great enthusiasm I submit my résumé for your serious consideration as the Operations Manager for your customer-care call center in Panama. Please allow me to share my enthusiasm, flexibility and availability in a personal interview at your earliest convenience. My contact information is as follows: PH: 555-555-5555, e-mail: dbgtr2@attbi.com, pager: 000-000-0000.

Sincerely,

David Gutierrez

Gracias!

29

Call Center Manager. *MeLisa Rogers, Victoria, Texas*

The writer wanted to convey the candidate's bilingual ability. This letter is a fictionalized version of an entry that was named "Most Eye-Catching Cover Letter" at the 2002 PARW Annual Convention.

Darlene L. Matheson

0000 Emerald Forest • Austin, Texas 78745 • (H) 555-555-5555 • (C) 000-000-0000

Star Communications
Attn: Daniel Rawlings
Human Resource Director
5555 7th Street, Suite Y
Dallas, Texas 75228

Dear Mr. Rawlings:

The Star Communications call center operation will not only reach but also **exceed** the 2004 goals and objectives under the leadership of an experienced and seasoned **CALL CENTER DIRECTOR**. With an extensive customer-care background in the fast-paced, demanding setting of a 24/7 environment—*servicing customers of the nation's premier companies*—my qualifications offer you the reality of a seamless transition into the world of a results-oriented, quality-focused operation.

My professional experience, spanning **14** years of multilevel responsibility, has been dominated by repeated successes in

- Enhancing client satisfaction and relations
- Increasing profits
- Exceeding client quality expectations
- Implementing process development strategies

I possess the confidence needed to face the toughest leadership challenges and have a proven track record as a solid achiever. In my current position, I administer internal **consultation to foreign and domestic call center operations** for Micro Systems Outsourcing Contact Center Solutions division.

With great enthusiasm I submit my résumé for your serious consideration as the Call Center Director for Star Communications. Please allow me to share my enthusiasm, flexibility and availability in a personal interview at your earliest convenience. My contact information is (H) 555-555-5555; (C) 000-000-0000.

Sincerely,

Darlene Matheson

> "Darlene has the keen ability to leverage her extensive call center operations expertise with creating master processes that are understood and followed by all levels of the operation...agent to Vice President...to achieve high-level success."
> Senior Human Resource Manager—Micro Systems Contact Center Solutions

30

Call Center Director. *MeLisa Rogers, Victoria, Texas*

The applicant's current assignment as a National Process Manager needed to be downplayed, and her extensive previous experience as a Call Center Manager needed to be emphasized.

March 29, 2004

Lockheed Martin Aircraft Center
ATTN.: Recruiting Manager
000 Terminal Rd.
Greenville, SC 22222

Dear Recruiting Manager,

Let me start by introducing myself and informing you of my intentions for employment. I am currently searching for an immediate full-time position as Designer, and in response to your ad posted at Monster.com, I am enclosing my resume for your review.

I held a Technical Designer position with XYZ Company and was part of that group for a year. Unfortunately, because of work reductions, a surplus action was initiated, resulting in my permanent layoff. Prior to working for XYZ Company, I joined the United States Navy, where I learned to work with gas turbines, along with all other duties required of a technician.

If you are seeking an individual who is as career-committed as it takes to achieve total success, please consider what I have to offer. I would be happy to have a preliminary discussion with you to see if we can establish a mutual interest. Thank you for taking the time to read this letter. I certainly look forward to exploring this opportunity further.

Sincerely,

Dious M. Souza
900 112th Ave. N.
North Bend, WA 99999
(555) 555-5555

Enclosures (3)

31

Technical Designer. *Diana Ramirez, Seatac, Washington*

This response to an ad begins with a paragraph that both introduces the applicant and indicates the targeted position. The middle paragraph states the applicant's Navy experience and reason for seeking employment.

— LYNN MATHEWS —

5 Spring Road • Riverside, Pennsylvania • (555) 555-5555 • lynnmat@aol.com

Dear _____:

Perhaps your graphics department needs a professional with demonstrated creativity and technical skills along with a strong desire to continue learning and to succeed. If so, the qualifications I can offer to your department include the following:

- **Design/illustration experience.** Earned a Bachelor's degree in Illustration from the University of Hartford and acquired extensive training in illustration and design/graphics, utilizing computer software programs such as Aldus FreeHand, QuarkXPress, and PageMaker with a Macintosh system.

- **Award-winning talent.** Recipient of several awards/honors for my artistic talent and academic achievements: the Faith Ferguson Art Award, first place winner in the Honors Art class, and membership in the National Art Honor Society. Many of my illustrations were selected and displayed in the Senior Illustration Show.

- **Technical skills.** Proficient in using various media, including oils, acrylics, gouache, scratchboard, pen and ink, cut paper, color pencils, watercolors, image processing, and etching. Credited for my innovative approach, a great eye for color, excellent technique, and an ability to generate clever ideas.

In both educational and employment settings, I have proven myself to be a dependable, hardworking individual who is always prepared, well organized, and able to manage multiple projects/assignments. I take great pride in the quality of my work, never having missed a single deadline. Additionally, I possess excellent interpersonal skills, am team-oriented, and am willing to "go the extra mile" as needed.

I would welcome a conversation to discuss the contributions I can make to your department, even if you do not have a position available now. I am eager to begin a career in my chosen profession and look forward to speaking with you soon. Thank you for your consideration of my qualifications.

Very truly yours,

Lynn Mathews

32

Graphic Designer. *Louise Garver, Enfield, Connecticut*

The applicant was a recent college graduate in the field of art. Bullets point to strong experience, talent, and skills. She secured a position as a graphic designer at a consumer products company.

CATHERINE T. LEBO

555 SW Morrison Street
Portland, OR 55555   ctlebo@yahoo.com

(000) 000-0000 Residence
(000) 000-0000 Mobile

October 28, 2004

Ms. Jill Horvath
Operations Manager
Starbucks Corporate
1000 Second Avenue
Seattle, WA 55555

Dear Ms. Horvath:

You will want to interview me for the Creative Director position with Starbucks because I have outstanding design/creative skills, am a perfectionist who always strives to improve what I do, and thrive on challenges.

In my current position, as creative director for a former start-up beverage company, the president of my firm came to me and asked if I could add an animation piece to the presentation that he was to give at a conference a couple of days from then. **He wanted an animated graphic of himself jumping up and down.** At that time, I didn't have any experience in creating animated graphics, but the request intrigued me. I found the application to design it in and was able to create an animated graphic of my boss jumping up and down while waving a white flag! It was very funny, and **my boss was very impressed that I was able to pull it off, especially in such a short timeframe.** He thought he was giving me an impossible request, but **I made it possible.** Most people would just say no when asked to do things they've never done before, but I see it as a personal challenge and an opportunity to learn something new.

After you review the enclosed résumé and visit with me, I think you'll agree that I'm the missing piece to your team. My experience in the creative field is solid, from developing a strong corporate image from the ground up to developing quirky traditions with a lasting impression. I have enclosed a puzzle (one of the traditions I have instituted in my current position) to challenge you and to remind you to give me a call.

I will follow up with you in the next few days and look forward to meeting you. Thank you for your time and consideration.

Sincerely,

Catherine Lebo

Enclosure

33

Creative Director. *Jennifer Rydell, Portland, Oregon*

The writer includes a funny story in the second paragraph to illustrate the applicant's skills. Boldfacing in that paragraph focuses attention on the applicant's accomplishment and its impact.

JENNIFER GEORGE

78 Holland Brook Road • Mooresville, NJ 22222 • (333) 333-3333 • jngrge@earthlink.net

January 10, 2004

Hiring Agent, Title
Company Name
Address

Dear Hiring Manager:

Your posting for a [position title] caught my attention as it seems an ideal match for my experience and talents. As an accomplished graphic designer with a broad range of industry experience, I believe I am someone who will be an asset to your company. With strong creative instincts and a proven record in producing visual designs and written copy that sell products, I would like to explore the possibility of putting my skills and experience to work for you.

As you can see from my enclosed résumé, my career encompasses roles in marketing, advertising, sales, and management. An award-winning graphic designer, I am also well-versed in managing all aspects of client projects to successful completion. Key to my success, the depth of my creative talents is fully matched by a disciplined focus on achieving outstanding results. Therefore, I am someone who consistently delivers top-quality projects no matter what the challenge.

Among my other strengths, I have solid sales instincts and have been successful in cultivating long-term relationships with key clients. With a strong customer focus, I often earn the repeat business of clients. Persuasive, self-confident, and effective, I have proven to be a respected and valued employee in the past. With a record of success behind me, I am confident that I will be an asset to you as well.

I would be pleased to have the opportunity to discuss future employment and look forward to speaking with you. Feel free to contact me at the address and phone number listed above.

Thank you for your consideration.

Sincerely,

Jennifer George

Enclosure

34

Graphic Designer. *Carol A. Altomare, Three Bridges, New Jersey*

This letter is for an applicant who had both creative and administrative/relationship management skills. Each of the first three paragraphs shows that she is a designer with extra talent.

SAMUEL LAFITTE

555555 Rio Grande
Valencia, California 91355
email: lafitte@earthlink.net

Voice mail: 555-555-5555
Residence: 000-000-0000

January 13, 2004

Goldcrest Graphics, Inc.
25517 16th Street
Santa Clarita, California 91321

Ensuring Quality Control requires an experienced staff with the expertise to analyze an independent contractor's or employee's ability to do the job correctly for the best price. I possess an innate ability to assess employees' work, equipment, and quality standards. My commitment is to quality while remaining price conscious.

As a Senior Graphic Designer for Adexa earlier this year, I acted as liaison for the director, writer, and printers and edited the full project. Through my supervision of others, I was able to develop a cohesive unit that worked toward a common goal. My management skills led to **greater efficiency** and **cost reduction** while easily meeting deadlines.

Others have pointed out my unparalleled imagination, which allows me to properly evaluate designs, whether for catalogs, Web sites, or software. My diverse background encompasses

- Work for the Los Angeles County Arts Commission
- Murals for Transamerica Insurance, Inc., toy stores, restaurants
- Fascias for Michael Jackson Enterprises
- 3-D animation for Mad TV
- Character design and model creation for a television pilot
- Animation, direction, and production of a short claymation film
- Logo creation

Additional strengths include

- Capability to handle many tasks at one time and meet every deadline, even when those deadlines occur hourly
- Motivation and desire to complete all projects in a timely manner
- Ability to remain respectful, patient, and level-headed under pressure

Artists are famous for being perfectionists, and it is a reputation that is well earned. Although I design on a Mac, I also use a real-world, hands-on approach to business and am confident I can make a significant contribution to Goldcrest Graphics. I can serve both your creative and post-production needs. I am available for any shift, for contract work, for travel, on any basis—you name it. I have no ego, only a desire to do my job to perfection and an ability to use technical skills with creativity to achieve an artistic end.

Eager to hear your ideas, I would appreciate a moment of your time. Could you spare a few minutes to discuss this with me in person?

Sincerely,

Samuel Lafitte

Enclosure

35

Senior Graphic Designer. *Myriam-Rose Kohn, Valencia, California*

Short paragraphs make a long letter easier to read. Bullets introduced by one or two sentences help to break up a page of short paragraphs. Both phenomena are used effectively in this cover letter.

215 Crestview Avenue
Indianapolis, IN 46220
555.555.5555
PhOstbg@earthlink.com

November 15, 2004

Mr. Douglas Shuck
Human Resources Manager
WTW Architects
609 Candlewood Street
Pittsburgh, PA 15212-5801

Dear Mr. Shuck:

Each architect holds his/her own unique paradigm. It has **always** been my dream to be an architect. As an elementary student, I remember drawing projects from my own perspective—viewing the world through different eyes than those of my classmates. Because I enjoy my work and know that success and fulfillment stem directly from working in one's passion, I submit my résumé and portfolio to you for consideration.

My résumé clearly shows that I have a variety of qualifying skills and abilities. Briefly, they are as follows:

(1) a Bachelor of Arts School of Architecture degree from Miami University with a respectable GPA achieved through hard work and attention to detail,

(2) a very strong background in computer-oriented design as evidenced by keen realistic imaging and detail-oriented visualization to provide innovative, practical design solutions while utilizing a consistent application of the fundamentals, and

(3) a sincere desire to apply these artistic and technical skills in a creative, fulfilling position in a firm such as yours.

I recently saw on the cover of *Buildings* magazine that WTW Architects was awarded "Best New Construction" for the Hetzel Union Building/Paul Robeson Cultural Center at Pennsylvania State University. The article caught my attention because I visited Penn State with my cousin in the spring and saw the "HUB." The building's oval interior commands a unique presence through the use of natural light and open spaces—a concept developed and perfected by Frank Lloyd Wright. One of your senior principals, Paul Williams, stated in the article, "The circle is symbolic of mankind—a symbol of civilization, a symbol of the town, the village, and the individual." The influence of Frank Lloyd Wright's design and expression is clearly evident through your firm's architecture—the same design and expression woven throughout my portfolio.

As you can see from my portfolio, I take pride in my work, too. It would be an honor to be a contributing member of your team and to work hard toward achieving WTW's goals and objectives. Because "proven skills" are best explained in person, I welcome the opportunity to introduce myself in an interview to discuss the value I offer WTW Architects. I will follow up with a phone call the week of July 21. Thank you for reviewing my portfolio, and I look forward to our meeting.

Sincerely,

Phillip Ostberg
Enclosures

36

Architect. *Sharon Pierce-Williams, Findlay, Ohio*

The writer used the AIDA style of business writing for persuasive sales letters, where Attention, Interest, Desire, and Action paragraphs sell the product—in this instance, the candidate.

MELISSA THOMAS
5 Janus Court • Four Bridges, New York 11111 • (555) 555-5555 • melissathomas@aol.com

January 18, 2004

Hiring Agent, Title
Company Name
Address

Dear Hiring Manager:

As a recent graduate with a background in psychology, extensive child care experience, and a strong interest in special education, I would like to be considered for a Teacher Assistant position at your school. I learned of your opening through one of my professors at Kearney University. She indicated that she thought I would be a good match for your needs.

As you can see from my enclosed résumé, I have more than eight years of experience as a nanny, providing day, overnight, and extended care to children. Currently balancing the needs of three different families, I care for six children on both a scheduled and as-needed basis. Among my charges is a special-needs child, an autistic boy whom I provide with ten hours of therapy each week.

With this background, the teacher assistant position seems particularly suited to my interests and strengths. I truly love working with children and enjoy being involved in their development. As a nanny, I earned a reputation as a responsible, caring, and effective employee. Energetic and organized, I also have a wealth of patience and a strong desire to learn and grow. With these traits, I have proven to be a valued employee in the past. I am confident that I will be an asset to you as well.

I would be pleased to have the opportunity to discuss future employment and look forward to speaking with you. Feel free to contact me at the address and phone number listed above.

Thank you for your consideration.

Sincerely,

Melissa Thomas

Enclosure

37

Teacher Assistant. *Carol A. Altomare, Three Bridges, New Jersey*

This recent graduate had eight years of experience as a nanny and wanted a position in education. The letter shows in turn her interest, experience, worker traits, and desire for an interview.

Wendy R. McClean

0000 Potter Street
Saginaw, MI 55555

555-555-5555

February 19, 2004

Discovery Center
Attention: Search Committee
9874 E. Maple Road
Troy, MI 48084

Dear Search Committee Members:

I was excited to read your advertisement in the *Oakland Press* for Director of the Discovery Center. It seems as if the ad could have been written for me! Most of my adult life has been spent working with or for children, culminating in an Associate degree in Early Childhood Education. I am enclosing my resume for your review.

As I said, I match the qualifications you are seeking. Let me elaborate:

Your Requirements	*My Qualifications*
♥ CDA	♥ I have applied for my CDA and expect approval soon.
♥ At least 12 credits in child development, child psychology, or early childhood education	♥ I recently earned an Associate degree with High Honors in Early Childhood Education.
♥ Strong leadership skills	♥ In addition to operating my own day care center for four years, I have been instrumental in planning and implementing several fund-raising events for the Easter Seals Society.

When you take a look at my resume, you will see that my quest to improve my knowledge hasn't stopped in the classroom. I regularly attend conferences, professional association activities and continuing education opportunities so that I can remain current in the field. The fact that I worked full time (operating my own day care center) while attending college exemplifies my motivation and commitment.

In conclusion, I am confident I have the training and experience to excel in this position. I hope you will contact me to arrange an interview at your convenience. Thank you for your time and consideration.

Sincerely,

Wendy R. McClean

Enclosure

38

Child Care Center Director. *Janet L. Beckstrom, Flint, Michigan*

The applicant had just earned her associate's degree and wanted to head a child care center. The Your Requirements… My Qualifications scheme calls attention to the applicant's relevant credentials.

KELLY MENDOZA

60 Maple Court • Princeville, NY 55555 • (222) 222-2222 Phone/Fax

November 30, 2004

Hiring Agent, Title
Company Name
Address

Dear Hiring Manager:

As an ambitious, self-motivated individual with a lifelong love of working with children, I believe I offer a set of skills that would make me a welcome and valuable addition to your teaching staff. With a keen ability to relate to children, demonstrated leadership ability, and outstanding communications skills, I would like to consider the possibility of putting my knowledge and experience to work for you.

As you can see from my enclosed résumé, in addition to two years of professional business experience, I have held an extensive array of child-focused positions, including that of camp counselor, care provider, and instructor. Throughout my life, I developed a reputation as a hardworking individual who can be depended on to get the job done no matter what the challenge. Keys to my success are strong planning and follow-through skills, a demonstrated commitment to achieving goals, and a genuine interest in helping others.

Among my strengths, I am a resourceful problem solver and an effective communicator with a passion for growth and learning. As an effective role model, I like to think that I can instill those same values in others. Assertive in my approach to life, I have always taken on tough challenges and succeeded in accomplishing goals. With a solid record of accomplishment behind me, I am confident I can do the same for you.

I would be pleased to have the opportunity to discuss your needs and how I might be able to meet them. I will call to follow up, or you can contact me at the address and phone number listed above.

Thank you for your consideration.

Sincerely,

Kelly Mendoza

Enclosure

39

Teacher. *Carol A. Altomare, Three Bridges, New Jersey*

This letter is the first of two variations for a young career changer who wanted to become a teacher (see Cover Letter 40). In this letter, the writer refers to two years of business experience and focuses on transferable skills.

KELLY MENDOZA

60 Maple Court • Princeville, NY 55555 • (222) 222-2222 Phone/Fax

March 1, 2004

Hiring Agent, Title
Company Name
Address

Dear Hiring Manager:

As an ambitious, self-motivated individual with a lifelong love of working with children, I believe I offer a set of skills that would make me a welcome and valuable addition to your teaching staff. With a keen ability to relate to students, demonstrated leadership ability, and outstanding communications skills, I would like to consider the possibility of putting my knowledge and experience to work for you.

As you can see from my enclosed résumé, I have nearly completed my first year of teaching at Canterbury School, where I am pursuing full certification through the alternative-route program. Already through Phase 2, I expect to have my full state certification in August. With a background that also includes an extensive array of prior child-focused positions, you can be sure you are getting someone with a solid history in supporting the development of children.

This year of preparation has been rewarding in many ways, and I have been successful in implementing new and exciting teaching methods in the classroom. Using game strategies, process-oriented training stations, and teaching methods that accommodate different learning modalities, I am able to reach my students while providing a creative and fun environment in which to learn. Incorporating Bloom's taxonomy in assessing students' understanding, I am confident that I am achieving my classroom goals.

Keys to my success are a solid grasp of pedagogical methods, a strong classroom presence, excellent planning and follow-through skills, and a genuine interest in helping others. In addition, I am a resourceful problem solver and an effective communicator who is passionate about instilling my love for growth and learning in others. Assertive in my approach, I have always taken on challenges and succeeded in achieving goals. With a solid record of accomplishment behind me, I am confident I can do the same for you.

I would be pleased to have the opportunity to discuss your needs and how I might be able to meet them. I will call to follow up, or you can contact me at the address and phone number listed above.

Thank you for your consideration.

Sincerely,

Kelly Mendoza

Enclosure

40

Teacher. *Carol A. Altomare, Three Bridges, New Jersey*

In this second variation, the writer refers to the applicant's one year of classroom experience and anticipated licensure. The third and fourth paragraphs indicate her successes and professionalism.

Susan Wiley

Permanent Address:	Swiley2222@msn.com	Current Address:
1111 Clinton Avenue	cell: (000) 000-0000	2102 Indiana Street #222
Houston, TX 00000		Lubbock, TX 00000
(281) 000-0000		(806) 000-0000

January 30, 2004

Jan Pearson, Principal
Hart Elementary School
2323 Middleton Street
Houston, TX 00000

"One hundred years from now it will not matter what my bank account was, the sort of house I lived in, or the kind of car I drove, but the world may be different because I was important in the life of a child."
—*Anonymous*

Dear Mrs. Pearson:

I love the preceding quote! Although it may be seen as too "sentimental" by some, I truly believe that being able to make a positive difference in children's lives is a worthwhile endeavor—and the *true* reward in life. I am excited about the opportunity to launch my teaching career and influence student growth, and I am certain that my enthusiasm and ability to motivate would be a welcome addition to your faculty.

My educational experiences have convinced me that being a teacher is a wonderful career choice. While taking upper-level courses in secondary education and completing observation hours at local junior high and high schools, I studied educational theory and, more importantly, realized the value of consistent discipline enforcement, student-centered learning, and classroom/lesson organization, among many other educator functions. Through my Cum Laude G.P.A. and performance on major grade projects, I demonstrated a strong background knowledge in these areas, and although theory does not always translate into practice, I am confident that my knowledge will transfer effectively in an educational setting.

I have had two very different, yet interesting experiences in my employment history that indirectly prepared me for some of the challenges I will face as an educator. As a server at The Olive Garden restaurant, I was recognized by management for providing excellent, prompt service in an environment that could best be described as fast-paced and highly stressful. As an intern reporter for the *Moore County News Press*, I developed a keen appreciation for the richness and value of small-town living through firsthand observations and interviewing local residents for human-interest stories. Although both experiences are quite different from working day-to-day in an educational setting, I do feel that these positions prepared me for handling difficult situations and relating to diverse individuals on a one-to-one basis.

My résumé is enclosed to provide details about my background and qualifications. If permissible, I will contact you to follow up on this letter of inquiry, or you may contact me at the number of my current residence. I look forward to meeting with you and discussing how I can contribute to the success of your school.

In addition, I have a particular interest in sponsoring extracurricular activities and would like to discuss with you how I could contribute to your school in this regard.

Thank you for your time and consideration.

Sincerely,

Susan Wiley

Enclosure

41

Entry-level Teacher. *Daniel J. Dorotik, Jr., Lubbock, Texas*

The anonymous quotation amounts to the applicant's philosophy of teaching and enables her to express in the first paragraph her excitement and enthusiasm at the beginning of her teaching career.

REBECCA POLLARD

1234 Manor Road
Cuyahoga Falls, OH 12345

(555) 555-1234
RPollard@email.com

January 2, 2004

Mrs. Sharon Price
Principal, Brighton Elementary School
1234 Weathers Road
Akron, OH 12345

Dear Mrs. Price:

I am writing to express my interest in obtaining a teaching position at Brighton Elementary School and have enclosed my résumé for your review. As you are aware, I have been a Substitute Teacher for Brighton Schools for the past two years and have received consistent positive feedback and requests for continued service from your teachers and staff.

During my time as a Substitute Teacher, I have had the opportunity to sub for grades K–6. I have thoroughly enjoyed my experiences as a Substitute Teacher and am confident in my career choice. I look forward to applying my knowledge and skills in the classroom consistently, completing lesson plans and meeting classroom objectives. Additionally, I am excited to develop relationships with students on a daily basis that will make a positive impact in their lives, from sharing simple activities together to exploring life lessons that will help them succeed in the future. I find value and satisfaction in sharing the day with middle school students and am dedicated to obtaining a permanent teaching position within the Brighton school system.

I will contact you next week to discuss potential teaching opportunities at Brighton Elementary School. I am sure you will agree that I possess the knowledge, skills, dedication and caring attitude required to excel as a Teacher in an elementary school environment.

Sincerely,

Rebecca Pollard

Enclosure

42

Teacher. *Tara G. Papp, Mogadore, Ohio*

After two years of substitute teaching, the applicant was looking for a full-time position. The middle paragraph conveys the applicant's positive attitude, confidence, and excitement toward teaching.

Julia Scully

20 Angela Street ◆ Colonie, NY 00000 ◆ (555) 555-5555 ◆ sclly@sage.edu

Date

Hiring Agent Name
Title
School Name
Address
City, State ZIP

Dear Mr. / Ms. _____:

As a dedicated, highly knowledgeable Teacher with certification to teach pre-Kindergarten through grade 6, I believe my skills and talents can make an immediate and long-term contribution to [name of school].

During my intensive teaching assignments with Russell Sage College, I have enjoyed teaching elementary and preschool students in a variety of positions and educational settings. I am skilled at developing and implementing stimulating lesson plans, administering and evaluating standardized tests, writing profiles, and conducting parent-teacher conferences. I am a team player capable of working well and building strong rapport with students, professionals, parents, and staff members. My educational background includes a Bachelor's degree in Elementary Education with a minor in Psychology from Russell Sage College. My proven ability to help children achieve their highest levels through positive motivation will be an asset to your team.

The accompanying résumé provides further details of my accomplishments and what I have to offer. I believe it would be mutually beneficial for us to meet and discuss your current or anticipated teaching positions. I will call next week to inquire about such a meeting.

Thank you for your time and consideration.

Sincerely,

Julia Scully

Enc. résumé

43

Elementary Teacher. *John Femia, Altamont, New York*

This letter is for a recent graduate. The opening paragraph indicates her occupational goal, the middle paragraph sells the candidate, and the third paragraph looks for an interview.

Christine Feathers
14 Hillard Place
Sayville, New York 55555
631.555.5555
christine23@aol.com

April 9, 2004

Charles Smith, Superintendent of Schools
Hicksville School District
124 Division Avenue
Hicksville, New York 55555

Re: <u>**Fourth-Grade Teacher**</u>

Dear Mr. Smith:

It has been reported that every individual will have had one or two teachers that had a profound impact on his or her life. I strive to be that teacher, and I am confident that my diverse student teacher experience and formal Elementary Education qualifications will enable me to do so.

I've learned that creating exciting lesson plans encourages an interactive classroom environment. This approach, along with integrating various subjects, helps address all learning experiences, and especially engages the student to learn on a more visual, tactile, and auditory basis.

As a student teacher in the second and fourth grades, I had the opportunity to work with gifted, ESL, and included students. This diverse experience helped me develop effective teaching techniques and unique classroom management strategies. I have created and instructed lesson plans in several disciplines, including but not limited to reading, mathematics, social studies, and science. In addition, I have designed bulletin boards, prepared weekly plan books, and participated in parent-teacher conferences.

I have enclosed my resume for your review and would love the opportunity to meet with you to discuss any Elementary Education teaching positions in the Hicksville School District.

Please call me at your earliest convenience to schedule an interview. I look forward to hearing from you and thank you in advance for your consideration.

Sincerely,

Christine Feathers

Enclosure

44

Elementary Teacher. *Deanna Verbouwens, Hicksville, New York*

The Long Island job market was saturated, and this applicant needed a letter that set her apart from thousands of other applicants. The writer regarded the last two paragraphs as "closers" for action from an employer.

LORRAINE SIMMONS

899 Forest Lane
Southland, PA 00000

(555) 555-5555
lorsim@aol.com

Date

Name
Company
Address
City, State ZIP

Dear Name:

My interest in contributing to your school system as an elementary teacher has prompted me to forward my resume for your consideration. With several years of service in different grade levels and all curriculum areas, my qualifications are a match for the position.

Specifically, I offer the following:

Education	◆ Master of Arts in Teaching from the College of Our Lady of the Elms.
Experience	◆ I have 8 years of experience in elementary school environments, including the past 5 years as a classroom teacher instructing fourth-grade students. ◆ I have taught diverse student populations representing various cultural and socio-economic backgrounds as well as different emotional/learning needs. ◆ My experience includes curriculum design and using a variety of creative teaching techniques to engage students with different learning styles and needs.
Leadership	◆ Extensive planning, program development, organizational and coordination skills combine with leadership strengths, including serving on a committee to develop and implement a performance-evaluation program for the faculty.
Philosophy and Attributes	◆ A skilled and dedicated teacher, I have excellent classroom-management, conflict-resolution, communication and interpersonal abilities. ◆ Monitoring, evaluating and actualizing teaching practices to facilitate the academic, social and personal needs of all learners are among my strengths.

If you are seeking a teaching professional who can stimulate elementary students' interests and focus their intensity and curiosity, then I may be the candidate you need. I enjoy challenges, and I work diligently and cooperatively to achieve common goals. Equally important, I am committed to the students, parents and community whom I serve. In addition, I strive to build effective relationships in my interactions with other educators and administrators.

I appreciate your serious consideration.

Sincerely,

Lorraine Simmons

45

Elementary Teacher. *Louise Garver, Enfield, Connecticut*

This letter helped the applicant secure an elementary teaching position. Bulleted items are clustered according to four criteria as bold side headings, making the items easier to comprehend.

Jennie S. Donaldson

000 Sheridan Place • Saginaw, MI 48601 • 555-555-5555

Date

Name
Company
Address
City, State ZIP

Dear Administrator:

The education field is in a predicament right now, isn't it? Many districts are faced with a need for teachers but may not have the funds to hire experienced educators, especially those with advanced degrees. I am one of those "seasoned" teachers, and I would like to explain why I believe my experience is valuable to your district.

This is my eleventh year of teaching at the early elementary level. Over time I have learned what works and what doesn't, what motivates children and what turns them off. Since I know what to expect from students at the beginning of each year, we can get right down to the business of learning. Given the importance of standardized test scores such as MEAP, it is important to start covering relevant material as soon and as often as possible. I don't have to teach by trial and error—I've been there, done that.

My ability to earn the trust and respect of my students is a key point as well. Getting parents involved in their children's education is important, too. My classroom is high energy and creative, and I'm not afraid to try new techniques. Completing a master's degree in teaching and curriculum has certainly helped round out *my* education.

I hope you'll give me an opportunity for an interview so that I can give you additional information about my teaching style, capabilities, and enthusiasm for the job. Please contact me at 555-555-5555. Thank you for your time and attention.

Sincerely,

Jennie S. Donaldson

Enclosure

46

Elementary Teacher. *Janet L. Beckstrom, Flint, Michigan*

Many teacher layoffs had created a huge applicant pool. Districts were hiring less-experienced teachers for less money. This letter explains why this experienced elementary teacher is "worth it."

CHRISTINE L. BERNARDO
000 ATTAWA ROAD
NEW VISTA, NM 88888

March 22, 2004

Dr. Stephanie Stasos, Assistant Superintendent
Human Resources Department
New Vista Public Schools
New Vista, NM 88888

Dear Dr. Stasos:

Recently, my neighbor, who teaches at New Vista High School, informed me that there may be several elementary and middle school teaching positions available for the coming school year. Since my last correspondence with you, I have received my middle school endorsement, in addition to my certification to teach in elementary grades. I am now certified to teach social studies at the middle school level through grade eight.

May I add that I feel quite honored to have been chosen from among more than 200 applicants to participate—along with mainly seasoned teachers—in a fully paid summer institute sponsored by the National Geographic Society. I am confident that this unique experience will add much interest to my own classes in project development and general class discussions.

As a substitute teacher in the New Vista schools this past year, I found administrators, supervisors, and faculty exceptionally helpful and pleasant. Such welcoming support from them is particularly assuring to entry-level teachers like me. I felt like one of the family!

Thank you, Dr. Stasos, for taking time from your busy schedule to see me last spring, and I look forward to another meeting with you soon to discuss in more depth my goals and long-range ambitions in the teaching profession. I would appreciate your scheduling me for a formal interview as I apply for a teaching position in the New Vista Public School District.

Sincerely,

Christine L. Bernardo

Enclosures: résumé; employment application packet

(555) 555-5555   ◊   Cell: (000) 000-0000   ◊   chrsbrnrdo@earthlink.com

47

Middle School Teacher. *Edward Turilli, North Kingstown, Rhode Island*

Networking breaks the ice in the first paragraph. The applicant strengthens her candidacy by informing the superintendent of her recent accomplishments and complimenting her school system.

DENNIS J. BAXTER
22 W. 25th Street
Aston, PA 19333
(555) 555-5555

January 16, 2004

Taylor School District
ATT: Donald E. Sanders, Director of Personnel
Alder Building, Second Floor
14 James Avenue
Drexel, PA 19000

Dear Mr. Sanders:

I am writing in reference to an elementary or middle school teaching position in the Taylor School District. I would like to be involved in extracurricular student activities as well, and I would be particularly interested in coaching in the school district where I am employed. A complete resume outlining my education and professional background is enclosed for your review.

I am currently under contract for the 2003–2004 school year at the Victory Valley Middle School as a long-term substitute in the Mathematics Department. I've also been fortunate to be involved as a coach in the school's athletic program. What a rewarding experience! More importantly, this past year has clearly defined where I belong—working with kids and making a difference to their lives, both in the classroom and on the field.

As you can see in the enclosed resume, I am also a professional carpenter. I bring a unique blend of experience and maturity to the classroom. It is my belief that teaching isn't just about lesson plans, report cards and parent conferences. In order to *capture* and *keep* the interest of students, a teacher has to be creative and interesting. I possess those qualifications, and I'm eager to apply them in a permanent teaching position.

It would be my pleasure to meet with you to discuss ways in which I can contribute to one of your elementary or middle schools. I will contact you in approximately a week to confirm that you have received my information and that I am a viable candidate for a teaching position in your district.

I sincerely appreciate your consideration and look forward to future discussions.

Sincerely,

Dennis J. Baxter

Enclosure

48

Teacher-Coach. *Karen Conway, Media, Pennsylvania*

This applicant not only had teaching and coaching experience, but also was a professional carpenter. The third paragraph calls attention to his "unique blend" of diversified experience and maturity.

Donald R. Jones

206 Hawkins Lane • Columbus, Ohio 43200 • 614.456.0000 • drjones@juno.com

April 17, 2004

Mr. Scott Trobough
Superintendent
Columbus City Schools
1234 Morse Road
Columbus, Ohio 43200

Dear Mr. Trobough:

After a successful career in government, I recently fulfilled a lifelong desire to become an educator at the secondary level. I have completed my education and licensure requirements and am excited to begin my teaching career. This letter is sent to inquire about possible teaching opportunities within the Columbus City Schools. The enclosed resume will provide detailed information regarding my background and experience in support of my candidacy.

To briefly highlight my qualifications, I offer you the following:

- Social Studies Comprehensive Certification (7–12) complemented by a Bachelor of Arts degree in Political Science

- Successful classroom teaching experience as a substitute and student teacher in diverse classroom settings—experienced in developing and implementing integrated lesson plans for cooperative learning

- More than 10 years of professional involvement in government at the local, state and federal levels providing invaluable insight and knowledge to bring into the classroom

In short, I bring a unique combination of education and "real world" experience not often found in today's classroom teachers. I believe the time I spent in government can only enhance my social studies teaching. Should you have a teaching position available, I would appreciate being considered a serious candidate. You should also know that I would be interested in serving as an advisor for extracurricular clubs and/or activities. Feel free to contact me to set up an interview or to answer any questions you may have regarding my background and experience.

Thank you for your time and consideration. I look forward to hearing from you.

Sincerely,

Donald R. Jones

Enclosure

49

Social Studies Teacher. *Melissa L. Kasler, Athens, Ohio*

The applicant was transitioning from government employment to teaching. Because of his background in real-world government and politics, he wanted to be a social studies teacher.

MICHAEL STACK

000 Lexington Drive / Albany, NY 00000 / (555) 555-5555

February 10, 2004

Dr. Taylor Raine Coleman
Putnam Valley Central School District
111 Peekskill Hollow Road
Putnam Valley, NY 10579

Dear Dr. Coleman:

Please accept this letter and enclosed résumé for the social studies position that is currently available within your district. As an experienced social studies teacher, I offer vast classroom exposure, a great deal of energy, and a commitment to the students.

Over the course of my career, I have taught both middle-school and high-school students in a variety of subjects, including U.S. History and Global History. Two years ago, my wife and I relocated to the Mohawk Valley from Albany, NY. Currently, I teach 8th-grade social studies in Herkimer Central School District. Prior to this, I taught for 14 years at Schenectady Central School District.

As a professional educator, my efforts extend beyond academics. I work hard at instilling a sense of school pride, building community awareness, and motivating students to set higher standards. In addition to general education, my teaching experience encompasses inclusion classes. With all my students, I take the time to connect with each one, demonstrating genuine sensitivity when working with those who have special needs. Through an ongoing process of planning, delivering, reflecting, and refining lessons, I am consistently successful at balancing individual needs with the NYS Standards & Assessments. I also have a proven record of success (98% passing rate) with the 8th-Grade Social Studies Assessment.

Most significant to my teaching ability is my enthusiasm for the material and appropriate sense of humor. Through these, I am able to engage students and facilitate the learning process. Daily lessons include classroom discussion of current events while activities focus on creating and using information for knowledge and understanding. I also highlight the modes of communication within the community and integrate technology and media into lessons. Whatever the topic, my goal is to emphasize the fact that knowledge and access to information are essential to responsible citizenship and participation in a democracy.

Thank you in advance for your time. I look forward to speaking with you to further discuss my qualifications.

Sincerely,

Michael Stack

Enclosure

50

Social Studies Teacher. *Kristin M. Coleman, Poughkeepsie, New York*

In this well-designed letter, the last sentence of the first paragraph indicates the key topics of the second, third, and fourth paragraphs, respectively. The letter gives the impression that the applicant has an orderly mind.

Wanda Ortiz

2 Fir Lane   (555) 555-5555
Smithtown, NY 11787   w_ortiz@aol.com

There is no more beautiful life than that of a student.
~ F. Albrecht

During my years as a bilingual educator, I have developed a keen understanding of the importance of student assimilation and respect for their native upbringing. These key principles make teaching bilingual students a rewarding and challenging career path.

As an educator, I wear many different hats: those of teacher, motivator, and leader. I am confident in my ability to create a "love of learning" environment for bilingual students that will enrich their academic growth.

I adhere to new procedures and commissioner regulations for LEP and have hands-on knowledge of the following academic standards: Language for Information and Understanding, Language for Literacy Response and Expression, Language for Critical Analysis and Evaluation, and Language for Social Interaction.

If your school district is looking for an enthusiastic and engaging educator who enjoys building brighter futures, I encourage you to give me a call at (555) 555-5555.

Sincerely,

Wanda Ortiz

51

Bilingual Educator. *Linda Matias, Smithtown, New York*

The applicant was going to use the cover letter at a teachers' job fair. Therefore, she could not personalize each letter. Instead of a salutation, the writer put first an inspirational quotation.

JAMES L. HAMMARLUND
63 Bay Vista Street, Westerly, WA 00000
(555) 333-4444
jlhamm@aol.com

February 22, 2004

Dr. Frank Kessler, Superintendent
Westerly School District
788 Whitman Road
Westerly, WA 00000

Dear Dr. Kessler:

Please accept this letter in response to your advertisements in *The Westerly Weekly Press*, January 20, 2004, and *The Westerly Sunday Journal*, January 22, 2004, for a Physical Education / Health teacher at Westerly High School. I have enclosed my résumé and a completed application for employment.

As a Washington State–certified, experienced, and successful teacher of Physical Education / Health and an athletic coach for nine years, I have consistently demonstrated my ability to motivate and handle youngsters, both in the classroom and on the playing field. Equally important, I possess a sincere caring for teenagers and extend myself to help ensure their success.

My strengths as a teacher include patience, dedication, and a strong sense of organization. Although I enjoy working within a rather structured curriculum, I am quite able to adapt to most working environments. Finally, of utmost importance to me is that my students receive physical education instruction of the highest quality. I strive to inculcate integrity in all that they do as students and future citizens and leaders of our city and country.

Thank you, Dr. Kessler, for considering my application for employment in the Westerly School District. I look forward to meeting with you to reveal and discuss my objectives during professional development.

Sincerely,

James L. Hammarlund

Enclosures: résumé / application

52

Physical Education/Health Teacher. *Edward Turilli, North Kingstown, Rhode Island*

This physical education teacher makes the point that he teaches the whole student instead of promoting only the student's physical well-being. This approach makes him appear unique.

Arthur Hampton, M.Ed.

1111 Parker Street
Brunswick, New Jersey 07777

Home: 222-999-5555
Office: 222-666-6600

January 16, 2004

Worthington Area School District
ATT: James Drury, Superintendent
14 Atherton Street
Worthington, New Jersey 06666

Dear Superintendent Drury:

Allow me to introduce myself.

For the past 19 years I have been involved in the educational leadership of two highly respected private schools. Two of my key responsibilities have been to introduce competitive and demanding instructional programs and to hire and develop the appropriate staff to meet those challenges. I'm happy to say that I have been successful in both areas, as reflected in the enclosed resume. Best of all, I have enjoyed making learning an exciting and enjoyable process for the students!

I am at a point in my professional career where I am ready for a new challenge. Key areas where I can make a contribution to your district are the following:

- Planning and developing curriculum
- Achieving accreditation
- Building teamwork and cohesive work groups
- Setting goals and high academic standards
- Budget management and fund-raising activities

It would be my pleasure to meet with you to discuss the ways in which I can make an immediate and positive impact on your fine district.

Thank you for your consideration and professional courtesy in reviewing my resume. I look forward to speaking with you soon.

Sincerely,

Arthur Hampton

Enclosure

53

Administrative Position. *Karen Conway, Media, Pennsylvania*

At a pivotal point in his long career, this educational leader wanted an administrative position in which he could further apply his leadership skills. Bullets point to his possible key contributions.

JANET SIMMONS

000 Old Farm Road • Sussex, NJ 11111 • (333) 333-3333 • jsmmns@msn.com

September 7, 2004

Hiring Agent, Title
Company Name
Address

Dear Hiring Manager:

Your posting for an Arts Coordinator caught my attention as it seems an ideal match for my experience, talents, and interests. As a successful art educator with a record of accomplishment not only in teaching but also in developing and coordinating stimulating programs that promote art in the classroom and the community, I believe I am someone who will be an asset to your organization. With a wealth of knowledge, proven planning and coordination skills, unbounded energy, and a passion for achieving goals, I would like to explore the possibility of putting my skills to work for you.

As you can see from my enclosed résumé, I have enjoyed a long, successful career in art education, having developed and taught a wide range of classes. Among my accomplishments, I take most pride in the influential role I had in expanding programs, improving curricula, and attracting students to art classes. As a testament to this, nearly 75% of students at Ridgemont High School, where I currently teach, have participated in elective art classes. I am also very proud of the annual art show, which I co-founded and then continued and expanded for more than 20 years. It is highly rewarding for me to see the wonderful talents of students professionally displayed and appreciated by attendees in these consistently well-received shows.

Through my school involvement, I have also had the opportunity to participate in other creative endeavors, such as set design, publication planning and layout, and special events coordination. Highly organized and detail-oriented, I have established a record of success in bringing all of these projects to completion. Resourceful and quick-thinking, I am undaunted by challenge and resilient in the face of problems. With these traits and a proven track record behind me, I am confident I will be an asset to you as well.

I would be pleased to have the opportunity to discuss future employment with you and look forward to speaking with you soon. Please feel free to contact me at the address and phone number listed above.

Thank you for your consideration.

Sincerely,

Janet Simmons

Enclosure

54

Arts Coordinator. *Carol A. Altomare, Three Bridges, New Jersey*

This art teacher was ready to retire and wanted to find related work in the community. A concern was to show not only her expertise in art education but also her creativity in other areas.

JOSHUA R. BENNETT

1234 Smith Road   (555) 555-1234
Kent, OH 12345   JRBennett@email.com

November 15, 2004

Search Committee for Academic Advisor
Attention: Andrea Miller
State University
P.O. Box 1234
Akron, OH 12345

Dear Ms. Miller:

I am writing to express my interest in the **Academic Advisor** position in the Student Advising Center, **Job Number 12345.** I became aware of this position through the State University job-posting Web site. I believe that I am well qualified for a position as Academic Advisor and have attached my résumé and qualifications for your review.

I possess a Bachelor's degree in Psychology, and a Master's degree in Education. Currently, I am an Academic Advisor at a community college and work in conjunction with the college's Career Center. My current role has provided me with valuable experience in assessing the career interest and development stages of a diverse population.

My work experience has also provided me with extensive knowledge of the academic advising process and the challenges of student life. I possess excellent interpersonal and communication skills, enabling students to trust in the guidance and information that I provide. Furthermore, I have experience in the area of training and development, which qualifies me for dealing with program development issues and implementing training programs for faculty and advisors. After a review of my résumé, I'm sure you will find that I am the best candidate for this position.

Thank you in advance for your consideration. I will contact you next week to discuss my ability to successfully fulfill the role of Academic Advisor at State University.

Sincerely,

Joshua R. Bennett

Enclosure

55

University Academic Advisor. *Tara G. Papp, Mogadore, Ohio*

With experience as an academic advisor at a community college, this applicant was looking for a similar position at a state university. The letter indicates his credentials and range of experience.

MICHAEL R. KELLEY

4567 Ridgeway Avenue • Lewiston, KY 44444 • 606.123.4567

July 22, 2004

Ms. Nancy Spires
Human Resources
Kenyon College
1234 Meadowbrook Avenue
Racine, Ohio 45771

Dear Ms. Spires:

First off, belated congratulations to everyone at Kenyon College for being listed in the *Kaplan/Newsweek* "How to Get into College" issue as one of the year's "hottest colleges." To that end, it would be an honor for me to join the Kenyon staff as the Head Men's Basketball Coach and strive to uphold the high standards of your institution. Please accept the enclosed resume as my sincere interest in this position.

With 18 years of coaching (14 of those at the collegiate level), extensive experience in Division III athletics and broad knowledge of the North Coast Athletic Conference, I have much to offer as the Head Coach of the Kenyon Lords.

In addition, my background as a Division III player and coach have greatly helped shape my coaching and administration philosophies regarding intercollegiate athletics. Those philosophies begin and end with academics and the true meaning of being a student-athlete.

I am eager to discuss with you my background and the position of Head Men's Basketball Coach. Feel free to contact me if you have any questions concerning my resume and references. I look forward to the opportunity of meeting with you to discuss my candidacy. Thank you for your time and consideration.

Sincerely,

Michael R. Kelley

Enclosure

56

Head Men's Basketball Coach. *Melissa L. Kasler, Athens, Ohio*

This coach wanted to convey his knowledge of the school/athletic program to which he was applying. To set a positive tone, the writer first congratulates the college on a recent achievement.

LAWRENCE CHIN, Ph.D.

0000 East State Street
Ithaca, NY 55555

(000) 000-0000 Home   lchn75@attbi.com   (000) 000-0000 Mobile

January 4, 2004

Professor Stephen Shinseki
Director, Laboratory of Solid State Physics
Harvard University
Cambridge, MA 55555

Attention: Experimental Physics Search

Dear Professor Shinseki:

I am responding to your advertisement for an assistant professor in experimental condensed matter physics and have enclosed my CV, publication list, and a statement of research interests for your review.

Some highlights of my research achievements include the following:

- Resolved a long-standing controversy about the nature of wide bands in rare earth-based, inter-metallic compounds by incorporating high-resolution photoemission, which **was cited in multiple papers in professional journals, including *Nature* and *Science*.**

- Mapped electronic and magnetic nature in Fe/Cr nanowedges by conducting depth-resolved hard X-ray standing wave spectroscopy with bright elliptically polarized light. **This work decorated the front page of *Science* as the work of the year for 2003.**

- Obtained the world record tunneling magnetoresistance and excellent thermal stabilities in metallic tunnel junctions by introducing a new type of deposition process and materials. **This work is patented and appeared in *Science* and *Physics* magazines.**

In my present position as a research associate professor at Cornell University, I have made several scientific and technological breakthroughs in the development of magnetic random-access memory devices. My work has not only made substantial contributions to the development of high-speed, high-density, low-power, and non-volatile magnetic devices, but also provided a fundamental understanding of the microscopic underlying mechanisms in the transport properties and the electronic structure of state-of-the-art magnetic nanostructures.

Thank you very much for your time and consideration. I look forward to discussing how my experience, credentials, and achievements meet your departmental needs.

Sincerely,

Lawrence Chin

Enclosures

Assistant Physics Professor. *Jennifer Rydell, Portland, Oregon*

The writer wanted to place the applicant's impressive achievements front and center "while still maintaining an understated feel for the academic world." Note the boldfacing of impressive info.

YVETTE SEITLIN

555 Andrews Road, Apt. 4   Pasadena, California 91030   555-555-5555   YvetteS@history.tulane.edu

---

March 6, 2004

Mr. James Goldberg
Cataloguing Operations Manager
Survivors of the Shoah Visual History Foundation
P.O. Box 3129
Los Angeles, California 90078-3168

Dear Mr. Goldberg:

It was a pleasure meeting you on Friday. I would like to join the Survivors of the Shoah Visual History Foundation project. My position at UCLA ends in December, and I am eager to win one of the research positions you mentioned at the tour's end. My experience in historical research, teaching, publishing and study qualify me for the position.

Your Needs	My Qualifications
M.A. degree in history	♦ Ph.D. Candidate in History, Tulane University, expected in 2005. Coursework focused on war and nationalism in the United States and in modern Europe.
	♦ Doctoral research focuses on civilians who faced enemy soldiers during the Civil War, much like the Holocaust survivors themselves.
	♦ M.A. in History, plus B.A. in History and English.
Superior research skills	♦ Doctoral research has taken me to more than 15 archives in 9 states. In addition, I have used countless other published, online and microfilm sources.
	♦ Awarded national and university funds to conduct research in field of study.
Ability to prioritize many tasks under deadline while displaying excellent attention to detail	♦ Selected as a research assistant for 2 noted professional historians. Completed many tasks while balancing my own coursework.
	♦ Conducted independent research for thesis, dissertation, conference presentations and research assistant projects.
	♦ Met all self- and institution-imposed deadlines for all research, coursework and publications.

58

Historical Researcher. *Gail Frank, Tampa, Florida*

The applicant found out about a "hidden" job by taking a tour of the Shoah Foundation. The tour-giver mentioned open research positions for which the applicant was a perfect fit. This letter highlights her eagerness and interest in the position. She was so confident in her ability that

YVETTE SEITLIN PAGE 2

<u>Your Needs</u>	<u>My Qualifications</u>
Strong interpersonal skills and excellent communication ability	♦ Taught as an adjunct instructor at UCLA for an upper-level history course.
	♦ Taught as a Teaching Assistant for an undergraduate history course at the University of Cincinnati.
	♦ Successfully presented 2 papers at History conferences with 2 more papers proposed for 2004.
	♦ Copy edited 2 books, one of which was a historical atlas with geographical terminology.
	♦ B.A. degree in both History and English demanded ability to write well.
Team player willing to make a commitment to the Foundation	♦ Strong, lifelong interest in Holocaust and its causes and significance. Belief in importance of this project.
	♦ Jewish ancestry makes this project even more significant to me.
	♦ Demonstrated ability to make long-term commitment to research and writing through achievement of thesis and pending dissertation.
Computer skills	♦ Strong skills in Microsoft Word and Excel, the Internet and database programs.

My resume/CV provides further details of my accomplishments. I have also attached a sheet of my references for your convenience. I will contact you next week to arrange a meeting so that we may discuss the Foundation's needs in greater detail.

Sincerely,

Yvette Seitlin

Enclosures

cc: Professor T. Smythe, Tulane University
Professor G. Ryder, Tulane University
Professor A. Roberts, UCLA

she included a set of references with her letter. Although this is not usually done, she wanted to provide all of the needed information right away (and she alerted her references to possible inquiries about her).

JOAN SMITH

6 Honeyberry Court • Frankston • Vic 3333 Australia
Ph: (613) 000 0000 (W) • (613) 000 0000 (H) • email: j.smith@hotmail.com

Date

Mr. De Kretzer
Head Dean
Melbourne University—Deakin Campus
65-150 Richmond Road
MELBOURNE, VIC 3000

Dear Mr. De Kretzer:

With the pending conferral of my Doctor of Philosophy, I am seeking a position as **Researcher / Educator** with your university and believe my academic accomplishments, extensive research and teaching expertise would certainly be transferable to this role.

My enclosed resume demonstrates my

☑ Distinguished record in teaching and technical innovation achieved through conceptualisation, development and implementation of flexible delivery style learning techniques. I have lectured to several campuses simultaneously through ISL (Distance) Education and through self-developed Online Course Web pages, and I am proficient in the operation of numerous popular software applications.

☑ Expertise in applying sophisticated quantative and qualitative research methodologies demonstrated in working towards successful completion of Ph.D.; numerous self-researched/published writings; continued professional development and conference attendance; and extensive research assistant work, utilising SPSS, N*VIVO and NUD*IST.

☑ Exceptional interpersonal, communication and presentation skills. Able to build and maintain strategic relationships with students and colleagues from diverse backgrounds. Recognised as a positive role model, teacher, lecturer, tutor and mentor.

☑ Facilitation of proactive classroom environments, encouraging active student participation to further enhance learning outcomes. Committed to holistic student development and learning experiences.

☑ Visionary, goal-driven work ethic, combined with solid team collaboration competencies and individual strengths utilising sound follow-through and detail orientation to plan and achieve projects from concept to successful conclusion.

Given the combination of these competencies, I am confident that I have developed a professional resourcefulness and personal diversity that will enable me to become a productive member of your faculty. Your consideration of my qualifications and academic and professional accomplishments will be appreciated.

Sincerely,

Joan Smith

Enclosure

59

Researcher/Educator. *Annemarie Cross, Hallam, Victoria, Australia*

This applicant was nearing the completion of her Ph.D. She had gained extensive experience throughout her short career. This letter sums up her experience and what she has to offer.

PATRICIA GREEN

444 Circle Drive • Brentwood, NY 55555 • (555) 444-2222 • Trainer@ITclass.n

Date

Name
Company
City, State ZIP

Dear Name:

Perhaps your organization is seeking to recruit a talented instructor to teach the complexities of advanced networking infrastructures to broad student populations. If this is the case, then please find the accompanying résumé, highlighting my career as an MCSE instructor, Systems Administrator, and Consultant, for your review and consideration for a position teaching advanced MCSE curriculums/Windows with your facility.

Currently, I maintain tenure as an MCSE instructor with InfoTech Training Solutions, a leading provider of high-end networking certifications in Microsoft, Novell, and Cisco; and as an innovator of the industry's first Hands-on-Technical Training Lab (HOTT™). In this capacity, I continue to effectively teach classes throughout InfoTech's headquarters and university-based satellite locations. I oversee the instruction of other trainers as part of the organization's Train-the-Trainer program, which I initiated, developed, and continue to implement.

My ability to teach curricula based on both theory and realistic business models not only has prepared students for today's competitive workplace, but also has resulted in an unprecedented 100% student passing rate on A+, MCP, and all MCSE core exams. I am confident that my verifiable track record, coupled with my personal and professional dedication to quality teaching, would greatly benefit your organization.

Although the accompanying résumé illustrates my background well, I feel that a personal interview would better demonstrate my knowledge and abilities. Therefore, I would appreciate an opportunity to meet with you for an in-depth interview to discuss the possible merging of my strengths with your organization's training objectives. Thank you for your review and consideration. I look forward to hearing from you soon.

Sincerely,

Patricia Green

Enclosure

60

MCSE Instructor. *Ann Baehr, Brentwood, New York*

The first paragraph is a probe to learn of any interest in an instructor, and the second indicates the applicant's current position and areas of expertise. The third attests to her effectiveness.

TED MICHAELS, EIT

0000 Snowcap Drive SW • Calgary, AB Canada T2V 4P5
Tel: 555-555-5555 • Cell: 000-000-0000
tedmichaels@emailnet.ca

March 10, 2004

Mr. Gordon Eberth
Vice President, Engineering
Fording, Inc.
205 9th Avenue SW, Suite 1000
Calgary, AB T2G 0R4

Dear Mr. Eberth:

The background and professional experience I can offer in reply to your ad for an entry-level engineer may prove ideal for your needs. I say "professional experience" because I have worked steadily throughout college, functioning as a professional engineer. Combine that professional experience with my recently earned Engineer in Training (EIT) credential and BSEE, and you have a fully equipped engineer ready to present your firm with advantages others may not offer.

For example, as a project engineer for an electrical company with $200M gross annual revenues, I acquired strong leadership and interpersonal skills. My experience with this company trained me to think on my feet while under high-pressured schedules that required quick assessment of key factors involved with project management, such as estimating and resource management. Dealing with the diverse concerns of management, unions, and customers, I have become adept at operating with the proper mix of authority, diplomacy, and tact.

While working in this demanding position, in which I held sole responsibility for project success or failure, I held down a full college schedule, achieving a 3.53 cumulative GPA. My formal academic training in electrical engineering provided me with a thorough foundation in principles that affect the business of engineering.

Let us arrange a convenient time to discuss further Fording's needs and my qualifications. I will contact you in a week to see about scheduling a meeting. Thank you for your time and consideration. I look forward to speaking with you.

Very truly yours,

Ted Michaels

61

Entry-level Engineer. *Nick V. Marino, Bishop, Texas*

This applicant recently graduated with his BSEE degree but had already gained valuable professional experience. He mentions also his recent experience and his Engineer in Training credential.

RYAN G. SMITH

555-555-5555
ryansmith@email.com

0000 Snowfall Drive
Colorado Springs, CO 80903

March 30, 2004

Mr. Robert Johnson
Lockheed Martin Corporation
6801 Rockledge Drive
Bethesda, MD 20817-1877

Dear Mr. Johnson:

➢ More than 13 years of professional experience in engineering sophisticated avionic systems, with a Bachelor of Science in Mechanical and Manufacturing Technology;

➢ Keen analytical and problem-solving skills;

➢ Proven ability to deliver quantifiable cost savings, whether leading the project, working independently, or operating as part of a cross-functional team;

➢ Experience in authoring ISO, process control writings, and training syllabi, as well as delivering the associated training; and

➢ A verifiable record of improving workflow and manufacturing processes that positively impact budgetary goals.

I would like to bring my expertise and experience as a **process engineer** to Lockheed Martin. My technical knowledge, drive, determination, and solid communication skills will allow me to make an immediate contribution to your organization.

Thank you for your consideration. I look forward to speaking with you.

Sincerely,

Ryan G. Smith
Enclosure

62

Process Engineer. *Cindy Kraft, Valrico, Florida*

Creating a simple vertical line and positioning the letter in the second "column" can make a letter stand out from a host of other letters. Starting the letter with bulleted items also is unique.

AVAILABLE FOR RELOCATION

Benito Hoover
maintenance reliability engineer

90 Carleton Drive
Macon, Georgia 00000
000.000.0000 — bh1@smartx.net

Thursday, June 17, 2004

Mr. Charles W. Moran
Crest, Inc.
2130 Interstate Parkway
Suite 400
Atlanta, Georgia 00000

Dear Mr. Moran:

If you think Crest's maintenance reliability engineer should go beyond the important functions of asset protection and regulatory compliance, we should explore adding me to your team.

To start, you'll find five solid, profit-building capabilities I can offer your company on the next pages. Backing them up are a half dozen examples of problems solved, thousands of dollars saved, durable measures to ensure compliance, and new corporate standards that boost productivity.

I am employed by one of the largest companies in the world. I love what I do and GE has promoted me four times in the last seven years. And, while there are always contributions to be made, the challenges I handle every day aren't as interesting as I would like them to be. Hence, I'm testing the waters with this confidential application.

I thrive when I can help management uncover and fix the problems so that firms like Crest get all the benefits of maintenance reliability. So let me suggest a next step: may I call in a few days to explore your special requirements? I'll do my best to make that time very well spent.

Sincerely,

Benito Hoover

Encl.: Résumé

63

Maintenance Reliability Engineer. *Don Orlando, Montgomery, Alabama*

Too often in the past, this applicant found jobs that turned out to be far below his abilities. This letter was designed to position the applicant as a key advisor to the management team.

ALVIN ENGINEER

1234 Autocad Street • Phoenix, Arizona 99999
aengineer@net.net • 999.999.9999

February 16, 2004

Name, Title
Company Name
Address
City, State ZIP

Dear Hiring Executive:

Your company's performance on a current contract will go a long way in determining your eligibility for subsequent work. As a fiscally responsible **Engineering Manager,** I will accept full ownership of every initiative, taking profit-and-loss responsibility for government work the same as for commercial environments. My expertise in strategic planning will ensure that technological capabilities keep pace with your evolving business requirements.

My diversified career includes spearheading multimillion-dollar R&D efforts for NCS Pearson and Raytheon. Prior to my tenure with these industry leaders, I gained experience in full-cycle development of prototype systems for various clients. Among the highlights of my technical leadership have been

- Serving as one of only five technical managers company-wide for a $3M initiative.
- Leading a CMM software accreditation project to achieve certification under budget and three months early.
- Being selected for participation in a corporate stock bonus plan.

I would appreciate the opportunity to discuss how I may be of service to <corporation name>. In the interim, I appreciate the time you have spent reviewing this letter and the accompanying material.

Thank you for your consideration.

Sincerely,

Alvin Engineer

Enclosure

64

Engineering Manager. *Cathy Childs, Pampano Beach, Florida*

This letter does not have all of the fields filled in yet but is almost completely written. The first paragraph displays unusual confidence, and the second exhibits leadership skills with its bullets.

DONALD E. STEWART
000 Orange Grove Lane
Boise, ID 83704

Day: 555-555-5555
SSN: 123-45-6789
Citizenship: United States

donstew@email.com

Cell: 000-000-0000
Federal Status: N/A
Veteran Status: N/A

Highest Federal Civilian Grade Held: N/A

March 7, 2004

Bureau of Reclamation
Snake River Area Office
214 Broadway Avenue
Boise, ID 83702-7298

ATTN: ROD-ASE-0-11-01

Dear Ms. Jane Winters:

This letter transmits my completed federal application in response to the federal vacancy announcement for the position of FACILITY ENGINEER, DD-2222-00, announcement number ROD-ASE-0-11-01. Enclosed you will find my résumé and supplemental narrative statements for the required Knowledge, Skills, and Abilities (KSAs), constituting all information requested by the announcement.

Thank you for your consideration of this application. I am eager to transition my career from commercial industry to federal service. Applying my extensive mechanical engineering knowledge and expertise in the service of the Federal Government would be an opportunity I would welcome greatly.

Let me direct your attention to my most significant qualifications:

- **20 years of engineering experience working in an industrial plant environment, managing the material condition of a wide variety of sophisticated equipment.**

- **Strong knowledge and ability in mechanical equipment operation and maintenance, supported by advanced degrees in mechanical and electrical engineering.**

- **Extensive professional training and certifications in safety, personal protective equipment, and OSHA requirements.**

Thank you, once more, for your consideration. I look forward to hearing from you.

Sincerely,

Donald E. Stewart

Enclosures

65

Facility Engineer. *Nick V. Marino, Bishop, Texas*

This applicant wanted to make a career change to government (federal) service. Bullets point to his most significant qualifications for the announced position of Facility Engineer.

EDWARD BAYER

November 3, 2004

Hiring Agent Name, Title
Company Name
Address

Dear Hiring Manager:

As a capable product engineer with extensive experience in the design and development of manufacturing methods for plastics and medical devices, I believe I offer a combination of skills that would benefit your company, and I would like to consider the possibility of putting my knowledge and experience to work for you.

As you can see from my enclosed résumé, I am a hands-on mechanical engineer with experience in extrusion and injection molding. My expertise lies in transitioning new medical devices from concept to manufacturing while ensuring the manufacturability of products. I am skilled in developing and tooling new manufacturing processes, setting specifications and generating manufacturing documentation, and producing and evaluating prototypes.

In addition to substantial technical skills, what distinguishes me from others is my innovative mindset and ability to take a fresh approach in critically evaluating systems and processes. It is this trademark that has allowed me to successfully release a multitude of new products over my career. It also has enabled me to create several new processes that expanded market opportunities and resulted in additional sales.

With a proven track record of success, I have demonstrated the ability to make contributions that positively impact the bottom line, and I am confident I can do the same for you. I look forward to speaking with you further about your company's goals and how I can help you achieve them. I will call to follow up, or you can reach me at the address and phone number listed below.

Thank you for your consideration.

Sincerely,

Edward Bayer

Enclosure

122 Majors Road ◆ Fairview, NJ 22222 ◆ (333) 333-3333 ◆ bayer@aol.com

66

Product and Process Engineer. *Carol A. Altomare, Three Bridges, New Jersey*

This mechanical engineer has experience in both product and process engineering, mentioned in the first and second paragraphs, respectively. The third paragraph indicates, in addition, his creativity.

HARRY STRONG

900 Starling Lane
Indianapolis, IN 00000

harrystrong@yahoo.com

Cell: (555) 555-5555
Office: (555) 555-5555

January 25, 2004

Name
Title
Employer
Address
City, State ZIP

Dear Mr. or Ms. _____:

Like many other recent graduates, I am searching for an opportunity to apply my skills while contributing to a company's growth. Unlike others, though, I don't believe that a new bachelor's degree is enough to qualify in today's highly competitive market.

As a result, I have worked diligently to supplement my college education with hands-on experience in financial environments, equipping me with a wide range of skills as a Financial or Business Analyst. Through my employment and educational training, I have developed the qualifications that will make me an asset to your company:

- **Financial Skills and Experience:** More than 2 years of experience in a corporate environment as a financial advisor, along with a solid background in financial analysis, reporting, budgeting, negotiating and business/financial planning. Apply financial tools to identify, manage and maximize investment funds.

- **Keen Research, Analytical and Quantitative Skills:** Adept at reviewing, analyzing and synthesizing financial data, as well as viewing challenges from different perspectives to arrive at creative solutions.

- **Computer Software Tools:** Demonstrated proficiency in learning new applications quickly. Skilled in using Microsoft Word, Excel and Access database software. I also use Morningstar extensively to research data on mutual funds.

- **Proven Communications, Organizational and Interpersonal Skills:** My collective experiences have enabled me to hone my interpersonal, written and verbal communications skills, which include developing financial reports, interfacing with internal and external customers and delivering presentations. Cultivating and maintaining positive relationships with a wide range of personalities have resulted in a large referral network from satisfied clients. Another strength is my ability to efficiently organize and manage my day-to-day responsibilities for maximum productivity.

Based on my talents and dedicated efforts, I have been recognized for my contributions to business growth and success. If you need a highly motivated professional who grasps new concepts quickly; loves to learn; and offers the personal drive, skills and confidence to succeed, I would welcome an interview. Thank you.

Sincerely,

Harry Strong

Enclosure

67

Financial or Business Analyst. *Louise Garver, Enfield, Connecticut*

This letter is for a new graduate who found an opportunity as a Financial Analyst. Bullets and boldfacing draw attention to the applicant's qualifications, which he gained from experience and education.

Angela T. Ingram

0000 Merritt Highway
Orlando, Florida 32821

555-555-5555
atingram@network.com

Director of Employment
Company
Address
City, State ZIP

Dear Director of Employment:

After a successful and satisfying career with Iowa's largest independently owned financial institution, I recently moved to Florida and am looking forward to embarking on a new career here. I am taking the liberty of enclosing a resume describing my background. When you review it, you may notice that I am experienced in and capable of stepping into a variety of areas. Let me elaborate.

Project Management. A consistent thread through my career at the bank was that I was often given the responsibility to oversee projects ranging from implementing new software to managing a major consolidation of branches. I have proven that I have the expertise to manage people and processes, resulting in minimal disruption to clients and/or staff.

Administration. I believe I have succeeded in providing administrative and technical support to management and users at all levels within the corporation. I am skilled in assessing others' needs and developing strategies to meet those needs. My communication skills are well developed, which facilitates my efforts.

Training and Supervision. My experience encompasses both. Because I had no formal technical training, I had to constantly self-teach and update my own skills. That gave me a unique perspective and helped me to become an effective trainer. As my resume indicates, I supervised a high-volume second-shift processing department.

In addition to the traits listed above, my performance reflects a dedication to my employer and a high degree of self-motivation. Performing beyond expectations is the norm for me. After you have examined my material, I hope you will contact me to arrange an interview. I am confident I can make significant contributions to your organization. I can be reached at home (555-555-5555) or on my cell phone (000-000-0000). Thank you for your time and consideration.

Sincerely,

Angela T. Ingram

Enclosure

68

Bank Supervisor. *Janet L. Beckstrom, Flint, Michigan*

The applicant was moving across the country and was qualified to work in diverse capacities. The writer capitalized on the applicant's broad experience and drew attention to it with boldfacing.

Eileen Gonzalez

00 Michalis Court
West Islip, New York 11795

Home Phone (555) 555-5555
E-mail: name@aol.com

Name
Company
Address
City, State ZIP

Dear Sir or Madam:

If your staffing requirements call for an articulate, well-trained professional with strong communication skills, superior leadership qualities and a talent for taking control, then I believe we have good reason to meet. The enclosed resume should be of interest to you.

My eagerness to learn and motivation to succeed should complement your staff well. I am confident that I can provide your facility with reliability and a quality work ethic that will maintain the integrity and dignity of the people it serves.

I have developed, acquired and currently maintain strong interpersonal skills and consider myself a professional, dedicated to providing the highest quality of service to the growing success of a progressive, growth-oriented facility. I pride myself in that I can readily take direction and provide creative input with an enthusiastic approach to various segments of a position.

I would welcome the opportunity to meet with you at a mutually convenient time to discuss ways in which my qualifications match your needs. You can reach me at the above address or by phone at (555) 555-5555. Thank you for your time and consideration.

Sincerely,

Eileen Gonzalez

69

Accounts Payable Professional. *Deborah Ann Ramos, Staten Island, New York*

Although a companion resume shows that this applicant has a strong Accounts Payable background, the letter is intentionally vague about a job target to keep possibilities open. See Resume 7 (page 369).

KELLY MENDOZA

60 Maple Court • Princeville, NY 55555 • (222) 222-2222 Phone/Fax

November 30, 2004

Hiring Agent, Title
Company Name
Address

Dear Hiring Manager:

As a self-motivated individual with a background in economics and finance, I believe I offer a combination of skills that would be of benefit to your company. With excellent analytical skills and leadership ability combined with outstanding interpersonal skills, I would like to consider the possibility of putting my knowledge and experience to work for you.

As you can see from my enclosed résumé, I have two years of experience in finance and investment analysis. Thus far in my career, I have developed a reputation as a hardworking individual who can be depended on to get the job done no matter what the challenge. Keys to my success are a strong set of skills, a demonstrated commitment to achieving goals, and a genuine interest in improving the way business is done.

Among my strengths, I am a resourceful problem solver and an effective communicator with a passion for growth and learning. Assertive in approach, I have taken on tough challenges and succeeded in accomplishing goals. With a solid track record behind me, I am confident I can do the same for you.

I would be pleased to have the opportunity to discuss your needs and how I might be able to meet them. I will call to follow up, or you can contact me at the address and phone number listed above.

Thank you for your consideration.

Sincerely,

Kelly Mendoza

Enclosure

70

Finance and Investment Analyst. *Carol A. Altomare, Three Bridges, New Jersey*

The applicant was seeking positions in education (see Cover Letters 39 and 40; pages 71 and 72). This particular letter was written to be used if the applicant was unsuccessful in finding a teaching position.

Diane Washington

300 Highland Avenue, Apartment 21 ♦ Boston, MA 02148 ♦ Home: (000) 555-5555 ♦ Office: (000) 000-0000

Date

Hiring Agent Name
Title
Company Name
Address
City, State ZIP

Dear Mr. / Ms._____ :

As a motivated, highly experienced Investment Executive with a strong background in selling and marketing investments to individuals and businesses, I believe my skills and talents can make an immediate and long-term contribution to the overall profitability and success of [company name].

During the past 8 years, I have successfully increased the quantity and quality of investments and built strong relationships with clients and businesses for several investment firms. I am skilled at coordinating large-scale seminars for high-profile organizations and developing business plans and sales strategies that achieve maximum revenues.

With outstanding presentation skills and thorough knowledge of the financial services industry, I am known for my unique ability to promote customer satisfaction by providing clients with investments that consistently meet their financial needs and goals. My professional credentials include a Master's degree in Marketing Communications and NASD Series 6, 7, 63 Brokerage Licenses. I am a team player who works well with clients, businesses, and management at all levels. My proven ability to generate new business and build relationships with individuals and businesses will be a significant asset to your team.

The accompanying résumé provides further details of my accomplishments and what I have to offer. I believe it would be mutually beneficial for us to discuss your company goals and how I can help you achieve them. I will call next week to inquire about such a meeting.

Thank you for your time and consideration.

Sincerely,

Diane Washington

Enclosure

71

Investment Executive. *John Femia, Altamont, New York*

This letter is for an experienced investment professional with considerable experience and strong credentials. The first three paragraphs make a strong case for the employer to meet with her.

RICHARD KIMBLE
rkimble@aol.com

12 Norwood Avenue   (555) 555-5555 (H)
Oakland, NJ 07420   (000) 000-0000 (W)

November 18, 2004

Hiring Authority
Company
Address
City, State ZIP

Dear Hiring Authority,

After 20 years as a successful small-business owner, I'm changing career directions to follow my longtime desire to be a financial planner. To that end, I am currently enrolled in a CFP program.

Although I have no professional experience as a financial planner, I have frequently advised others on investment strategies. In my own case, I developed an investment strategy for my portfolio that yielded an annual return of 10.5% for a 10-year period ending 12/31/01. I also managed the disbursement of assets for 2 estates.

I can be characterized as an entrepreneur with sound business judgment, maturity, good sales skills, and high integrity. I enjoy challenges that require learning new skills and interacting with the public. I am steady and patient, having built my own business from the ground up to more than $500,000 in annual revenues.

My goal is an exciting and rewarding position with a company facing new prospects. I am eager to participate in any training process that will build on my skills and provide the knowledge I need to be successful.

I prefer to stay in the metropolitan New York City area, but will consider attractive opportunities in the tri-state region. I would prefer to travel no more than 50% of the time.

Sincerely,

Richard Kimble

Enclosure

72

Financial Planner. *Igor Shpudejko, Mahwah, New Jersey*

This professional photographer wanted to transition to being a financial planner without related experience. The writer emphasized the applicant's maturity and sound business judgment, which are needed by FPs.

BRITTANY LYONS
000-000-0000   lyons@email.com

0000 S. Front Street, Tulsa, OK 74107

March 12, 2004

Ms. Lisa Hart
First Bank of Columbus
1383 Main Street
Columbus, OH 43204

Dear Ms. Hart:

Numbers drive good business decisions … collecting and analyzing data is critical to sound decision making.

My career experience within the banking industry has been broad-based, but it has always involved generating the necessary data to foster decisions that positively impact an organization's bottom line. My ability in this area is well documented in my résumé. I have …

➢ Held full decision-making authority for *deploying, expanding, and optimizing the banking delivery network* within the Florida region for the past three years.

➢ Ensured the *successful transition of employee incentive plans* following Barnett Bank's merger with Bank of America.

➢ Developed *uniform reporting mechanisms* to promote efficient line-management activities.

➢ *Reengineered and standardized* national sales incentive programs.

➢ Taught *staffing needs calculations and employee utilization* to branch offices to ensure delivery of top-notch customer service while controlling costs.

➢ Created a *cost analysis system* to effectively track internal profitability.

I will be relocating to the Columbus, Ohio, area within the next few months and would appreciate the opportunity to discuss how I might deliver similar results for your organization. May we talk?

Sincerely,

Brittany Lyons

Enclosure

---

*Ability is what you're capable of doing. **Motivation** determines what you do.
Attitude determines how well you do it. — Lou Holtz*

73

Bank Executive. *Cindy Kraft, Valrico, Florida*

A number of features make this letter distinctive: the partial line in the contact information, the business axiom in boldface, the bulleted items enhanced with italic, and the Lou Holtz quote.

KIMBERLY A. CARTER

888 West Road • Anywhere, Michigan 55555 • 555.222.2222

January 8, 2004

Marcy Johnson
ABC Accounting Company
333 Capital Avenue
Anywhere, Michigan 55555

Dear Ms. Johnson,

As a well-qualified credit account specialist, I demonstrate my ability to effectively communicate with clients, resolve payment issues, and collect past-due payments. I bring more than 18 years of accounts receivable experience in addition to being involved in all processing stages of collections. The scope of my experience includes, but is not limited to, commercial, automotive, and manufacturing environments.

My focus is to deliver results and provide superior service by quickly identifying problem areas in accounts receivable and developing a solution strategy to ensure that issues are resolved. My expertise lies in my strong ability to build rapport with clients, analyze accounts, and manage all aspects related to my appointed position and areas of responsibility. I find these qualities to be my greatest assets to offer employers.

Because of an unforeseen circumstance, I was unable to continue my employment as a cash applications analyst with a well-known automotive industry leader. Since my employment with A-1 Corporation, I have accepted a temporary position as a billing assistant with a local company. My objective is to secure a position in accounts receivable and credit collections with an established company. As you will note, my résumé exhibits a brief review of contributions I have made to my employers, and I enjoy challenges.

A complete picture of my expertise and experience is very important. Therefore, I will follow up with you next week. I look forward to speaking with you soon to answer any questions you may have regarding my background.

Regards,

Kimberly Carter

Enclosure

74

Credit Account Specialist. *Maria E. Hebda, Trenton, Michigan*

This letter is strong because of four carefully crafted paragraphs. These indicate in turn the applicant's experience, areas of expertise, career objective, and follow-up plans.

Regina Openhence

125 S.E. Stanley Court • Palance, Utah 99999

555-555-5555 *cell*   home **555-555-5555**

December 16, 2004

Attention: Lindsey Harold
Codder County Bank
P.O. Box 9229
Palance, UT 99999

Dear Ms. Harold:

In response to your recent advertisement for an experienced Commercial Loan Officer, I have enclosed a copy of my résumé for your review. As you will note, I have spent more than 20 years in the banking industry in a variety of positions. My expertise is in working in the commercial loan department and one-on-one with the customers, walking them through the loan process, educating them, and making sure they are receiving the fullest benefits possible.

I have achieved numerous accomplishments and have a record for developing a strong bottom line for the bank. My personal passion as a "people person" shines through in the successes I've achieved. I am computer literate, analytical, thorough, and well experienced in the complete loan process.

I would like the opportunity to meet with you personally where we may further discuss your bank's requirements and my qualifications. It appears from your advertisement that our needs may be a very close match. Please call me at your earliest convenience to schedule a time when we may meet and review how we may mutually benefit each other. Thank you for taking the time to review my résumé, and I look forward to meeting you personally.

Sincerely,

Regina Openhence

Enclosure

75

Commercial Loan Officer. *Rosie Bixel, Portland, Oregon*

This strong letter contains just three strong paragraphs. The first directs attention to the resume and the applicant's expertise, the second mentions worker traits, and the third asks for a meeting.

Paula Santiago

0000 Royal Sydney Street
Gainesville, GA 20155

Home Phone: (555) 555-5555
Alternative Phone: (000) 000-0000
psantiago@aol.com

Date

Hiring Agent Name
Title
Company Name
Address
City, State ZIP

Dear Mr. / Ms. _____:

As a highly successful, motivated Loan Officer with more than 13 years of experience in the real estate and auto industries, I believe my skills and talents can make an immediate and long-term contribution to the overall profitability and success of [name of business].

Throughout my career, I have increased the profits and volume of business for all of my employers, as evidenced by perfect customer satisfaction ratings and consistently earning top producer awards. I am skilled at coordinating and selling heavy volumes of loans per month and work well with clients, professionals, and sales staff throughout every phase of the loan process.

With strong leadership skills and a keen eye for detail, I am proficient at employee training, recruiting, leading of sales teams, and relationship building. I have contributed to the success of my employers by designing and implementing new processes and programs, as well as authoring manuals for improving sales and business practices. My proven ability to generate new business and increase profits will be a significant asset to your team.

The accompanying résumé provides further details of my accomplishments and what I have to offer. I believe it would be mutually beneficial for us to meet and discuss your company goals and how I can help you achieve them. I will call next week to inquire about such a meeting.

Thank you for your time and consideration.

Sincerely,

Paula Santiago

Enc. résumé

76

Loan Officer. *John Femia, Altamont, New York*

In this letter, the writer discusses as recurring topics the applicant's skills, contributions, sales expertise, achievements, profitability, worker traits, leadership ability, and creativity.

GAHRAM MEESHAN

0000 Central Avenue
Glendale, California 91208

555-555-5555
g_meeshan@earthlink.net

March 10, 2004

HORIZON MORTGAGE LENDERS, INC.
522 N. Purdham Avenue
Glendale, California 91203

Attention: Robert Vesag, Sales Manager

RE: **Loan Officer**—Monstertrak no. 1039888

Dear Mr. Vesag:

Once in a while, someone wakes up to find himself living in the wrong life.

As a forensic biomechanics assistant and a personal trainer, I have extensive experience in dealing with people, difficult or otherwise, as well as in research and data collection. These are skills that would be easily transferable to the loan industry since I would also have to deal with people and data, albeit in a different environment.

My current goal is to explore new career options that fit better with my personality. I like numbers, but would rather deal with them in a financial environment.

In your ad under qualifications, it states "No experience necessary." As my résumé indicates, I am a quick learner and problem solver while dealing with new concepts, systems, and procedures; therefore, a good fit exists between your requirements and my abilities. I do have a bachelor's degree, although not in the discipline you prefer. Again, this should not be an obstacle as I have a strong desire to learn and to succeed.

I will call you on Thursday to set up an appointment and further explore the possibilities of our working together.

Thank you for your time and consideration.

Sincerely,

Gahram Meeshan

Enclosure

77

Loan Officer. *Myriam-Rose Kohn, Valencia, California*

This applicant was a forensic biomechanic's assistant and wanted to become either a broker or a loan officer. The letter therefore mentions transferable skills, the reason for a switch, and motivation.

Susan E. Williams

0000 Indianwood Road
Clarkston, Michigan 48348

555-555-3333
susiew@network.net

Dear Director of Employment:

A BBA degree, 20+ years of experience in the banking industry, and a comprehensive understanding of probate law—that's what I have to offer your organization. After a rewarding career at Michigan National Bank, I find myself in the position of seeking new career opportunities. My resume is enclosed for your review.

My recent experience at the bank has been in the Personal Trust/Probate department. In my capacity as Trust Officer, I was responsible for personal trust, estate, and investment accounts. I settled estates, coordinated the administration of legal documents, and directed the disbursement of funds according to the trust and/or applicable laws (among many other things). This comprehensive background would be a distinct asset to your firm.

In addition to my fiduciary responsibilities, I took a personal interest in every client. There were cases that necessitated my intervention to arbitrate differences between feuding beneficiaries. Sometimes I was called on to schedule doctor appointments or arrange for home repair. But serving the client (or the client's estate as the case may be) was always my top priority.

When you review my resume, you will see that I also managed the corporate trust division and provided administrative support in the employee benefit area. This experience adds to my versatility.

Thank you for taking the time to review my credentials. I hope you feel a personal meeting would be beneficial; I am available at your convenience. If you have any questions—or when you are ready to schedule an interview—please give me a call at 555-555-3333.

Sincerely,

Susan E. Williams

Enclosure

78

Trust Officer. *Janet L. Beckstrom, Flint, Michigan*

The applicant had extensive experience in a bank's trust/probate department. She was looking for a position with a law firm that could benefit from her experience and transferable skills.

RAYMOND MARLIN

12 Main Street
New York, New York 00000
(555) 555-5555 • raymon44@cox.net

February 8, 2004

Mr. Fred Johnson
President/CEO
Reynolds Corporation
666 Mason Road
New York, New York 00000

Dear Mr. Johnson:

Perhaps your company could benefit from a strong chief financial officer with a record of major contributions to business and profit growth.

The scope of my expertise is extensive and includes the full complement of corporate finance, accounting, budgeting, banking, tax, treasury, internal controls, and reporting functions. Equally important are my qualifications in business planning, operations, MIS technology, administration, and general management.

A business partner to management, I have been effective in working with all departments, linking finance with operations to improve productivity, efficiency, and bottom-line results. Recruited at The Southington Company to provide finance and systems technology expertise, I created a solid infrastructure to support corporate growth as the company transitioned from a wholesale-retail distributor to a retail operator. Recent accomplishments include the following:

- **Significant contributor to the increase in operating profits from less than $400,000 to more than $4 million.**

- **Key member of due diligence team in the acquisition of 25 operating units that increased market penetration 27% and gross sales 32%.**

- **Spearheaded leading-edge MIS design and implementation, streamlining systems and procedures that dramatically enhanced productivity while cutting costs.**

A "hands-on" manager effective in building teamwork and cultivating strong internal/external relationships, I am flexible and responsive to the quickly changing demands of the business, industry, and marketplace. If you are seeking a proactive finance executive to complement your management team, I would welcome a personal interview. Thank you for your consideration.

Very truly yours,

Raymond Marlin

79

Chief Financial Officer. *Louise Garver, Enfield, Connecticut*

This senior-level applicant wanted a finance executive position that encompassed all areas of finance and not just treasury operations (his most recent position). He was successful in reaching his goal.

DAVID JOHNSON
5 Mulberry Street
Simsbury, CT 00000
(555) 555-5555
davidj@compusa.com

February 3, 2004

Mr. George Meadows
Chief Executive Officer
Danaher Corporation
678 City Center
Hartford, CT 00000

Dear Mr. Meadows:

As a manufacturing executive, I have consistently delivered strong performance results through my contributions in cost reductions, internal controls and technology solutions. The comparison below outlines some of my accomplishments as a Chief Financial Officer in relationship to the position requirements.

Your Requirements	My Qualifications
Full range of finance, accounting and treasury experience; operational focus; strong internal controls.	Built and led strong finance organizations, creating solid infrastructures and strengthening internal controls. Instituted formal budgeting, forecasting, cash management and other management processes. Proven record for designing growth strategies and financial consolidations to achieve business objectives.

Recruited by Halstead Company to provide expertise in acquisitions, financing and MIS and to orchestrate an IPO. Comprehensive background in all areas of finance, accounting and treasury. Recognized for strengths as a consensus/team builder and effective arbitrator/negotiator. |
| Mergers and acquisitions experience. | Acquired extensive experience in the analysis of new business opportunities and with mergers and acquisitions throughout career history. Effectively merged and streamlined two divisions, which resulted in substantial savings and positioned company for future growth.

Spearheaded acquisition of several operating businesses with sales ranging from $1 million to $220 million, which included personally handling all negotiations, performing due diligence, developing tax structure and coordinating legal and accounting activities. |
| MIS background. | Led installation of state-of-the-art MIS technology in different companies. Improved inventory management, boosted sales and cut annual operating expenses through MIS technology implementation. |

I would welcome a personal interview to discuss how my experience would contribute to the achievement of your company's objectives for growth and success.

Very truly yours,

David Johnson

80

Chief Financial Officer. *Louise Garver, Enfield, Connecticut*

Some resumes and cover letters for executives have smaller type to fit in more information. This letter is an example. This two-column format was successful in generating interviews and offers.

Beverly Armstrong, C.P.A.

0000 Harbour Walk Road
Weston, CT 06883

555-555-5555 • Cell: 000-000-0000
bevarmstrong@yahoo.com

January 17, 2004

The Azure Group
P.O. Box 21648
Weston, CT 06883

Dear Hiring Professional:

The position of **Director of Finance** advertised online accurately describes my skills and abilities. I may be the ideal candidate for you—I not only have the experience you request, but also additional perspective from other fields and positions to draw on.

Your Needs	My Qualifications
Minimum of a B.A. in Accounting or Finance	◆ Certified Public Accountant
	◆ Bachelor of Business Administration from Colby with a concentration in Accounting and Finance
5–7+ years of progressively responsible experience providing high-level financial analyses	◆ More than 14 years in a variety of financial positions of escalating responsibility for large and small companies in different fields
	◆ VP of Finance and Controller for $250 million public company, managing monthly financial close, daily cash flow analysis, overall financial and profitability analysis, acquisition and systems integration, coordinating audits, health and property & casualty insurance, and human resources
	◆ Results include negotiating competitive contracts to reduce expenses from $250K–$400K annually, reducing cash outlay by $1.25 million due to creative financing deals, and achieving post-merger synergies of $3–$4 million annually
A strong insurance background	◆ More than 4 years at Commercial Insurance company, promoted to Director of Reinsurance, reported directly to CFO
Ability to create and implement new procedures and systems	◆ At Director and VP levels, implemented new processes to improve cash management, credit card processing, staffing, cost reduction, automated reporting systems, and many others
Experience in reviewing contracts and agreements	◆ As Director of Acquisitions, reviewed and revised documents, including all confidentiality/nondisclosure agreements, letters of intent, and stock/asset purchase agreements
	◆ In VP of Finance and Controller positions, reviewed and improved cash management procedures, health insurance agreements, reinsurance contracts, and fronting agreements

81

Director of Finance. *Gail Frank, Tampa, Florida*

This similar two-column format extends to a second page. The size of type would be too small if you tried to fit all of this letter's information on one page. The visible "weight" of the second column gives the impression that this candidate's qualifications more than adequately meet the

Beverly Armstrong, C.P.A. **page 2**

<u>**Your Needs**</u>	<u>**My Qualifications**</u>
High degree of personal integrity and effective interaction skills with executives, clients, vendors, and other internal/external parties at all levels	◆ Excellent relationship-development, problem-solving, negotiation, and presentation skills; manage sensitive relationships with executive management, directors, employees, clients, bankers, insurance regulators, venture capitalists, investment bankers, joint-venture partners, and acquisition targets

My resume provides further details of my accomplishments. I look forward to discussing yet another career opportunity with you. Please give me a call or e-mail if you would like to sit down for an interview.

Sincerely,

Beverly Armstrong

Enclosure

prospective employer's needs. If you feel that long paragraphs slow down reading of a letter, you can see that the tempo of reading across columns from left to right is quicker, which makes the format successful.

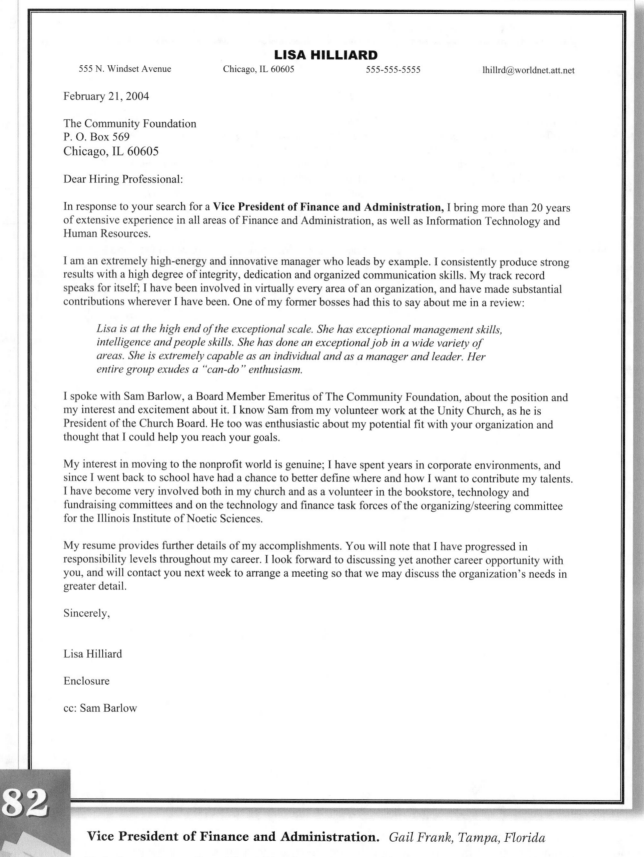

LISA HILLIARD

555 N. Windset Avenue   Chicago, IL 60605   555-555-5555   lhillrd@worldnet.att.net

February 21, 2004

The Community Foundation
P. O. Box 569
Chicago, IL 60605

Dear Hiring Professional:

In response to your search for a **Vice President of Finance and Administration,** I bring more than 20 years of extensive experience in all areas of Finance and Administration, as well as Information Technology and Human Resources.

I am an extremely high-energy and innovative manager who leads by example. I consistently produce strong results with a high degree of integrity, dedication and organized communication skills. My track record speaks for itself; I have been involved in virtually every area of an organization, and have made substantial contributions wherever I have been. One of my former bosses had this to say about me in a review:

> *Lisa is at the high end of the exceptional scale. She has exceptional management skills, intelligence and people skills. She has done an exceptional job in a wide variety of areas. She is extremely capable as an individual and as a manager and leader. Her entire group exudes a "can-do" enthusiasm.*

I spoke with Sam Barlow, a Board Member Emeritus of The Community Foundation, about the position and my interest and excitement about it. I know Sam from my volunteer work at the Unity Church, as he is President of the Church Board. He too was enthusiastic about my potential fit with your organization and thought that I could help you reach your goals.

My interest in moving to the nonprofit world is genuine; I have spent years in corporate environments, and since I went back to school have had a chance to better define where and how I want to contribute my talents. I have become very involved both in my church and as a volunteer in the bookstore, technology and fundraising committees and on the technology and finance task forces of the organizing/steering committee for the Illinois Institute of Noetic Sciences.

My resume provides further details of my accomplishments. You will note that I have progressed in responsibility levels throughout my career. I look forward to discussing yet another career opportunity with you, and will contact you next week to arrange a meeting so that we may discuss the organization's needs in greater detail.

Sincerely,

Lisa Hilliard

Enclosure

cc: Sam Barlow

82

Vice President of Finance and Administration. *Gail Frank, Tampa, Florida*

To indicate the applicant's breadth of experience and high standards, the writer provided in the center of the letter a quotation in italic from one of her performance reviews. The reader's eye goes right to it.

Dorothy Bond
555 Winding Lane
Pleasant Park, IL 00000
555-555-5555
xxxxxxx@aol.com

January 15, 2004

Job Code M5555
Chicago Tribune
P.O. Box 806883
Chicago, IL 00000

Dear Sir/Madam:

In response to the advertisement you placed in the *Chicago Tribune* for Administrative Supervisor, Hospital Fundraising Development Department, I have enclosed my résumé for your review. My successful experience in administrative management, new business development, marketing, and promotion, combined with my strong work ethic and MPA/Healthcare degree, would be a good match for this position.

In my career, I have enjoyed creating strategies that expand and improve the client relationship base and marketing efforts. I have also developed a variety of effective administrative procedures and programs. From the beginning, I have maintained an interest in public administration and completed a Master's in Public Administration–Healthcare through City University in 2000. I am now targeting positions in the field of public administration that would combine these skills and experiences, and I would appreciate the opportunity to talk with you about your plans and philosophies. In my search, I am targeting a compensation range in the mid-thirties to mid-fifties.

You can reach me at the phone number or e-mail listed above. Thank you for your time and attention.

Sincerely,

[signature]

Dorothy Bond

Résumé enclosed

83

Administrative Supervisor. *Christine L. Dennison, Lincolnshire, Illinois*

The first paragraph indicates the target position and the applicant's suitability for it. The wide compensation range in the second paragraph gives ample room for coming to an agreement.

Cindy Springs
2016 Warm Avenue
Seattle, WA 88888
(555) 555-5555
cindysprings@msn.com

April 16, 2004

Steve Franklin
Canyon Sheriff's Youth Foundation
1632 Barley Drive
Seattle, WA 88888

Dear Mr. Franklin,

As a highly organized professional with experience in coordinating fundraising events and office management, I invite you to consider the enclosed résumé in support of my application to secure a position with Canyon Sheriff's Youth Foundation.

I have successfully implemented and monitored strategic objectives and projects to meet the diverse needs of the Seattle Chamber of Commerce as the Manager, consistently completing projects within or under budget. My experience and knowledge will bring immediate improvements to your current and future projects. Please consider the following in addition to my enclosed résumé:

- **In-depth project management,** planning, organizing, and evaluating programs for effectiveness and efficiency. Held presentations with officials and community leaders addressing all concerns and showcasing solutions.
- **Decisive, innovative, and dedicated team leader,** inspiring strong team morale as shown by building a team of professionals, coupled with promoting high-quality work supported by a community-oriented attitude.
- **Developed strong relationships with customers,** subordinates, senior management, volunteers, council officials, and community representatives through outstanding communication skills and business etiquette.

It is with great interest that I encourage you to consider my résumé, as I am confident that your organization will benefit from my focus on achieving company objectives as a dedicated leader and team member. I am certain that a personal interview would more fully reveal my skills and desire to join your team, and I invite you to contact me, at your convenience, at the above number.

Sincerely,

Cindy Springs

Enclosure

84

Fund-raiser and Office Manager. *Denette D. Jones, Boise, Idaho*

This three-paragraph letter is enhanced with three bulleted statements after the second paragraph. Boldfacing enhances the key topic of each bulleted statement, making the topics readily visible.

Benjamin Hall

56 Sunny Knoll Drive ✦ Poughkeepsie, NY 12601 ✦ 555-555-5555

February 20, 2004

Ms. Taylor Coleman, Director
The American Heart Society
12 Tucker Drive
Wappingers Falls, NY 12590

Dear Ms. Coleman:

I am a beauty industry professional who is writing to express interest in employment opportunities within your organization. My goal is a promotional position where I can use my marketing expertise and industry contacts in the area of events planning. With my commitment to social advocacy and enthusiasm for cause-related marketing, I believe that I could positively contribute to your endeavors.

For more than six years I have been working as an events planner for various social causes and issues. Currently, I am responsible for leading the marketing and fund-raising efforts for b•cause—a foundation that I established. Throughout my career I have served in a volunteer capacity in an effort to generate philanthropic support and galvanize industry professionals to embrace issues affecting our community.

My career accelerated after Revlon recognized my ability to spot trends and deliver results. Revlon signed me as its National Fund-raising Director. In only a few years, I conceptualized and brought to fruition countless fund-raisers and events, raising more than $500,000. I was successful in planning and executing these programs through a substantial knowledge of the beauty industry (its business, leaders and experts) and a broad understanding of fund-raising.

While I have an innate ability to take charge and interpret complex issues, my skills focus on the actual raising of revenues through donor acquisition, corporate giving and personal solicitation. Equally notable has been my ability to identify opportunities, gain high-profile support and negotiate corporate sponsorship. More specifically, I have consistently demonstrated an ability to establish credibility and confidence with individuals or large groups. Further, I am experienced and comfortable in dealing with top public and private community leaders.

Enclosed is a copy of my resume for your review. I look forward to the opportunity to provide you with further details of my professional value and personal commitment during an interview. Thank you for your time.

Sincerely,

Benjamin Hall

Enclosure

85

Events Planner. *Kristin M. Coleman, Poughkeepsie, New York*

Striking in this letter is the amount of white space in relation to the great amount of information it supplies. The writer accomplished this feat through smaller-than-average type and narrower left and right margins.

35–12 Cottonboll Drive
Selma, AL 00000

Yasheika Ojimobi

Banquet Management Specialist

yasheika@partytime.com

Phone: (000) 000-0000
Pager: (000) 000-0000

January 14, 2004

Victor Gibson
Director of Human Resources
Sheridan Corporation
1674 Eldridge Avenue
Montgomery, AL 00000

Dear Mr. Gibson:

In speaking recently with Maxine Ray, who works for Jake Levitz, your Convention Services Manager, I learned that there may be several positions open for persons who are skilled in setting up banquets or managing on-site activities for convention services and trade shows. Because I was intrigued by these opportunities, I am acting on Maxine's suggestion to send you my resume and this letter of interest.

Having spent the past 15 years performing every imaginable task associated with putting together successful banquets and events attended by hundreds of people, I know I have the essential qualifications to be an asset to your organization. As you review my resume, you will see the scope of my involvement and the versatility I can offer. I take great pride in my work, and I am totally dedicated to meeting and even exceeding the expectations of a demanding clientele for their social or corporate functions.

Throughout my career, I have been most effective in orchestrating a team effort while recognizing individual talents to accomplish project goals. The key to my success has been my ability to efficiently manage multiple and varied activities, all taking place simultaneously. Given the opportunity, I can demonstrate this in any project situation calling for broad cooperation.

In addition, I am receptive to new learning experiences, welcome challenges, and have no objection to travel, late hours, or weekend work.

I would appreciate meeting with you personally to discuss your organization's plans and how I may be able to contribute to their accomplishment. I will call you within the next week to determine your interest and perhaps arrange a time when we can meet. Thank you for any consideration.

Sincerely,

Yasheika Ojimobi

Enclosure: Resume

86

Banquets and Events Planner. *Melanie Noonan, West Paterson, New Jersey*

Extra-wide left and right margins provide satisfying white space in this letter. The first paragraph mentions a referral, and the next three paragraphs play up the applicant's merits. See Resume 8 (page 370).

Ashina Hartnett
555 55th Avenue, Rochester MN 55555
(555) 555-5555

January 24, 2004

Mr. Samuel Gleason
James T. Conference Coordinators
555 Salome Boulevard
Chicago IL 66666

Dear Mr. Gleason:

Banquet and Conference Coordinator

My work with a highly diverse clientele has been very rewarding, and the experience has reinforced my need to work in an independent capacity that draws together decision-making, problem-solving and superior people skills.

Staff and the general public respond positively to my managerial, leadership and communication style. I would like to continue working in a business or people-related position with public visibility, and have enclosed a resume for your review. Some of the other qualities I offer are

- Ability to listen closely and react to what people actually say or mean
- Diplomacy, discretion and consistent style
- Positive attitude
- Flexible nature attuned to changing markets and needs
- Attention to details and concerns
- Efficient multitasking and performance under pressure
- Professional manner, with strict adherence to confidentiality
- Awareness of the importance of professional networking—willingness to attend Chamber of Commerce and other relevant meetings

I've enjoyed assisting in the sales department of a major hotel the last two years and have been called on to fill in when the Conference Coordinator needed additional help with the multitude of details for an unusually large conference. I have not only done some of the "grunt" work but also conferred with various clients, set up the technical logistics, handled last-minute changes and coordinated with the banquet department. Testimonials from the Conference Coordinator and General Manager will back up my skills and abilities and will verify their opinion that I would be a good fit for a full-time banquet and conference coordinator.

I am highly responsible and trustworthy, and clients and employees alike feel comfortable that I'll do what I say, and that promises won't "fall between the cracks." My genuine concern for quality customer service and improved worker motivation is readily apparent, as is interest in professional development and ongoing learning.

It is difficult to determine from resumes career potential and in which areas a person can make a difference to a company. I am looking forward to meeting with you to discuss your needs, to exchange information, and to address any questions.

Sincerely,

Ashina Hartnett

87

Banquet and Conference Coordinator. *Beverley Drake, Rochester, Minnesota*

The applicant was moving from sales to conference work. Unique "multisheet" bullets suggest that each bulleted quality is multifaceted. The third paragraph refers to relevant experience.

Beverly Chase Ryan

0000 Big Horn Road
Bldg. 12, Apt. C
Vail, Colorado 89898

(555) 666-8888   beverlyryan4@aol.com   Cell: (555) 666-7777

January 12, 2004

Leonard R. Victors, Human Resources Manager
AAA Giant Events, Inc.
222 Johansen Boulevard
Vail, Colorado 89898

Dear Mr. Victors:

I was thrilled to find your firm's advertisement in the *Vail Sunday Times*, January 12, 2004, for a Senior Winter Events Consultant. My broad management experience in events planning, coupled with my enthusiasm for working in the skiing industry, clearly matches your stated requirements for the ideal candidate to fill this position.

Most of my professional adult life has been occupied with sports, sports marketing, public relations, successful promotional endeavors, and executing all operations within a high-end catering business in Newport, Rhode Island. My athletic achievements and participation in numerous activities in college point to my early accomplishments in building a solid foundation for the intensive responsibilities of planning and successfully executing such events as AAA regularly engages in.

In addition, my experiences as advertising account executive for North American Skiing Companies, director of retail marketing for a radio station, and director of public relations for a baseball team have strengthened my abilities to meet any challenges that may lie ahead in my focused ambition to go further in this growing field of sports events planning.

I would appreciate meeting with you to discuss my candidacy for the position as Senior Winter Events Consultant with AAA Giant Events, Inc. Please contact me for an appointment if you agree that my qualifications are sufficient, or may I call your office to request a meeting date convenient to you?

Thank you for considering my application. I eagerly look forward to our meeting and the opportunity to discuss my credentials and career aspirations for this position.

Sincerely,

Beverly Chase Ryan

Enclosure: résumé

88

Senior Winter Events Consultant. *Edward Turilli, North Kingstown, Rhode Island*

This letter displays the applicant's enthusiasm toward the advertised opening and the prospect of pursuing further her field of athletics. She mentions key experiences for sports events planning.

Sarah Lemareaux

oooo Southern Street   *sarah@greenson.net*   *Home (ooo) 555-5555*
Miami, Florida ooooo   *Work (ooo) 888-8888*

October 14, 2004

Attn: Marianne Burger
Comstock Enterprise
8787 Rampart
New York, New York 00000

Dear Ms. Burger:

As you will note from the enclosed resume, I am <u>not</u> "your average, everyday person" who seeks a position in international relations. I am an energetic, creative, driven individual who enjoys people and adventure and does not shy away from hard work.

With a degree in International Relations, some speaking/writing capabilities in Spanish and German, and world travel experience, I feel I have something to offer a company in event coordination, protocol, or administration. For five years, I have worked in the family's finance business where I honed skills in office management, advertising, public relations, accounting, and investments. Starting a music production company in 2000 with two partners paved the way for extensive travel and interaction with strange and fascinating people in the industry. Other "adventures" in and after college have contributed to my skills in directing and coordinating special events and professional conferences; I can manage multiple tasks simultaneously with ease.

Your organization appears to offer the unique challenges I desire. I would very much like to explore career opportunities in a personal interview at your convenience. Please contact me at either of the numbers provided.

Thank you for your interest,

Sarah Lemareaux

Enclosure

89

Events Coordinator. *Sally Altman, Tulsa, Oklahoma*

The graphic and the distinctive horizontal lines enclosing the contact information at the top of the letter support the letter's claim that this applicant is not just average and is worthy of serious consideration.

NINA ALTONSON

Chauncey Court #16
Rochester MN 55555

(555) 555-5555

MEDICAL OFFICE PROFESSIONAL

♦ ♦ ♦

BUSINESS SKILLS

Data Entry 12,500 KPH
Telephone Skills
Pneumatic Record Transport System
Facilitation
Problem Solving
Customer Service
Filing (Numeric & Alpha)
Training of Staff

CULTURAL DIVERSITY & LANGUAGE

Four Years of Spanish
Extensive Travel–Western U.S.
Multicultural Experience

March 21, 2004

Mr. William Babinski
Staffing Director
Chambers Medical Clinic
Duluth, Minnesota

RE: MEDICAL TRANSCRIPTIONIST

Dear Mr. Babinski:

Enclosed is a resume for the posted position.

Graduating with honors in 2003 from the medical transcription certification program at Manchester Community and Technical College, I am ready to begin the career for which I have worked so hard.

My medical records experience will be especially helpful in this position. Not only am I highly familiar with patient record management, but also I bring the following:

- ♦ Positive collaboration with physicians and other medical personnel
- ♦ Understanding of team concepts, legalities, confidentiality, hospital code and patient rights
- ♦ Experience working with pneumatic record transport systems
- ♦ Multicultural experience

General business skills complement my experience. This includes data entry, word processing, strong communication skills and accuracy, as well as the ability to monitor my own work. I've established a good track record for a positive attitude, initiative, organizational skills, pride in my work, confidence and team spirit.

I very much look forward to hearing from you regarding this position.

Sincerely,

Nina Altonson

90

Medical Transcriptionist. *Beverley Drake, Rochester, Minnesota*

Making a cover letter look different from others is a challenge. Using a multicolumn format can produce good results. The vertical line can be in a narrow, separate column or as a side border of a text column.

Ariel Adams
111 Washington St.
Hunterville, IL 60030
(111) 222-2222
aadams@email.com

October 27, 2004

Human Resource Manager
Lucas County Health Department
Human Resources Office
111 Greenich Rd.
Lucasville, IL 00000

Dear Human Resource Manager:

When I read your advertisement for a ***Patient Care Representative*** on Lucas County's Web site, I thought that you had written the job description with me in mind. As you require, I am fluent in both English and Spanish and have excellent interpersonal skills. Additionally, I have experience in handling cash and performing inventory.

For the past 3 years, I have been caring for an elderly relative who is now deceased. During that time, I gained a considerable amount of experience scheduling appointments and communicating with medical staff and patients. I can be very empathetic and patient with sick individuals who may be confused or upset.

As soon as I complete my GED next month, I am available to start work. As you will see on my attached resume, I am actively working to improve myself. For 10 hours each week, I have been practicing typing and am confident that I can meet your expectations in this area.

I am eager to make a difference at the Lucas County Health Department. I will contact your office at the end of the week to verify that you have received my letter and resume and to talk to you further about this opportunity. In the meantime, feel free to contact me at (111) 222-2222.

Thank you for your time and consideration,

Ariel Adams

Enclosure: Resume

91

Patient Care Representative. *Eva Locke, Waukegan, Illinois*

The writer cast as strengths the skills this applicant used in caring for a sick relative. Because the applicant lacked GED and typing requirements, these are mentioned as being met in the near future.

JENNIFER E. EMERSON, LPN

000 PEABODY AVENUE   MELROSE, MA 00000
(444) 888-2222   CELL: (444) 888-0000
         E-MAIL: JEMERSON@AOL.COM

February 5, 2004

Madeline Detweiler, Practical Nurse Administrator
Lowden Family Health Centers
4444 South Main Road
Pohasset, MA 00000

Dear Ms. Detweiler:

I am writing in response to your advertisement in *The Melrose Daily News* for a full-time Licensed Practical Nurse. I believe that I can fill that position well due to my education, health care experience, and professional sincerity.

A recent LPN graduate of the Pohasset Regional Technical School in Taunton, MA, I currently hold a license in Massachusetts and have also applied for a New Hampshire license.

My demonstrated strong organizational and communication skills derive from my successful employment experiences in business offices, as my enclosed résumé confirms. These skills, coupled with my LPN education and training, should prove to be of great benefit to your family health center.

I am confident that you will agree that my qualifications match your requirements for this position. Therefore, I would greatly appreciate an opportunity to meet with you to fully reveal my keen interest in the health care field and to determine how I may fit your staff profile. I can be reached by e-mail, home phone, or cell phone days or evenings to arrange for an appointment. If I do not hear from you by Monday, February 15, I will call your office to request a meeting at a time convenient to you or another member of your staff.

Thank you for considering my application for employment at Lowden Family Health Centers.

Sincerely,

Jennifer E. Emerson, LPN

Enclosure: résumé

92

Licensed Practical Nurse. *Edward Turilli, North Kingstown, Rhode Island*

The challenge was to convince a recruiter that the entry-level applicant's proactive manner in obtaining her degree and another state license outweighed her minimal nursing experience.

Frances C. MacSorley

1212 Juniper Circle
North Kingman, CT 66666
francesmac@earthlink.com

(000) 222-1111   Cell: (000) 222-3333

January 27, 2004

Philippe J. Desjardin
Director of Human Resources
New Haven Memorial Hospital
111 Brently Street
New Haven, CT 00000

Dear Mr. Desjardin:

This letter is in response to your advertisement in *The New Haven Sunday Times*, January 27, 2004, for a Licensed Practical Nurse to be employed at the Leone Mathieu Life Care Center.

I believe that my qualifications are strong for this position, for my 15 years in practical nursing have given me excellent professional experience in addition to my personal career objective of providing and maintaining the highest level of nursing care and quality of life to patients under my charge. My total nursing experience has been, and continues to be, full-time, direct patient care.

Always deeply committed to the nursing profession, I have striven to keep abreast of the latest data through in-service learning and reading various journals and selected publications. Courses taken in the liberal arts are in direct preparation for my Associate degree as a Registered Nurse. Moreover, they have broadened my capacity to deal with humanitarian issues that are so much a part of healing.

If you agree with me that my credentials are sound for this position at the Leone Mathieu Life Care Center, I would very much appreciate an opportunity to meet with you to discuss my candidacy for this opening at Memorial Hospital. I can be reached by e-mail, at my home after 5 p.m., or at any time by my cell phone to schedule an appointment at a time that is convenient to you.

Thank you for considering me for this position; I look forward to hearing from you soon.

Sincerely,

Frances C. MacSorley

Enclosures: résumé / application

93

Licensed Practical Nurse. *Edward Turilli, North Kingstown, Rhode Island*

After 15 years in practical nursing, the applicant wanted another LPN position while she worked on her registered nursing degree. The letter shows her commitment to nursing and humanitarian issues.

Grace Messenger, R.N.

000 Oak Grove Place ▪ Canandaigua, NY 14424 ▪ 585/555-0000

March 19, 2004

Dr. David Mansfield
Superintendent of Schools
Canandaigua City School District
99 North Street
Canandaigua, NY 14424

Dear Dr. Mansfield:

As a Licensed Registered Nurse with five years of related experience, including public school nursing, I have great interest in your opening for a School Nurse.

For the past two school years, I have been employed at Phelps Central School, providing routine and emergency health services to the staff and school population of 1000+ students. In addition, I gained experience in school nursing on a substitute basis with your district as well as Manchester-Shortsville. In these roles, I have been able to apply and hone my generalist skills, most notably in assessment, emergency care, and health counseling. Notable accomplishments in my current position include

- Completion of School Nurses Orientation Program.
- Training in Section 504 regulations.
- Automated External Defibrillator Training and Certification, as well as involvement in school policy development for defibrillator use and placement selection; I also manage the equipment maintenance program.
- Management of student attendance using a custom software application.

As a lifelong resident of Canandaigua and parent of school-aged children, I have been actively involved in the community and the school for more than a decade. I believe this offers me a unique perspective and understanding—of the environment in which I would work, of the individuals receiving care and their families, and of the impact to our community.

A collaborative professional, I am both dedicated and visionary. I will use my clinical and personal skills in partnership with the administration to support the school's mandate to provide and maintain a healthy and safe environment for its students and employees.

It is my hope that we can meet to discuss your School Nurse opening and my background in greater detail. I will follow up this letter and résumé with a call to your office but invite you to contact me anytime at 555-0000.

Thank you for your consideration and time.

Sincerely,

Grace Messenger

Enclosure

94

School Nurse. *Salome A. Farraro, Mount Morris, New York*

The applicant earned her credentials after seeing her three children through elementary school. The second paragraph and the bulleted items show that she had solid experience in school nursing.

Jan Marie Saint

000 Pelton Avenue, Staten Island, New York 10310 • Phone: (555) 555-5555/Cell: (555) 555-5555 • E-mail: name@aol.com

Name
Company
Address
City, State ZIP

Dear Sir or Madam:

If you are interested in a creative and dynamic individual with superior leadership qualities and a talent for taking control, then I welcome you to take a good look at my resume. The combination of skills and experience I am offering should be of interest to you.

Throughout my college career, I have gained valuable insight into the task of working effectively while maintaining quality relations and interfacing regularly with a diverse staff and a variety of professionals. Having a strong initiative in decision making and assumption of responsibilities, I am prepared to play an integral part in an atmosphere where I can apply my creative and innovative talents.

I am sure that I will, through persistent efforts, meet mutual objectives and feel confident that my experience and skills can be used to the advantage of your facility. My eagerness to learn and motivation to succeed should well serve to complement your staff.

I am dedicated to providing the highest quality of service and welcome the opportunity to discuss ways in which I can excel in a position as Physician Assistant within your healthcare facility. I can be reached at the above address or by phone at (555) 555-5555. Thank you for your time and consideration.

Sincerely,

Jan Marie Saint

Enclosure

95

Physician Assistant. *Deborah Ann Ramos, Staten Island, New York*

This letter shows that the applicant has more to offer than skills and experience: She will be a Physician Assistant with leadership strengths, creativity, motivation, initiative, and team spirit.

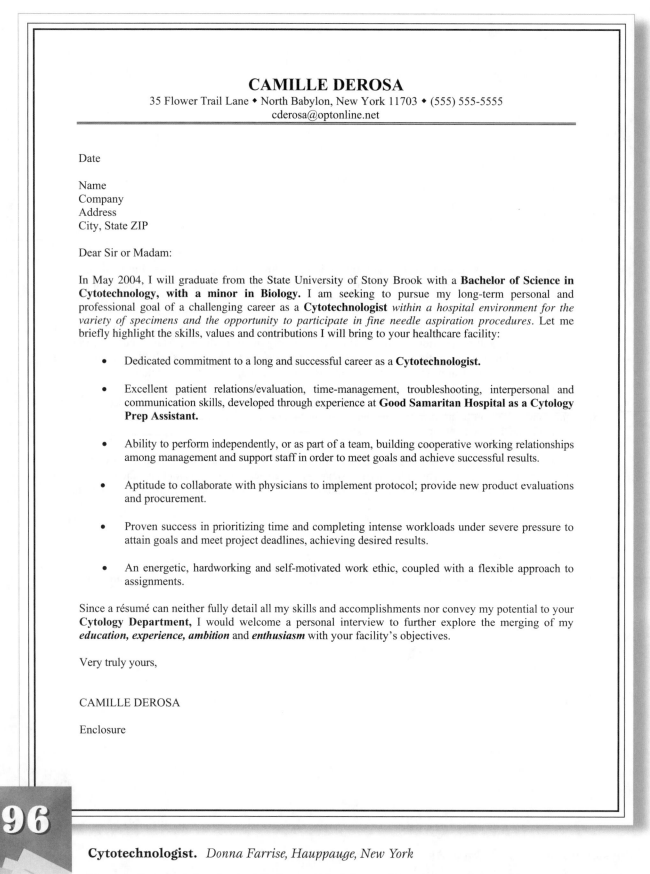

CAMILLE DEROSA

35 Flower Trail Lane ◆ North Babylon, New York 11703 ◆ (555) 555-5555
cderosa@optonline.net

Date

Name
Company
Address
City, State ZIP

Dear Sir or Madam:

In May 2004, I will graduate from the State University of Stony Brook with a **Bachelor of Science in Cytotechnology, with a minor in Biology.** I am seeking to pursue my long-term personal and professional goal of a challenging career as a **Cytotechnologist** *within a hospital environment for the variety of specimens and the opportunity to participate in fine needle aspiration procedures.* Let me briefly highlight the skills, values and contributions I will bring to your healthcare facility:

- Dedicated commitment to a long and successful career as a **Cytotechnologist.**

- Excellent patient relations/evaluation, time-management, troubleshooting, interpersonal and communication skills, developed through experience at **Good Samaritan Hospital as a Cytology Prep Assistant.**

- Ability to perform independently, or as part of a team, building cooperative working relationships among management and support staff in order to meet goals and achieve successful results.

- Aptitude to collaborate with physicians to implement protocol; provide new product evaluations and procurement.

- Proven success in prioritizing time and completing intense workloads under severe pressure to attain goals and meet project deadlines, achieving desired results.

- An energetic, hardworking and self-motivated work ethic, coupled with a flexible approach to assignments.

Since a résumé can neither fully detail all my skills and accomplishments nor convey my potential to your **Cytology Department,** I would welcome a personal interview to further explore the merging of my *education, experience, ambition* and *enthusiasm* with your facility's objectives.

Very truly yours,

CAMILLE DEROSA

Enclosure

96

Cytotechnologist. *Donna Farrise, Hauppauge, New York*

The two-line page border, boldfacing and italicizing of key information and keywords, and bulleting of skills and worker traits make this letter attractive, strong, and easy to grasp at a glance.

Elizabeth Santiago

11 Riverside Drive   (555) 555-5555
New York, NY 10023   esantiago@xyz.com

April 23, 2004

Michael Kahn
Director of Human Resources
St. Luke's–Roosevelt Hospital Center
Roosevelt Division
1000 Tenth Avenue at 58th Street
New York, NY 10019

Dear Mr. Kahn:

After reading about your organization's new health care initiatives, as described on the hospital's Web site, I was excited to learn of an opening for a Clinical Laboratory Scientist. My background in developing and implementing testing and instrumentation procedures can bring an immediate benefit to the hospital as it strives to improve patient care. I am enclosing my resume for your review.

With 15 years of experience in the hematology and pathology departments of two major teaching hospitals, I am able to prioritize workflow and resolve problems to ensure the efficiency and accuracy of department operations. In particular, I have reviewed and revised operating procedures to achieve regulatory compliance. Among my key accomplishments are the following:

- Managed installation and implementation of new coagulation system, including writing procedures and training staff. Coordinated with multiple departments for successful completion within a one-month time line.

- Integrated a standardized coagulation system across two hospital campuses to ensure better patient care and quality assurance.

- Established, wrote, and set up a preventative maintenance schedule for hematology instrumentation to ensure the quality of performance.

I look forward to the opportunity to talk with you in person about the contribution I can make to your hospital. You can reach me at (555) 555-5555.

Thank you for your consideration.

Sincerely,

Elizabeth Santiago

Enclosure

97

Clinical Laboratory Scientist. *Wendy Gelberg, Needham, Massachusetts*

The applicant did background research on the prospective employer's Web site and links her accomplishments directly to the mission of the company. Bullets point to the accomplishments.

KATHERINE TEOJEN
555 Caswell Avenue
Charlotte, NC 28888
(000) 000-0000

March 27, 2004

Dr. John Irving
Director of Clinical Recruitment
Carolinas Medical Center
Charlotte, NC 28888

Dear Dr. Irving:

On the high seas, navigation is very important. In fact, few persons could play a more significant role than the captain of a large cargo vessel.

When the cargo vessel approaches the mainland or nears port, a towering beacon of golden light flashes and revolves to guide ships and warn of obstacles. Here, the lighthouse and its keeper bring the ship through the maze of rocks, atolls and barnacled debris, to safe harbor.

The speech-language pathologist is comparable to the lighthouse keeper; she is the beacon, the guiding light, with the training to show the way to those less fortunate. I understand, intimately, the importance of such training. At age six, to correct the mispronunciation of the letter "r," I went to a speech therapist. This was a pivotal moment, for I realized that *I* could be helped and that speech-language problems were correctable.

Over the years, this interest has grown and taken on a new meaning. Two years ago, I volunteered for Operation Smile, a project in which local physicians travel to Third-World countries and perform reconstructive surgery (usually pro bono) to correct cleft palates of children.

Since then, I have worked as a volunteer at Lake Forest School for the Deaf, teaching basic life skills using sign language. And at Mercy Speech & Hearing Center, a clinic sponsored by the United Way, I currently volunteer, observing and evaluating children with articulation and audiology problems.

Since August 2000, while completing requirements for a master's degree, I have been employed at The Center for Speech Excellence in Charlotte, administering tests and tutoring children in the Fast-Forward Program, an intensive six-week interactive program, with emphasis in receptive language skills, auditory processing and central processing disorders. Working under the auspices of Pamela Wright, a speech pathologist, I have shadowed her while working with children with cochlear implants. The Center treats hearing-impaired children and also works with adults (e.g., accent reduction, voice pitch alteration, and stuttering).

My goal is to provide diagnostic, therapeutic and associated counseling services within a hospital or other clinical setting. I am particularly interested in working with children with articulation, fluency, language, voice and neurological deficits. If your hospital needs a speech pathologist—to be that "guiding light"—I would appreciate the opportunity to discuss your needs in a personal interview. I look forward to hearing from you. A brief résumé of my background is enclosed.

Sincerely,

Katherine Teojen

Enclosure

98

Speech Pathologist. *Doug Morrison, Charlotte, North Carolina*

The ambition of this young speech-language pathologist to help others overcome obstacles (because of her own early problems with speech) is embodied in the opening and closing analogy.

DOMINIC FALCUCCI

November 3, 2004

Hiring Agent, Title
Company Name
Address

Dear Hiring Manager:

Your posting for a [position title] caught my attention as it seems an ideal match for my experience, talents, and interests. As a pharmacy supervisor with experience in customer service, relationship management, inventory control, and process improvement, I believe that someone with my background and skills would be an asset to your company. Innovative and driven, with a proven ability to deliver results, I would like to explore the possibility of putting my skills and experience to work for you.

As you can see from my enclosed résumé, in my current position I brought substantial improvements to store operations while gaining a solid understanding of the pharmacy business. Among my successes, I implemented initiatives that improved workflow and efficiency, simplified inventory management, minimized unpaid claims, and reduced employee turnover. In addition, by developing strong, long-term relationships with vendors, doctor's offices, and insurance company reps, I have been able to enhance service to the customer as well.

My success has been defined by my leadership, dedication, focus on effectiveness, and openness to new ways of doing business. Skilled at identifying improvement opportunities, I am also adept at finding and implementing appropriate solutions. At the same time, with strong communications skills, I am a capable team builder with the ability to motivate others. In the past, I have proven to be a respected and valued employee—someone who learns quickly and is able to apply my knowledge in practical applications. With a record of success behind me, I am confident that I will be an asset to you as well.

I would be pleased to have the opportunity to discuss future employment and look forward to speaking with you. Feel free to contact me at the address and phone number listed below.

Thank you for your consideration.

Sincerely,

Dominic Falcucci

Enclosure

45 APPLE ORCHARD LANE ▪ HOLLOW HILLS, NEW YORK 22222 ▪ (333) 444-5555

99

Pharmacy Supervisor. *Carol A. Altomare, Three Bridges, New Jersey*

This drugstore pharmacy manager wanted to transition to a corporate position. Each of the first three paragraphs indicates experience, skills, or worker traits that would be transferable to a corporate setting.

Winthrop "Lee" Kent

0000 Carlton Circle — Memphis, Tennessee 00000
winlee@extra.com — ✆ 000.000.0000 – 555.555.5555 (Cellular)

Friday, January 30, 2004

Dr. Charles Fleming, MD
Medical Associates of Crofton, P.C.
500 Elm Street
Suite 400
Crofton, Alabama 36100

Dear Dr. Fleming:

If you could "design" the best practice manager for Medical Associates, would the following meet your needs?

❑ A **cash-flow expert** who combines the realistic outlook of an auditor with the profit-building drive of an entrepreneur,

❑ A **productivity multiplier** with a proven track record of leading diverse employees to greater productivity and loyalty,

❑ A manager with a gift for **freeing decision makers** for the tasks only they can do, and

❑ A dedicated administrator who can replace the distractions of business with **peace of mind** that comes from lessened liability and greater profits.

You have just read the 76-word version of my résumé. You'll find the complete document on the next pages. What you won't find are the usual "summary of qualifications" and lists of responsibilities. In their places are more than a half dozen documented contributions that helped moved organizations forward.

I enjoyed working for the state. And they promoted me twice in just eight months because they valued my contributions. But my real calling is working in the private sector.

Because I have a natural desire to fill people's needs, I would like to hear about Medical Associates' special requirements in your own words. May I call in a few days to find a few minutes to do that?

Sincerely,

Winthrop Kent

Encl.: Résumé

100

Medical Practice Manager. *Don Orlando, Montgomery, Alabama*

This letter helped a state employee transition to a medical practice manager. The letter opens with an engaging question, and the answers—as bulleted items—appeal to the needs of the reader.

SAMANTHA DOYLE

November 3, 2004

Addressee
Company Name
Company Address

Dear Hiring Manager:

Your posting for a medical malpractice litigation manager caught my attention as it seems an ideal match for my experience and talents. As an accomplished R.N. with high-level experience in the settlement of medical liability claims, I believe I am someone who will be an asset to your company. With proven negotiation and management skills, along with the ability to build productive relationships with professionals in the medical field, I would like to explore the possibility of putting my skills and experience to work for you.

As you can see from my enclosed résumé, during my career I held a series of positions of increasing responsibility with MedPartners, a company that provides medical liability insurance to physicians. In my current position as Litigation Supervisor, I established a record of success in bringing some of the highest-profile cases to appropriate resolution, implementing effective strategies that minimized potentially large payouts. Keys to my success in this area are a strong understanding of the medical industry, a keen ability for recognizing meritorious cases, and a demonstrated talent for building trust and partnering successfully with physicians.

Among my other strengths, I am articulate and persuasive, an incisive decision maker with strong assessment skills. Credible and influential, I have proven to be a respected and valued employee. With a record of success behind me, I am confident that I will be an asset to you as well.

I would be pleased to have the opportunity to discuss future employment and look forward to speaking with you. Feel free to contact me at the address and phone number listed below.

Thank you for your consideration.

Sincerely,

Samantha Doyle
Enclosure

101

Medical Malpractice Litigation Manager. *Carol A. Altomare, Three Bridges, New Jersey*

The first paragraph indicates the applicant's skills and experience to show a match between her and the prospective company. The second paragraph tells of the applicant's success and strengths.

Julie Windham
1111 Madison Avenue
Boise, ID 00000
(000) 000-0000
jwindham@earthlink.net

January 30, 2004

Human Resources Department
Access Health Care
2323 Woodhaven Street
Boise, ID 00000

Dear Human Resources Representative:

It is with great interest that I forward my resume for consideration as Program
Director. Currently, as Admissions Coordinator for the ABC Rehabilitation and
Care Center, I spearhead marketing efforts for this health care service
provider, ranked #1 in a heavily competitive market, drawing clients from all
parts of Idaho. My results have been significant and include the following:

* Occupancy rate increase from 90% to 98% (highest rate among facilities in
Idaho);

* Patient increase from 6-7 to 18-19 through strategic marketing communications;

* Cost-effective service rate wins through tactical negotiations with insurance
companies.

My resume is attached to provide you with specific details concerning my
background and qualifications. Thank you for your time.

Sincerely,

Julie Windham

102

Program Director. *Daniel J. Dorotik, Jr., Lubbock, Texas*

This e-mail letter in text (.txt) format shows that online letters (and resumes) are preferably
shorter than those in traditional format. Readers like window-size documents that require little
scrolling.

DIANA ROGERSON ARQUETTE
0000 North Roundtree ▪ Chandler, AZ 85750 ▪ 555-555-5555

March 23, 2004

Mr. John J. Jackson, Board of Directors
Van Nuys Mental Health Services
345 North Seney Boulevard
Van Nuys, CA 93214

Dear Mr. Jackson:

In today's intensely competitive healthcare market, the ultimate success of any enterprise requires management that can

- Clarify and strengthen the organization's core values and principles to facilitate dynamic business growth and profitability enhancement, while keeping the people side of the business strong.
- Instill self-confidence and motivation in managers, supervisors and support staff and train them for maximum achievement in service and patient satisfaction.
- Restructure and organize the facility to draw maximum quality and performance from available staff, resources and databases.

I believe my track record, as outlined in the enclosed résumé, demonstrates that your facility would benefit from my business reengineering ability and prior successes. In my current position as Behavioral Health Administrator, I have been the catalyst in a major turnaround of the facility, spearheading the reduction of expenses, FTEs, and professional fees, while increasing patient satisfaction. In addition, I sit on various task forces and committees within the corporate structure and the local and state community to offer support and proactive solutions to the constantly changing environment in the healthcare industry.

I would welcome the opportunity to explore my potential contributions to your facility's quality, revenues, and bottom line. Thank you for your consideration of my qualifications, and I look forward to discussing the possibilities soon.

Sincerely,

Diana Rogerson Arquette

Enclosure

103

Behavioral Health Administrator. *Kay Bourne, Tucson, Arizona*

Bullets point to healthcare-facility survival needs in a tight economy. The second paragraph indicates how the applicant might help the facility to be economically successful with patient satisfaction.

FOSTER M. CLAYTON
9 Cranberry Lane ▪ Oxford Hills, PA 19666
Home: (555) 888-9999 ▪ Mobile: (555) 555-6666 ▪ E-mail: Clay212@aol.com

December 16, 2004

Ms. Liz Carter
MHS Recruiters
999 Old Nathan Road
Suite 333
Eagleville, PA 19777

RE: Orthopedic/Musculoskeletal Product Line Director
Main Health Systems

Dear Ms. Carter:

It is with great interest that I submit my resume and collateral materials for consideration as Orthopedic/Musculoskeletal Product Line Director at Main Health Systems. It is my understanding that the successful candidate will possess qualifications and experience that closely match those detailed in my resume, and it would be my pleasure to meet with you to discuss this exciting opportunity.

Highlights of my professional career include

♦ More than 20 years of top-flight management experience in the healthcare services and products industries.

♦ Expertise in the start-up of new healthcare ventures and accelerated growth within existing provider organizations.

♦ Delivery of strong revenue and profit growth within extremely competitive healthcare markets.

♦ Strong qualifications in new business development, strategic planning, marketing, risk management, program development, and teaching.

♦ Broad-based general management skills in human resource affairs, training, financial planning and analysis, and presentations to various boards and professional groups.

♦ Extensive network of professional, technical, and medical contacts throughout the healthcare community.

My leadership style is direct and decisive, yet I am flexible in responding to the constantly changing demands of the industry, customers, and the market. I am familiar with most regulations governing healthcare practice, and have been actively involved in several professional organizations within the field.

I look forward to speaking with you to discuss this opportunity. I would be pleased to provide professional references, additional biographical information, and work samples in preparation for an interview. Thank you for your consideration.

Sincerely,

Foster M. Clayton

Enclosure

104

Orthopedic/Musculoskeletal Product Line Director. *Karen Conway, Media, Pennsylvania*

This letter's first paragraph directs the reader to the resume, and the bullets draw the reader's attention to the applicant's most relevant experience, expertise, qualifications, and skills.

BRIAN IRVING, M.D.
89 Rowlings Road
Buffalo, NY 00000
(555) 555-5555 ~ BIMD@aol.com

July 1, 2004

John Murdock, M.D.
Vice President, Medical Research & Drug Safety
Johnson & Johnson
2344 Connecticut Avenue
Norwalk, CT 06856

Dear Dr. Murdock:

Currently Director of Scientific Affairs at Bennington Pharma, I am exploring
employment opportunities in clinical research with your company. I recently learned
from Dr. Brian Peterson of your need for a Director of Research and Development.
My 12+ years of experience in clinical research and department management in
pharmaceutical organizations both in Europe and the United States may interest you.

Complementing my medical degree is expertise in the development, design,
implementation, staffing and management of clinical studies for pharmaceutical,
cosmetic and OTC skin care products. The scope of my responsibilities extends well
beyond research and development to include collaboration with Marketing and
Consumer Affairs to provide scientific, advertising, promotion and customer-relations
support. I have been highly effective in building relationships with industry opinion
leaders, resulting in the successful promotion of our company's full range of products.

In addition, I am experienced in sourcing, auditing, negotiating and managing contracts
with independent product test sites both in the U.S. and overseas. My international
business qualifications include partnering with our company's affiliate organization in
Asia to design and conduct clinical trials to address market needs.

I would welcome the opportunity to meet with you and discuss the contributions I would
make toward your company's continued growth and success.

Sincerely,

Brian Irving, M.D.

105

Director of Research and Development. *Louise Garver, Enfield, Connecticut*

The applicant used this letter successfully to identify new employment opportunities with
another organization in the same industry. The referral in the first paragraph captures attention
immediately.

PAUL JOHNSON

14 Westlake Drive
Framingham, MA 01702

Email: paul@johnson.com

Cell: 000 000 0000
Residence: 555 555 5555

11 February 2004

Mr. David Paul
ATCT Hospital
18 Saddleback Road
Framingham, MA 01702

Re: Chief Executive Officer

Dear Mr. Paul:

For almost 20 years, I have been at the forefront of initiatives that have positioned organizations to support significant growth, and turned around floundering and problematic divisions to regain the respect of the people they serve. I have conceived new ideas to strengthen core services to customers, project-managed new infrastructure initiatives, and maintained the morale of "the troops" despite periods of instability and change.

Considered a senior executive with a combination of vision and corporate realism, I have been acknowledged for my capacity to harness the enthusiasm and talents of others, identify core issues, and exploit the necessary resources available to stretch funds and achieve management objectives in healthcare and medical environments.

Experience of this magnitude hasn't been developed overnight; successes have been hard won, and commitment has been tireless. Yet the rewards of seeing an idea take hold of people's imaginations for better and more responsive service delivery remains to this day one of my greatest motivators, and it is a skill I'm keen to demonstrate for my next employer as I meet the next challenge of my professional life.

Eager to tackle new opportunities, my last major role as Vice President, Business Delivery, consulting primarily to medical, healthcare, and education sectors, has now concluded. I have transformed what was a new business unit into a vital, responsive operation that delivered strong productivity increases and growth in just two years.

And now the time is ripe for a new challenge. Broad-based knowledge across diverse sectors and specialist executive consultancy experience in healthcare and medical sectors position me well for joining your leadership team.

Experienced in hospital operations, case management, and all the economic, procedural, and staff issues inherent in such environments, I believe I can bring a unique skill set to the role of hospital CEO. Having worked closely with senior executives in major healthcare facilities and hospitals, I know and understand the complexities of the healthcare system, the infrastructure, and how to position the organization for genuine growth. I see significant opportunities in aligning myself with ATCT Hospital, opportunities I'm keen to tackle and achieve measurable successes in, for our mutual benefit.

Naturally I would be delighted to explore your needs in detail at an interview and can arrange to meet at a mutually convenient time. In the meantime, my résumé is attached for your review, and I can be contacted at the numbers provided. Thank you for your time and consideration, and I look forward to speaking with you soon.

Sincerely,

Paul Johnson

106

Chief Executive Officer. *Gayle Howard, Chirnside Park, Melbourne, Australia*

The challenge of this cover letter was to convince the reader that this senior consultant, who had worked in healthcare for many years, was qualified to assume the role of a hospital CEO.

CATHERINE SITTON
555 N. Johnson Avenue, Apt. 5
Brookhaven, Pennsylvania 19333
(555) 555-8888

December 16, 2004

Sodexo Marriott Corporation
ATT: Franklin Hunt, Director of Personnel
5 Landon Way
Princeton, NJ 08888

Dear Mr. Hunt:

I would like to express my interest in joining Sodexo Marriott in a management capacity. I am particularly interested in a senior-level position involving corporate dining, catering, and banquet events. Enclosed is my resume, reviewing my extensive background and accomplishments in staff and operations management, for your consideration.

As an effective manager and chef, I have a proven track record in all facets of the food service industry. My greatest strength would have to be my ability to generate employee loyalty and create a team environment. Equally strong is my ability to control labor and food costs. I am especially proud of the fact that former staff members often request to join me when I accept a new assignment. I provide extensive training, direction, and feedback; they are clearly aware of my expectations and interest in their welfare.

Other key attributes include attention to detail, the ability to work effectively in high-pressure situations, a high level of motivation, and emphasis on sanitation. Here are several career highlights that may be of interest:

- ◆ Significantly reduced Workers' Compensation costs in all locations through close attention to safety.
- ◆ Acquired an excellent reputation as a chef, skilled in the areas of menu planning, timing, presentation, and food quality.
- ◆ Hired as a consultant to assist a new center-city restaurant during its start-up phase.
- ◆ Developed training manuals and completed staff training for all positions.

On a final note, it goes without saying that guest satisfaction is key to a successful operation. I consistently stress to my staff the importance of communicating effectively with guests. Not only does the guest feel unique and special, but also it demonstrates confidence on the part of the employee. That equates to a successful dining experience and repeat business, which has been the norm in each of my operations.

I believe my education and background have provided the tools and experience necessary to manage a large-scale operation, and I would welcome the opportunity to discuss employment prospects at Sodexo Marriott in a personal interview. I believe your organization would be an ideal work setting for someone with my skills and personality.

I'll look forward to hearing from you.

Sincerely,

Catherine Sitton

Enclosure

107

Hotel Manager. *Karen Conway, Media, Pennsylvania*

A series of equally short paragraphs makes this longer-than-average cover letter relatively easy to read. The bulleted items provide relief from the series and draw attention to career highlights.

Michael J. Fisher, C.M.C.

56 Madison Avenue
Summit, New Jersey 07901
(555) 555-5555

Dear Sir/Madam:

Enclosed is my resume for your review. I am confident that my extensive experience as an executive chef and hotel/restaurant manager would serve as an asset to a position in your organization. My career began 23 years ago as an apprentice training under several notable, internationally known chefs. Since that time I have been involved extensively in the area of food services management and marketing.

I am currently General Manager and Corporate Executive Chef of Hague Nieuw-York. In 1999, I was hired to start up this 225-seat restaurant. The casual dining establishment is part of Avanti Brands, Inc., USA. I am responsible for all financial reporting and instituted key control systems to meet the standards of the parent company. Additional achievements include gaining excellent media publicity, creative menu development, and directing on- and off-site catering for many New York City premieres. I was asked to coordinate all aspects of our new construction and assist in the design aspects of the kitchen.

As Director of Operations for Town Square Katering and Times Square Restaurant in Hoboken, New Jersey, my staff and I expanded the business to accommodate parties ranging from 10 to 4,000 people and grossed more than $1.5 million in sales.

Working as Vice President of Operations and Executive Chef for Pine Ridge Country Club, I oversaw all profit-and-loss functions for a 165-seat, a la carte restaurant and a 1,000-seat banquet facility. The club had an 18-hole championship golf course that I managed, with an active membership of 1,000 members.

I gained extensive international experience working as Executive Chef for Ordini's, a five-star-rated restaurant in New Zealand, preparing food for the Prime Minister, various heads of state, and visiting dignitaries. I obtained my New Zealand Master Chef's Certification. In addition, I served as an Executive Pastry Chef and Chef for a Hawaiian hotel owned and operated by the Sheraton Corporation.

Thank you for your consideration. I look forward to speaking with you personally regarding my qualifications and how I can contribute positively as a member of your management staff.

Sincerely Yours,

Michael J. Fisher, C.M.C.

Enclosure

108

Executive Chef and Hotel/Restaurant Manager. *Beverley and Mitchell I. Baskin, Marlboro, New Jersey*

Inferior cover letters wallow in generalities and abstraction. This letter is unusually interesting because of its many references to restaurants in specific locations around the world.

JONATHAN BRANSON
Nimrod Acres, Fifth Estate, Rochester, MN 55555
cell phone: (555) 555-5555   home phone: (555) 555-5550

February 4, 2004

Mr. Jack Bloomwell
Jake's Quality Constructing and Estates
40 Main Way, Suite Two
Eden Prairie, MN 55555

RE: Project Manager, Peregrine Estates and Country Club

Dear Mr. Bloomwell:

It is with great interest that I submit the enclosed resume and this letter for the position of Project Manager in your company, which would make use of the following experience and skills:

- Management and coordination of resources and activities
- Knowledge of the real estate and construction industries
- Property management
- Decision making and troubleshooting
- Supervision and hiring
- Customer service
- Technology and technical skills
- Long-time membership in area country clubs

As my resume will show, I am extremely competent in juggling multiple priorities simultaneously. A high energy level, combined with strong people skills, dedication and good business sense, contribute to success at whatever challenges I tackle. Without those skills, I would not have been able to finance my education through full-time work, while maintaining a full load of courses. In addition, I was able to balance family needs—difficult without lots of flexibility, good intentions and total commitment to dependability. Understanding when to delegate and how to manage time well have served me throughout my efforts to be successful.

Areas of special interest include management, oversight, coordination and contact with a variety of customers and contractors. My experience thus far has been diverse—often more than one job at once while I was finishing my degree. I've worked with my hands as a dishwasher and construction worker, and worked directly with people from the viewpoints of manager, customer service representative and electronic technician.

A resume can provide only an introduction. I look forward to the opportunity to meet with you to review your needs and the company's overall goals. At that time, I can address any questions you may have. Within the next week, I will contact your office to see whether you are scheduling interviews or need additional information.

Sincerely,

Jonathan Branson

109

Country Club Project Manager. *Beverley Drake, Rochester, Minnesota*

The "RE:" line makes the position easy to spot, and the bullets help the reader see that the applicant has experience and skills for the position. The next paragraphs show other relevant competencies.

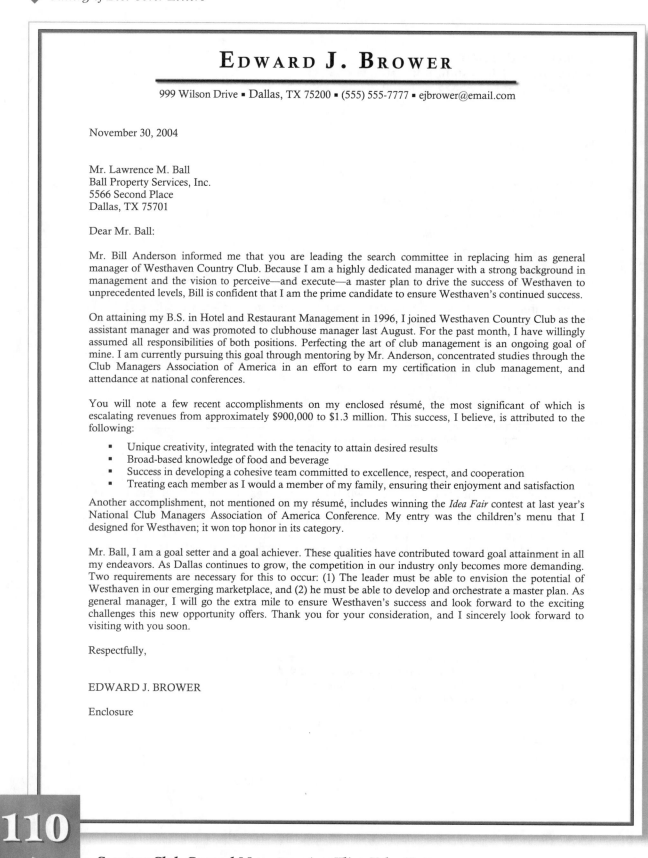

EDWARD J. BROWER

999 Wilson Drive ▪ Dallas, TX 75200 ▪ (555) 555-7777 ▪ ejbrower@email.com

November 30, 2004

Mr. Lawrence M. Ball
Ball Property Services, Inc.
5566 Second Place
Dallas, TX 75701

Dear Mr. Ball:

Mr. Bill Anderson informed me that you are leading the search committee in replacing him as general manager of Westhaven Country Club. Because I am a highly dedicated manager with a strong background in management and the vision to perceive—and execute—a master plan to drive the success of Westhaven to unprecedented levels, Bill is confident that I am the prime candidate to ensure Westhaven's continued success.

On attaining my B.S. in Hotel and Restaurant Management in 1996, I joined Westhaven Country Club as the assistant manager and was promoted to clubhouse manager last August. For the past month, I have willingly assumed all responsibilities of both positions. Perfecting the art of club management is an ongoing goal of mine. I am currently pursuing this goal through mentoring by Mr. Anderson, concentrated studies through the Club Managers Association of America in an effort to earn my certification in club management, and attendance at national conferences.

You will note a few recent accomplishments on my enclosed résumé, the most significant of which is escalating revenues from approximately $900,000 to $1.3 million. This success, I believe, is attributed to the following:

- Unique creativity, integrated with the tenacity to attain desired results
- Broad-based knowledge of food and beverage
- Success in developing a cohesive team committed to excellence, respect, and cooperation
- Treating each member as I would a member of my family, ensuring their enjoyment and satisfaction

Another accomplishment, not mentioned on my résumé, includes winning the *Idea Fair* contest at last year's National Club Managers Association of America Conference. My entry was the children's menu that I designed for Westhaven; it won top honor in its category.

Mr. Ball, I am a goal setter and a goal achiever. These qualities have contributed toward goal attainment in all my endeavors. As Dallas continues to grow, the competition in our industry only becomes more demanding. Two requirements are necessary for this to occur: (1) The leader must be able to envision the potential of Westhaven in our emerging marketplace, and (2) he must be able to develop and orchestrate a master plan. As general manager, I will go the extra mile to ensure Westhaven's success and look forward to the exciting challenges this new opportunity offers. Thank you for your consideration, and I sincerely look forward to visiting with you soon.

Respectfully,

EDWARD J. BROWER

Enclosure

110

Country Club General Manager. *Ann Klint, Tyler, Texas*

The referral in the first paragraph is especially strong because the retiring general manager is recommending that the applicant be considered seriously in the search for a replacement.

Cliff Stanton

February 1, 2004

John Smith
Hyatt Hotel
1234 Larimer Street
Denver, CO 80000

Re: Position HY123456

Dear Employment Director:

It's all about heads and beds and customer satisfaction in the hospitality industry. It takes an innovative and tenacious manager to face successfully the tremendous challenges confronting today's leading hotels. I have made a career out of turning around faltering properties, raising service standards, increasing organizational efficiency, and significantly improving bottom-line profits.

I am currently the General Manager of the Executive Hotel, Denver. The owners have decided to convert the property into an assisted-living facility, and while they have asked me to stay with the property, my passion for the hotel business necessitates that I move on. I am seeking a management position with an upscale hotel such as yours.

My résumé speaks to my history of decisive leadership as well as strong financial and operating results. Most notably I have

- Turned unprofitable properties into consistently performing, multimillion-dollar organizations.
- Streamlined operations and eliminated duplicate functions to reduce costs and increase productivity and revenue.
- Integrated finance and operations, creating proactive business units focused on the bottom line and positioned for long-term growth and profitability.

The value I bring to Hyatt Hotels is broad experience spanning all core business functions with a primary focus on operations and finance. My success is directly attributable to my ability to unify organizations, initiate action, and deliver results.

I welcome the chance to explore any current assignments commensurate with my management skills. I am willing to relocate for the right opportunity.

Thank you for your time and consideration, and I look forward to hearing from you.

Sincerely,

Cliff Stanton

Enclosure

P.O. Box 1234 · Denver, CO 00000 · Home (555) 555-5555 · Mobile/Pager (555) 555-5550 · cliffs@yahoo.net

Hotel General Manager. *Roberta Gamza, Louisville, Colorado*

The applicant wanted to move to a luxury, full-service hotel chain. To get the reader's attention, the writer began by getting to the point about what is important in the hospitality industry.

000 Sharps Boulevard NE
Norfolk, Virginia 55555

☎ (555) 555-5555

December 20, 2004

Mrs. Linda Thorndyke
Director of Human Resources
Heritage Companies
PO Box 555
Houston, Texas 55555

RE: Human Resources Assistant

Dear Mrs. Thorndyke:

I am very interested in re-careering to the Human Resources field and have enclosed a resume for your review. Originally an accountant, I am now returning to the paid workforce after a period of extensive community and volunteer work.

Balancing a number of general business skills, I also have a valuable complement of human-service-related strengths, including the following:

facilitation, interviewing and assessment   training and tutoring
patient and customer service   client research and analysis
client data gathering and consultation   listening and communicating

One of the main things I missed in accounting work is direct interaction with people and the opportunity to feel as if my work would make a difference in the lives of others. My nature is one of compassion, patience and responsibility. Solution-oriented, I believe that all problems can be worked out. Research and assessment skills, time management, decision making and multitasking add to the value of my people skills. Adding more flexibility, my working style is one that easily lends itself to either an independent or a group work environment.

Others describe me as highly professional, sensitive to the needs of others, a positive thinker, detail-oriented and dependable. I feel that my maturity and combination of business and people skills are assets and would like to meet with you to discuss your needs, including how I might contribute to those goals.

I will contact your office to see whether additional information is needed, and to determine a suitable time to meet with you.

Sincerely,

SHANNA COLLINS

Human Resources Assistant. *Beverley Drake, Rochester, Minnesota*

After a period of volunteer work, this accountant wanted to return to the workforce but in the field of human resources. The letter identifies her transferable strengths, skills, and worker traits.

BRIAN THOMAS

000 Dennis Drive • Ridgewood, NY 11385 • (555) 555-5555 • BThomas@overway.com

March 9, 2004

Ms. Mary Jones
Director of Human Resources
Human Resources Department
International Paper Distribution
South Main Street, Rte. 27A
Brentwood, NY 11717

Dear Ms. Jones:

The accompanying résumé is presented for your review and consideration for an entry-level/trainee position with International Paper Distribution's Human Resources Department. Although not yet defined, this position will take advantage of my ability to learn quickly, easily grasp complex concepts, assume increased levels of responsibility, and complete assignments independently or as part of a team with a high level of performance.

I offer a Bachelor of Arts degree in Psychology along with seven years of experience working in increasingly responsible store-management positions while attending school full time. In my current position as Assistant Manager with Bagel Café, my primary responsibilities are centered on overseeing day-to-day store operations in areas of customer service, vendor relations, inventory control, regulatory compliance, and staff supervision.

In 1999, I was selected by management to assist with the revamping of personnel management practices involving 12 full- and part-time employees. Utilizing my academic knowledge and prior experience, I successfully redefined job descriptions and responsibilities, provided hands-on training, and implemented new policies and procedures resulting in a more structured and supportive workplace where employees currently enjoy incentives to work hard and maintain their terms of employment.

It is with your organization that I hope to contribute in the same vein. Therefore, I would welcome the opportunity to meet with the appropriate managers to discuss the possibility of my joining your organization's team of Human Resources professionals. Thank you for your review and consideration. I look forward to speaking with you soon.

Sincerely,

Brian Thomas

113

Human Resources Position, Entry Level. *Ann Baehr, Brentwood, New York*

While working as assistant manager for Bagel Café, the applicant learned that he had an aptitude for human resources activities. This letter is part of his application for full-time work in this field.

MARIGOLD TRUMAN

555 Windy Way East • Brentwood, NY 11717 • (555) 555-3333 • HR@TheBranch.net

June 25, 2004

Ms. Mary Smith
Recruitment Administrator
Human Resources Department
THE BRANCH BANK
One Branch Plaza
Brentwood, New York 55555

Dear Ms. Smith:

The enclosed résumé and supporting documentation are presented for your review and consideration for acceptance into The Branch Bank's Human Resources Associates Program. Ideally, this opportunity will develop and strengthen my skills and knowledge while exposing me to a broad spectrum of areas and challenges conducive to professional growth in the field of Human Resources.

I offer a Bachelor of Arts degree in Psychology and tenure with The Branch Bank since June of 1997 in the position of Senior File Clerk, Pre-Arbitration/In-Coming Collections Department. Initially, I joined this department as a temporary employee and proved myself as a team player capable of handling a heavy caseload while significantly improving the quality of office procedures. As a result, my current position was created for me on a permanent basis.

Further, to ensure the continuity of positive changes that I have brought to the department, I provide ongoing training to employees, a role I greatly enjoy. To date, I have been recognized and rewarded for my drive to go above and beyond what is expected of me, with recent contributions that include an interim position as a fully trained Auto Call Directory representative. I am confident that my education, record of excellence (including perfect attendance), and personal attributes (strong organizational, overall communication, and computer skills), combined with a firm aspiration to further my career in Human Resources, qualify me as a suitable candidate.

Although this application, along with my personnel file, illustrates my background well, I feel that a personal interview would better demonstrate my knowledge and abilities. Therefore, I would appreciate an opportunity to interview with you at a convenient time. Thank you for your review and consideration. I look forward to hearing from you soon.

Sincerely,

Marigold Truman

114

Bank Human Resources Position. *Ann Baehr, Brentwood, New York*

The unusual horizontal lines are eye-catching. With its filled circle on the left, the top line balances the contact information. With a filled circle on the right, the bottom line balances the top line.

KIMBERLY BLAKELY

000 Romeo Drive
Commack, New York 11725
(555) 555-5555

Dear Sir or Madam:

Reflecting on my professional experience within the insurance industry, it is at this point in my career that I am seeking to pursue my long-term personal and professional goal of a challenging career within **Human Resources.** Let me briefly highlight the skills, values, and contributions I will bring to your organization:

- Dedicated commitment to a long and successful career within **Human Resources.**

- Excellent customer service/relations, time-management, troubleshooting, and communications skills, developed through many years in the insurance industry as a **Claims Specialist.**

- Ability to perform independently or as part of a team, building cooperative working relationships among management and support staff in order to meet goals and achieve successful results.

- An energetic, enthusiastic approach with proven success in prioritizing time and resources to attain goals and meet project deadlines.

My personal and professional education, work experiences, interests, and strengths have all contributed to outstanding business achievements. I am accountable for diverse responsibilities, including servicing clients and the general public. My acquired knowledge and experience as a contributing individual in the business world will prove to be a quality that will enhance the goals and standards of any Human Resources department.

Please take the time to review the aforementioned credentials. I firmly believe you will find them to meet the needs of your company, and I am confident my contributions to your organization will prove to be lasting, if given the opportunity. Thank you for your time and consideration.

Very truly yours,

KIMBERLY BLAKELY

Enclosure

115

Human Resources Position. *Donna Farrise, Hauppauge, New York*

This insurance claim specialist wanted a position in any human resources department. Boldfacing highlights Human Resources as a goal. Bullets point to values, transferable skills, and worker-trait contributions.

Available for relocation

Sue Allard

000 Roberts Road, Martinville, Alabama 00000
☏ 334.555.5555 (home) — 334.555.6666 (cell)
suealla@clark.com

November 2, 2004

Ms. Deborah Montiel
States Bank
44 Charleston Street
Montgomery, Alabama 00000

Dear Ms. Montiel:

I want to make it as easy as possible for States Bank to add me to its team as a Human Resources Assistant. Moving toward that goal starts with my résumé.

I wanted to give you something more valuable than the usual job titles, responsibilities, and college course work. That's why I've included examples of HR-related problems solved. At school, my problem-solving skills were reviewed by senior HR professionals who were paid to evaluate my work against tough industry standards. At work, everyone saw my workforce management abilities—from supervisors, to coworkers, to customers. In fact, it was my work experience that motivated me to get a degree in Human Resources while I continued learning on the job.

My development program is almost finished. I have just obtained my BS in Human Resources. But I want to start putting my energies and skills to work in that field as soon as I can.

So, as a next step, I would like to hear about States Bank's specific HR needs in your own words. May I call in a few days to set up time to do that?

Sincerely,

Sue Allard

Encl.: Résumé

116

Human Resources Assistant. *Don Orlando, Montgomery, Alabama*

The applicant had a recent HR degree but never had held an HR position. The third sentence in the second paragraph counters any view that college instruction is out of touch with the real world.

PATRICIA THOMAS

1234 Vancouver Street
Akron, OH 12345

(555) 555-1234
PThomas@email.com

January 7, 2004

Wake-Up Call Staffing
Attention: Melissa Brown
1234 E. Miles Street
Akron, OH 12345

Dear Ms. Brown:

It was nice to speak with you on the telephone recently regarding potential career opportunities with Wake-Up Call Staffing. As we discussed, I have worked as a temporary for Wake-Up Call Staffing in the past and received excellent reviews from employers. Now that I have completed an advanced degree in Human Resources, I am prepared to excel in a career as a Recruiter. I have attached my résumé and qualifications for your review and am certain that you will be quite impressed.

I recently obtained a Master's degree in Human Resources and currently work as a Consultant. As a result of my degree requirements, internship and current position, I have gained valuable experience with critical aspects of the selection process, such as

- Developing and administering employment tests
- Researching legal properties of tests
- Conducting job analyses
- Developing and conducting behavioral interviews
- Reviewing and critiquing resumes
- Conducting training sessions for employees

I feel that my background would prove valuable to the recruitment process at Wake-Up Call Staffing in many ways. For example, I am experienced in standardized test development, administration and legal issues of fairness involving the testing process. This would certainly benefit the preemployment testing process at Wake-Up Call Staffing. My work experience has also enhanced my analytical and organizational skills, which are critical to success in any position. In fact, my current supervisor has stated that my organizational skills are one of my greatest assets.

Overall, I seek to integrate my interpersonal skills, positive attitude, perseverance, determination and knowledge of the selection process in order to recruit qualified candidates. I would thoroughly enjoy the opportunity to implement my recruiting skills at Wake-Up Call Staffing, and I look forward to speaking with you again soon.

Sincerely,

Patricia Thomas

Enclosure

117

Human Resources Recruiter. *Tara G. Papp, Mogadore, Ohio*

This letter begins as a follow-up to a phone call—a sure way to capture attention. The first paragraph specifies the target position, and each successive paragraph highlights the applicant's merits.

Cliff Barnes
0000 Jefferson Avenue • Lewiston, ID 99999 • (555) 555-5555

January 2, 2004

James Hall
Director of Parks and Recreation
Lewiston City Personnel Department
PO Box 162
Lewiston, ID 99999

Dear Mr. James Hall,

I am writing to express interest in Superintendent of Recreation Services with your organization and am enclosing my résumé for your review. I offer a distinguished record of achievements in directing process improvements and designing action plans to achieve company goals.

One of my greatest strengths lies in my ability to devise strategies that immediately boost operating efficiency, generate revenues, reduce costs, and eliminate excess. While serving as Director of Food and Beverage at Terrace Lakes Golf Course, the accomplishment I am most proud of is not doubling the revenue in two years. It is not the handling, hiring, firing, and scheduling of personnel. It is not the writing and producing of an employee manual, which had never been done before. My most significant accomplishment, which displays creativity and problem-solving skills, is the successful use of cooking facilities no more extensive than that of the average family: a range, a microwave, and an outdoor barbecue. It is truly like feeding several hundred people every day out of your own kitchen. This requires a lot of planning and inventing of ways to do the extraordinary under the most ordinary of conditions.

I offer innovative approaches to financial management that enable organizations to maximize existing capital. As a seasoned supervisor, I offer expertise in a wide range of HR functions, including organization design, restructuring, downsizing/rightsizing, staff training and development, recruitment and retention, and employee relations.

Unlike many of my peers, I have equally strong experience leading organizations from a broader point of view, encompassing strategic planning, operations and facilities management, and general business administration. Successes in these areas, as well as my expertise in finance and human resources, have provided me with the qualifications to initiate the action and deliver the results so critical to your organization's long-term performance.

In summary, I believe I am uniquely qualified to take on a superintendent of recreation services leadership role with your organization. If you would like to schedule a time for us to meet, please contact me at (555) 555-5555.

Sincerely,

Cliff Barnes

Enclosure

118

Superintendent of Recreation Services. *Denette Jones, Boise, Idaho*

The applicant uses the second paragraph to capture the reader's admiration. The paragraph tells of the applicant's feat of using limited cooking facilities to meet a golf course's food demands.

MICHELE M. CROWN

00000 East 47th Avenue, #10
Denver, Colorado 80239
555.555.5555 ▪ mcrown@aol.com

March 1, 2004

Mr. William R. Wilkison, Director
Appleone Employment Services
Sales/Marketing
487 South Broadway
Denver, Colorado 80219

RE: HR Recruiter—Account Executive, Denver Office

Dear Mr. Wilkison:

If you seek an individual with the behavioral characteristics to deal effectively with people, build relationships, influence and persuade, and provide superior customer sales and service, we should meet. More than a decade of experience in human resources recruiting, screening, placing, and training qualifies me as the individual you seek.

During 11 years with United Airlines (most recently as Station Operations Supervisor for the Denver site), I have performed extensive recruitment and training functions, including contributions in the areas of presentation, negotiation, sales, and customer service. From my enclosed résumé, you will find that my experience and skills translate well to human resources recruitment.

To explore fully my abilities as a human resources recruitment professional, I acquired the services of a professional career development firm. Let me share with you some confirming comments from a recent behavioral assessment I completed that shows the work style I offer to Appleone (each excerpt begins with "Michele is"):

- "Good at maintaining friendly public relations. She believes in getting results through other people and prefers the 'team approach.'"

- "Places her focus on people and prides herself on her 'intuition.' To her, strangers are just friends she hasn't met."

- "Likes to develop people and build organizations. She is good at creating enthusiasm in others and enjoys the uniqueness of each human being."

Mr. Wilkison, let's set up an informal meeting to discuss the ways that my record of successful recruitment, people development, and staffing management can benefit Appleone Employment Services. I will call you next week.

Thank you for your time. I look forward to speaking with you.

Very truly yours,

Michele M. Crown

119

Human Resources Recruiter–Account Executive. *Nick Marino, Bishop, Texas*

After 9/11, the applicant was laid off from an airline involved in the terrorist attacks and wanted to transition to human resources. The testimonials from an assessment are strong support.

REBECCA B. STILLS
0000 Prosperity Road • Monroe, NC 28888 • (555) 555-5555

March 20, 2004

Ms. D. Finnegan
TICS Corporation
P.O. Box 7488
Charlotte, NC 28241

Dear Ms. Finnegan:

Why did Abraham Lincoln win log-splitting contests so easily?

You've heard the reason: He knew exactly where to place his wedge to give his blows the most power. When Lincoln won these contests, he was the same age as I am now; and I, too, want to enter a log-splitting contest.

I have a good, strong wedge and a sturdy hammer, but I need a log: a company whose growth I can contribute to and build a career with.

In the first place, I want to get into the field of human resources—as a generalist—starting as a **human resource assistant.** I have strong computer skills (Word, Excel) and the ability to master new things. In addition, I possess strong communication skills, honed through four years as a waitress and as a customer service representative within a fast-paced, quality-minded call center environment.

In May, I will receive my baccalaureate degree in Psychology; I lack only one three-hour course, which is offered at UNCC in the evening this summer. During my college years, I worked to provide 75% of all expenses, so I have grown accustomed to long hours and hard work. And during this time I have been molding my wedge: working as an HR intern (please see enclosed résumé) and learning about employee benefits plans and procedures.

This, then, is my wedge into the field of human resources: to be a human resource assistant, acquire experience and advance to more responsible positions. Your company and its opportunities can be my log.

Will you let me enter the contest?

I can be reached at (555) 555-5555. I look forward to hearing from you.

Sincerely,

Rebecca B. Stills

Enclosure

120

Human Resources Assistant. *Doug Morrison, Charlotte, North Carolina*

This recent graduate was keenly interested in entering the field of human resources. The letter displays her motivation, strong interest, enthusiasm, youthful vitality, and career goals.

PHYLLIS MARTIN, PHR   **(555) 555-5555**
5555 Maxwell, Clearview, Texas 79000

February 12, 2004

Sid Critefelder
Vice President of Human Resources
NATURAL GAS COMPANY
P.O. Box 5555
Panhandle, Texas 79408

RE: HUMAN RESOURCES GENERALIST

Dear Mr. Critefelder:

Your recent HR generalist vacancy has prompted me to send you my résumé for review. As you will discover, I offer the depth of experience necessary to successfully administer safety, benefits, and compensation programs; recruit, train, develop, and retain staff; build community relations; assess and fulfill staffing needs, and evaluate / revise policies and procedures. **Thirteen years of collective HR experience** also enforce comprehensive knowledge of state and federal personnel regulations. Additionally, my history reflects a loyal, stable employee who thrives on increasing responsibility and progressive learning. It would be an honor to contribute to a corporate culture such as yours, which values people and appreciates differences.

The following attributes and well-developed skills are additional reasons to take a close look at my credentials:

HUMAN RESOURCES ADMINISTRATION
- Integrity, loyalty, and diligence earn respect and reflect distinction.
- Ownership of responsibility and accountability demonstrate leadership and character.
- Time management and organization skills help streamline tasks and cultivate efficiency.
- Investigation and decrement foster effective problem resolution.
- Analysis and interpretation skills assist in understanding guidelines, policies, and procedures.

COMMUNICATION / INTERPERSONAL SKILLS
- Direct communication and appropriate interpersonal style enhance understanding.
- Enthusiastic presentation stimulates interest in and retention of material.
- Attentive listening enhances interviewing, counseling, and mediating.
- Professional / personal security reflect a genuine person who easily integrates into teams.
- Ability to build rapport strengthens community ties and maintains valuable resources.
- Persuasiveness sells ideas and promotes acceptance of change.

PERSONAL CHARACTERISTICS
- Friendly, personable, helpful attitude contributes to an accommodating environment.
- Attention to details and focus on excellence inspire others to excel.
- Capacity to easily learn and retain procedural information suggests decreased training time.
- Willingness to embrace challenging, changing situations indicates flexibility and adaptation.
- A sense of humor and positive outlook help ease stress in the workplace.

Experience, confidence, and drive will enable me to make significant contributions to your HR goals. Because a personal interview would benefit us both, I will contact you within the week to schedule an appointment at your convenience. In the meantime, thank you for your consideration.

Sincerely,

Phyllis Martin, PHR

Enclosure: Résumé

121

Human Resources Generalist. *Edie Rische, Lubbock, Texas*

This letter is full of keywords relevant to the field of human resources. The clustering of the bulleted items according to three categories breaks up a long list and makes the items easier to grasp.

RUBY SLATER
RubySlater@email.com

5555 Arguello Avenue	**Residence (310) 555-5555**
Los Angeles, California 55555	**Mobile (310) 555-0000**

[Date]

[Name]
[Title]
[Company]
[Address]
[City, State, ZIP]

Dear [Ms./Mr. Name]:

Strong human resources leadership can have a tremendous impact on operating results. By building and managing an effective HR infrastructure, developing successful productivity, efficiency, quality and performance management, I have consistently made a direct contribution to corporate goals. Highlights of my professional career include

- 15 years of senior-level experience as an HR Generalist, providing HR planning and leadership in union and nonunion environments across diverse industries
- Implementation of HRIS technology and applications to improve information flow and use in strategic planning initiatives
- Strong qualifications in employee relations with ability to build confidence and trust between employees and management
- Introduction of loss control, safety and Workers' Compensation fraud programs
- Authoring employee manuals to provide employee guidelines in compliance with changing regulatory environments

Most significantly, I have positioned myself and the HR function as a partner to senior management in working together toward producing top-performing workforces able to meet operating challenges. Currently I am looking for a new opportunity as a senior-level HR professional with an organization seeking talent, drive, enthusiasm and leadership expertise. I would welcome a personal interview to explore such positions with your organization. Thank you.

Sincerely,

Ruby Slater

Enclosure: Resume

122

Human Resources Generalist. *Vivian VanLier, Los Angeles, California*

The applicant was seeking a position as a senior-level HR professional. Bullets point to highlights of her 15-year career. In the last paragraph, she places her HR role on a par with senior management.

Lynette Hadley

000 E. Ogden Avenue
Bolingbrook, Illinois 60460   lhadley@internetservice.com   (000) 555-5555—home
(000) 000-0000—mobile

January 25, 2004

Mr. Robert Smith
V.P., Sales
ABC Company
1116 E. Washington Street
Chicago, IL 60606

Dear Mr. Smith:

Having achieved a solid record of success in Human Resource Management roles, I am presently seeking a new challenge. My resume, which is enclosed for your review, outlines my career accomplishments, including

- Progressive advancement to responsible positions within two major corporations.
- In-depth experience in all aspects of human resource management, personnel development, and corporate planning.
- Active participation in a variety of projects involving design, implementation, and employee training of company-wide and client policies and procedures.

My dedication to excellent performance, ability to interact effectively and professionally with all levels of personnel, and continuing growth make me a value-added asset to an organization. Please contact me at (000) 555-5555 to schedule a confidential interview to discuss how I might be of benefit to your human resource team. Thank you for your time and consideration.

Sincerely,

Lynette Hadley

Enclosure

123

Human Resources Manager. *Pat Chapman, Naperville, Illinois*

This broadcast letter, devised to be sent to a number of companies, indicates the sender's search for a new challenge, summarizes her career accomplishments, and tells of her worth as an employee.

KATHLEEN BEST

33 Wells Road ◆ Hillsdale, NJ 88888
(333) 333-3333 Home ◆ (444) 444-4444 Cell ◆ kbest@att.net

March 4, 2004

Hiring Agent, Title
Company Name
Address

Dear Hiring Manager:

Your posting for a Human Resources Director caught my attention as it seems an ideal match for my career goals and interests. As a knowledgeable human resources professional with a broad generalist background, I believe I offer expertise that would be of benefit to your company. With a proven record in developing and implementing best practices, along with a flair for creating work environments that attract and hold top-notch talent, I would like to explore the possibility of putting my skills and experience to work for you.

As you can see from my enclosed résumé, I am someone who gains satisfaction from bringing about improvements in the workplace. With a genuine integrity that is readily recognized, I have established a reputation as an employee advocate who can be trusted and relied on to champion the needs of the employee while serving the best interests of the company. Among my accomplishments, I have

- Introduced outstanding benefits and compensation programs that support organizational goals.
- Successfully recruited high-caliber candidates for positions at all levels in the organization.
- Improved staff performance through the implementation of a full range of training and development programs.
- Initiated performance-driven management processes for all levels of staff.

With strengths in recruiting and retention, training and development, and benefits and compensation, my career success is defined by an innate enthusiasm for seizing challenges and driving projects. Dedicated and accessible, I am adept at building the commitment necessary to make programs successful. A respected leader, I pride myself on excellent communications skills and the ability to reach employees. In the past, I have proven to be a productive and valued company resource. With a record of success behind me, I am confident that I will be an asset to you as well.

I would be pleased to have the opportunity to discuss your needs and how I might be able to meet them. Please feel free to contact me at the address and phone number listed above. I look forward to speaking with you soon.

Thank you for your consideration.

Sincerely,

Kathleen Best

Enclosure

124

Human Resources Director. *Carol A. Altomare, Three Bridges, New Jersey*

The opening paragraph refers to the applicant's suitability for the posted position. Bullets point to noteworthy accomplishments, and the third paragraph indicates strengths, skills, and worker traits.

Denise Herman

000 Peacock, Amarillo, Texas 79105　　C: 000-000-0000　　O: 000-000-0000　　e-mail: dherman3@email.com

Will you ever find time for that career path project? How about those first-quarter goals...are they still incomplete on the white board?
Then please call...together we can do it all!

HUMAN RESOURCE PROFESSIONAL
Available Immediately for:

Temporary or Permanent

❖

Short-term or Long-term

❖

Full-time or Part-time

Dear Mr. Coleman,

It is with great enthusiasm that I respond to your posting for a Human Resource Director for Shady Oak Center. My professional employment history is a great match for the qualifications you have listed, and...I am available immediately!

Six years of increasing human resource responsibility in a 24x7 environment defines my flexible work ethic and supports your requirement of holidays and weekends. My professional background relative to your position is highlighted as follows:

- **Human Resource Management**—state / federal employment law; unemployment compensation; organizational policies / procedures; safety / health; benefits administration; departmental budget; job descriptions.
- **Training and Development**—agent / management training programs; organizational development strategies; quality improvement programs.
- **Employee Climate Survey**—employee feedback for improved workforce solutions.
- **HRIMS Utilization**—records management; employee database reports.

Additionally, I am available to relocate, travel or assume special assignments at your request. I can also offer you a variety of employment status options to meet your budget.

Your satisfaction is guaranteed with this win-win opportunity!

The downsizing of my previous Human Resource Manager position coupled with my desire to return to the Houston area makes this offer possible. A personal meeting at your earliest convenience to discuss our mutual employment goals would be greatly appreciated. You may reach me at my personal cell phone number (000-000-0000) to arrange a meeting place and time.

I look forward to hearing from you soon.

Sincerely,

Denise Herman

> "Denise has a great attitude and will do everything from data entry and filing to
> flying across the country to assist in interviewing and hiring."
> —Quote from a fellow HR Professional who utilized Denise on a contract assignment

125

Human Resources Director. *MeLisa Rogers, Victoria, Texas*

This HR Manager candidate was downsized and needed an immediate assignment, preferably in Texas. The writer marketed the person's flexibility and sold her availability into a contract assignment.

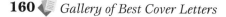

JACK BARRY

000 Drummond Boulevard
Campbell, CA 95008

jbarryweb@yahoo.com
555-555-0000

February 15, 2004

Ms. Harriet Tallant
Director of Corporate Web Development
Reaching Out, Inc.
444 Dublin Avenue
San Jose, CA 95100

Dear Ms. Tallant:

Your requirement for an Interactive Web Designer interested me because of my enthusiasm for Web development/design and my strong desire to continue working and building a career in that field. My résumé is enclosed for your consideration.

In recent years, I have utilized my creative, analytical and problem-solving skills to complete several Web-related projects, both independently and as a project team member. These include the following:

- Building, programming, testing and refining an enrollment-tracking application with an intuitive user interface
- Designing and developing one module for the successful, timely release of a new product
- Designing and implementing a Web user interface
- Creating a process and templates for production of JPEG images for hotel Web sites

Prior to that time, I gained solid experience as a programmer/analyst, a software architect and a software /support engineer. Key activities included database development and troubleshooting, small-business application development and interactive product testing. My ability to understand and analyze complex problems; communicate with clients to assess their needs; and develop innovative, practical solutions enabled me to make a worthwhile contribution to each of my employers during that period.

As I prepare to close out my work on the software application I developed for A Higher Experience, I am beginning to search for an employment situation that will allow me to use my existing experience and skills in Web development/design while also offering potential opportunities to expand and enhance my professional strengths.

I am definitely interested in being considered for the position of Interactive Web Designer with Reaching Out and would like to arrange an interview at your earliest convenience to discuss how I can contribute to your team. I look forward to hearing from you soon.

Sincerely,

Jack Barry

Encl.

126

Interactive Web Designer. *Georgia Adamson, Campbell, California*

This letter is easy to read because of its chronological organization: In recent years.... Prior to that time.... As I prepare.... Bullets point to completed projects. The last paragraph shows interest in the job.

Sami Sosa
5941 Glendower Lane
Plano, TX 75093
Res: (555) 555-5555
Cell: (555) 000-0000
s.sye@iee.org

Dear Hiring Executive:

I am exploring leadership opportunities with your company. With a strong background in the launch of software applications and services such as Intelligent Networks, as well as operational support systems in North and South America, Europe, Asia, Africa and the Middle East, I maintain excellent customer relationships and deliver on commitments. As a hands-on team builder with solid management, operation and product development skills, I am certain I could make a valuable contribution to your goals. Areas of expertise and transferable skills include

P&L Responsibility	Strategic Planning	Problem Analysis & Resolution
Budget Planning & Forecasting	Project Management	Team Leadership
Product Management	Product Development	Business Development
Training & Development	Network Applications	Systems Integration
Technology Management		

Throughout my career I have

→ Combined in-depth technical knowledge with operational business knowledge.
→ Managed P&Ls of more than $400 million and staff of 1,500 throughout the world.
→ Developed an exceptional ability to build strong, long-term customer relationships.

My peers can confirm that I thrive in an atmosphere of challenge. An in-depth knowledge of all phases of business activity, along with specialized abilities that set my performance apart, enables me to offer a truly unique talent. I'm confident I can bring to the table a package of skills, experience and abilities that will provide you with an invaluable resource.

I will follow up with you in a few days to answer any questions you may have. In the meantime, you may reach me at (555) 555-5555 home, (555) 000-0000 cell or through email at s.sye@iee.org. I look forward to our conversation and thank you for your time and consideration.

Sincerely,

Sami Sosa

Enclosure

127

Information Technology Position. *Steven Provenzano, Schaumburg, Illinois*

The opening paragraph is impressive because of its global connections. The three-column list of areas of expertise and transferable skills is useful because it can be modified for each targeted employer.

ROBERT J. LITTLEFIELD

0000 Indiana Avenue ◆ St. Paul, MN 00000 ◆ (000) 000-0000 ◆ name@aol.com

January 30, 2004

Mr. Ted Morrison, IT Director
ABC Computers
3434 Smith Street
St. Paul, MN 00000

Dear Mr. Morrison:

I read your advertisement for a Software Developer with considerable interest, as my background and skills meet your requirements for this position. Therefore, please accept my résumé for your review and allow me to explain briefly the positive qualities I can bring to your company.

Because my résumé contains the specifics regarding my BBA degree, educational awards, and technical competencies in areas such as object-oriented programming, I will not need to go into detail here about these particular items. Instead, I'd like to point out a few of my qualities not covered on the résumé that I would contribute to help your organization meet its development project objectives:

- **Highly focused work ethic**—I maintain a strong focus on "getting the job done right" in a field where the back-and-forth nature of the project cycle can lead to getting sidetracked and committing errors.
- **Ability to modify communications**—I am skilled in altering my communications to gain understanding from end users with minimal IT knowledge and team members with limited English skills.
- **Enthusiastic attitude**—I truly enjoy software engineering and the challenges inherent in an ever-changing, leading-edge field. To this end, I always enjoy learning about emerging industry trends.

Companies today need more than "technologists" to ensure the success of high-priority goals; they need individuals who can also master the teamwork, the communications, and the relationship-building side of projects. I am the type of person who would bring this balance of technical and nontechnical skills to help your firm achieve success.

I am available immediately for a personal interview and offer you competence, dedication, and a strong work ethic. Thank you for your time and consideration, and I look forward to the opportunity to meet with you.

Sincerely,

Robert J. Littlefield

Enclosure

128

Software Developer. *Daniel J. Dorotik, Jr., Lubbock, Texas*

A resume typically presents details not found in a cover letter. This cover letter is different in indicating qualities not covered in the resume. Bullets and boldfacing call attention to these qualities.

Leonard Curtis

123 Circle River Drive · Littleton, CO 00000
555.555.5555 · Lencurt@msno.com

January 21, 2004

John Jones
Vice President, Software Development
Axis Technologies
Table Mesa Drive
Boulder, CO 00000

Re: Position 1234, Software Development Manager

Dear Mr. Jones:

I am passionate about developing products that provide real-world solutions and have an impact on customers' business. Understanding the challenges our customers face, combined with practical implementations of product concepts and technologies, is key to successfully designing and delivering value-rich, profitable products.

I noted with great interest your advertisement in the *Denver Post* for a Software Development Manager. My technical management expertise, leadership skills, and extensive experience in VC++ are an excellent fit with your position.

My strengths are in creatively applying or modifying industry products to job requirements and incorporating new technologies quickly and proficiently. My track record as outlined in the enclosed resume demonstrates that I can

- Manage programs from initial concept through deployment at customer sites.
- Supervise/mentor cross-functional teams as well as software and hardware engineering teams.
- Serve marketing with my technical expertise, influencing product development, client presentations, and contract negotiations.

I admire the corporate culture and core beliefs that Axis Technologies exemplifies. I am eager to apply my knowledge and expertise, and I welcome the opportunity to explore my potential contributions with you.

Thank you for your consideration; I look forward to speaking with you soon.

Sincerely,

Leonard Curtis

Enclosure

129

Software Development Manager. *Roberta F. Gamza, Louisville, Colorado*

The person was applying to a company known for its friendly and laid-back corporate culture and wanted to refer to the company's culture in the letter. Short paragraphs help to make it easy to read.

WILLIAM SHINDLEY

783 NE Fremont Drive
Lake Oswego, OR 55555
wil.shindley@hotmail.com

(000) 000-0000 Residence   (000) 000-0000 Cell

March 14, 2004

Mr. Edward Hosack
Human Resources Manager
PacifiCorp
1843 SW First Avenue, Suite 200
Portland, OR 55555

Dear Mr. Hosack:

I read your recent ad for a Software Program Manager on Monster.com with interest, as it seems a perfect match to my background and experience. As a software program manager with expertise in managing successful software projects in the $10K to $5 million range, **I bring the kind of experience needed to get the job done, on time and at or under budget.** Allow me to highlight my skills as they relate to your stated requirements and interests:

YOUR REQUIREMENTS	MY QUALIFICATIONS
Bachelor's degree in related area or 3+ years of project management experience in a software development environment.	Bachelor's degree in computers and 3+ years of project management experience in a software development environment. **Strong record of delivering project results.**
Demonstrated knowledge of development processes, metrics, project planning, and project management.	Significant background as a programmer/software developer, 3+ years of project management experience, and **project management certification (PMP).**
Good working knowledge of MS Word and Excel. Experience with MS Project a plus.	**Strong skills in MS Word, Excel, and Project.**

As an additional plus, I possess an **understanding of user interface design and usability** through my experience as both a programmer and a project/program manager.

I look forward to an interview with you so that we can discuss specific examples where I have used these skills to positively influence my employer's bottom line. I will follow up with you in the next week.

Thank you for your time and consideration.

Sincerely,

William Shindley

Enclosure

130

Software Program Manager. *Jennifer Rydell, Portland, Oregon*

The Your Requirements... My Qualifications format was used because the applicant was a perfect match to the job ad he was responding to. This format and boldfacing show off the applicant's skills.

SETH JACOBS

000 Pine Road, Emerson, NJ 07360, (555) 555-5555, sjacobs@aol.com

March 24, 2004

Dear Hiring Authority,

As a computer professional with more than 15 years of experience providing client support services, I'm now focusing on using my recent training to manage various networking systems.

In the past, I have installed, configured, and maintained hardware and software such as Windows 95/98, Professional 2000 and Windows Server 2000. Most recently, though, I earned certifications for

- Cisco Certified Network Associate (CCNA)

- Microsoft Certified Systems Engineer (MCSE) for Windows 2000

- Microsoft Certified Professional (MCP)

In addition to my strong computer skills, I have an excellent background in working with customers and am especially skilled in building relationships, resolving problems and training new employees. I also work well under pressure and am used to meeting tight deadlines.

Currently I am looking for a position in network administration where I can offer my computer and interpersonal skills to a company that is facing new prospects.

Thank you in advance for your consideration.

Sincerely,

Seth Jacobs

Enclosure

131

Network Administrator. *Igor Shpudejko, Mahwah, New Jersey*

The applicant was changing direction in the IT industry. He started in computer operations but then wanted to get into network administration. He went back to school and got three certifications.

Bruce Barnes
000 Ichabod Crane Lane
Montgomery, New Jersey 08502
000-000-0000
E-mail: Bruce_Barnes45@email.com

Date

Name
Company
Address
City, State ZIP

Dear Sir/Madam:

As a senior **Operations and Systems Professional,** I understand that success depends on the ability to merge the strategic with the practical, to understand needs and expectations in the corporate environment, and to communicate those needs to appropriate managers. I believe that my background and accomplishments reflect a commitment and an ability to find solutions to these challenges.

My career includes 15 years with Merrill Lynch, four of those years as First Vice President of Fund Operations, Systems and Infrastructure. More recently, I served as President of GovXcel, a specialty software firm; and as Chief Information Officer / Senior Vice President of VerticalNet, an Internet company that acquired and maintained 59 virtual scientific and engineering communities. In all positions, I was responsible for streamlining their operations.

One of my greatest strengths is hiring and developing motivated, long-term employees and building strategic teams. I have developed contacts in several industries, enabling me to work with people on all levels. Among the people I have managed are Ph.D. scientists and engineers, systems and technical professionals, and accounting personnel.

Many of my assignments have been with start-up operations. I approach my work with a strong sense of urgency, working well under pressure and change. I am a forward thinker and a team player who has a strong commitment to my people and the organizations I work for.

Thank you for your consideration. I look forward to meeting with you personally so that we may discuss how I can make a positive contribution to your corporation.

Sincerely yours,

Bruce Barnes

Enclosure

132

Operations and Systems Professional. *Beverley and Mitchell I. Baskin, Marlboro, New Jersey*

In five short paragraphs, the applicant indicates his views on success, the shape of his 15-year career, his people skills, his worker traits, and his anticipation of a positive interview with the reader.

ALEX MARTINEZ

March 10, 2004

Hiring Agent Name, Title
Company Name
Address

Dear Hiring Manager:

Perhaps you are seeking a capable IT professional with extensive industry experience and excellent leadership and problem-solving skills for your project manager opening. I have a strong record as a project manager and applications engineer and believe I have the right combination of skills to succeed in such a position.

As you can see from my enclosed résumé, my career spans 19 years of experience in information technology, including more than 10 years in management roles. I have directed more than five major projects representing investments in excess of $100 million and have a proven track record of success in building Web-based e-commerce sites, client/server applications, and data warehousing projects. I am a certified Web master and have extensive experience with many Web development tools. I am also an expert SQL programmer. This means that you get someone who has the knowledge and experience to find solutions.

Among my strengths, you will find that I am a capable project manager with effective team-building skills. I am able to communicate effectively and work well with staff and clients at all levels of the organization. In the past, I have used these skills to contribute to bottom-line profitability, and I am confident I can do the same for you.

I would enjoy the opportunity to discuss future employment and look forward to speaking with you. I will call next week to follow up, or you can reach me at the address and phone number listed below.

Thank you for your consideration.

Sincerely,

Alex Martinez

Enclosure

9 Farm Road ◆ Trenton, NJ 11111 ◆ (333) 444-4444 ◆ AlexM@aol.com

133

IT Project Manager. *Carol A. Altomare, Three Bridges, New Jersey*

This IT project manager had a wealth of experience. The second paragraph directs the reader's attention to the resume; the letter then summarizes the applicant's career, achievements, and skills.

STEVE BRODY

999 Royal Augusta Road, #234
Pinehurst, Ontario A1A 1A1   stevebrody@email.com   Home: 555.222.8888
Cell: 444.777.6666

February 2, 2004

Ronald Kleinberg
Senior VP, Technology Management
IBC Technology
600 Century Place
Pinehurst, Ontario
B2C 3D4

Dear Mr. Kleinberg,

Stan Morrisey of Suntech and Ellis Cantasi of Levinson Solutions both suggested that I contact you, as they believe that my skills, expertise, and leadership in technology development are a perfect match for IBC. Having reviewed your Web site, I am very impressed with your successes and aggressive plans for the future and would like to draw your attention to the value I can offer.

Put simply, my expertise lies in delivering high-performance, enterprise-class technology solutions, and throughout my career, I have leveraged the following skills and experience to exceed expectations in service bureau, government, and national retail environments:

> - More than 15 years of experience in leading and developing enterprise data centres, voice and data communications, and information-storage technologies
> - Shrewd business skills with a solid grasp of the "business" of technology
> - Full-cycle project management, including strategic planning, design, implementation, and maintenance
> - Superior leadership capabilities with outstanding people skills and a customer-centric focus

Results have been consistent and significant, and include the following:

> - **Recently negotiated $12 million annual savings** in strategic print-sourcing initiative
> - Spearheaded consolidation of two corporate print shops, realizing an **annual savings of $600,000**
> - **Under-cost critical UNIX and Data Warehousing acquisition** project by $2.5 million
> - Introduced and supported new **debit and POS technologies across 8,000 retail registers nationally**
> - Successfully proposed innovative Y2K solution, **saving more than $2.5 million in application upgrades**

I invite you to review the attached résumé, which further outlines the value I can offer your technology team, and would welcome the opportunity to discuss how I could contribute to IBC's future growth and success. If you are interested in a dedicated professional with a reputation for generating real results, then I believe we would have much to discuss.

I thank you for your time and look forward to the opportunity to meet in person.

Sincerely,

Steve Brody

Encl.

134

Technology Development Position. *Ross Macpherson, Whitby, Ontario, Canada*

The letter first refers to some mutual acquaintances and then indicates the applicant's expertise and achievements. The company had no opening, but he got an interview to discuss another position.

JON VERNON

48 White Pine Road • Union City, NJ 11111
(333) 444-4444 • jvernon@aol.com

November 4, 2004

Hiring Agent, Title
Company Name
Address

Dear Hiring Manager:

Your posting for a [position title] caught my attention as it seems an ideal match for my experience, talents, and interests. As a capable network engineer with a solid technical background and a proven record in building and troubleshooting computer systems and networks, I believe I offer a set of skills that would benefit your company. With extensive knowledge and strong analytical skills complemented by excellent interpersonal skills and a commitment to customer satisfaction, I would like to explore the possibility of putting my talents to work for you.

As you can see from my enclosed résumé, I have held several technical positions in computer support and electronics. Common to these positions is a strong focus on providing exemplary support to the user or client. An eager learner, I pride myself on my ability to successfully take on new challenges and develop ever-expanding areas of expertise. In addition, with outstanding problem-solving skills combined with the ability to develop an easy rapport with users, I am someone who can effectively diagnose and resolve all types of computer problems, whether related to software, hardware, servers or individual workstations. Calm and easygoing, I am effective in meeting goals even when faced with difficult circumstances.

Among my strengths, I am disciplined and hardworking with a demonstrated ability to balance the competing demands of multiple projects. Passionate about providing service excellence, I have established a long-standing reputation as an effective and valuable employee. With a record of success behind me, I am confident that I will be an asset to you as well.

I would be pleased to have the opportunity to discuss future employment and look forward to speaking with you. Feel free to contact me at the address and phone number listed above.

Thank you for your consideration.

Sincerely,

Jon Vernon

Enclosure

135

Network Engineer. *Carol A. Altomare, Three Bridges, New Jersey*

The opening paragraph explains why the applicant seems an ideal match for the position. The remaining paragraphs indicate in turn the individual's skills, strengths, and worker traits.

Vicker T. Seed
0000 N. Lincoln Avenue
Altadena, CA 91001
Home: (555) 555-5555
Cell: (000) 000-0000
VTSeed@msn.com

VENTURE CAPITAL ■ FUNDRAISING ■ IT ACQUISITION

February 15, 2004

Bill Gates, CEO
Microsoft Corporation
One Microsoft Way, Ste. 303
Redmond, WA 98052-8303

Dear Mr. Gates:

An IT expert, I have 20 years of real-world experience in fundraising and acquisitions. I have a track record for raising seed and venture capital and originating and closing IT acquisitions—of both products and businesses.

My potential value to an employer includes the following:

➤ Seasoned fundraising, acquisition, and negotiation for multimillion-dollar IPOs and technology investments.

➤ Multiyear relationships with technology markets. Expertise in Venture Capital, Seed and Growth Companies, and IT Acquisitions.

➤ Exceptional "brand" loyalty from IT institutions and investors—based on multiple business investments and joint ventures.

I am seeking opportunities to perform capital fundraising and acquisition services for a growing technology firm and its investors. I will contact you within the next week to discuss any needs you may have and to schedule an interview.

Sincerely,

Vicker T. Seed

Enclosure: Résumé

136

IT Fundraising and Acquisitions Position. *Helen Oliff, Reston, Virginia*

The applicant was older and lacked the blue-chip credentials typical among investors. The challenge was to demonstrate—through bullets and boldfacing—the candidate's potential value to an employer.

MARY LAWSON, 84 Swan Lane, Blaine MN 55555
(555) 555-5555   Email: mllaw@network.com

February 5, 2004

Mr. Charles Phillip
Gantry Communications
303 Mountain Pass
Denver, CO 55555

INFORMATION TECHNOLOGY IN EDUCATIONAL AND NONPROFIT SECTORS
MARKETING ▶ ANALYSIS ▶ DATA ▶ APPLICATIONS

Dear Mr. Phillip:

Promoted 11 times in 21 years by Nelson International Technologies, I have an extensive background in information systems and project-based work. Since leaving traditional employment in 2003, I've been challenged by entrepreneurial ventures, career exploration, and civic work.

Enclosed is a resume detailing my strengths and abilities, with particular emphasis on marketing and technical skills. Other relevant areas of knowledge and expertise include the following:

- ▶ leadership, consulting, and relationship building
- ▶ strategic analysis and creativity
- ▶ speech writing, presentations, instruction, and training
- ▶ data synthesis and research
- ▶ applications for academic learning approaches
- ▶ marketing programs and client relations

Achievements, awards, and recognition attest to my ability to think "out of the box," apply theory, test concepts, and contribute to breakthrough ideas. Leading edge ... change-oriented technology ... resourceful ... self-motivated—these are qualities describing my style and approach to whatever I do.

An interview would provide the opportunity to exchange information, address issues, answer questions, and determine applicant suitability. I am most interested in discussing your company's goals and needs and will call within the next week to schedule a time to meet. I look forward to speaking with you.

Sincerely,

Mary Lawson

Enclosure

137

Information Technology Position. *Beverley Drake, Rochester, Minnesota*

A banner between the reader's address and the salutation indicates the applicant's target fields and areas of expertise. After the second paragraph, bullets point to additional areas of knowledge and expertise.

Florence Finch

1234 W. Berkley St.
Round Lake, IL 60000
(222) 222-2222
ffinch123@email.com

Ms. Sylvia Smith
Jimpsom Corporation
4321 E. 176th
Deerfield, IL 60000

Dear Ms. Smith:

I recently graduated from Comp Technical Institute with a Computer Programming Certificate representing 350 hours of IT studies. Jason White, who also graduated from this course and is currently employed with your company, tells me that Jimpsom is seeking IT professionals with up-to-date programming skills. I believe I am just the person you are seeking!

With advanced training in Java and C++, I possess the communication and problem-solving skills to design and troubleshoot virtually any software. As you will see on my enclosed resume, I have more than 10 years of experience in office positions that required extensive computer use and have a firsthand knowledge of the needs of the end user. Previous supervisors have described me as patient and logical.

I would appreciate the opportunity to speak with you further about a future role at Jimpsom. I will call you at the end of this week to ensure that you received this letter and to answer any questions that you may have. In the meantime, feel free to contact me at (222) 222-2222. I look forward to speaking with you soon.

Many thanks,

Florence Finch

Enclosure

138

Information Technology Professional. *Eva Locke, Waukegan, Illinois*

This recent graduate had a certificate in computer programming but did not have formal experience in that field. The letter emphasizes her training, transferable skills, and useful experience.

Kate Dobson
0000 Autumnbrook Drive ▪ Atlanta, GA 00000 ▪ (000) 000-0000 ▪ name@aol.com

January 30, 2004

Human Resources Department
ABC Solutions
3434 Pinetree Avenue
Atlanta, GA 00000

RE: Position as Systems Administrator

Dear Staffing Representative:

It was with great interest that I noted your advertisement for the position of Systems Administrator.
I believe I am the ideal candidate for your consideration, with qualifications correlated to your
requirements. Thus, please allow me to explain briefly how I might contribute to your firm's
operational performance.

Throughout my career, my expertise has been in providing systems integration solutions for multimillion-
dollar clients. As a Senior Systems Integrator for IBM, I have instituted technology assimilations and
changes for our clients that produced cost savings and positioned them for success in their respective
markets. I would now like to use my systems management and integration skills to help your company
maintain a strong customer base and improve productivity.

Additionally, my background in help desk administration, project management, and IT applications could
benefit your firm in specific need areas. I enjoy being a diverse "team player" within an organization and
contributing to my employer's success in various capacities.

To provide you with details concerning my qualifications and accomplishments, my résumé is enclosed. I
will contact you next week to follow up on this letter of inquiry; perhaps we could arrange a meeting to
discuss our mutual interests.

Thank you for your time and consideration. Please do not hesitate to contact me if I can answer any
questions.

Sincerely,

Kate Dobson

Enclosure

139

Systems Administrator. *Daniel J. Dorotik, Jr., Lubbock, Texas*

This letter is a response to an ad. Short paragraphs mention in turn the applicant's qualifications; areas of expertise and skills; background and worker traits; and resume, providing details.

Victoria A. Future

0000 Woolery Lane, Dayton, OH 45415
Phone: (555) 555-5555 | E-mail: vfuture@jitaweb.com

Date

Contact
Company
Address
City, State ZIP

Re:

Dear Mr(s). _____:

In desktop support and as a network administrator, I handled a number of technical, maintenance, and support issues for the corporate and branch computers at S³ Business Techs. I configured and installed hardware, software, and peripherals—and diagnosed and troubleshot complications pertaining to the local area network (LAN). I worked with virus-protection software and utility programs, ensuring that company policies and procedures were followed and that each new feature addressed technological advancements.

Stepping up to the plate, you'll discover that I've applied key performance by installing the LAN system at S³ Business Techs in only 7 months, saving $1.5 million in fines by integrating an EDI system and Ordernet mailboxes. I saved up to $256,000 the first year by implementing a self-help process for end users that eliminated the need for costly technical support on small problems.

Skills recap includes the following:

- Managed LAN network life cycles on a Windows platform, from software and hardware applications to equipment layout and technical support

- Have in-depth knowledge of LAN maintenance and troubleshooting, including desktop support, configuration, and workstation issues, from initial problem analysis to final end resolution

- Integrate amongst technical support, ensuring that multiple tasks and parallel deadlines are met and in line with technological advancements and company growth

Contact me at (555) 555-5555 should you require clarification of my skills or would like to schedule a meeting time for us to discuss this position.

Sincerely,

Victoria A. Future

Attachment

140

Network Administrator. *Teena Rose, Huber Heights, Ohio*

This direct letter indicates immediately the applicant's experience and quantified accomplishments. Bullets point to network experience, network knowledge, and technical-support expertise.

James Madison, CCNA, MCSE

00000 Autumnwind Drive • Houston, TX 00000 • (000) 000-0000 • name@ev1.net

January 24, 2004

ABC Systems
2323 Smith Avenue
Housprint, TX 00000

RE: Senior WAN Engineer position, ID #6970

Dear Hiring Authority:

It was with great interest that I read about your opening for a Senior WAN Engineer, as my background and abilities meet your requirements for this position. Please allow me to explain briefly what I can offer your organization.

With several years of experience as a Network Engineer, Manager, and Administrator, I have demonstrated the ability to fulfill business goals through network solutions, maintain excellent client relationships, and make bold decisions to achieve corporate and client objectives on critical projects. The following accomplishments illustrate these skills:

- As a Network Engineer and Director of Engineering Services with Cisprint, I completed a complex VPN installation project involving 20 bank locations within an aggressive one-week deadline.
- As a Network Engineer and Special Projects Manager with IED Communications, I received commendations for my work on implementing Cisco VPN networks using PIX and 1720 VPN routers.
- As a Network Administrator for Top Networks, I built loyal client relationships through constructing, installing, and configuring desktops, workstations, servers, and all network-essential equipment.

I have found that the most effective skills for a network engineering position lie in an understanding of both the technological and business goals within an organization. What I would bring to ABC Systems is a combination of technical expertise and business intelligence to help fulfill your company's ongoing and future objectives.

I have enclosed my résumé to provide additional details regarding my background and qualifications, and I welcome the opportunity to interview for this position.

Thank you for your time and consideration.

Sincerely,

James Madison

Enclosure

141

Senior WAN Engineer. *Daniel J. Dorotik, Jr., Lubbock, Texas*

This well-organized letter displays ABC, A+B+C thematic structure. Three roles indicated in the second paragraph (Network Engineer, Manager, and Administrator) appear again as bulleted items.

Robert M. Joyner

0000 North Sunland Circle
San Jose, CA 98771
555-555-5555
robmjoyner44@email.com

February 12, 2004

Ms. Margery Wilson
City of Palm Springs Human Resources
10 North Landing Way
Palm Springs, CA 96112

Dear Ms. Wilson:

As an experienced IT manager/consultant with a record of success, I am interested in the posting for an Information Technology Manager in the City of Palm Springs. A review of your requirements suggests a good fit with my background and skills.

Your Requirements	My Experience
Selection, procurement, and design of computer equipment	Managed projects requiring systems, design, vendor interface, selection decision.
Manage development, maintenance, and modification of applications	Hired, trained, and mentored teams that participated in creating, reengineering, and servicing systems used company-wide.
Consult with departments on software development	Consistently interfaced with senior and middle management and other staff to ensure that all requirements were met while limiting risks.

Personal attributes I offer include strong interpersonal and communication skills, an honest and conscientious approach to the job, and a flexible attitude. I am very much a team player and have the ability to motivate employees to achieve team success.

A copy of my résumé is enclosed for your review. I would welcome the opportunity to further discuss your needs and how I could benefit the IT department and the City of Palm Springs in the near and long term. Thank you for your consideration, and I look forward to speaking with you.

Sincerely,

Robert M. Joyner

Enclosure

142

Information Technology Manager/Consultant. *Kay Bourne, Tucson, Arizona*

After many years as an independent contractor, this applicant was seeking to become an employee in a city/county or corporate setting. The Your Requirements… My Experience scheme is effective.

Steven Brooks

1111 Lawrenceville Road ◆ Haven, CT 00000 ◆ 000-000-0000 ◆ user@adelphia.net

(Date)

(contact name)
(company name)
(street address)
(city, state ZIP code)

Dear Hiring Professional (or insert contact name):

As a goal-oriented, progressive individual with more than 20 years of combined experience in positions that allowed for the development of diverse skills and proactive management in the areas of Recruiting and Information Technology, I feel my skills and qualifications are ideal to fill the position of (insert job title) in your (insert department), as listed with (insert source) on (insert date).

My background has positioned me to accept employment where I can use a wide range of skill sets within a small- to mid-range organization. The ideal position will allow me to provide a wealth of experience to employ a combination of strategic marketing, budget-administration, technological and sourcing skills to grow revenues and increase bottom-line profitability.

I have enclosed a copy of my résumé for your review. Please feel free to contact me, at your convenience, if you have any questions or would like to schedule an interview. I look forward to discussing the mutual benefit of our association.

Thank you for your time and consideration.

Sincerely,

Steven Brooks

Encl.

143

Information Technology Recruiter. *Lea J. Clark, Macon, Georgia*

This letter template with fill-in fields is adaptable to different kinds of job targets. You can make the changes necessary to reflect your own experience, qualifications, skills, and follow-up plans.

TIMOTHY L. MICHAELS

000 King Street • Fairport, New York 14450 • 555-555-5555 • timm2@localnet.net

January 25, 2004

Mr. I. M. Important, CIO
Important Industries, Inc.
1234 Industrial Parkway
Rochester, New York 14699

Dear Mr. Important:

Capitalizing on a 12-plus-year career with Eastman Kodak Company that has encompassed Systems Administration, IT Project Management, and Business Analysis experiences, I am seeking to use my broad-based IT knowledge in a challenging position with your firm. In pursuit of that goal, I have enclosed for your review a résumé that outlines my professional background.

Some of the key capabilities that I can bring to a position with your firm include the following:

- **Supporting precision manufacturing operations, including clean room environments. During the start-up and launch of Kodak's thin film manufacturing facility, I was accountable for setting up and maintaining process control, inventory management, and resource planning applications that contributed to the efficient and profitable operation of that plant.**

- **Managing database tools that allow sales and marketing teams to capture customer information, track market trends, and plan sales/marketing strategies. In my current assignment, I maintain applications that are utilized by 100 managers in the field, plus close to 100 marketing and headquarters staff, to manage relationships with a customer base exceeding one million total accounts.**

- **Implementing and maintaining HR applications and e-mail utilities to serve up to 500 end users. As a Senior Systems Analyst with the team that launched the Office Imaging Group, I had responsibilities in these areas, including controlling user access and establishing accounts.**

- **Serving in Business Analyst roles that have included using innovative IT solutions to streamline and optimize various materials-forecasting functions.**

I believe that the knowledge and expertise developed over the course of my career can be a valuable asset to a smaller firm on the rise. I would enjoy meeting with you to explore how I can best serve your current and future needs, and I encourage you to contact me to arrange an initial interview.

Thank you for your time and consideration. I look forward to speaking with you soon.

Sincerely,

Timothy L. Michaels

Enclosure

144

IT Project Manager/Systems Administrator. *Arnold G. Boldt, Rochester, New York*

To avoid a bland list of technical proficiencies, the writer presented this applicant in the context of his project-management and customer-relation skills. Bullets and boldfacing make these skills stand out.

FRANK D. ZAZZARA, MCP

0000 Ocean Avenue • Huntington, New York 11740 • (555) 555-5555
frankzazz@optonline.net

Dear Sir or Madam:

As an **IT / Systems Engineer / Network Specialist,** I am routinely faced with the challenges to evaluate specific technologies and their ability to meet operating requirements. I am seeking an **MIS** opportunity where I can continue to contribute to company growth and technological expansion through change, refinement and improvement. Highlights of the experience, qualifications and contributions I would bring to your organization include the following:

- Design, lead and supervise the development and delivery of cost-effective, high-performance technology solutions to meet challenging business demands—developed through IT support efforts with Fortune 500, marketing, graphic arts, litigation and insurance companies.

- Offer extensive experience in business process reengineering and workflow analysis techniques.

- Provide the flexibility to expand technical support services systems competency through internal development and external acquisition initiatives.

- Have extensive qualifications in all facets of project lifecycle development, from initial feasibility analysis and conceptual design, through documentation, implementation, user training and enhancement.

- Provide contributions to the vision, strategy and long-range development of technical support services infrastructures through organizational, leadership, team building and project management qualifications.

Because a résumé can neither fully detail all my skills and accomplishments, nor predict my potential to your organization, I welcome the opportunity to meet, discuss and explore the possible merging of my talent, experience and qualifications with your organizational **MIS** system needs.

Very truly yours,

FRANK D. ZAZZARA, MCP

Enclosure

145

IT Systems Engineer/Network Specialist. *Donna M. Farrise, Hauppauge, New York*

Boldfacing and bullets help to focus this applicant's multifaceted letter. The letter relies especially on the bulleted items to highlight the applicant's experience, qualifications, and possible contributions.

Lydia Cunningham
4444 Alapaha Drive
Golden, Maryland 00000

✆ [000] 555-5555 — [000] 555-6666 (Mobile) — lcunningham4012@propser.net

Wednesday, 07 March 2004

Drayton Nabers
Director of Finance
c/o State of Maryland Personnel Department
Post Office Box 00000
Annapolis, Maryland 00000-0000

Dear Mr. Nabers:

As soon as I saw your announcement for Chief Information Officer, I made writing this application my first priority. Because my natural inclination is to anticipate and try to fill needs, I thought you deserved a good deal more than the standard application and résumé.

I designed my résumé in a new way. Gone are the usual "summary of qualifications" and sterile lists of responsibilities. In their places, starting right at the top, are eight capabilities I want to offer the Governor and the people of Maryland. Backing them up are 14 sample contributions made to organizations of all kinds — from large public-sector agencies to small businesses to nationally known IT leaders. Finally, I wanted you to have a detailed list of my technical skills. Nevertheless, there is important information no résumé format or application form can transmit well.

I've already begun a personal, professional development program. I designed it to make me productive right from the start. I am studying the National Association of State Chief Information Officers' Transition Handbook, Governor's Transition Team IT Assessment Template, and the Chief Information Officer Transition Handbook. And I've begun to form professional relationships with CIOs in several states. They've given me invaluable insights into tough problems they are dealing with right now — problems that are similar to ones we face in Maryland today.

Normally, I would take the next logical step and ask for a little time on your schedule so that I could hear about your specific IT needs and goals in your own words. However, I am sensitive to the instructions that accompanied the announcement. If a personal meeting isn't possible now, I encourage you to test me for yourself in an interview soon.

Sincerely,

Lydia Cunningham

Enclosures:
1. Application for Examination
2. Résumé
3. IT Capabilities the State of Maryland Can Use at Once
4. College-Level Course Work Applicable to CIO Performance

146

Chief Information Officer. *Don Orlando, Montgomery, Alabama*

The challenge was to find a way to get the hiring decision maker's attention. The letter shows that the applicant was already learning about state government and could be effective at once.

ROBERT P. BARNES, CBCP
Certified Business Continuity Professional

1434 Madison Boulevard
Orlando, FL 38917
Residence: 555-555-5555
Mobile: 000-000-0000
RobertPBarnes@earthlink.net

April 8, 2004

Samuel Ryan, CIO
Global Financial Services, Inc.
495 Central Avenue
Orlando, FL 38917

Dear Mr. Ryan:

Development of a comprehensive, state-of-the-industry business-continuity program is critical to a company's ability to achieve its core mission. Employee safety, shareholder value, corporate reputation, revenues and profits, data integrity and IT systems—these are some of the corporate interests that an effective business-continuity program is designed to protect. My expertise is the ability to deliver, within a complex multinational organization, innovative business-continuity plans that are integrated with overall corporate strategy and aligned with corporate goals.

In my work as Business Recovery Manager at Morgan Summers Financial Services, I established just such a program. My groundbreaking thinking and writing promotes business-continuity planning as a strategic, business-driven process in which IT plays a supporting role. My contributions helped ensure that the company would mitigate risk, survive potential disruptions and recover in a timely manner. Achievements included the following:

— Developed and executed business-continuity plans for an organization with $176 billion in assets under management, 40 business units, 800 employees and 19 different IT systems running 200 applications.
— Promoted my visionary concept of the role of business-continuity planning throughout the organization and achieved buy-in for plan initiatives from 40 business units (including six IT business units) and two disaster-recovery vendors.
— Implemented a multifaceted employee-awareness program to help ensure that employees knew how to implement plans in the event of a business disruption.

I came up through the ranks as an IT professional and earned both my M.B.A. degree and my Bachelor's degree in Business Computer Information Systems. As an experienced BCP manager who is a Certified Business Continuity Professional, I am well credentialed for assuming a leadership position in business-continuity planning.

Please contact me if you are interested in my demonstrated ability to help a company mitigate risk and protect critical assets. I look forward to an opportunity to speak with you in person about your business requirements. Thank you.

Sincerely,

Robert P. Barnes

Enclosure

147

Business Recovery Manager. *Jean Cummings, Concord, Massachusetts*

This cover letter is for a position in an increasingly important field: business continuity planning. Dashes serve as bullets to indicate the applicant's achievements with "heavy numbers."

Danielle Quinones

danielleq@homenet.com

Current Residence:
515 Abernathy Court
Richland, NJ 00000
(000) 000-0000

After March 1, 2004:
70 Turtleback Trail
San Jose, CA 00000
(000) 000-0000

January 3, 2004

Stevenson, Pellegrino & Delacruz, P.C.
Attorneys at Law
194 Morse Avenue
San Jose, CA 00000

Attention: Law Office Administrator

Please accept this letter and resume in application for the position of Legal Administrative Assistant you posted recently on the Internet.

Although I presently reside in New Jersey, I will be relocating to California in the near future. I am extremely interested in the position you describe and precisely meet your qualification requirements. As I plan to complete my undergraduate education at Los Gatos University and then continue on to pursue a law degree, this position seems like an ideal opportunity to expand my knowledge in the various aspects of a legal practice.

In my current position as a legal secretary for an attorney specializing in personal-injury litigation, I have had extensive experience in organizing workflow and meeting multiple deadlines. I can assess what needs to be done and take appropriate action with minimal direction. Having no prior legal experience, I quickly learned on my own initiative how to open and keep track of a large number of case files varying in complexity. Managing a variety of responsibilities in an environment with deadline pressures is a challenge that I truly enjoy.

I hope you will give me the opportunity to prove my ability to make a significant contribution to your organization. If you are interested in speaking with me further, I will gladly fly to California to interview for this position. Please contact me by leaving a message with Joe or Katy Ventura at (000) 000-0000. They will also serve as my personal references.

Sincerely,

Danielle Quinones

Enclosure: Resume

148

Legal Administrative Assistant. *Melanie Noonan, West Paterson, New Jersey*

The opening paragraph identifies the position, and the second paragraph tells of the applicant's relocation plans. The third mentions crucial experience and skills. See Resume 12 (page 374).

CHRYSTAL SCOTLAND

55 Horrace Drive
Brentwood, New York 55555
(555) 555-5555
CS@LawandOrder.net

Date

Name
Company
Address

As a second-year law student at The Long Island University School of Law, I look forward to realizing my long-held dream of practicing law. As I move toward receiving my Juris Doctor in May 2004, my career focus has remained steadfast with a strong interest in the emotionally charged world of Family Law. After careful research, I have chosen to seek a summer position with your law firm that will allow me the opportunity to further develop myself professionally. Ideally, this position will build upon recent undergraduate internship experience working within a progressive Domestic Violence Clinic headed by the Long Island Law Service Committee.

In this position, my oral advocacy skills, technique for conducting witness examinations, and ability to effectively negotiate on behalf of clients played a vital role in achieving a favorable outcome for my client when given the opportunity to try a case in Family Court. This achievement, coupled with my experience as a Student Editor on Long Island University's Family Court Review, solidified my interest in Family Law.

Prior experience includes three years as an Administrative Assistant with The Law Offices of McLaughlin & Meyers, P.C., a position held while attending school full-time. In this capacity, I exercised strong research, communication, and problem-resolution skills, along with the ability to handle pressing assignments in the office and at the courthouse. It is with your firm that I hope to continue in this vein as I strive to further my education and develop myself professionally.

The accompanying résumé illustrates well my experience, academic achievements, and community service. However, I feel a personal meeting would better convey the value I could bring to the appropriate position. I welcome the opportunity to participate in a confidential interview to discuss in person the possibility of my joining your law firm.

Thank you in advance for your consideration. I look forward to hearing from you soon.

Sincerely,

Chrystal Scotland

149

Legal Administrative Assistant. *Ann Baehr, Brentwood, New York*

This law student was looking for a summer position to continue her professional development. The letter shows that she is already an effective worker who could help a law firm significantly.

TINA NELSON

1234 Skyline Drive • Wickham, MA 22222 • (333) 333-3333 • tnelson@aol.com

December 6, 2004

Hiring Agent, Title
Company Name
Address

Dear Hiring Manager:

Your posting for a Court Executive caught my attention as it seems an ideal match for my experience, talents, and interests. As an attorney with several years of business management experience, I believe I offer a combination of skills that would be of value to your department. With a broad knowledge of business operations and a proven track record in establishing effective policies, procedures, and programs, I would like to explore the possibility of putting my expertise to work for you.

As you can see from my enclosed résumé, following a three-year period in private law practice, I assumed management responsibilities for a small start-up venture. Directing operations, I have been involved in all aspects of the business, from developing and managing budgets; to hiring, training, and evaluating staff; to developing and implementing policies and procedures; to setting up and maintaining the financial books. Focused on efficiency and cost-effectiveness, the infrastructures put in place have proven to provide solid foundations for continued business success.

Among my strengths, I offer a full understanding of legal proceedings, excellent administrative skills, and an analytical mind-set. In addition, I pride myself on sound fiscal policies and a supportive, open management style that brings out the best in my staff. Driven and determined, I have established a reputation as a sharp business leader who gets the job done. With a proven track record behind me, I am confident I will be an asset to you as well.

I would be pleased to have the opportunity to discuss future employment with you and look forward to speaking with you. Please feel free to contact me at the address and phone number listed above.

Thank you for your consideration.

Sincerely,

Tina Nelson

Enclosure

150

Court Executive. *Carol A. Altomare, Three Bridges, New Jersey*

This lawyer wanted a job that used her legal training as well as her newly acquired business operations experience. The second paragraph indicates the breadth of her management expertise.

THOMAS QUARTER

490 Apple Lane   Villa, Indiana 11111   222-222-2222   tomquarter@letter.com

Date

Address Block

Dear XXXX,

In 2000, an unexpected opportunity presented itself, and I left the practice of law to found a niche confectionary company specializing in Swiss chocolate. Although I have enjoyed running my own business and met with success, I feel that my entrepreneurial curiosity has been satisfied and I am now in a position to step away from my company. Consequently, I am ready to return to the challenges of a legal career and am interested in joining your firm as an associate.

My experiences as an entrepreneur have allowed me to look at the business of law from a fresh perspective. I can better appreciate the pressures that the partners of a law firm feel and understand why they expect so much of their associates and other employees. I have no doubt that my work ethic, motivation, and recent experiences will allow me to quickly become a valued member of your legal team.

A brief and partial listing of my qualifications includes the following:

- Extensive experience in marketing and business generation and outstanding customer/client relations skills.
- Proven abilities in negotiating and drafting high-dollar power purchase and sales agreements as well as mediation experience.
- Exemplary educational background that includes a BA from New York University and a JD from Columbia University School of Law.

My main desire is to resume the practice of law; therefore, I am flexible with regard to graduation-year classification. I hope to speak with you in the near future to further discuss how I can benefit your practice. Thank you for your time and consideration.

Regards,

Thomas Quarter

151

Lawyer. *Alyssa Pera, Los Angeles, California*

This individual had taken a break from the legal profession to open his own business and now wanted to return to the practice of law. His entrepreneurial experiences are cast as positive.

Jane Tripper
488 Flower St.
Roseville, KY 44444
(444) 444-4444

Date

Name
Company Address
City, State ZIP

Dear Salutation:

Few attorneys only a few years out of law school can claim experience managing a multimillion-dollar business, proven skills in dispute resolution, and the ability to negotiate contracts that result in the savings of millions of dollars. I am just such an attorney, and I am interested in joining your firm as an associate.

As Manager of Corporate Development at Telecom Inc. in Louisville, I managed all legal and financial matters for the Midwest Region. Although I was not working in a legal capacity, I consistently demonstrated my legal savvy by resolving contract disputes and earning favorable results for my company. Using my communication and client-management skills, I was able to gain consensus among the parties and identify and manage the strategic issues.

In addition to my negotiation skills, I am at ease with numbers and complex financial matters. I have done extensive budget analysis and revision and proven skillful in estate planning matters. My keen financial sense will allow me to increase your firm's revenue, guaranteeing that your investment in me will pay off quickly.

I am a decisive, focused individual who excels under pressure, and I have a unique set of skills to offer your firm. If you are interested in an attorney with an already proven track record of accomplishments and a strong business background, I urge you to contact me at your earliest convenience.

Sincerely,

Jane Tripper

152

Associate Lawyer. *Alyssa Pera, Los Angeles, California*

The applicant had not been practicing law directly but wanted to get into a law firm. She did have much business and professional experience, so the writer played that up as much as possible.

Kevin Finn

000 Horseback Lane • Stamford, CT 33333 • (111) 111-1111 • Kevin@finn.com

Postdate

Address Block

Dear _____:

My ambition to become an attorney has always been synonymous with my desire to practice labor and employment law. In pursuit of this goal, I recently earned both a Juris Doctor with a Labor and Employment Law Certificate and a master's degree in Human Resources from Antioch University. Presently, I am planning to relocate to the Washington, D.C., area to be at the forefront of this rapidly evolving field. As such, I wish to apply for a position as a first-year associate at your firm.

My graduate studies in both law and human resources have enabled me to gain valuable insight into the most current legal issues affecting the workplace. I conducted classroom presentations on many of these issues, such as employment discrimination, sexual harassment, union disputes, and Workers' Compensation. As employment law is an expansive discipline, I have also gained experience in areas such as administrative and criminal law in order to understand this area from diverse perspectives.

Throughout law school, I have taken advantage of every opportunity to apply what I learned in the classroom to real-world situations. Through internships and numerous community-service activities, I have assisted people from diverse backgrounds with a variety of concerns. As a result, I have developed excellent communication skills and a keen ability to assess individual clients' needs. Each experience, both academic and work related, also afforded me the opportunity to develop the necessary research, writing and analytical skills required of a first-class attorney.

I would appreciate the opportunity to meet with you and further discuss my qualifications. Please contact me at your convenience. Thank you for your time and consideration.

Very truly yours,

Kevin Finn

153

Labor and Employment Lawyer. *Alyssa Pera, Los Angeles, California*

This graduate was enthusiastic about practicing labor and employment law. His enthusiasm is evident in all three main paragraphs. His master's degree in Human Resources shows his commitment.

SIMON D. HARRIS
89 Fledgling Plaza ▪ Columbus, OH 33333
(111) 111-1111 ▪ simon@harris.com

Date

Address

Dear Salutation:

I am an experienced legal professional with an LL.M. in Taxation, interested in joining your firm as an associate. Although my desire to practice tax law represents a career change for me, it is a change made with a great deal of planning and resolve. As outlined below, I have spent the past few years preparing myself for this shift, and I am eager and feel well prepared to begin this new stage of my career.

For 13 years, my practice focused on the litigation of large and complex personal-injury cases. Seeking a more transactional practice, I left private practice in 1996 to work for JRO—an insurance industry leader. My work with JRO somewhat satisfied my interest in transactional work; however, I desired a more significant change. After evaluating my strengths and interests, I eventually settled on taxation as the area that would best fulfill me as a professional.

Understanding that such a transition could not be made without the proper educational background, I enrolled in the University of Ohio's six-course program in business finance while still employed with JRO, earning a certificate in 2001. This program re-enforced my desire to move into taxation, and I consequently entered the University of Ohio's LL.M. program in that area of concentration.

Now I am ready to put my academic training into action. I offer highly transferable skills that will be assets as I enter this practice area. As a result of my background, I have developed excellent drafting skills and an acute attention to detail. Additionally, I have experience providing effective counsel and engaging in frequent client contact.

I am confident that I can be of value to your practice and hope to further explore how I might benefit your firm. If you would like to set up a meeting or speak with me in more detail about my qualifications, please contact me at your earliest convenience. I look forward to hearing from you.

Sincerely,

Simon D. Harris

154

Estate Planning Lawyer. *Alyssa Pera, Los Angeles, California*

The applicant wanted to transition to a new legal practice area, and the letter explains his reasons and qualifications for doing so. The change is not hasty but based on years of preparation.

Dennis L. Richards

1234 Oak Tree Drive • Bloomington, IL 61704 • 309.555.5555 • dlrichards@aol.com

CORPORATE COUNSEL

Litigation Management ~ Attorney Management

Dear Sir/Madam:

I am an accomplished corporate attorney with a successful career and have enclosed my resume for your review. Throughout my positions at State Farm Insurance, I have been praised for my ability to direct multiple legal cases and manage a large staff of lawyers.

I believe I have mastered the art of contact management, corporate networking, and personal relationship building. In doing so, I developed a thorough knowledge of all aspects of business law. Listed below are some accomplishments of which I am proud:

- Promoted twice over a five-year period to my present position as Legal Counsel after demonstrating exceptional legal and managerial expertise.

- Acknowledged for leadership skills in corporate and governmental affairs. Serve as an advocate and liaison between clients and corporations.

- Experienced in the areas of litigation, arbitration, mediation, and budgetary management.

Thank you for your consideration. I believe my success as a professional reflects my personal integrity, extensive communication skills, and willingness to work hard. I look forward to speaking with you to discuss how I may make a positive contribution to your executive team.

Sincerely yours,

Dennis L. Richards

Enclosure

155

Corporate Counsel. *Beverley and Mitchell I. Baskin, Marlboro, New Jersey*

This applicant was a successful lawyer with management skills. Managerial expertise is a theme that appears repeatedly in this letter: in the first two paragraphs and in the first and third bulleted items.

ROGER LEVY

48 Green Grove Lane
Greenville, SC 33333

(333) 333-3333   rlevy@green.com

Date

Address

Dear Salutation:

I am a widely experienced professional seeking an opportunity to combine my skills in law and technology in a position with your company. Since graduating from law school, my career has followed a dual trajectory in technology and law—I have provided counsel to numerous companies regarding software development and contracts, and, as an associate with Wolf & Green, represented individuals and entities in complex litigation. At this juncture, I desire to move into an in-house role where I can employ my ability to evaluate and understand technology in the protection of the company's interests.

My background well prepares me to counsel on strategic direction as well as how to protect developed intellectual assets once that direction has been solidified. With extensive experience as a computer programmer, I possess an exceptional capacity to advise on highly specific issues that impact agreements and intellectual property matters. I can also present complex technical issues to others in a way that is easy to comprehend.

In addition to technical expertise, I am an effective mediator who can see all sides of an issue and patiently work out agreements between parties. Further, my skills in analysis and presentation allow me to successfully present my position with regard to intellectual property disputes. I believe this combination of traits and professional history will serve me well in a corporate environment, and I look forward to beginning this next stage of my career.

I welcome the opportunity to further discuss my potential to benefit your company. Please contact me at your earliest convenience if you wish to arrange an interview.

Sincerely,

Roger Levy

Enclosure

156

Corporate Counsel. *Alyssa Pera, Los Angeles, California*

The individual had two backgrounds: one in computer technology and the other in law. After graduating from law school, he integrated both areas of expertise in software-development contracts.

Luis Colón

000 East 19th Avenue, Allentown, PA 00000 ■ ■ ■ ■ ■ ■ ■ ■ ■ ■ ■ (000) 000-0000

February 17, 2004

Mr. Eugene Zontag
Lehigh County Prosecutor
1015 Malcolm Street
Allentown, PA 00000

Dear Mr. Zontag:

I am writing to you and sending my resume at the suggestion of Dr. William
Jarvis, who recently spoke to you regarding my potential for a field position
with the County Prosecutor's Office. I would be interested in exploring the
possibilities for employment in a criminal investigative unit such as narcotics,
homicide, robbery, arson, or fraud.

In 2000 I was honorably discharged from active duty, having served for three
years in the U.S. Army. I am currently in the Army Reserves and also have four
years of experience as an Emergency Medical Technician. As you will see from
my resume, these experiences as well as my volunteer work with urban youth
have trained and prepared me for any challenge requiring a physically fit and
highly disciplined individual. Because I grew up in a tough neighborhood, I
learned street survival skills early in life. I am not intimidated by anyone, and
have mastered the art of unarmed self-defense in addition to the proficient use
of firearms and other weapons.

I feel I could contribute significantly to the law enforcement efforts in your
district by taking an active part in the thorough investigation of alleged
criminal offenses. I would appreciate the chance to meet with you personally to
discuss how my skills and experience could best be utilized to meet your needs.

Thank you for your consideration, and I look forward to hearing from you soon.

Sincerely,

Luis Colón

157

Criminal Investigator. *Melanie Noonan, West Paterson, New Jersey*

The referral in the opening paragraph establishes a connection immediately with the reader of
the letter. The second paragraph explains why the applicant's background makes him fit for a
position.

JOSHUA ABERNATHY

January 9, 2004

Raritan Bay Police Department
5 Hunters Square
Brunswick, PA 22222

Dear Hiring Manager:

Your advertisement for a Police Office Recruit caught my attention as it seems an ideal match for my experience and talents. As a disciplined, self-motivated individual with experience in corrections and three years of military service, I believe I am someone who can be an asset to the Raritan Bay Police Department. With a demonstrated commitment to service and a solid set of skills to offer, I would like to explore the possibility of putting my skills to work for you.

As you can see from my résumé, my background in corrections and in the military has afforded me extensive training opportunities, and I am knowledgeable in many areas that relate to law enforcement. In addition, I have nine years of service to the community as a rescue squad member. Currently CPR-certified, I previously held certification as an EMT as well. Among my other strengths, I have demonstrated the ability to accurately assess difficult situations, make sound judgments and respond appropriately. With strong interpersonal skills, I am effective in dealing with people and building trust. In addition, I am a fast learner, someone who is eager to continue to develop and grow.

Law enforcement holds great appeal for me as it is my ambition to make a difference in the community. Therefore, I would enjoy the opportunity to discuss your needs and how I might be able to meet them. Please feel free to contact me at the address and phone number listed below. I look forward to hearing from you soon.

Thank you for your consideration.

Sincerely,

Joshua Abernathy

Enclosure

20 GREEN STREET ◆ FARMINGTON, NJ 88888 ◆ (222) 333-4444 ◆ nathy1@att.net

158

Police Officer. *Carol A. Altomare, Three Bridges, New Jersey*

This corrections officer wanted to become a police officer. As in Cover Letter 157, the second paragraph shows that the applicant's background makes him especially suitable for the new position.

MARK STALLONE

February 3, 2004

Hiring Agent, Title
Company Name
Address

Dear Hiring Manager:

Perhaps you are seeking a promising police officer with strong analytical abilities who is motivated by challenge and has a large capacity for growth. As a self-confident individual with a commanding presence and excellent interpersonal skills, I believe I offer the right combination of skills and traits to be just that person.

As you can see from my enclosed résumé, I have accumulated two years of professional experience since earning my degree. In my current position in the Consumer Affairs group of a major pharmaceutical company, I have the opportunity to serve both internal and external clients. Always exercising good judgment, I have demonstrated the ability to deal effectively with people from all backgrounds, earning their trust and respect. Often faced with frustrated or angry callers, my record shows that I am able to respond in a calm manner, defusing tensions through patient, but persuasive, discussions.

While in college, I was a member of the Corp of Cadets, a full-time ROTC leadership program. Coming from a family of police officers and firefighters, the disciplined, regimented lifestyle suited me well, and by senior year, I was second-in-charge to a group of 50 junior cadets. An advocate of giving back to the community, I was also a frequent volunteer for numerous service activities.

Among the strengths I offer, you will find that I am proactive, observant, disciplined and thorough. I am also known as a team player with excellent communication skills who works hard to get the job done. These are traits that have served me well in the past, and I am confident they can be put to good use on your police force as well.

I would be pleased to have the opportunity to discuss future employment and look forward to speaking with you. Feel free to contact me at the address and phone number listed below.

Thank you for your consideration.

Sincerely,

Mark Stallone

Enclosure

---

48 LAMONT LANE ▪ JUNCTION STATION, PA 09999 ▪ (444) 444-4444 ▪ stallone@att.net

159

Police Officer. *Carol A. Altomare, Three Bridges, New Jersey*

This applicant without law-enforcement experience wanted to become a police officer. The second, third, and fourth paragraphs explain why he considers himself qualified for a position.

BILL STEADMAN, CPP

CORPORATE EXECUTIVE ● CHIEF SECURITY OFFICER

"Security is always too much...until it's not enough."
—Daniel Webster

«Date»

«First_Name» «Last_Name»
«Title»
«Company»
«Postal_Address»

Dear «Courtesy_Title» «Last_Name»:

Within minutes, the disastrous events of September 11, 2001, transformed our conceptualization of corporate security—changed its significance, scope, and strategy—from an optional "diligence" to an absolute requirement. Undoubtedly, the 15,000+ companies that were directly affected that day have since created, expanded, and / or upgraded corporate security.

In these perilous times, today's socially and financially conscientious enterprise is obligated to take a serious, urgent, and comprehensive approach to protecting infrastructure, property, and people from internal and external threats. Globally, companies are reprioritizing corporate security in their plans and actions, despite the soft economy.

Today's conundrum? Do more with less—again! This is where I come in! Through 20+ years of experience in the planning, deployment, and management of full-scale corporate security programs, I can provide <Name of Company> with the capacity to efficiently and cost-effectively avoid / mitigate risk and loss. In addition, I bring the added value of senior-level executive achievement, advanced academics, and an understanding of technology.

The following are highlights of my successes:

- Served as Head of Security for all of Your Cable's corporate entities and assets and managed related strategies, projects, inventories for corporate headquarters and two operating divisions. Controlled $7 million capital and expense budget.

- Assisted SVP of Security (solid line to CEO) with enterprise-wide budget and team oversight ($24+ million / 800+ employees).

- Contributed to $1+ million in annual cost savings related to corporate security.

- Formed and managed an internal organization—Intelligence Services Group—as a solution to employee and vendor security issues.

- Planned and managed technology-based security—personnel, proprietary, and intellectual property protection—systems projects representing investments, some in excess of $1 million.

- Contributed to post-9/11 strategic plans and actions for high-profile venues and events (e.g. West Side Arena, Lyman Recital House, and Senior GMA Tournament). Consulted on Metropolis Plaza security issues after the '93 bombing.

<Name of Contact>, if you see value in the breadth of my experience, scope of my knowledge, and caliber of my management qualifications, please get in touch so we can set up a meeting. I look forward to discussing your needs and my solutions. I can guarantee you a substantial ROI.

Sincerely,

Bill Steadman

Enclosure

vulnerability assessment ● access security ● event security ● workplace / employee security
executive protection ● electronic surveillance / countermeasures ● competitive intelligence / countermeasures
emergency preparedness ● crisis response ● intellectual / proprietary property protection

25 Bristol Road, Smallville, New Jersey 33333 ● Home: 444-444-4444 ● Cell: 777-777-7777 ● E-mail: bstead@verizon.net

160

Corporate Security Officer. *Deborah Dib, Medford, New York*

Contact information is put at the foot of the page in order to start selling the need for security at the top with the Webster quotation. The bulleted successes and the keywords near the foot are strong.

JONATHAN A. EAGEN
4444 Martin Road • Allentown, PA 19222 • (666) 888-0000

March 17, 2004

Thomas Ridge, Director of Homeland Security
White House
ATT: Office of Homeland Security
1600 Pennsylvania Avenue
Washington, DC 20502

Dear Secretary Ridge:

As you build your Homeland Security team, it is my hope that you are looking for individuals like me—people who have been in the trenches and who are willing to "do what it takes" to accomplish a task. If you spoke to Jack Long in Lt. Governor Justine's office, he would tell you that I *am* that person, and that I would be a strong contributor to this uncharted and unprecedented challenge you face.

Until August, I was a Research Analyst and Campaign Coordinator for Senator Don Thornton. Following Senator Thornton's retirement, I served as a Campaign Coordinator for Representative Lisa Carpenter, working closely with the Republican State Committee. At this point, I am ready for a new challenge, and I can envision no other personal or professional opportunity more fulfilling and rewarding than being a member of the Homeland Security team.

From the time I was a young man, I have had an interest in public service. You will note in my resume that I have served as a Councilman and Committeeman in my home borough. Although I didn't realize it at the time, I was taking the first steps toward a career serving the public and my country. When I envision the perfect job and work environment, there are three things that rank high on my list of priorities:

- I work best on a team...particularly one that is targeting a meaningful goal such as homeland security;

- I *must* be aligned with a leader who is known for his/her integrity, character and strength of purpose...an individual who leads by personal example; and

- I want to be given the opportunity to tackle any challenging, responsible assignments that I'm deemed capable of handling. I make it my business to learn all I can about my organization's mission, strategies and functions so that I can work from a standpoint of knowledge.

On a personal level, you should be aware that I am single, available for travel and open to working extra hours to accomplish the team's objective. To say I am organized and work well under pressure would be an understatement. I've had to in order to balance full-time employment with my educational requirements. And whether large projects or small—you can count on me to get the job done. I have a "can-do" attitude and plenty of persistence, and I enjoy doing the footwork.

I would be proud to join this top-flight team concerned with protecting our nation and its citizens. I have enclosed my resume, outlining my experience and credentials, for your consideration. I realize that a resume is only a brief overview, so I can be available to meet with you for a personal interview at your convenience. Please note that I have submitted my resume online as well. I look forward to talking with you in the near future.

Respectfully,

Jonathan A. Eagen

Enclosure

161

Homeland Security Position. *Karen Conway, Media, Pennsylvania*

Referrals in the first two paragraphs help to catch the reader's attention. The letter then turns to building a case for regarding this applicant as a worthy candidate for a Homeland Security position.

CST. DANIEL TURCOTT #544

000 King Street, Apt. #212   Phone: (555) 444-8888
Augusta, Ontario A1A 1A1   Pager: (905) 444-5555

January 12, 2004

RE: PROMOTIONAL REVIEW BOARD

Dear Sir/Madam,

It is with great interest that I submit my qualifications for the Promotional Review Board. I am a highly skilled and highly regarded police officer with recent experience working as an Acting Sergeant and considerable international leadership experience. In all capacities, I have consistently distinguished myself as a dedicated, well-organized, and highly capable leader.

In addition to the experience and expertise outlined in the attached résumé, I offer strengths in the following specific areas:

> **Leadership**—Through my current role as Acting Sergeant with the Augusta and Pinehurst Community Police Services, and additionally from my experience in Kosovo as the Chief of Border Police Unit, I have demonstrated strengths in leading officers through example, coaching, and the clear communication of expected performance standards. In delegating responsibilities and specific tasks to subordinate officers, I am mindful of developing officers and ensure that they are part of the team. I provide leadership by example, showing compassion and respect for fellow officers while maintaining good guidance and direction.

> **Communications Skills**—My communication is clear and concise, and I have excellent listening skills. In Kosovo, I was responsible for representing our United Nations Border Policing efforts in politically tense meetings with Yugoslav, Macedonian, NATO, and UN representatives. These meetings were extremely volatile at times, and required the highest levels of diplomacy, clarity, and interpersonal expertise.

"Mr. Turcott enjoys a natural ability to interact and converse well with people of all walks of life. His interpersonal skill is the trait that is far superior and the envy of many."
Everson W. Summerset, Inspector
Chief of Training for United Nations Mission in Kosovo

> **Organizational Skills**—I have consistently been commended for my organizational and logistical skills. While in Kosovo, I effectively managed all resources and coordinated the activities of 130 officers and 60 police vehicles across five international border crossings. Most recently, I reviewed and updated 433 ARPS files on outlaw motorcycle gang members and their associates.

"There were always logistical problems and bureaucratic issues to be handled. These circumstances never deterred Turcott from accomplishing his mission, even under difficult circumstances"
Willis B. Redfield, Senior Case Agent, Narcotics Division
New York Police Department

> **Above-Standard Proven Work Record**—As a Uniform Officer, I maintain one of the highest levels of statistics with regards to drug and criminal investigations within my division. Additionally, I am consistently identified for special projects and investigative work within my division, the Intelligence Unit, and other police services.

Page 1 of 2

162

Police Constable. *Ross Macpherson, Whitby, Ontario, Canada*

This Police Constable had to "apply" for a promotion to Sergeant. Because hundreds of officers applied for the promotion and the letter and resume carried so much weight, the standard one-page length was replaced with a powerful two-page letter that included achievements and

CST. DANIEL TURCOTT #544

000 King Street, Apt. #212
Augusta, Ontario A1A 1A1

Phone: (555) 444-8888
Pager: (905) 444-5555

continued…

➢ **Dedication**—Extremely self-motivated and driven to succeed, I have a consistent desire to improve skills and exceed expectations. Proven flexibility and adaptability.

➢ **Self-Discipline**—I was personally selected by Division Inspector to develop, coordinate, and implement a 6-week Street Level Drug Investigation within the Pinehurst community. As Officer in Charge, I successfully managed budget allocation, vehicle rentals, and undercover buys, and directed junior and senior officers in the execution of all search warrants.

➢ **Conflict Resolution**—I successfully created a 130-officer Border Police Unit in Kosovo, requiring advanced conflict-resolution skills in a post-war restoration scenario. Given that no such police unit existed in the region when I arrived, our presence in such a volatile region created considerable conflict among residents and the international police officers I was responsible for training and supervising. In spite of these obstacles, I was able to create an effective Border Police Unit covering five international border locations between two sovereign countries.

"[Officer Turcott's] sensitive, honest, and positive team approach garnishes the mutual respect between himself and others that permit effective conflict resolution."

Everson W. Summerset, Inspector
Chief of Training for United Nations Mission in Kosovo

I am confident that my work experience, reputation, and dedicated work ethic will exemplify the type of officer you require. Thank you for your consideration.

Sincerely,

Constable Daniel Turcott #544

testimonials in seven top functional areas. Boldfacing and underlining make these areas stand out. Italic is used for the important testimonials. This candidate got the promotion over more than 200 other officers.

BRUCE T. THOMASON

98 Ben Franklin Drive • Austin, TX 78734
Home: (555) 222-2222 • ThomasonB@aol.com • Work: (555) 333-3333

<Date>

[Company Name]
[Department]
[Address]
[City, State, ZIP]

Dear [Name],

It is with great interest that I am forwarding my résumé for consideration as Major within your agency. As a highly motivated Director of Informational Systems within your law enforcement agency, and having served in many capacities within this agency, I am confident that I possess the skills, the knowledge, and—most important—the dedication and commitment to ensure that citizens are provided with safe, efficient, quality protection.

My desire to make a difference in the community and in the lives of the people in that community led me to a career in law enforcement. The teamwork, dedication, and commitment involved in serving the community make this work extremely rewarding, as does the continual effort to be the "Best of the Best." Law enforcement is a physically demanding and dangerous occupation, requiring physical fitness, discipline, and teamwork. My team-building, leadership, and motivational skills will be an asset to your agency, as will my stamina and capacity to act decisively in emergency situations.

With more than 25 years of law enforcement experience, I will bring to this position extensive expertise and departmental knowledge. With a vision of a progressive Sheriff's Office with a continuing tradition of exemplary service, I believe my values of honesty, embraced diversity, respect, commitment, and full accountability, combined with knowledge gained from extensive experience, will guarantee my ability to do this important work.

Throughout my career, I have demonstrated my ability to handle full responsibility and leadership. My responsibilities have been diverse, and have included departmental management, strategic planning, project management, and financial analysis. Having successfully executed tactics to cut costs and improve efficiency, I possess the ability to conceive and implement business solutions to problems while working closely with personnel and projects, building a reputation for quality and overall results. My mission is for a Sheriff's Office by and for the people, committed to justice by serving and protecting our community.

Thank you for your time and consideration of my application. I look forward to discussing in detail with you the ways in which I can make a significant contribution to your agency, and I invite you to contact me, at your convenience, at either of the above numbers.

Sincerely,

Bruce Thomason

Enclosure

163

Police Officer, Major. *Jennifer Rushton, N. Richmond, New South Wales, Australia*

The individual was applying for an internal position as Major within his agency. He wanted to show both his commitment to law enforcement and his ability to lead and implement changes.

DARWIN E. TOHALT

637 Lazey L Road • Ginsville, Missouri 64730
Office: 555-555-5555 • Wireless: 000-000-0000 • Fax: 000-000-0000
Email: darwintohalt@ctcis.net

LETTER OF INTRODUCTION

This letter is to introduce Darwin E. Tohalt, Accredited Traffic Accident Reconstructionist. As a retired highway patrolman and a member of the Major Crash Investigation Unit, I possess the knowledge, specialization, training, and experience to investigate and analyze traffic accidents beyond the normal investigation performed by the police.

Attached is a professional profile that highlights my qualifications. I have investigated and reconstructed hundreds of accidents involving passenger and commercial vehicles, pedestrians, and bicycles. These credentials will render my opinion in court as an "expert" in traffic accident reconstruction. My experience extends to consulting with attorneys and insurance companies in any accident case, for the prosecution and defense, along with civil cases representing both the plaintiff and the defendant. Also, I have performed extensive research and evidence documentation.

There are many areas of an accident that can be analyzed. Vehicle speed is the most common issue, and there are several methods, including speed from skid marks, conservation of energy, crush damage, and conservation of linear momentum, that can be applied. There can be questions of collision avoidance or the ability of a driver to see a hazard. Most accident cases require that several issues be analyzed and correlated so that an overall picture of the situation can be presented. Computer programs are used to assist in reconstruction of accidents. These programs are very complex and require considerable training to use them correctly. Various types of scale diagrams, photos, animations, and scale models are prepared.

There is no set fee for the reconstruction or analysis of a traffic accident. My services are provided on an hourly fee basis. A simple situation may take very little time, while a complex situation may take several days just to collect the required information. Then there is the time required for trial or deposition appearances. There is no charge or obligation for the initial review and consultation on any traffic accident case. With this review, a cost estimate can be provided.

From responding to an accident scene, to documentation and preservation of the evidence, to determination of vehicle speeds or avoidability, to courtroom presentations and exhibits, I can assist you in all of your needs for traffic accident reconstruction.

Sincerely,

Darwin E. Tohalt

Attachment

164

Traffic Accident Reconstructionist. *Gina Taylor, Kansas City, Missouri*

The applicant was a retired highway patrolman who wanted to go into accident investigation for insurance and law firms. The writer developed this letter of introduction for the new company.

Tom Clancey

0000 35th Street ▪ Springtown, AR 00000 ▪ name@aol.com
Home: (000) 000-0000 ▪ Work: (000) 000-0000 ▪ Cell: (000) 000-0000

January 20, 2004

Christine Farner, City Secretary
City of Springtown
P.O. Box 0000
Springtown, AR 00000

Dear Ms. Farner:

Please accept the enclosed résumé in application for the position of Chief of Police with the City of Springtown. Having served as the Assistant Chief of Police of Springtown for over 15 years, I am now prepared to take the next step and provide our growing community with strong, progressive leadership.

My résumé will verify that I meet all the necessary experience, educational, and skill-based requirements for this position. However, what my résumé may not fully indicate is the level of dedication I offer to the community of Springtown. Being the public safety leader of a community with close to 15,000 residents is a substantial responsibility; not only is the Chief of Police the prime media spokesperson, head investigator, and lead program coordinator for the police department, but he or she is also one of the most visible role models in the community.

Throughout my career, as various community members will verify, I have demonstrated deep involvement in Springtown's civic activities and community improvement programs, and my efforts as the Assistant Chief of Police have been recognized through awards from both Springtown College and the Springtown Rotary Club. As the Chief of Police, I would bring an even greater level of devotion to the Springtown community.

In addition, I am a strong advocate of progressive ideas and continual development. As laws, technologies, and times change, so must Springtown adapt with new law enforcement strategies, policies, and implementations. One of my central goals if selected as Chief of Police would be to introduce new programs that further promote Springtown's reputation as a safe, attractive community. I envision the police department doing even more to make Springtown the type of community that encourages businesses and families to make it their permanent home.

Again, my résumé is enclosed to provide you with additional details concerning my background and qualifications. I look forward to the opportunity to interview for this position.

Thank you for your time and consideration.

Sincerely,

Tom Clancey

Enclosure

165

Chief of Police.   *Daniel J. Dorotik, Jr., Lubbock, Texas*

The applicant was responding to an ad but was seeking an internal promotion. The second, third, and fourth paragraphs indicate in turn the individual's credentials, record, and interest in future growth.

TED PELLETIERE

Home:	E-mail: pellted@cox.net	*Mailing Address:*
000 Mullen Road	(555) 555-5555	P.O. Box 445
Peekskill, NY 00000		Peekskill, NY 00000

March 23, 2004

New York Times
Box 990
New York, NY 00000

RE: INVESTIGATIONS MANAGER

As a professional with extensive hands-on and supervisory experience in law enforcement, private industry and the military, I believe that my expertise is a match for this position. Accordingly, I have enclosed for your review a resume that summarizes my skills and accomplishments in investigations management.

I have achieved a successful record as an investigator and supervisor in delivering results to corporate clients as well as in community and executive protection. My skills encompass undercover criminal investigations • background checks • fraud investigations • arrests and extradition • fugitive location and apprehension • electronic surveillance and detection • employee dishonesty.

Currently as Chief Inspector at the Chief State's Attorney's Office, I direct a team in security, safety, and investigation operations. As a supervisor, I am accountable for the development, training, and supervision of a diverse workforce. I also am well versed in security program planning and critical incident/crisis management based on my experience as a member of the Federal Anti-Terrorism Task Force.

Previously employed with the New York Police Department, I progressed through increasingly responsible law enforcement positions that included development of the training division, establishing and overseeing the department's narcotics unit and training new staff. In addition, my diverse experience includes providing successful investigative services for corporate clients in the insurance industry, as well as conducting criminal/counterintelligence investigations during my military reserves tenure.

I am confident that my expertise and professionalism would allow me to meet the challenges of this managerial role and protect your clients' interests. Thank you for your consideration.

Sincerely,

Ted Pelletiere

166

Investigations Manager. *Louise Garver, Enfield, Connecticut*

This applicant wanted an investigations management position in a corporate setting. The letter refers to the individual's experience, skills, current position, and previous NYPD employment.

ALLEN JURGENS

0000 Red Barn Road
Agua Dulce, California 91350

555-555-5555
ajurgens@netzero.net

January 5, 2004

Benson Security
35000 Sierra Highway
Agua Dulce, California 91350

Proficient Loss-Prevention Expert
Committed to Helping You
Achieve a Healthier Bottom Line!

Each year, retailers lose an estimated $26 billion in merchandise to shrinkage, primarily through theft and employee error. This means 1 to 2 percent of total sales are lost, and for larger companies, this loss totals in the millions. Some companies find themselves in this predicament because of an ineffective loss-prevention program or lack of one.

Here's how I can help...

- Draw on practical experience to identify and solve loss-related problems.
- Develop and implement sound strategies to arrive at effective solutions.
- Use effective management techniques to train loss-prevention staff.
- Collaborate with team members to address current problems and anticipate future challenges.

I believe in the *Golden Rule* and have always applied it; it was one of the first things I instilled in my staff. Throughout my law enforcement career, I have focused on empowering my subordinates to succeed by encouraging them to develop their strengths and grow professionally. In many cases where individuals were dissatisfied, I resolved the underlying problems and turned their attitude around. This approach consistently produced highly effective, supportive teams under my command.

Qualifications I bring to your company [use name of company if you have it] include

- Proven performance in fast-paced and high-stress working environments.
- Strong analytical skills with exceptional attention to detail.
- High motivation and ability to aggressively take on great responsibility.
- Hands-on experience with classified documentation.
- Experience in intelligence report writing, including in-depth reports on high-interest areas of operation.

Based on my experience, strong work ethic, and commitment (no one will "outwork" me), I am confident that I can add significant value to your security function. If appropriate, I would like to schedule a meeting to discuss your needs and the contribution I can make to the success of your organization. Should any questions arise regarding the information on my résumé, please contact me; otherwise, I will call you next week [if you have or can look up contact number] to set up an appointment. I look forward to speaking with you soon.

Sincerely,

Allen Jurgens

Enclosure

167

Loss Prevention Expert. *Myriam-Rose Kohn, Valencia, California*

This letter's pattern includes these items in turn for the reader: your problem, how I can help, my work with subordinates, my qualifications, and my confidence in being useful to your organization.

Thomas J. Sonner

333 West Boulevard
Hansing, WA 98888-8888
(777) 777-7777
email: TJS777@email.com

March 18, 2004

General Manager
Senior Gardens
77 Mystery Drive
Hansing, WA 98888

RE: Community Relations Director

I enclose my résumé in response to your March 8, 2004, ad in *The Hansing Bee* for a Community Relations Director. It seems a surprisingly good match for my background, and I would welcome an opportunity to discuss it with you personally.

My considerable experience as a highly successful, respected, and beloved pastor / counselor / teacher, briefly summarized on the enclosed résumé, testifies to my relationship-building expertise—I am confident in my ability to represent Senior Gardens to prospective residents and their families. My work with diverse populations has honed my innate ability to recognize needs and present workable solutions—I can easily relate to your customers. Of course, successful networking with civic and religious leaders in local and state communities, office personnel, administrators, executives, children, and adults is one of my fortes.

With my experience in recruiting volunteers, public speaking, presentations, and training, I have well-developed powers of persuasion—easily translated to sales and marketing skills— and certainly ministry and teaching can be considered long-term-care industries.

I hope you can see the potential here for my making a significant contribution to your business and will give me a call. Thank you for your consideration.

Sincerely,

Thomas J. Sonner

enc: résumé

168

Community Relations Director. *Janice M. Shepherd, Bellingham, Washington*

The applicant was a Roman Catholic priest who had decided to transition to secular work. This letter was successful in getting an interview for him, and he was successful in landing the job.

Paul Patton

15711 Clinton Avenue
Houston, TX 00000

Home: (000) 000-0000
Email: name@aol.com

January 14, 2004

Dr. Ken Woolforth
Vice President for Enrollment Management
University of Houston
P.O. Box 00000
Houston, TX 00000-0000

Dear Dr. Woolforth:

It was with great interest that I learned about the opening for a Director of Professional Services, as my qualifications match your requirements for this position. Please allow me to explain briefly how my skills and abilities can contribute to the success of the University of Houston.

In reviewing the requisition for this position, I noted that you are seeking a candidate with the ability to "apply universal business principles to a variety of environments"; as the Director for my advertising firm and a General Manager in several other capacities, I have held full responsibility for a broad range of business disciplines and functions, including marketing, accounting, budgeting, sales, production, customer service, staffing, and general administration. In addition, I meet the following specific requirements:

Your Requirements:	**My Qualifications:**
▪ 7 years of management experience	▪ 15+ years of experience in various management positions
▪ Bachelor's degree from accredited university	▪ BS from the University of Houston
▪ Knowledge of printing, copying, and mailing processes	▪ Experience in printing, mailing, and copying functions as Director of XYZ Advertising
▪ High level of financial and administrative management skills	▪ Track record of meeting tight budgets, streamlining processes, and ensuring workplace efficiency

My résumé is enclosed to provide you with additional details regarding my background and achievements, but I am certain that a personal interview would more fully reveal the diversity of my management experience and the unique contribution I can make to your university. Thank you, Dr. Woolforth, for your time and consideration.

Sincerely,

Paul Patton

Enclosure

169

Director of Professional Services, University. *Daniel J. Dorotik, Jr., Lubbock, Texas*

This letter was a response to an ad. The writer used a Your Requirements… My Qualifications format to draw attention to the excellent match between the applicant and specific ad requirements.

Shemaka Drew
414 Chapel Hill Road Morraine, Georgia 30000 ☎ [678] 555-5555 (Home) sd200@charge.com

Friday, April 9, 2004

Mr. Charles W. Moran
Chairman, Board of Directors
The Wentworth Foundation
2230 Corona Boulevard
Suite 100
Atlanta, Georgia 30000

Dear Mr. Moran:

I want to be the one who translates your vision for The Wentworth Foundation into results as your Executive Director. Over the years, I've done just that for not-for-profit entities that range from a large university to a humane society to a minority arts festival to a science museum to a family and career services provider.

How well did I do? On the next pages, you'll read about some two dozen documented contributions. But I thought you deserved more than a typical résumé, with its sterile lists of job titles and responsibilities.

In their place are examples of donors found and retained, funds raised, staff and volunteers inspired, services expanded—in short, everything The Wentworth Foundation should have to be the center of excellence in the field. However, even a specially tailored résumé format can't show *how* I've built my track record.

Behind the results is this professional code that guides all I do:

- ❑ Building financial support is good; keeping financial support growing is better.
- ❑ Making your organization more visible is good; having it synonymous with its function is better.
- ❑ Recruiting volunteers is good; keeping them is not only better, it's more fun.

Now I am ready to put all my energy to work for The Wentworth Foundation. However, when it comes to your special needs, words on paper are no substitute for personal conversations. May I call around the middle of next week to hear about your organization's special needs?

Sincerely,

Shemaka Drew

Encl.: Résumé

170

Executive Director, Foundation. *Don Orlando, Montgomery, Alabama*

The applicant had many positions during the last few years. The letter refocuses attention away from the applicant's job history and to the benefits the person can bring to the foundation.

Donald Hilton

000 Glendale Road, Apartment 3 ♦ Schenectady, NY 12302 ♦ (555) 555-5555 ♦ brasso607@aol.com

Date

Hiring Agent Name
Title
Company Name
Address
City, State ZIP

Dear Mr. / Ms. _____ :

As an experienced, motivated professional with a Bachelor's degree in Environmental Science and a strong background in environmental planning, conservation, laws, consulting, health, and safety, I believe my skills and talents can make an immediate and long-term contribution to the overall success of [name of company / organization].

I am proficient at planning and implementing environmental projects, conserving land and resources, gathering and interpreting field data, and consulting clients on environmental issues. In my current position as an Air Technician, I collect and analyze air samples and help clients and businesses meet safe, legal limits. Additional environmental experience includes the study of trout habitat selection in the Lake Champlain Watershed, wetlands management, wildlife control, landscape improvement, and writing environmental reports and documents.

With excellent organization, leadership, and communication skills, I am capable of managing major projects, large groups of people, and multiple priorities simultaneously. I am a team player who works well with coworkers, clients, businesses, and management at all levels. My proven ability to complete projects and assignments from concept to completion with meticulous detail will be a significant asset to [name of company].

The accompanying résumé provides further details of my accomplishments and what I have to offer. I believe it would be mutually beneficial for us to discuss your company's goals and how I can help you achieve them. I will call next week to inquire about such a meeting.

Thank you for your time and consideration.

Sincerely,

Donald Hilton

Enc. résumé

171

Project Manager. *John Femia, Altamont, New York*

The applicant is a recent graduate in environmental science. Currently an air technician, he wants to expand his activities in planning and managing a wider range of environmental projects.

GEORGE CARRIZALES, EIT

800 Indiana Avenue
Austin, TX 79423

Home: (000) 000-0000
name@msn.com

January 30, 2004

ENERGY Corporation
200 Apple Center
Houston, TX 00000

Dear Hiring Manager:

Please accept the enclosed résumé in application for current openings the ENERGY Corporation has available. After researching your company's Web site, I recognized the dedication you have for your clients' best interests and I fully agree with your mission statement in that ***"management of environmental and public health risk is integral to the successful operation of a business."*** I am confident that I could contribute to your organization's and clients' future needs.

My graduate and undergraduate studies at the University of Texas provided me the opportunity to study and analyze key concepts, principles, and practices in environmental engineering. Subsequently, I demonstrated in-depth knowledge of environmental issues and problem-solving strategies through my work in upper-level class assignments and projects. Because I am a strong advocate of continuing education and intend to maintain professional development throughout my career, you can be assured that I will stay on top of emerging, critical environmental matters.

Of course, there is a notable difference between academic studies and practical field experience. While I completed my Bachelor's and Master's degrees, I worked as a Research Associate and Assistant for the University of Texas. In this environment, I learned the importance of precise analysis and attention to detail in field research. Also, I gained experience in examining and solving problems with environmental concerns such as wastewater treatment and brush control. Both my experience and education demonstrate the level of performance I would bring to your organization.

My résumé is enclosed to provide additional details concerning my background and achievements. Thank you for your time and consideration.

Sincerely,

George Carrizales

Enclosure

172

Environmental Engineer. *Daniel J. Dorotik, Jr., Lubbock, Texas*

This letter was written in response to an ad. The student conveys convincingly that he should be interviewed despite a lack of strong experience. Boldfacing highlights his agreement with the company's mission.

John J. Doe

333 222ⁿᵈ Place, Seattle, WA 98100
206.333.3333 home // 206 444-4444 cell // JohnDoe@hotmail.com

January 13, 2004

Mr./Ms_____
Recruiting
Nordstrom Direct
One Union Square
Seattle, WA 98101

RE: Assistant Inventory Manager, Job Code 3333

Dear _____,

I'm writing because I share Nordstrom's core values and genuinely want to work for your company. I value the company's commitment to service and quality, its dedication to its employees and the exemplary way it conducts business. Wishing to leave a successful career in hospitality, I offer a sound sense of customer service, often-commended initiative, and a track record of teamwork and meeting stated objectives. I'm enclosing my resume for your current position, Assistant Inventory Manager.

In the Nordstom family tradition, my family owned a well-known retail store in Spokane, WA. I was raised to value hard work. Starting at age five, I stocked shelves, moving to managing books and inventories, monitoring profits, making sales and keeping customers happy, day in and day out. I sincerely want to advance this mutual family tradition, growing customer relationships and profits for Nordstrom. Per my resume, skills matching those listed in the posted job include the following:

> **Teamwork and Leadership:** Advanced within current restaurant position to oversee all areas of operations, working cohesively as part of an 8-person team.
> **Sales, Goal Achievement and Time Management:** Received numerous bonuses, exceeding sales quotas for an auto-glass installer while attending college.
> **Inventory, Delivery Assurance and Project Management:** Accurately handled ordering, tracking and delivery assurance for 30 custom jobs simultaneously.
> **Management, Initiative and Business Expertise:** Owned a profitable catering company while simultaneously attending school and manning a busy bartending position.

I am confident that my values and personality will fit within your team and meld well with your mission. While I may not have every skill listed in your ad, I'm one who learns quickly, asks pertinent questions and works efficiently to help my next employer advance competitively. I am commended by supervisors for managing my time well, working positively with the public and meeting any target put before me. I can offer very positive references, upon request.

I look forward to talking with you to discuss how I can become a contributor to Nordstrom's continued success. Sincere in my wish to join a quality company, I plan to e-mail you next week to check on the status of your hiring process and discuss opportunities.

Thank you for your consideration. I truly feel we have something to talk about and look forward to meeting you soon.

Sincerely,

JOHN J. DOE

173

Assistant Inventory Manager. *Alice Hanson, Seattle, Washington*

The letter did not get an interview for the posted job but did get an interview with a Nordstrom recruiting manager to explore other opportunities. Boldfacing highlights important skills.

Rodney Bain
79 West Seminole Circle
Butte, MT 55555
Cell: (555) 555–5555
Home: (555) 555–5555

May 28, 2004

Paul Sharpy
Human Resources Director
Valley Medical Center
1632 Arlington Avenue
Butte, MT 55555

Dear Mr. Sharpy,

Please accept this letter as application for the Plant Operations Supervisor position currently available with Valley Medical Center, as advertised in the *Montana Chronicle*. My confidential résumé is attached for your review and consideration, and I believe you will find me well qualified.

You will find that I possess a solid background in plant operations within the healthcare industry, with more than 20 years of experience. In this capacity, I have developed an expertise in clinical engineering and facilities maintenance and am confident that my expertise in these areas will prove to be an asset to Valley Medical Center.

Additionally, I am familiar with maintenance and repair of medical equipment; buildings and building systems, including boilers; and other equipment that provides air-conditioning, heating, steam, hot water, electricity, sanitation, and medical gases. I have been instrumental in several successful JCAHO surveys, and I am known for effectively identifying and resolving problems before they affect related areas, personnel, or patients.

I would welcome the opportunity to discuss with you how I might make similar contributions to the success of Valley Medical Center. I look forward to hearing from you to schedule a personal interview at your convenience. Thank you for your consideration.

Sincere regards,

Rodney Bain

Enclosure

174

Plant Operations Supervisor. *Denette Jones, Boise, Idaho*

The opening paragraph indicates the targeted position, and the second refers to the applicant's background and expertise. The important third paragraph shows the breadth of his knowledge.

ALLEN T. BORNEO
8001 Satchel Drive
Greenfield, MA 00000
Home: (555) 555-5555 • Cell: (555) 555-5555
E-mail: allentb@aol.com

January 24, 2004

Mr. John Deering
Director of Facility Maintenance
Marietta Manufacturing
Marietta Plaza
Greenfield, MA 00000

Dear Mr. Deering:

Although I opted for retirement at a young age, I have come to realize that I have too much energy and many skills that I still enjoy using. Retirement is definitely not for me. Therefore, your ad for a maintenance specialist caught my attention as I offer the key qualifications your company needs.

Specifically, I have an excellent performance record in the operation and maintenance of building systems and equipment, including electrical, HVAC, telecommunications, pneumatic, electro-mechanical and hydraulics. I am also knowledgeable of state building codes, safety and other regulatory guidelines.

My expertise encompasses multisite facilities oversight, staff supervision, project management and vendor relations. Examples of relevant accomplishments include reduction in annual maintenance costs and improved functional capabilities while consistently delivering quality service.

Equally important are my planning, organization and communication strengths. Despite the challenges that can often be encountered, I have completed projects on time and under budget consistently. I welcome a personal interview to discuss the value I would add to your company.

Sincerely,

Allen T. Borneo

175

Maintenance Specialist. *Louise Garver, Enfield, Connecticut*

This individual was bored with retirement and wanted to return to work at a lower level. The letter displays his zeal for work. He received an interview and a subsequent offer, which he accepted.

VICTORIA L. WILLIAMS

555 Hillcrest Circle • Anywhere, Michigan 55555

April 8, 2004

Dale Peterson
ABC Corporation
555 Logan Street
Anywhere, Michigan 55555

Dear Mr. Peterson,

My career experience in retail operations management along with working for one of the largest housewares manufacturing companies has provided me great opportunities to demonstrate my strengths in operations management and merchandising while undertaking full P&L responsibilities.

Equally notable are my strengths in developing effective programs and finding creative solutions to meet or exceed corporate objectives. The achievements noted in my résumé reflect the most recent contributions I have made to my employer. I am a proactive business leader and manager with a reputation for developing innovative programs, enhancing productivity and efficiency while developing teams that provide bottom-line results.

I am currently exploring new professional challenges and am willing to relocate. I would welcome the opportunity to discuss my background with you further so that I may provide you more detail on the organizational leadership I can offer your company.

Next week I will contact you to see if we can schedule a meeting at your convenience. I look forward to speaking with you soon.

Regards,

Victoria L. Williams

Enclosure

176

Retail Operations Manager. *Maria E. Hebda, Trenton, Michigan*

The four brief paragraphs indicate in turn the applicant's experience and career field, strengths and achievements, willingness to relocate and interest in an interview, and follow-up plans.

John R. Dover

0000 Ridgeway View
Easterling, North Carolina 00000

Office (444) 333-2222
jdover@home.com

February 22, 2004

Daniel R. Cummings
Director of Human Resources
Wellington Company
1212 Severnson Drive
Waco, Texas 00000

Dear Mr. Cummings:

I'm looking for trouble ... chaos ... problems.

And, no, I am not kidding. My expertise in the industrial management arena is solving problems. I thrive on problems because I know how to handle them and have the track record to prove it. No brag, just fact.

Talk to the company I'm currently managing—they'll tell you what a mess they started with and where we stand now. The plant is running smoothly, profits are growing, and morale is high. I'm ready to move on. There are no more significant problems here.

I did not purposely seek out your company because I, or anyone else, think there is something wrong. I would like to relocate to Houston to be closer to my family and am simply asking various companies if they could use someone with my talents and penchant for "trouble." I deal in people, issues, and in-house adversity. My philosophy is to involve everyone in the company to identify the problem(s), develop a strategy to solve it, and follow through with the appropriate action. Throughout my career in all types of companies, I have been successful in streamlining production, reducing operating expenses, and updating equipment or systems. These are actions that make companies <u>successful</u>. And that's my obsession—I want to make your company more successful.

I would appreciate the opportunity to talk to you about my joining your organization in a managerial capacity. For your review, my résumé is enclosed. And to further put you at ease, you can give me a test: Allow me to talk to your Front Line Supervisor and Controller. With their input, we will know quickly whether I can honestly help your company.

I am eager to hear from you. Please contact me at the above number.

Sincerely,

John R. Dover

Enclosure

177

Industrial Manager. *Sally Altman, Tulsa, Oklahoma*

With an unusual horizontal line at the top of the page and the unexpected statement in italic, this letter is designed to catch the reader's attention. The letter successfully keeps the reader's attention.

RON BATTISTA

999 Augusta Crescent
Pinestone, Ontario L1N 8G7

Home: (555) 666-4444
Cell: (555) 777-9999

March 3, 2004

Salvatore Bosso
Bosso Associates Inc.
333 Bayfield Avenue
Suite 1550, P.O. Box 16
Pinestone, ON A1A 2B2

Re: Manager, Technical Services

Dear Mr. Bosso,

To be a truly effective manager, you have to get your hands dirty.

Throughout my management career, this has a been a major key to my success—getting in the trenches, spotting opportunities for improvement and cost savings, leading the team by example, and knowing firsthand that things are running at optimum levels. If this is the type of manager you're looking for, then I'd welcome the opportunity to speak with you about the contribution I can make.

In recent management positions, I have been responsible for overseeing and optimizing the logistics and operations of expansive, high-volume environments. In every position, I have considered my mandate not only to manage activities, but to find opportunities to improve processes, eliminate redundancies, cut costs, increase revenues, and improve service. The results have been dramatic:

- **Slashed distribution costs by $500,000 for National Review**
- **Inherited district with lowest customer satisfaction rating and turned it around to first place in less than one year**
- **Increased dealers from 600 to 1,150 in less than 7 months**
- **Reduced inventory costs by $16,000 within one year**

I believe I can offer you the very same level of expertise, and I am confident that the results would speak for themselves. I would welcome the opportunity to meet in person to discuss the value I can bring, and I am available for a personal interview at your convenience.

Thank you for your consideration. I look forward to hearing from you.

Sincerely,

Ron Battista

Enclosure

178

Technical Services Manager. *Ross Macpherson, Whitby, Ontario, Canada*

The candidate wanted to convey in the opening paragraphs his hands-on management style. The bullets then communicate strong quantified achievements he has provided for previous employers.

SAMUEL RYAN

January 19, 2004

Hiring Agent, Title
Company Name
Address

Dear Hiring Manager:

As a successful business manager with a broad background and a wealth of experience in developing and delivering innovative programs that increase revenues, I am someone who can be a great asset to your company. With demonstrated successes in identifying promising business opportunities and mobilizing effective teams to put them into practice, I would like to explore the possibility of putting my expertise to work for you.

As you can see from my enclosed résumé, my background includes roles in sales, marketing, operations, and information analysis that recently culminated in business management positions where I have been able to implement programs that significantly improved operations and reduced costs. For example, in my current position as Manager of a central Business Information Center, I successfully introduced a new sales protocol designed to optimize how sales calls are planned and carried out, reducing center costs by more than $2 million. Prior to that, as Business Unit Manager for several lines of business, I was instrumental in identifying and implementing new opportunities that allowed the company to realize $5 million in additional income.

My success has been defined by my strong analysis skills, solid business instincts, considerable practical experience, and ability to rally staff around a common goal. In addition, my communications skills are top-notch, and I am quick to recognize and address project disconnects when they arise, expertly keeping programs on track. In the past, this combination of skills has allowed me to make a significant impact on bottom-line revenues. With a solid track record behind me, you can be confident that I can do the same for you.

I would be pleased to have the opportunity to discuss your needs and how I might be able to meet them. Feel free to contact me at the address and phone number listed below.

Thank you for your consideration.

Sincerely,

Samuel Ryan

Enclosure

000 FENWAY WAY ▪ ELM RIDGE, NJ 22222 ▪ (555) 555-5555

179

Business Manager. *Carol A. Altomare, Three Bridges, New Jersey*

The applicant was a business manager with a diverse background and a strong record of bringing about organizational and operational improvements. The second paragraph quantifies achievements.

LESTER SIMPSON

0000 North Page • Tulsa, OK 00000 • (333) 444-5555

MANAGEMENT PROFESSIONAL

Seeks career opportunity which will effectively utilize an extensive background developed through the cable industry. Expertise in Marketing, Public Relations, Financial Management, Operations, Construction and Engineering. Not quite able to leap tall buildings in a single bound, but very effective in achieving many of the objectives set forth by owners, shareholders, or upper management. Numerous transferable skills for business; adaptable to any industry. Call Lester Simpson at 1-333-444-5555.

Dear Sir or Madam:

If I could be assured that the right company would respond to an ad such as the one above, you would be reading this in your local classifieds. But, because business protocol dictates a different approach, please note that I have enclosed my résumé for your review and consideration.

I believe this ad and my résumé disclose the gist of what I have done and can do for you in several areas of management or operations. The strength of my leadership, strategic planning methods, and procedure for handling various personnel situations are the types of business matters that we would need to explore together, in person, to determine whether my expertise and character fit the needs of your company.

As indicated, I have been in the cable television industry for most of my career. I stepped into numerous roles and advanced successfully, whether it was P.R., finances, or even electronics. Versatility and the wherewithal to learn and keep pace in a rapidly changing environment enhanced my business skills and left me with a great deal more to offer you.

I would appreciate the opportunity to meet with you personally. I can be reached at the above number and would be available for a meeting at your convenience. Thank you for your consideration. I look forward to your reply.

Sincerely,

Lester Simpson
Résumé enclosed

180

Operations Manager. *Sally Altman, Tulsa, Oklahoma*

The tongue-in-cheek, position-wanted ad is the unique hook that captures the reader's attention and directs it also to the resume. The embedded ad is a "filled" text box with a top and bottom border.

Jon W. Nederstein
0000 Winchester Court, #2B
Alexandria, Virginia 22314-5780
(555) 555-5555

March 22, 2004

Todd Norling
Human Resource Director
Artesia Drilling Equipment Company
14502 Highway 14 East
Stafford, Texas 77700

Dear Mr. Norling:

Over the years, I have seen many examples of great leadership. What separates the truly successful from the rest is a higher level of contribution toward the organization's most important goals. Are you looking for a vice president of operations who can motivate a team to implement plans that not only meet but also exceed growth and financial goals? If so, I am the person who can deliver these contributions.

As you will note on the enclosed résumé, the breadth of my expertise covers a wide area of responsibilities. I am a hardworking, ambitious leader and motivator. I am consistently recognized for team-building, creative problem solving and a high degree of expertise in the manufacturing field. Would you like to see some of these events take place in your facility?

- Turnover rate of 12% per month brought to 3% per month
- Scrap rate cut 50%
- Increased output threefold
- Profits raised 200% in 2 years

These accomplishments demonstrate what I have done in the past for other manufacturing facilities and can do in the future for you. At your convenience, I would like to meet with you and explore the possibility of using my experience and knowledge to benefit Artesia Drilling Equipment Company. I will call later this week to see if we can arrange an appointment. Thank you for your time and consideration.

Sincerely,

Jon W. Nederstein

Enclosure: Résumé

181

Vice President of Operations. *Michele Angello, Aurora, Colorado*

Bullets in the body of the letter emphasize accomplishments that are commented upon in the resume. The text refers to the applicant making the same type of improvements for the next employer.

Brad Atkins
00000 Pinehill Drive
Harrisburg, PA 17101

Office: 555.000.2334
brad@aol.com
Cell: 555.000.0191

Dear Hiring Manager,

I had an early start to my management career in the trucking services/logistics industry when I launched a truck repair facility in Harrisburg, PA. I grew the shop from a one-man operation to a successful business, serving 100 carrier accounts nationwide. RUAN Leasing Company liked my style, recruited me after I sold the business, and provided me with an avenue to use my talents in managing their Northeast region. Unfortunately, companies reorganize and in doing so, let go of good people. I have had the misfortune of being one of those "good people" and find myself among the "chosen" to be "RIFed."

If your organization is in need of an Operations Manager with a proven track record in building and leading effective teams that set the standard for preventative maintenance currency, employee commitment to the job, creative approaches to quality improvement, and controlling operational costs, then you should give me a call or email me.

For the last 10 years I have worked remotely from a home-based office and traveled extensively throughout my region to ensure face-to-face, personal attention. With this arrangement in mind, I see no need to confine my search to any particular geographic area. For the right opportunity, I would consider expanding my reach beyond my Western Pennsylvania home base and relocating to a new area.

My resume follows.

Sincerely,

Brad Atkins

182

Operations Manager. *Norine Dagliano, Hagerstown, Maryland*

This letter was created for posting to online job banks in the logistics industry. The opening paragraph explains why the candidate is a job seeker. The second tells of his worth as a manager.

Richard B. Silverman

3434 Smith Avenue
Newark, NJ 00000
Home (000) 000-0000
Work (000) 000-0000 x0000
name@yahoo.com

January 30, 2004

Ms. Renee Wilson, Human Resources Director
AFA Manufacturing
1111 Lafayette Lane
Trenton, NJ 00000

ATTN: Job Number A-5846

Dear Ms. Wilson:

It was with great interest that I learned of your opening for the position of Operations Manager. I believe I am a worthy candidate for your consideration, with qualifications matching your requirements. Thus, please allow me to explain briefly how I might contribute to your firm's operational and financial performance.

Throughout my career, my expertise has been in leading production operations to profit growth through continual improvement and efficiency. For the past six years, I have built a track record with Builders Depot that demonstrates my ability to lead dramatic profit and organizational growth, indicated through the following sample of highlights:

* Coordinated and executed both improvement and relocation projects, completed on time and on budget, that produced savings ranging from $575,000 to $9 million;
* Forged strategic relationships with vendors and external business partners that enabled quick resolution of problems and positioned Builders Depot for business development and expansion;
* Led departments consistently to multimillion-dollar sales and profit increases through strategic cost-slashing initiatives, workforce performance improvements, and quality-control management.

To provide you with details concerning my qualifications and accomplishments, my résumé is enclosed. Thank you for your time and consideration, and please do not hesitate to contact me if I can answer any questions.

Sincerely,

Richard B. Silverman

Enclosure

183

Operations Manager. *Daniel J. Dorotik, Jr., Lubbock, Texas*

Almost all formatting features have been removed from this letter to make it scannable for job search databases. Bullets point to accomplishments. The first is quantified with dollar amounts.

Mark Forbart, Operations Manager

555 Frank Road, Winthrop, MA 02152 ◆ (555) 555-5555
forbartj@yahoo.com

February 15, 2004

ATTN: HR DEPT.
GENCO MANUFACTURING
451 Andover Street
Lowell, MA 01852

Dear Hiring Professional:

In response to your search for a quality Manufacturing Management professional, I bring 8 years of extensive, hands-on experience in Operations. This includes project and facility management, people development, quality procedures and new product development.

I am an extremely high-energy and innovative engineer who leads by example. I consistently produce strong results with a high degree of integrity, dedication and problem-solving skills.

Many of my achievements are due to my ability to create and maintain rapport with individuals within the organization. This quality, coupled with a drive to think analytically and manage deadlines, has given me a track record of success. Some highlights include the following:

◆ Promoted from Process Engineer to Manufacturing Supervisor to Productions Engineer to Manufacturing Manager to current Operations Manager position within an 8-year time frame
◆ Succeeded with both ISO 9001 and ISO 9002 programs
◆ Led new product introduction, pilot plant production and national expansion
◆ Set up new facilities in record time
◆ Made several process improvements, inventory-level improvements and reductions in stand product costs
◆ Hired, trained and developed team of 38 employees with 21 direct reports

My resume and a summary page provide further details of my accomplishments. You will note that I have progressed in responsibility levels throughout my career. I look forward to discussing yet another career opportunity with you. I will contact you next week to arrange a meeting so that we may discuss your company's needs in greater detail.

Sincerely,

Mark Forbart

Enclosure

184

Operations Manager. *Gail Frank, Tampa, Florida*

The applicant's plant was closing. The writer points out his top accomplishments and emphasizes that he is a "people person" who builds strong relationships and values teamwork and integrity.

Daniel E. Parsons
0000 Shoreham Drive   Charlotte, NC 28211
(H) 555-555-5555 (C) 000-000-0000 e-mail: dparsons@carolina.rr.com

January 6, 2004

Mr. Robert McCaine
Production Manager
BF Goodrich Tire Company
8925 Springsteen Blvd.
Windsor, NY 13865

Dear Mr. McCaine:

Throughout my 19 years of professional employment, I have always been recognized as someone who could *"get the job done."* Being a multitasker who thrives on responsibility and achievement, I excel in a fast-paced, production-oriented environment. Jon Peterson, a mutual friend and colleague, suggested that I contact you to discuss the contribution that I could make to BF Goodrich Tire Company in potential positions at your facility. Your review of my résumé in consideration of my qualifications with regard to these opportunities would be greatly appreciated.

In review of my background, you will note a comprehensive career that spans eight years in the tire industry. Six of those eight years are associated with **Michelin Tire and Rubber.** While my management background is defined by successes in **safety, team building, logistics management, quality and communication,** my operations knowledge is extremely strong in the **curing and final finish** operations. I have directed 100% of operations in curing and final finish, inclusive but not limited to

- Manpower Planning
- Team Building
- Quality Control
- Inspection and Classification
- Warehousing
- Defect Management

As an operations manager and department leader, I believe strongly in giving employees ownership of their work while motivating them to achieve success. **This empowerment model results in an increase in employee retention, loyalty, production, efficiency and safety awareness.**

At this juncture in my career I am seeking the opportunity to transition my qualifications into a high-growth corporation in need of strong leadership. BF Goodrich Tire Company is the corporation I am interested in. An opportunity to personally meet to discuss my qualifications in consideration of the following positions would be greatly appreciated:

- Department Manager
- Shift Coordinator
- Supervisor (willing to enter at this level to prove my potential for growth opportunities)

I am extremely enthusiastic about the possibility of joining the team at BF Goodrich Tire Company, and I can be reached at 555-555-5555 or 000-000-0000 at your convenience. Thank you again for your professional consideration, and I look forward to hearing from you soon.

Sincerely,

Daniel E. Parsons

185

Operations Manager. *MeLisa Rogers, Victoria, Texas*

This candidate was eager to get his foot in the door and was therefore willing to accept a position of lesser responsibility to prove himself. The writer emphasizes his abilities and proven track record.

ANTHONY QUINN

February 22, 2004

Hiring Agent, Title
Company Name
Address

Dear Hiring Manager:

As a driven operations director with extensive experience in packaging and production, and a proven record of accomplishment in bringing about efficiency improvements, I believe I offer an expertise that would be of benefit to your company. With a hands-on approach, strong leadership skills, and a focus on achieving operational excellence as my strengths, I would like to explore the possibility of putting my knowledge and skills to work for you.

As you can see from my enclosed résumé, my background includes ground-up experience in all aspects of facility operations. Currently, my responsibilities encompass the oversight of a 100,000-square-foot facility that specializes in clinical packaging for the pharmaceutical industry. My record speaks to my ability to effectively implement operations improvements that directly impact bottom-line revenues. Most notably, I was instrumental in helping the company realize revenues that surpassed goals by over $2 million. In addition, I am credited with leading the successful implementation of an Oracle Manufacturing module that automated our existing inventory and purchasing systems as part of a company-wide move to enterprise resource planning.

My success in achieving results has been defined by my progressive mind-set, sound problem-solving skills, strong decision-making ability, and effective follow-through. Equally important is my passion for teamwork. A lifelong involvement with football makes me a firm believer in the power of teamwork, and I am an avid supporter of its principles in the workplace. My open and inclusive management style and my commitment to training and developing staff arise from my belief in teamwork. I feel strongly that staff members are an intrinsic part of the success I have had in achieving goals. With this combination of skills and traits to offer, as well as a solid track record behind me, I am confident I can produce results for you as well.

I would be pleased to have the opportunity to discuss your needs and how I might be able to meet them. Feel free to contact me at the address and phone number listed below.

Thank you for your consideration.

Sincerely,

Anthony Quinn

Enclosure

25 BRIDGE STREET ▪ FRAMINGHAM, NY 11111 ▪ (333) 222-1111
aquinn@earthlink.net

186

Operations Director. *Carol A. Altomare, Three Bridges, New Jersey*

This person with a strong record wanted to highlight his passion for teamwork. The third paragraph indicates this especially. A small font size presents much information with plenty of white space.

BETH SMITHEY

000 Reynolds Court   **Valrico, Florida 33594**   **(555) 555-5555**   bethsmithey@aol.com

April 9, 2004

Cargill Animal Nutrition
ATTN: Florida Position
P.O. BOX 8250
Montgomery, ALABAMA 36108

Dear Hiring Professional:

The Cargill Animal Nutrition management position you advertised recently accurately describes my skills and abilities. I am a professional with a strong track record of success who would love to join your company!

Your Needs	Examples of My Qualifications
Team Player	◆ Currently a case manager for a juvenile offender release program after completion of boot camp. Have to create a team environment with the juvenile, drill instructor, psychologists, teachers and parents to ensure post-release success. Our program has the highest success rate in Florida.
Adaptability	◆ Ran a retail store and performed any and all functions that had to be completed, from sales to administrative to customer service. ◆ Set up and ran a new branch of a company that provided auto financing. Had to adapt rules and procedures to accommodate car dealers and customer needs.
Communication Skills	◆ Have developed and given numerous presentations and classes to groups and organizations. ◆ In Human Resources position, gave new-employee orientations, completed and filed paperwork and answered employee questions.
Decision-making skills	◆ All my jobs have required exceptional decision-making ability: from developing case-management and release plans to running a store or managing human resource benefits for employees.
Manage multiple tasks simultaneously	◆ Currently supervise and oversee the cases of up to 30 juveniles who are in different phases of release, simultaneously managing their needs, program plans and paperwork. ◆ Background in Human Resources, where conflict management and multitasking were essential to successful performance.
Conflict-resolution skills	◆ As case manager for a youth offender program, am constantly resolving and mediating conflicts among the juveniles, their parents, the system, teachers and other authority figures.

My resume provides further details of my accomplishments. I look forward to discussing a new career opportunity with you. I will contact you next week to arrange a meeting to discuss your company's needs in greater detail.

Sincerely,

Beth Smithey

187

Case Manager. *Gail Frank, Tampa, Florida*

A poorly worded, "loose" want ad asked for a lot of generic skills. The applicant had little experience in the field. The writer played up the applicant's communication skills and team-player achievements.

William L. Peterson
0000 N.E. 22nd Avenue • Camas, Illinois 99999

555-555-5555 *cell*   bycdtv5213@eastystreet.com   *home* 555-555-5555

Winston & Collier Company
1111 NW Venture Highway
Camas, Illinois 99999

Dear Hiring Executive:

In response to your recent opening, I've taken the liberty of enclosing a copy of my résumé for your review. As you will note from my résumé, I have progressively accepted the business challenge, increased profits, and completed projects under budget and ahead of schedule.

I am highly committed to strong project management and not afraid of putting in the work to succeed regardless of the commitment. My work is highlighted by a unique ability to engage each member of our group in working together as a strong team, matching duties to skills and producing a winning team and outstanding projects. I have learned a lot about the "business world" from the athletic arena. I've discovered that a combination that will produce a successful finished project is one where we have strong analytical skills, a thorough understanding of the requirements involved, the development of a strong team, and the ability to work together efficiently. I thoroughly enjoy people, possess a well-developed sense of humor, and have a strong belief that you must enjoy what you do. I believe these concepts have greatly assisted in the successes I have achieved.

I would like the opportunity to meet with you personally to explore where your company's needs and my abilities may blend. It appears that your requirements and my skills may be a close match. Please call me at your earliest convenience to set a mutually convenient appointment. Thank you for taking the time to review my résumé, and I look forward to your call.

Sincerely,

William L. Peterson

Enclosure

188

Project Manager. *Rosie Bixel, Portland, Oregon*

The first paragraph does the letter's job of referring the reader to the resume. The middle paragraph sells the reader on the applicant, and the third expresses interest in an interview to explore a match.

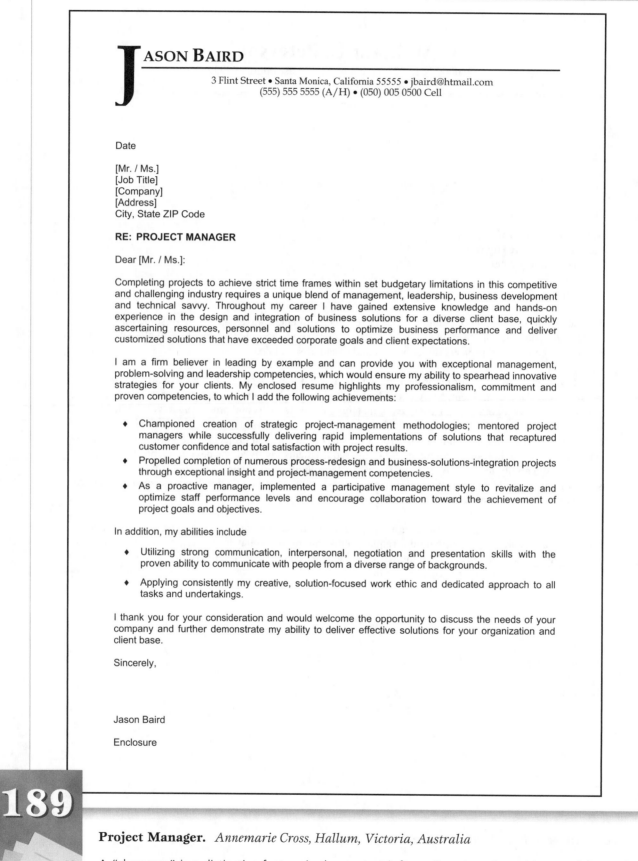

Jason Baird

3 Flint Street • Santa Monica, California 55555 • jbaird@htmail.com
(555) 555 5555 (A/H) • (050) 005 0500 Cell

Date

[Mr. / Ms.]
[Job Title]
[Company]
[Address]
City, State ZIP Code

RE: PROJECT MANAGER

Dear [Mr. / Ms.]:

Completing projects to achieve strict time frames within set budgetary limitations in this competitive and challenging industry requires a unique blend of management, leadership, business development and technical savvy. Throughout my career I have gained extensive knowledge and hands-on experience in the design and integration of business solutions for a diverse client base, quickly ascertaining resources, personnel and solutions to optimize business performance and deliver customized solutions that have exceeded corporate goals and client expectations.

I am a firm believer in leading by example and can provide you with exceptional management, problem-solving and leadership competencies, which would ensure my ability to spearhead innovative strategies for your clients. My enclosed resume highlights my professionalism, commitment and proven competencies, to which I add the following achievements:

- ♦ Championed creation of strategic project-management methodologies; mentored project managers while successfully delivering rapid implementations of solutions that recaptured customer confidence and total satisfaction with project results.
- ♦ Propelled completion of numerous process-redesign and business-solutions-integration projects through exceptional insight and project-management competencies.
- ♦ As a proactive manager, implemented a participative management style to revitalize and optimize staff performance levels and encourage collaboration toward the achievement of project goals and objectives.

In addition, my abilities include

- ♦ Utilizing strong communication, interpersonal, negotiation and presentation skills with the proven ability to communicate with people from a diverse range of backgrounds.

- ♦ Applying consistently my creative, solution-focused work ethic and dedicated approach to all tasks and undertakings.

I thank you for your consideration and would welcome the opportunity to discuss the needs of your company and further demonstrate my ability to deliver effective solutions for your organization and client base.

Sincerely,

Jason Baird

Enclosure

189

Project Manager. *Annemarie Cross, Hallum, Victoria, Australia*

A "drop cap" is a distinctive feature in the contact information, together with a partial horizontal line that extends to the right margin. The RE line in boldfacing makes it easy to spot the targeted position.

BART SAVARD

April 10, 2004

Expertise Technology Consultants
ATT: V.P. of Development
565 West Highlands Street
Chicago, IL 60605

Dear Hiring Professional:

In response to your search for a strong technical team member, I bring more than 15 years of experience at IBM. As a Senior Development Manager, I provided the technical, planning and operational management on several key projects for the company. Developing and launching complex computer systems is my expertise.

I am an extremely creative and innovative leader who is always looking for new ways to approach a project. Many of my achievements are due to my ability to create and maintain rapport with individuals—peers, subordinates and management. These qualities, coupled with a drive to think strategically and excellent technical ability, have given me a track record of success. Some areas I can help you with include the following:

- Project management: setting objectives, critical path planning and allocation of resources
- Planning and coordinating test strategies and release analysis
- Problem resolution and creative solutions
- Hiring, interviewing and training
- Budget development, administration and tracking
- Creation and presentations to management regarding project status

I am eager to relocate to your city within the next year and plan to be in town next month interviewing for positions at several companies. I would love to meet with you then and discuss your company's needs and my relevant experience in greater detail. Please call or email me if you would like to meet.

Sincerely,

Bart Savard

Enclosure

555 Benoit Circle   **Rochester, MN 55901**   **555-555-5555**   **savard55@yahoo.com**

190

Senior Development Manager. *Gail Frank, Tampa, Florida*

This technical applicant's three-page resume listed his many accomplishments. The letter is purposely nontechnical to emphasize the areas in which he can help a future company at a new location.

Kevin Kennedy

0000 Sierra Mar Drive	Residence: (555) 555-5555
San Jose, CA 95118	Office: (000) 000-0000
www.svcrojects.com	kennedy1@msn.com

Date

Hiring Agent Name
Title
Company Name
Address
City, State ZIP

Dear Mr. / Ms. _____:

As a motivated, highly experienced management professional with a strong background in project management, supply management, and product marketing, I believe my skills and talents can make an immediate and long-term contribution to the overall profitability and success of (name of company).

During the past 14 years, I have held positions of progressive responsibility at a variety of fast-paced information technology companies in multilocation, multistate, and international locations. I am skilled at providing companies with profitable project solutions, bringing new products to market, and developing business and marketing plans.

With outstanding leadership skills and an extensive management background, I am known for my unique ability to coordinate large teams of professionals and multimillion-dollar budgets and projects with proven results. My professional credentials include an M.B.A. in Marketing, a Bachelor of Arts degree in Economics, and a Project Management Certificate from the University of California at Berkeley. I am a dependable, results-oriented team player capable of working with professionals at all levels. My demonstrated ability to generate new business and manage large-scale projects will be a significant asset to your team.

The accompanying résumé provides further details of my accomplishments and what I have to offer. I believe it would be mutually beneficial for us to discuss your company goals and how I can help you achieve them. I will call next week to inquire about such a meeting.

Thank you for your time and consideration.

Sincerely,

Kevin Kennedy

Enc. résumé

191

Project Manager. *John Femia, Altamont, New York*

The applicant's skills are mentioned in each of the first three paragraphs, which indicate also in turn his background, past positions, and credentials. The fourth paragraph shows interest in an interview.

CLYDE T. PHELPS

0000 SE Melrose Drive
Lake Oswego, OR 55555
(000) 000-0000
ctphelps@msn.com

April 10, 2004

Mr. David Lawson
Operations Manager
Turner Construction Company
563 NW Pettygrove Street
Portland, OR 55555

Dear Mr. Lawson:

Could your company use a results-oriented problem solver with a thirst for new challenges? As a seasoned **Construction Project Manager/Owner's Representative** experienced in successfully completing diverse commercial construction projects ranging in value from $250K to $40 million, I bring

- 10+ years of experience managing successful projects from initiation to completion
- a B.S. in Architecture
- strong commitment to customer service and quality in everything I do
- exceptional skills in fostering team rapport through direct communication
- proven ability to develop, monitor, and meet construction deadlines, finishing at or under budget

Here's a sampling of some of my successes:

- Completed construction of $8.5 million hotel project three weeks ahead of schedule and $250K under budget, while exporting and replacing 50,000 cubic yards of contaminated soil.
- Maintained a nearly 100% within-budget and on-schedule success rate in completing construction of 12 fast-food restaurants within a 12-month period.
- Reduced time required creating punch lists by 50%. Created and facilitated efficient hotel-room construction inspection process.
- Decreased time required to track and expedite units to jobsite by 50% through development of unique estimating spreadsheet that categorized custom door and window unit types and prices.

Could you use someone like me on your team? If so, I look forward to discussing how my skills and experience could benefit your organization. I will follow up with you by phone in the next week and look forward to speaking with you soon.

Sincerely,

Clyde Phelps

Enclosure

192

Construction Project Manager. *Jennifer Rydell, Portland, Oregon*

The writer developed this "cold" inquiry letter for an applicant with strong experience and accomplishments. Bullets point first to an experience list and then to quantified accomplishments.

FRANK CREESHER

000 South Stewart Way · Sacramento, CA 99999 · (555) 555-5555 · fcreesher@aol.com

March 28, 2004

Thomas Lindsay
Projects Manager
Evinco Metus
1632 Artic Avenue
Sacramento, CA 99999

Dear Mr. Lindsay,

Leading construction management projects for high-growth companies within the microelectronics industry is my area of expertise. I am currently exploring opportunities where I can contribute significant experience in project management—hence, my interest in Evinco Metus.

As you will note on the enclosed résumé, the breadth of my expertise covers a wide area of responsibilities, thereby providing me with insights into the total operation. My experience includes microelectronics cleanroom facilities, hazardous occupancies, laboratories and workspaces to support integrated micro systems research and development, as well as production. Allow me to highlight several key projects of particular relevance to Evinco Metus:

- Project Manager for **Command Semiconductor project** (Manassas, VA) through Marrow Contractors, Inc.;
- Senior Project Manager for **Hysteria E-4 Wafer Fab project** (Eugene, OR) through M+W/Marrow joint venture;
- Pre-Construction Manager for **Miasma Technologies Fab 6 project** (Boise, ID) through Morose.

You will find me to be a dedicated project manager who leads by example and is accustomed to a fast-paced environment where deadlines are priority and handling multiple jobs simultaneously is the norm. I have more than 15 years of experience and throughout my career have built a reputation as an individual who takes charge and responsibility for planning and executing challenging projects and for being a talented and determined manager who accomplishes results.

I am confident that the mixture of my work experiences, along with my strong communication skills, would benefit your company. I welcome the opportunity to meet with you to explore how my expertise and talents could best meet the facilities and construction project needs of Evinco Metus.

I appreciate your time and consideration and look forward to speaking with you soon.

Sincerely,

Frank Creesher

Enclosure

193

Construction Project Manager. *Denette Jones, Boise, Idaho*

The applicant wanted to move from construction management to project management. Bullets and boldfacing highlight key projects relevant to the targeted company, which is mentioned three times.

Lynn Struck

0000 Eagle Drive
Sterling Heights, MI 48310

555-555-5555
lynnst@network.net

April 12, 2004

DaimlerChrysler
Employment Division
1000 Chrysler Drive
Auburn Hills, MI 48326

I am contacting you to apply for a production position with Daimler-Chrysler. I have eight years of valuable production experience. My husband, Adam Struck, is a current DaimlerChrysler employee at Warren Assembly. He suggested I send my resume for consideration.

My first production position was with Plastics Research in its Brighton, Michigan, plant. I learned a lot about assembling parts and operating machinery. Since 1998 I have held a seasonal position with Conrad Foods on a packaging line. To say that I'm a hard worker is an understatement. For example, my first summer on the job I packed an average of 3,000–4,000 jars a day (the standard is about 1,200 jars/day). Because of my performance, the next year I was promoted to Crew Leader, the only seasonal employee to hold that position. I get along well with my coworkers and am constantly on the lookout for ways to improve my performance.

I really enjoy the fast-paced production environment, and it would be great to work for DaimlerChrysler. Once you've read my material, I hope you will forward my resume to the specific units that need production workers. I am available anytime for an interview. Thank you for your time and consideration.

Sincerely,

Lynn Struck

Enclosure

194

Automotive Production Position. *Janet Beckstrom, Flint, Michigan*

The applicant wanted a production position in an automotive plant. She mentioned her husband's name because the company offers hiring preference to those recommended by current employees.

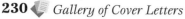

SHANNON HEWLETT

| 0000 Fourth Street | New York, NY 10012 | 555.555.5555 | SHewlett@hotmail.com |

April 3, 2004

Mr. John Wyle
Director of Human Resources
Broadcasting Company USA
30 Madison Avenue
New York, NY 10017

Dear Mr. Wyle:

As an experienced Associate Producer with a steadfast career that reflects several years in responsible positions for major clients across new media production, including HBO and Hewlett Packard, I am enthusiastic about my decision to move my career in the direction of broadcasting.

I bring an accomplished background that encapsulates my ability to conceive, create, and manage the production of independent and high-profile projects with a sense of purpose and a record of achievement. As a renaissance professional who continues to push the envelope of creativity while meeting the demands of workflow and people-management requirements, I continue to prove my ability to cut through red tape and confusion by providing clarity and direction with a demonstrated combination of intellect, artistic talent, and business savvy.

Whether working on proposals, negotiating with vendors, consulting clients, or traveling cross-country to conduct large group training seminars, I deliver results and secure the respect of senior management based on my high performance level. Through hands-on leadership of cross-functional teams, I maintain a cohesive synergy between clients and production teams from point of planning to market launch of multimillion-dollar projects. My ability to work in the present and anticipate what's ahead continuously ensures that deadlines are met on time and within budget with superior results. It is with your organization that I hope to continue in this vein while taking on new challenges in the field of broadcasting.

If, on reviewing my accompanying résumé, you feel there is a mutual interest, I would welcome the chance to meet with you to discuss the possibility of my joining your production team as Associate Producer. Thank you for your time. I look forward to speaking with you soon.

Sincerely,

Shannon Hewlett

195

Associate Producer, Broadcasting. *Ann Baehr, Brentwood, New York*

The applicant sought to move as Associate Producer from one career (in media production) to another (broadcasting). The letter refers to the many areas in which her experience is relevant to the new field.

Jeremy N. Fisher
0000 North Street
Evanston, Illinois 00000
(000) 111-2222

Coming Soon to Your City ...
The Answer to Your Production
Needs!

Dear General Manager or Production Manager:

Once in a great while, genuine talent and experience shows up at your doorstep. Someone with the engineering expertise, technical versatility, and production know-how to get the job done *right* the first time. Someone you can rely on to deliver quality work. Someone you can rely on for creative input. Heck, just someone you can *rely on!*

Well, that's me, Jeremy N. Fisher.

I've been in the broadcast industry for quite some time and am certified in Television Production from the Center for Media Arts in New York. I've come a long way since my studies in production and communications, having worked as a master control operator, producer, director, editor, and cameraman for television and radio stations and corporate/governmental video production departments. As you will see on the attached résumé, my career has been diverse, yet held together by that connecting strand called production. I love television production and it shows—as does my appreciation for the people with whom I work. Even with the pressures and strict deadlines of the business, I have always maintained my poise, sense of humor, and good rapport with associates.

I truly believe that I can bring some answers to your station's production needs and would like to discuss this with you in person. Like a summer movie release, I will be "appearing in your city" on August 8th, 9th, and 10th and would appreciate the opportunity to meet with you then. I will contact you in a few days to schedule a convenient time.

Thanks for your consideration and your confidentiality in this matter.

Sincerely,

Jeremy N. Fisher

Résumé enclosed

196

Television Producer. *Sally Altman, Tulsa, Oklahoma*

The filled, shadowed box is a strong bid to make this letter stand out from the competition. The centered sentence that repeats the applicant's name is another bid to make this person distinctive.

Jillian K. Young

000 Hawkeye Court   Iowa City, IA 52242   *jcyoung@network.net*
                                                          555-555-7777

Date

Name
Company
Address

Dear Hiring Manager:

How many times do resumes cross your desk from individuals who have extensive warehouse experience *plus* mail-handling experience? I imagine not a lot. So I hope you will review my material and consider my interest in an appropriate position with your organization.

I gained the bulk of my experience during seven years of service in the military, much of which was as a Supply/Warehouse Manager. Not only did I keep track of 10,000 parts in a 10,000-square-foot depot, but I also coordinated repair requests for equipment and vehicles, processing about 300 work orders per day. Additionally, I have been trained in hazardous materials handling, manual and computerized inventory control, and overall warehouse management. Since I left the military in 1999, I have been a Mail Carrier. One of my periodic assignments is to reduce the accumulation of mail that has been designated *nondeliverable*. It takes research and perseverance, but eventually I whittle down the pile.

My experience in the military cultivated a strong work ethic and helped me develop many personal skills, not the least of which are organization and communication. In fact, my superior officer commended me for my efficient and accurate methods. I have no problems delegating and supervising others.

I will soon be joining my husband in our new home in Cedar Rapids, and I am eager to begin working in the area. If you believe my skills match your needs, I would appreciate a telephone call to discuss employment opportunities. Of course I can make arrangements to be available for an in-person interview as well. Thank you for your time and consideration.

Sincerely,

Jillian K. Young

Enclosure

197

Warehouse Manager. *Janet Beckstrom, Flint, Michigan*

The applicant had warehousing experience in the Army and worked for the U.S. Postal Service. She could not transfer to a Post Office in her area, so she sought a warehouse management position.

PATRICK M. FINLEY

21 Madison Avenue
New York, NY 10000
Phone: 555-555-5555
Finley1243@msn.com

March 22, 2004

Attention: Mr. Green
ABC Company
15 Green Street
New York, NY 10011

Dear Mr. Green:

Managing and motivating large groups of personnel under high-pressure circumstances while maintaining 100% accuracy is what I do best. I have coordinated and directed groups in excess of 5,000 during complex operations with responsibility for multimillion-dollar equipment, and have consistently received commendation from superiors for outstanding performance.

I chose not to reenlist after 10 successful years with the United States Marine Corps in favor of a civilian career. I am seeking the opportunity to transition my experience into a corporate organization where I can continue to plan, strategize, and direct projects.

The energy, professionalism, and discipline I will bring to ABC Company, paired with my responsiveness to ever-changing business conditions, will streamline operations, improve morale, and ensure continued success. This will positively impact your company's productivity and bottom line.

Although my resume is detailed, it cannot convey the full level of my team-mentality and communication skills. My desire to intensively interact with others has sharpened my ability to quickly build rapport and gain trust from superiors and subordinates. You will find that I am a fast learner who knows both how to give and how to take direction.

I would welcome the opportunity to meet with you to discuss your challenges and my qualifications. I will call in a few days to arrange a time that is convenient for you. In the meantime, if you need more information, please feel free to call me at 555-555-5555.

Sincerely,

Patrick M. Finley

Enclosure

198

Corporate Manager. *Ilona Vanderwoude, Riverdale, New York*

After 10 years in the Marine Corps, this individual wanted to transition to a corporate position. The first paragraph indicates what he did; the third suggests what he might do for the company.

Deputy Director Resource Development

Timothy Cavanaugh
0000 Muroc Drive Burleson Air Force Base, Texas 00000
✉ 000.000.0000 (Office) — 000.555.5555 (Home) — 999.0000 (DSN)
tim.cavanaugh@burleson.af.mil

Monday, 12 July, 2004

Colonel Jordan Cliff
Director of Staff
Headquarters Resource Command
1100 Operations Drive
Burleson Air Force Base, Texas 00000-0000

Dear Colonel Cliff:

Just as you suggested, I have nominated myself for the upcoming GS-14 position that will convert the Deputy DS to a civilian slot. But as I focused on filling out the required AFPC Résumé Writer, I became convinced that you deserved a great deal more than just data constrained by character limits of that online form. This package is the result.

Because the next deputy will likely have long-lasting impact on Resource Command, it seemed that two vital pieces of information had to be documented. As a baseline, I had to show my understanding of the kinds of problems I'll be asked to solve. And supporting that baseline had to be vivid examples of my ability to solve similar problems very well.

For the baseline to be valuable, I went beyond the usual consideration of traits or staff skills. I focused on capabilities I must provide to make enduring contributions to the RC mission. You'll find nine of them right at the top of my résumé. For proof of capabilities, I had to go beyond just summarizing past problems solved. And so I selected 16 contributions to my organizations that illustrated those capabilities in action.

However, there is some vital information no format, no matter how tailored, can provide. As you read, I hope this central idea stands out clearly: All my efforts are aimed at maximizing long-term returns on every resource investment RC and the Air Force make. I want every tasking, every initiative, to be an opportunity to motivate, lead, and educate others to that same point of view. For me, that vision stands behind every duty, every standard, every KSA, and every classification criterion that might appear in the job announcement.

It's difficult for me to be distracted from the daily business of Resource Command, particularly when that distraction requires me to focus on myself. Therefore, if I have overlooked any information you need, I know you will not hesitate to call on me.

V/R,

Timothy Cavanaugh, Colonel, USAF

Atch: Résumé

199

Deputy Director, Resource Development. *Don Orlando, Montgomery, Alabama*

This retiring senior Air Force officer wanted to stay on in his position as his own civilian replacement. Some Air Force jargon is evident in the letter. For example, "V/R" means "Very respectfully."

SAM SAFETY

1234 Toxic Drive • Anyton, Ontario L9T 5K9
ssafety@net.ca • 999.999.9999 • 999.999.9999

May 1, 2004

Name, Title
Company Name
Address
City, State ZIP

Dear Hiring Executive:

Having worked for 15 years in chemical engineering for the power metallurgy industry before beginning coursework for my forthcoming Certificate in Occupational Health and Safety, I have both the theoretical knowledge and practical, hands-on experience in loss prevention and control in industrial settings to qualify for a challenging position as an **Occupational Health & Safety Professional** in your organization.

Offering outstanding team and project-management skills and a strong operations background in hazardous chemicals environments and training of technical emergency response crews, I am ever flexible and accepting of increased responsibilities. My work has enabled me to develop expertise in a broad range of industrial applications, including chemical processing, machine tooling, fabrication, hazardous material handling, manufacturing, building controls, and laboratory setup and experimentation. In addition to my full-time job as a research technologist, I have devoted my spare time to serve as an instructor for rural volunteer fire departments in techniques for environmental emergency response. Among the highlights of my work are the following:

♦ Lessening handling risks for a dangerous industrial gas by configuring available technology to provide a means of evaluating levels of concentration.
♦ Co-managing a respiratory-protection program for a chemicals research department and facilitating the formation of a chemical-spill response team.
♦ Leading project teams to develop new products and processes, including environmental health and safety procedures.

I would appreciate the opportunity to discuss how I may be of service to your company. In the interim, I appreciate the time you have spent reviewing this letter and the accompanying resume.

Sincerely,

Sam Safety

Enclosure

200

Occupational Health and Safety Professional. *Cathy Childs, Grand Island, Florida*

The applicant had 15 years of industrial experience and was receiving a Certificate in Occupational Health and Safety. The middle paragraph and bulleted items indicate his skills and areas of expertise.

GWEN LARSEN

January 14, 2004

Hiring Agent, Title
Company Name
Address

Dear Hiring Manager:

Your posting for a [position title] caught my attention as it seems an ideal match for my experience and talents. As a capable industrial health and safety professional with a solid technical background and a wide range of experience, I believe I am someone who will be an asset to your company. With a proven ability to implement health and safety initiatives that get results, I would like to explore the possibility of putting my skills and experience to work for you.

As you can see from my enclosed résumé, I have nearly three years of industrial health and safety experience. Currently working as a Health and Safety Consultant for an insurance company specializing in Workers' Compensation, I am mainly responsible for auditing client work sites to evaluate health and safety risk. Working throughout the metropolitan New York region, I have audited various facilities and have developed a keen eye for safety infractions and improvement opportunities. Prior to that, I was safety coordinator for a metal-recycling company, leading all safety efforts at one of their export facilities. Implementing new training programs, introducing a "Return to Work" program, and developing positive relationships with staff at all levels, I successfully put renewed focus on safety. In my two and a half years in that position, on-the-job injuries were reduced by 30%.

My success in these positions is defined by my dedication, team approach, and strong interpersonal skills. Skilled at identifying problem areas and recommending remedial action, I am also adept at building the individual commitment necessary to make a safety program successful. An acknowledged leader with excellent communications skills, I have proven to be a respected and valued resource. With a record of success behind me, I am confident that I will be an asset to you as well.

I would be pleased to have the opportunity to discuss future employment and look forward to speaking with you. Feel free to contact me at the address and phone number listed below.

Thank you for your consideration.

Sincerely,

Gwen Larsen

Enclosure

45 CONSTITUTION AVENUE ◆ RIVER VIEW, CONNECTICUT 22222 ◆ (222) 999-9999
GWENLARSEN@MSN.COM

201

Industrial Health and Safety Professional. *Carol A. Altomare, Three Bridges, New Jersey*

In this response to an ad, the applicant states her purpose in the opening paragraph. The middle paragraph indicates the breadth of her experience, and the third paragraph tells of her skills.

Patrick D. Wilder
11 Monroe Street, Salt Lake City, UT 55555
(555) 555-5555 home   patrickw@prodigy.net   (555) 555-5555 cell

March 25, 2004

Todd Hazeltine
Safety and Health Management
St. Jude's Hospital
16 Rock Lane
Salt Lake City, UT 55555

Dear Mr. Hazeltine:

The purpose of this letter is to introduce myself and then to meet with you about the opportunity for me to provide my expertise in managing safety and health programs to your organization. My confidential resume is enclosed for your review, and I am certain that you will find me very well qualified. Highlights of my resume include

- More than 20 years of experience in Occupational Health and Nursing
- Significant expertise working with OSHA regulations and regulatory compliance
- Ability to develop, conduct and oversee safety and health programs
- Effective communication, preparing technically sound reports, including recommendations for correction of hazards

My professional background, along with my sincere interest in helping others, has enhanced my desire to excel. As a highly motivated professional, I enjoy the challenge of complex, demanding projects.

I am available to meet with you to discuss my qualifications at your convenience and can be reached at either of the above telephone numbers. I would like to thank you in advance for your time and any consideration you may give me. I look forward to hearing from you.

Sincerely,

Patrick D. Wilder

Enclosure

202

Occupational Health and Safety Professional. *Denette Jones, Boise, Idaho*

Bullets point to resume highlights concerning the applicant's experience, areas of expertise, field-related skills, and communication skills. The rest of the letter shows his motivation and interest.

LISA ABRAHMS

14 South Houston Street • New York, NY 22222
(333) 333-3333 Home • (444) 444-4444 Fax • abrahms@earthlink.com

January 4, 2004

Hiring Agent, Title
Company Name
Address

Dear Hiring Manager:

Perhaps you are looking for someone who is energetic yet sophisticated, creative yet focused, and analytical yet great with people. I am a well rounded, multitalented individual and could be just the person you are looking for.

As you can see from my enclosed résumé, I have a wealth of experience in positions requiring both strong quantitative aptitude and top-notch interpersonal skills, and I have filled these roles with aplomb. Most recently, I have served as a financial assistant to a well-known movie actor, providing thorough oversight while winning trust and respect.

In the past, I have proven to be a creative problem solver with excellent analytical skills. I have built productive and enduring business relationships. In addition, I have demonstrated strong leadership and oversight skills. I have proven to be an asset to every organization in which I have worked, and I know I can do the same for you and your company.

I would be pleased to have the opportunity to discuss future employment with you and look forward to speaking with you. I will call to follow up, or you can reach me at the address and phone number listed above.

Thank you for your consideration.

Sincerely,

Lisa Abrahms

Enclosure

203

Personal Assistant. *Carol A. Altomare, Three Bridges, New Jersey*

This applicant was a very intelligent, talented individual without a clear career path. Each of the first three paragraphs indicates her exceptional merits, skills, and worker traits any employer would like.

Bethann Goodman

111 Lake Shore Drive
Cleveland, OH 99999
bgoodman@dotresume.com
555-555-5555

April 21, 2004

Ms. Jayne Atherton, Director
Personal and Domestic Services
279 Parkside Avenue
Doylestown, PA 99999

Dear Ms. Atherton:

I noted with interest your ad for a personal assistant in the April issue of *The Personal Caretaker.*

A nonsmoker whose children are grown, I have experience as a personal assistant and home caretaker. The duties of my current position include operating a household, maintaining gardens and a greenhouse, running errands, cooking, light housekeeping, serving as hostess, arranging transportation, and accompanying individuals and groups on outings and trips to medical appointments.

While attending to my duties, I always look for ways to improve service. For my current employer, I have made the following contributions:

- Increased income potential through development of a new management system.

- Restored an empty greenhouse and created new flower beds from scratch.

- Reorganized the household to operate more efficiently.

- Provided extra support to individuals in need.

A copy of my résumé is enclosed for your review. I would welcome the opportunity to discuss the personal assistant position or related positions in the Bucks County area for which I am qualified. You can reach me at 555-555-5555, where I am currently on a leave of absence.

Thank you for your consideration, and I look forward to hearing from you soon.

Sincerely,

Bethann Goodman

Enclosure

Personal Assistant. *Jan Holliday, Harleysville, Pennsylvania*

This letter is a response to an ad requesting a nonsmoker without children. After addressing these issues, the letter summarizes the applicant's duties and accomplishments in her current position.

ANGELA S. FAGAN
333 South Street ▪ Philadelphia, PA 19111
Home: (555) 999-3333 ▪ Mobile: (555) 444-1111 ▪ e-mail: afagan@aol.com

January 29, 2004

Ms. Rose Mayer, Director
Celebrity Associates, Inc.
44 Lake Road
Malvern, PA 19484

Dear Ms. Mayer:

I was excited to discover **fabjob.com** on the Internet. I've known for some time that a *9 to 5 job* wasn't the right fit for someone with my background and personality, and I would like to explore the possibility of becoming a Celebrity Personal Assistant.

The Guide certainly clarified the unique skills and expectations of a Celebrity Personal Assistant. Many of the qualifications mirrored my responsibilities as Entertainment/Promotions Coordinator for Harrah's Entertainment. On any given day, I had multiple balls in the air—from coordinating arrangements for celebrities (lodging, transportation, meals) to selecting costumes and overseeing myriad administrative duties associated with a popular entertainment site. I had an excellent reputation for putting out fires and **going the extra steps** to achieve success. Flexibility and the ability to remain calm were the key elements that allowed me to function effectively in such a high-pressure environment.

On an administrative level, I am very organized and meticulous. Careful follow-up is important when coordinating special events and projects, particularly when you are involved with senior-level executives and celebrities. Of course, it goes without saying that I am familiar with various technology and equipment, including a Palm Pilot, since my background has always involved administrative duties.

Wearing multiple "hats" keeps my daily calendar at maximum capacity, an environment in which I tend to flourish. Overall, I feel my organizational skills and my ability to handle different personalities with varying degrees of understanding and maintenance, regardless of the time element involved, would serve me well as a Celebrity Personal Assistant.

Would you allow me to formally introduce myself? I am very interested in expanding my professional horizons and eager to discuss a future association.

I can be available at your convenience with somewhat minimal notice. My employer is not aware I am contacting you, however, so I would appreciate your confidentiality. A complete resume is enclosed for your review.

Thank you in advance for your consideration.

Sincerely,

Angela S. Fagan

Enclosure

205

Celebrity Personal Assistant. *Karen Conway, Media, Pennsylvania*

Each paragraph conveys the applicant's enthusiasm toward becoming a Celebrity Personal Assistant. Her organizational skills, technological expertise, and evident maturity temper well her excitement.

Kathryn Tamburro

0000 66th Avenue North ◆ Frankfort, NY 00000 ◆ 555.555.5555

April 2, 2004

The Ritz-Carlton
3000 Central Florida Parkway
Orlando, FL 32837

Dear Employment Specialist:

I am writing to express my interest in the esthetician position that is posted on your Web site. I was very interested to see this opportunity as my background and qualifications match the requirements outlined in the posting. My goal is to relocate to the Orlando area and secure a position where I can utilize my esthetic training and sales experience.

As you will see from the enclosed résumé, I am a newly licensed esthetician (New York State). Since earning my certificate, I have been working in an upscale salon in Millbrook, NY—an affluent town outside New York City. Working in this salon has helped develop my business competency and enhanced my knowledge of service delivery for high-end clientele. In addition to my certification and licensure, I hold a bachelor's degree from Vassar College in Poughkeepsie, NY.

The value I bring to the Ritz-Carlton is not only a broad-based background, but a strong business sense and creative flair. More important, I know how to comport myself with high-profile clientele and understand the level of service required from clients seeking world-class spa treatment.

While my esthetic training emphasized specialized techniques and provided exposure to the most up-to-date methods (influenced by Manhattan's progressive market), I also gained valuable product sales experience through the school's operational storefront. Working in the store sharpened my sales, marketing and general business skills. It also contributed to my understanding of the financial impact of daily decisions as well as an awareness of the importance of maintaining positive customer relations.

I am confident that these qualifications will enable me to make immediate contributions toward your overall service goals. I would be happy to make myself available for a personal interview at any time. Thank you in advance for your time and attention. I look forward to hearing from you.

Sincerely,

Kathryn Tamburro

Enclosure

206

Esthetician. *Kristin M. Coleman, Poughkeepsie, New York*

A task of this letter is to show an upscale employer that the applicant is suitable for the employer's clientele. Every paragraph indicates that she is more than a match for high-profile clients.

Richard Chisholm

15 Clubhouse Drive
Stony Point, NE 00000

(000) 000-000
richpix@verizon.com

March 10, 2004

Mr. John Ambrose
News/Picture Assignment Editor
Seward Daily Journal
229 West Rugby Street
Seward, NE 00000

Dear Mr. Ambrose:

As a follow-up to our phone conversation, I am very interested in joining your photo department in a part-time photography position, eventually leading to full-time employment. As you review my resume, please note that I have thorough technical knowledge of shooting and editing as well as a creative personal style to envision and tell a story through the lens.

In the photo-intensive environment of a newsroom, I know the importance of teamwork and the ability to adapt to different formats. I am also accustomed to the pressures of constant deadlines and dealing with temperamental personalities. When problems arise, I remain calm, think clearly, and resolve the issues as quickly as possible. In addition, my flexible schedule will allow me to be available on holidays or at other times you may be shorthanded.

If you are seeking candidates who have a strong passion for photojournalism and subscribe to high NPPA standards, I would appreciate your consideration of my qualifications. I am confident that I can make a significant contribution to your photo department and look forward to discussing potential employment.

Sincerely,

Richard Chisholm

Encl. Resume

207

Photographer. *Melanie Noonan, West Paterson, New Jersey*

This applicant wanted to give the impression of being someone with creative talent. The writer chose a nonconventional font to convey the idea that his photographer had aesthetic taste and was flexible.

HAROLD VEETER
000 Tidewater Road
Springfield, MA 00000

(555) 555-5555

HARVT@home.com

February 4, 2004

Mr. Fred Jones
Director of Procurement
Technologies Corporation
3229 Polumba Drive
Springfield, MA 01087

Dear Mr. Jones:

During a recent conversation with Paul Browning, he suggested that I contact you about my interest in a procurement position in your department. Although you may not have an opening at this time, I would welcome the opportunity to learn more about your procurement function and industry.

As you may know from Paul, I recently sold my business and am enthusiastic about the prospect of new challenges. In anticipation of the business closure, I have taken the time to evaluate my career interests, skills and strengths to determine my options.

Procurement was one of my primary responsibilities and a function I enjoyed tremendously. As a result, I have decided to pursue a search in this field. Briefly, my qualifications include a bachelor's degree plus 10 years of experience in supplier/broker relations, cost-effective contract negotiations and managing a multimillion-dollar purchasing volume.

Well-organized with excellent communication and interpersonal skills, I am confident in my ability to add value to an organization. My conversation with Paul reaffirmed my interest in your company, and I look forward to meeting with you to explore the possibilities in relationship to your department's needs.

Sincerely,

Harold Veeter

208

Procurement Position. *Louise Garver, Enfield, Connecticut*

The individual wanted to make a career change and used this letter to obtain a networking meeting that ultimately led to a job offer. The purpose of networking is made clear in the first paragraph.

ELIZABETH GREEN

5555 Oak Tree Lane • Northridge, CA 55555
(555) 555-5555 • egreen@email.com

[Date]

[Name]
[Address]
[City, State ZIP]

Dear _____:

If you are seeking a motivated and detail-oriented Purchasing Professional with a proven ability to streamline operations, motivate teams and achieve significant cost savings in a multimillion-dollar environment, then my enclosed résumé should be of interest to you.

Common themes that have run throughout my professional career have been outstanding team-building and leadership strengths as well as my ability to see the "big picture"—integrating the purchasing function into corporate goals. Representative of my past accomplishments are the following:

- Directed $200 million purchasing unit for West Coast Entertainment Company…
- Hired, trained and motivated top-performing team members…
- Consistently identified and developed talent in others…
- Employed technology to streamline procedures, including automating the download of purchasing orders to the Letter of Credit system, improving on-time issuance from 20% to 75% within two years…
- Consolidated supplier base from 1,200 to 650 within one year…
- Sourced and developed excellent working relationships with outside and internal vendors…
- Participated in key negotiations…

I am currently seeking a new professional challenge where I can make a positive contribution to future goals and success. I possess a high level of energy and motivation, learn quickly, adapt well to new environments and enjoy challenges. I look forward to a personal meeting, at which time we can discuss your needs and my qualifications in detail. Please don't hesitate to call me at the above number to set up a meeting. Thank you in advance for your time and consideration.

Sincerely,

Elizabeth Green

Enclosure

209

Purchasing Professional. *Vivian VanLier, Los Angeles, California*

The middle paragraph with bulleted accomplishments is the key paragraph in this letter. Quantified representative achievements sell the reader on the superior worth of this candidate.

GARRY FUNG

1234 Augusta Crescent
Pinehurst, Ontario A1A 1A1

Phone: (555) 333-7777
Email: gfung@email.com

January 24, 2004

Joseph Neiman
Chief Technology Officer
Sandoz Investments
123 Young Boulevard, Suite 2305
Pinehurst, Ontario

Dear Mr. Neiman,

> ➢ **Is your organization fully prepared to safeguard its technology services, information, and facilities in the event of a disaster?**
> ➢ **Are you taking full advantage of high-value and cost-effective vendor agreements?**
> ➢ **Do you benefit from high team performance and low turnover?**

If you answered "No" to any of the above questions, then allow me to introduce myself and the expertise I can offer your organization. With a proven and award-winning track record of achievement, I offer a unique combination of expertise in disaster recovery/business continuity planning, vendor management/negotiations, and team leadership. I am currently offering my services to organizations within the Durham region and would like to draw your attention to the value I offer.

Put simply, my expertise is delivering results. In previous positions, I have designed, implemented, and optimized comprehensive enterprise-class disaster recovery and information security procedures, saved millions in vendor negotiations and third-party service agreements, and led a variety of cross-functional teams to consistently achieve and exceed organizational mandates.

If the following interests you, I invite you to review the attached résumé, which further illustrates my experience, achievements, and expertise:

- **Expert in Disaster Recovery, Information Security, and Business Continuity**—expertise includes planning, protection, and off-site recovery of technology services, databases, and facilities
- **Superior contract procurement, negotiation, and vendor-management capabilities**—proven record for negotiating agreements that improve service quality and save millions in vendor costs
- **Strong, decisive, and motivating leader**—reputation for building and leading high-performance teams to breakthrough achievement
- Available for **full-time, part-time, contract, and consulting opportunities**

If you believe that you could benefit from a highly motivated and talented professional with a reputation for generating results, I would welcome the opportunity to meet and discuss the specific value I can offer your organization.

I thank you for your consideration, and I look forward to speaking with you soon.

Sincerely,

Garry Fung
Enclosure: Résumé

210

Vendor Contract Negotiator. *Ross Macpherson, Whitby, Ontario, Canada*

This candidate offered a variety of expertise, so this broadcast letter opens with a few questions to get the reader thinking. The candidate landed five interviews and a lucrative contract in six weeks.

WALTER E. ELLIS
75 Clover Street
Rochester, New York 14610-4261
555-555-5555 (Home) / 000-000-0000 (Cellular)
walteree@rochester.rr.com

February 27, 2004

Mr. B. Thomas Golisano
President & CEO
Paychex, Inc.
911 Panorama Trail, South
Rochester, New York 14625

Dear Mr. Golisano:

Capitalizing on a career that encompasses broad-based experience in brand marketing, public relations, and customer relations, I am seeking an opportunity to apply these skills in a marketing communications position that will offer the potential for advancement based on performance. I believe that I possess knowledge and expertise that can be an asset to your firm and have, therefore, enclosed for your review a résumé that outlines my professional background.

Some key points that you may find relevant to a marketing communications role with your organization include the following:

- *Identifying target audiences and developing marketing messages that reach those audiences. In both business-to-business and consumer products settings, I have been successful in researching potential market segments and creating strategies that effectively communicate product features and promote brand awareness.*

- *Implementing innovative, technology-based approaches to marketing, including championing e-commerce initiatives that both augment product sales and afford opportunities to gather information about customers.*

- *Spearheading public relations efforts that coordinate with marketing strategies and advance overall business goals. These have included placement of features in both electronic and print media, participation in high-profile public events, and implementation of "strategic philanthropy" initiatives.*

- *Directing an array of brand management activities, which have encompassed graphic design, copy writing, and production of collaterals, point-of-sales materials, and product packaging.*

I am confident that my experience, education, and enthusiasm will allow me to make a meaningful contribution to your ongoing business success. I would enjoy meeting with you to discuss in detail how my capabilities can best serve your marketing communications needs. Please contact me to arrange a mutually convenient date and time when we might initiate a dialogue.

Thank you for your time and consideration. I look forward to speaking with you soon.

Sincerely,

Walter E. Ellis

Enclosure

211

Marketing Communications Position. *Arnold G. Boldt, Rochester, New York*

The applicant was transitioning from a marketing position with a small firm to a corporate setting. The challenge was to show that his marketing skills were transportable to a corporate environment.

Tina Nestavez

| 0000 W. Inman Ave | Tampa, FL 33609 | (555) 555-5555 | t.nestavez@juno.com |

March 20, 2004

Mr. Gary Frank
Director of Marketing
Nike, Inc.
One Nike Drive
Seattle, Washington 98744

We hope Tina joins our team!

Dear Mr. Frank:

"Just Do It." That is what I said to myself after hanging up the phone with my friend Jim Heald. He had just described his conversation with you—about needing a new public relations person in Brazil. I had to write after hearing your requirements! Jim said they are the following:

YOUR NEEDS	MY EXPERIENCE
Communicate in Portuguese and Spanish	✓ Fluent in reading, speaking and writing Portuguese, Spanish and English ✓ Translated an entire book from Portuguese to English ✓ Lived, worked and studied in Brazil
International Experience	✓ B.A. in International Relations ✓ Currently have 100% travel job with extensive foreign travel ✓ U.S. citizen who has lived in Brazil, Japan, Australia and Africa
Public Relations/Liaison/ Communications/Sports Experience	✓ Completed Sporting Goods Analysis on Brazil's economy for U.S. Department of Commerce ✓ Effective multiorganizational liaison as a relief worker in Africa ✓ Resolve ongoing public relations and communications challenges as the "flight attendant in charge," American Airlines

My enclosed résumé provides further details of my accomplishments and experience. I look forward to reviewing them with you. I will call you in a few days to see if we can meet next week and discuss how I can help you meet the goals for "Brasil futebol." I'm ready to go!

Sincerely,

Tina Nestavez

Enclosure

212

International Public Relations Position. *Gail Frank, Tampa, Florida*

This letter appeared in the first edition of this book. The applicant needed a letter that made her stand out. The check marks under Experience serve as a "YES!" for each qualification.

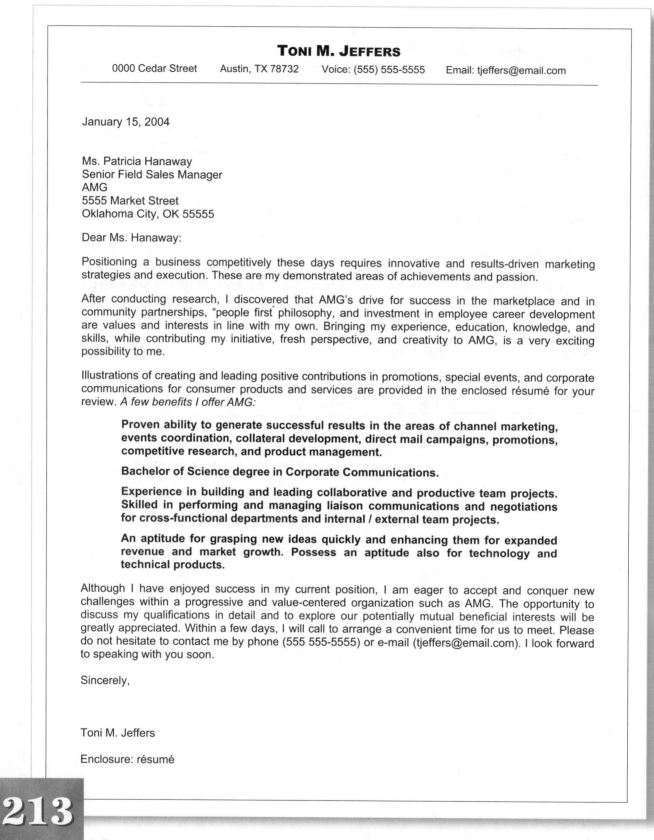

TONI M. JEFFERS

0000 Cedar Street   Austin, TX 78732   Voice: (555) 555-5555   Email: tjeffers@email.com

January 15, 2004

Ms. Patricia Hanaway
Senior Field Sales Manager
AMG
5555 Market Street
Oklahoma City, OK 55555

Dear Ms. Hanaway:

Positioning a business competitively these days requires innovative and results-driven marketing strategies and execution. These are my demonstrated areas of achievements and passion.

After conducting research, I discovered that AMG's drive for success in the marketplace and in community partnerships, "people first" philosophy, and investment in employee career development are values and interests in line with my own. Bringing my experience, education, knowledge, and skills, while contributing my initiative, fresh perspective, and creativity to AMG, is a very exciting possibility to me.

Illustrations of creating and leading positive contributions in promotions, special events, and corporate communications for consumer products and services are provided in the enclosed résumé for your review. *A few benefits I offer AMG:*

> **Proven ability to generate successful results in the areas of channel marketing, events coordination, collateral development, direct mail campaigns, promotions, competitive research, and product management.**
>
> **Bachelor of Science degree in Corporate Communications.**
>
> **Experience in building and leading collaborative and productive team projects. Skilled in performing and managing liaison communications and negotiations for cross-functional departments and internal / external team projects.**
>
> **An aptitude for grasping new ideas quickly and enhancing them for expanded revenue and market growth. Possess an aptitude also for technology and technical products.**

Although I have enjoyed success in my current position, I am eager to accept and conquer new challenges within a progressive and value-centered organization such as AMG. The opportunity to discuss my qualifications in detail and to explore our potentially mutual beneficial interests will be greatly appreciated. Within a few days, I will call to arrange a convenient time for us to meet. Please do not hesitate to contact me by phone (555 555-5555) or e-mail (tjeffers@email.com). I look forward to speaking with you soon.

Sincerely,

Toni M. Jeffers

Enclosure: résumé

213

Corporate Communications Position. *Karen D. Wrigley, Austin, Texas*

The applicant displays in this letter her knowledge of the company's corporate culture. She hints at her motivation for targeting the company without being negative toward her current employer.

Katherine Lacey Elliot

999 Kettlepond Circle
Salesbury, CO 22222

(000) 999-6666
Cell: (000) 999-9898
kathy5@earthlink.net

February 12, 2004

Susan Mary Anthony, Human Resources Manager
ABC Advertising Corporation
000 Weybosset Street, Suite 1000
Whitehead, CO 55555

Dear Ms. Anthony:

Your advertisement in the *Whitehead Sunday Globe,* February 11, 2004, for a copywriter to work in ABC's media relations department excited me, for this position would fulfill my ideal goal. Although a recent college graduate, I believe that my experience and academic training may be just what you are seeking in a candidate to fill this post. Please note that my enclosed résumé illuminates my practical field experiences in written communication.

As an English major at Newberg State College, with a concentration in writing, I have worked beyond traditional courses of study by planning and completing independent study projects that took place here and abroad. My cross-cultural studies in Ireland have given me not only a better understanding of education and business in Europe, but also a more global vision of the world marketplace and the tremendous influence that America exercises there. In addition, I would like to share my research article on psychology and the media.

Another independent-study project that has strengthened my base of preparedness for employment in communications was in journalism at *The Salesbury Citizen News.* You may be interested in looking over my portfolio of samples as evidence of substance and style in written communication. I believe that I have excelled in working independently to plan and execute programs on my campus radio show, although I learned that cooperating in teams often brought about stimulating ideas and results.

If you agree that my qualifications meet your standards for this position in the media department, please contact me to make an appointment for an interview at a time convenient to you. I can be reached at my telephone or cell phone, both equipped with voice mail. Thank you for considering my application; I look forward to meeting with you soon.

Sincerely,

Katherine Lacey Elliot

Enclosure: résumé

214

Copywriter, Advertising. *Edward Turilli, North Kingstown, Rhode Island*

This entry-level job seeker indicates her wide experience in communications and zeal to enter this field. Her time in Ireland points to her global awareness as an edge over traditional competitors.

Tim K. Petersen

0000 Groveland Avenue ♦ Kalamazoo, MI 49004 ♦ 555-555-2222 ♦ tkpetes@network.net

March 5, 2004

Mr. Roger Sanderson
National City Bank
3291 Westnedge Avenue S.
Kalamazoo, MI 49008

Dear Mr. Sanderson:

Marjorie McCarthy suggested I contact you regarding the Public Relations Manager and Communications Specialist positions that were recently posted on your Web site. When you have a chance to review the enclosed resume, you will see that I meet or exceed the qualifications for both positions.

You will notice that over the last 15+ years I have worn many hats. Because the organizations with which I was associated were small, I was responsible for everything from writing press releases to community outreach, grant writing to marketing, and fundraising to budget management. The common thread among these responsibilities: **communication.** Putting the organization's best foot forward was always the priority. I believe my accomplishments (described on my resume) reflect my ability.

My personal assets lend themselves to your positions. For example, you will find that I am

- Highly organized (I had to be to wear all those hats!)
- An accomplished writer (newsletters, marketing material, scripts)
- A strategic thinker (erased red ink and turned a significant profit in 3 years)
- Versatile (all those hats, remember?)

That's why I am confident I can become a successful team member of National City's Communications/Marketing Department. I hope you'll give me an opportunity to speak with you personally so I can elaborate on my qualifications and motivation. Please contact me at 555-555-2222 (or tkpetes@network.net) at your convenience. Thank you for your consideration and I'll look forward to hearing from you.

Sincerely,

Tim K. Petersen

Enclosure

215

Public Relations Manager/Communications Specialist. *Janet Beckstrom, Flint, Michigan*

The applicant was transitioning from work primarily in a nonprofit arena to work for a for-profit organization. The second paragraph displays a variety of experience from which he could draw.

Jonathan Crosswilt

0000 S.E. Mountain Road
Milwaukie, Oregon 99999

(555) 555-5555

January 28, 2004

Trailblazers, Inc.
555 NE MLK Blvd.
Portland, Oregon 99999

Dear Hiring Executive:

I appreciate this opportunity to apply for the position of *Executive Director of Communications* for the Blazers. Enclosed is a copy of my résumé, which shows that I have obtained outstanding experience in a variety of areas, including expertise in communications and public relations.

With more than 26 years of business experience, I have developed strong communication techniques and a unique ability to work effectively with the media. As a successful business owner, I have had the direct responsibility for planning and directing all aspects of the business, developing policies and procedures, and detailing strategic plans. I also have a strong background in promoting concepts while at the same time securing a strong position in the market. While working with Tim Owen's Autogroup, I was responsible for the organization and public relations relating to sponsored auto races at Portland International Raceways, including working with celebrity guests such as Paul Newman.

In working with various basketball teams over the years, I have had the privilege of developing teams from scratch, promoting the team concept to various school districts, and marketing the sport to the public. You will find me to be highly energetic, diplomatic, and results-oriented with a history of success that will support my achievements.

Needless to say, submitting a brief review on paper does not give you a complete picture of my abilities. I would very much like the opportunity to meet with you personally to detail more in depth the qualifications I can share with your organization. I believe that your requirements and my skills are a close match. I look forward to your call to set up an interview time. You can reach me at 555-555-5555.

Sincerely,

Jonathan Crosswilt

216

Executive Director of Communications. *Rosie Bixel, Portland, Oregon*

The opening paragraph indicates the targeted position and focuses the applicant's expertise. Experience is the topic of the second and third paragraphs. The fourth is an interview request.

Diane C. Cartwright

0000 Main Street
West Nyack, NY 00000

000.000.0000
dcc41@mydomain.com

April 20, 2004

Ms. Allison Campbell
The ACME Agency
151 West Third Street
Somerset, NJ 00000

Dear Ms. Campbell:

Creativity. Power. Results.

With more than ten years of experience in writing business-to-business and direct-mail copy, I have a diversified agency background that has exposed me to several different industries, including health care, financial services, insurance, medical, retail, real estate, and pharmaceuticals. As a seasoned professional, I have consistently created captivating and powerful copy that captures target-market attention and gets the desired results.

Looking for someone who can multitask?

Multitasking has become second nature for me. On average, I balance anywhere from 15 to 20 assignments at any given time. What's more, many of my assignments consist of multiple parts (letters, reply cards, brochures, etc.) and require not only creativity but refined editing skills to ensure that the copy is polished and sharp.

As you required, I have enclosed three representative samples from my portfolio along with my résumé. I am confident that, if chosen for this position, I will be able to take The ACME Agency's copy assignments and produce attention-grabbing results.

I welcome the opportunity to discuss with you The ACME Agency's objectives, and share how I believe I can contribute to the desired end results. Please contact me at (000) 000-0000 to arrange an appointment. I look forward to hearing from you.

Sincerely,

Diane C. Cartwright

Enclosures

217

Writer, Business Communications. *Patricia Traina-Duckers, Edison, New Jersey*

The line between this occupational group and the preceding one is a thin one. Besides writing ad copy, however, this applicant wrote different documents for different industries.

EILEEN ANDERSON

April 2, 2004

Name, Title
Company Name
Address

Dear Hiring Manager:

Perhaps you are looking for a development officer or grant proposal writer who can think critically and is able to develop compelling arguments. As a well-organized, detail-oriented educator and administrator, I believe I offer the right combination of skills to be just that person.

As you can see from my resume, I have more than 20 years of experience in education, including more than 13 years in administrative leadership roles, where I had the opportunity to write grants for the Los Alamos Board of Education. In addition to having excellent writing and communications skills, I have demonstrated an ability to effectively handle multiple tasks and keep them on track. I also have excellent relationship-building skills and a proven track record of working cooperatively with and getting results through others.

In the past, I have been able to combine my ability to think critically with strong administrative and organizational skills and a willingness to learn new things to contribute to a better organization. I would be most pleased to be considered for a position within your organization, as I know I could put these same skills to good use for you. I have enclosed my résumé for your review and look forward to hearing from you to discuss how I might be able to meet your needs. Please feel free to contact me at the number listed below.

Thank you for your consideration.

Sincerely,

Eileen Anderson

Enclosure

52 YORK ROAD • READING, NJ 11111
HOME (222) 222-2222 • FAX (333) 333-3333 • E-MAIL anderson@aol.com

218

Grant Proposal Writer. *Carol A. Altomare, Three Bridges, New Jersey*

This applicant had some grant-writing experience and now wanted to become a full-time grant writer. The second paragraph indicates the individual's experience and skills for the position.

CHARLENE C. JOHNSON

0000 Maplewood Drive
Silver Spring, MD 20904

Residence: (555) 555-1212
Business: (000) 555-5555

Email: CharleneJohnson@email.com

May 6, 2004

Ms. Debra Channing
Human Resources Manager
Vianet Technologies, LLC
13842 Leland Avenue, NW
Washington, DC 20015

Dear Ms. Channing:

I am writing in response to a job posting I found at www.dccomputerjobs.com for your Technical Publications Manager opening. As a professional in technical communications with more than 20 years of experience in writing and editing, including 9 years of managing a technical publications team at Avery Technology, I believe that I am a great candidate for this position.

What attracted me to Vianet was your astonishing success in the past four years as leaders in wireless and cellular technology. My experience in documenting wireless technology, as well as working with others to craft the customer documentation to support the latest cutting-edge features in wireless technology, would surely be an asset to your organization. My track record in management includes such accomplishments as the following:

- Managed annual budget of $120K to $250K for 12 years.
- Delivered $15K to $100K of training for major product launches.
- Created first departmental style guides that led to formatting standards that created a consistent corporate image for a family of publications and enhanced documentation usability.

I am excited about this opportunity to continue my career in management and confident that my abilities and expertise will make a fresh, welcome contribution to Vianet. I will call later this week to discuss when we can meet and go into detail about how my expertise can benefit your company.

Sincerely,

Charlene C. Johnson

Enclosure

219

Technical Publications Manager. *Daree Allen-Woodard, Upper Marlboro, Maryland*

This letter was a response to a job posted on the Web. The first two paragraphs indicate the applicant's background, and the bullets point to quantified relevant achievements.

Glen Stamos

**0000 Nightingale Lane
Yale, Arkansas 00000
(444) 333-2222**

Attn: Human Resources

I am an energetic, early-retired, gotta-find-something-to-do administrator who wants to put my experience and know-how of the real estate business to work for you. Having languished in several temporary jobs recently, I have found this planned, "temporary state of being" unsatisfactory. I'd really rather put my expertise to work full-time.

Not too long ago, I completed certification as a Real Property Administrator at City Community College, and while there, I also took a basic computer operations course. Several years earlier, I acquired my sales and broker's licenses and worked for a few real estate companies, but found the travel outside of Yale to be a bit much. The challenge of putting this licensure to work in a management or administrative capacity seems much more suitable to my tastes and talents. I love the business and enjoy meeting and talking with all kinds of people. I am a person who likes to plan, organize, and implement—a good formula, I think, for a position with your company. Having supervised and maintained three large facilities for an international petroleum firm, I am well qualified.

A personal interview at your convenience would be most appreciated. Please contact me at the above number or address. Thank you for your consideration and reply.

Sincerely,

Glen Stamos

Attachment

220

Real Property Administrator. *Sally Altman, Tulsa, Oklahoma*

The opening paragraph explains the applicant's reason for seeking full-time employment, and the second paragraph indicates his credentials, interests, skills, worker traits, and experience.

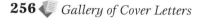

PHILLIP MILES PORTER, JR.
9 CINDYANNE PLACE
WESTPORT, MA 00000

(222) 555-6666   PORTERPM@PROPERTY.NET   CELL: (222) 555-7777

March 28, 2004

R. Bruce Billings, Human Resources Manager
Markham Management Corporation
287 Chadworth Street
Boston, MA 02222

Dear Mr. Billings:

Your advertised position for a property manager at a prestigious condominium development in Watertown, published in the Sunday *Boston Globe*, March 21, 2004, captured my immediate attention. I firmly believe, and hope you agree, that my long, embedded, and rich experience in residential and commercial property management meet the standards, drawn from your profile of the ideal candidate, to fill this position.

My background and foundation in real estate and property management are well documented in the enclosed résumé, which highlights my notable competence and wide experience in rentals, leasing practices, inspections, financing, maintenance, and budgeting. Having successfully managed and advertised rental properties for M.P. Valois Real Estate, Ltd., during the past five years has given me a solid footing in this field.

In addition, I am very familiar with all the Boston real estate developments over the past 17 years, having worked extensively with the J. Varnum Corporation as Project Manager for such impressive developments as Windham Heights and Patriot Towers. At the latter development, I leased 19,000 square feet of condominium space and capably negotiated leasing contracts to tenants for commercial space that totaled 40,000 feet at the concourse.

Mr. Billings, if you agree with me that my qualifications match your specific employment requirements for this position, I would appreciate an opportunity to meet with you or another representative to review my candidacy in more depth. I look forward to hearing from you and thank you for your consideration of my application for this employment opportunity.

Sincerely,

Phillip Miles Porter, Jr.

Enclosure: résumé

221

Condominium Property Manager. *Edward Turilli, North Kingstown, Rhode Island*

In this ad response, the first paragraph identifies the target position and begins to indicate the person's experience. The next two paragraphs elaborate on his experience and suitability for the job.

DAN FARRON

1111 Autumnbrook Drive
Houston, Texas 00000

home: 713.000.0000
name@aol.com

January 19, 2004

Mr. Jonathan Trammel, President
XYZ Corporation
3434 Main Street, Suite 100
Houston, TX 00000

Dear Mr. Trammel:

I noted your advertisement for a Vice President of Operations in *The Houston Chronicle* with a great deal of interest. Your candidate description and position requirements appear to be an excellent match with my background and qualifications.

As Senior Vice President of a diversified Texas real estate firm, I have more than 18 years of expertise in all property types and all facets of commercial real estate investments, including acquisitions, dispositions, development, management, renovation, reuse, finance, and asset management. Some of my skills and experiences that indicate the value I can bring to your company are the following:

- Handled more than 150 commercial transactions nationally, examining every angle and determining appropriate resolutions. I have been successful in acquiring and marketing underdeveloped or mismanaged properties and repositioning them into profitable real estate.
- Built extensive relationships, networks, and alliances with brokers, lenders, and third-party consultants, allowing me to obtain one of the most important value-driven components in real estate: information.
- Developed experience in commercial real estate and demonstrated ability to structure financial loans, venture equity, and troubled debt restructuring, as well as market commercial property.

With commercial foreclosures up, bankruptcies increasing, and long-term interest rates at a 40-year low, opportunity is "knocking at the door" again to recognize and take advantage of these significant market changes and acquire distressed or underperforming properties.

I believe that my experience and qualifications, along with my drive and enthusiasm, make me an excellent candidate for your opening. Perhaps we could arrange a meeting to discuss your current needs and the strategies I could contribute toward their fulfillment. Thank you, Mr. Trammel, for your time and consideration.

Sincerely,

Dan Farron

Enclosure

222

Vice President of Operations. *Daniel J. Dorotik, Jr., Lubbock, Texas*

The opening paragraph claims a match between the applicant and the advertised position. The next two paragraphs, together with the bulleted items, give evidence of expertise and achievements.

Melinda H. Jacobson

0000 Westwood Drive NE   Grand Rapids, MI 49505   555-555-4444

Date

Name
Company
Address
City, State ZIP

Dear Employment Director:

What does it take to be an excellent appraiser? Accuracy. Thoroughness. Attention to detail. Understanding of the process. I believe you will find that I have these assets and more. That's why I am contacting you—to learn about opportunities in commercial appraising, appraisal review, appraiser management or other related positions with your organization. My resume is enclosed for your review.

You will see that I have been appraising commercial properties for several years. I have found that my skills are particularly geared toward commercial lines in that I am very analytical and I understand how the process actually works. The challenges that commercial appraising present are also exciting.

The breadth of my experience is described on my resume. I have generated many complex files and appraised diverse properties, from vacant land to manufacturing plants and strip malls. In addition to my commercial and residential experience, I have been training appraisers and reviewing/releasing their work. This has presented its own challenges, which have solidified my knowledge of the field.

I sincerely hope you will agree that I have the potential to join your team as a great commercial appraiser. A personal interview would give me a chance to expand on my qualifications and give you an opportunity to see firsthand how motivated I am. I can be reached at 555-555-4444 to make arrangements. Thank you for your consideration.

Sincerely,

Melinda H. Jacobson

Enclosure

223

Commercial Appraiser. *Janet Beckstrom, Flint, Michigan*

The applicant's experience was mostly in residential appraising, but she wanted to transition to the more profitable realm of commercial appraising. The focus is on previous commercial experience.

James Wallbert

0000 S.E. Webber Court • Jacksonville, Texas 99999

222-333-4444 *cell*　　　　wallbert.james@jjj.com　　　　*home* 222-666-7777

March 3, 2004

HR Manager
1909 W. 32nd Avenue Suite 205
Jacksonville, TX 99999

In response to your recent advertisement in *The Republic*, I've enclosed a copy of my résumé for your review.

As you will note, I have had more than 12 years of experience in the coffee industry, with outstanding results in sales. I meet people well and am able to ascertain their needs quickly and fulfill their requirements in an above-average manner. Account management is an area where I have had outstanding success by increasing accounts, developing active accounts to a higher dollar volume, recapturing former accounts, and creating a strong repeat business with my customers.

I am enthusiastic, not afraid of hard work, and eager to meet new customers. I am confident you will find my skills to be an exact match to fill the position you have available. I would like to meet with you personally so that we can further discuss your needs and my abilities. You may contact me at the numbers listed above to set a mutually convenient appointment. Thank you for taking the time to review my résumé, and I look forward to your call.

Sincerely,

James Wallbert

Enclosure

224

Account Manager. *Rosie Bixel, Portland, Oregon*

When a hiring manager has too little time to read many letters, a short letter is more apt to be read than a long letter. This brief letter indicates experience, achievements, worker traits, and motivation.

Joseph Inaisa

000 E. Ogden Avenue
Naperville, Illinois 06060
jianisa@internetservice.com

000-555-5555—home
000-000-0000—mobile

February 25, 2004

Mr. Byron Davis
Human Resources Manager
General Motors Corporation
555 W. Milwaukee
Detroit, Michigan 08082

Dear Mr. Davis:

Having established a successful sales and marketing background in the automotive industry, I am currently pursuing a new, challenging fleet sales position with General Motors. Please review the enclosed resume, which provides an overview of my career history and accomplishments.

My experience includes assuming progressively more responsible sales positions through which I have successfully developed new business, retained and expanded existing territories, and built strong client relationships. My key strengths include prospecting, analyzing market trends, relating to clients, managing accounts, paying attention to detail, and closing deals. I employ a vigorous and persistent approach toward achieving corporate goals and expectations.

If you are seeking a highly qualified, energetic account manager with a proven track record of success, we should meet. I look forward to the opportunity to further discuss how I would quickly become a valued member of your sales and marketing team. Please contact me at 000-555-5555.

Thank you for your time and consideration.

Sincerely,

Joseph Inaisa

Enclosure

225

Account Manager. *Patricia Chapman, Naperville, Illinois*

This broadcast letter was for an automotive sales and marketing individual. The opening paragraph indicates his goal, and the second tells of his experience, success, skills, and strengths.

Eric Hamlin

0000 North Way ◆ Atlanta, GA 00000
Phone: (770) 000-0000 ◆ E-Mail: name@yahoo.com

January 30, 2004

Todd Worthington, Director
XYZ Company
1111 Stenson Avenue
Atlanta, GA 00000

Dear Mr. Worthington:

Perhaps you are in need of a dependable, skilled Account Director who can help you manage accounts and contribute to performance and revenue increases. Please allow me to explain briefly how my ability to manage operations, staff development, and client relationships can contribute to your organization.

Through my ten years of experience in sales, data, and project management, I have built a track record of increasing assets, revenues, and productivity for each of my employers. Some of my achievements include the following:

➢ Equifax: Awarded recognition by executive management for surpassing production goals.
➢ Prudential: Boosted number of assets by 30% within first year with firm.
➢ Progressive: Increased sales by 15% through strategic marketing plans.

Above all, I have demonstrated the ability to lead others both by example and direct instruction/mentoring. My teams maintain excellent performance and productivity gains, and I earned the respect and trust of numerous representatives and associates whom I trained and coached. You can be assured that I would add value to your operations as well through my leadership and staff-development initiatives.

I have enclosed my résumé to furnish you with additional details concerning my background and achievements, but I am certain that a personal interview would more fully reveal my strengths and what I have to offer your organization. Thank you for your time and consideration.

Sincerely,

Eric Hamlin

Enclosure

226

Account Director. *Daniel J. Dorotik, Jr., Lubbock, Texas*

In this broadcast probe for an unadvertised need, the letter indicates the individual's job goal, experience, and record. Bullets highlight achievements. The third paragraph stresses leadership.

MIKE A. STEVENS

(555) 555-5555 ❖ mstevens@email.com ❖ 255 Alimony Cove ❖ Austin, TX 78727

February 15, 2004

Mr. Jake Thomas
President
Thomas Manufacturing
815 Mopac Lane
Austin, TX 78888

Dear Mr. Thomas:

As a former NFL football player, I was continually challenged to overcome adversity. In fact, my career began with rejection from college recruiters because of my size and lack of speed. Through persistence and a lot of hard work, I was not only drafted into the professional leagues, but also achieved recognition as the fastest receiver for the Washington Redskins. I was able to accomplish this by setting my own objectives to overcome any obstacle preventing me from playing ball.

Tenacity, competitiveness, team contributing, and goal setting were crucial qualities that drove my successful professional football career. It is with confidence and determination that I have applied these same qualities to excel in **sales and account management** and achieve both personal and company success.

The attached résumé highlights my experience and proven ability to

❖ **Increase revenues by bringing in new key clients, with minimal ramp-up time.**

❖ **Manage all aspects of the sales cycle from leads generation to negotiation to delivery.**

❖ **Penetrate and sign major national accounts by using strong relationship-building and creative problem-solving skills.**

The opportunity to discuss with you personally how my demonstrated sales skills will contribute to the vision and success of Thomas Manufacturing will be greatly appreciated. I will contact you within the week to arrange for a convenient time to meet. I look forward to speaking with you soon.

Sincerely,

Mike A. Stevens

Enclosure: résumé

227

Account Manager. *Karen D. Wrigley, Austin, Texas*

The writer used the applicant's former NFL experience as an attention-getter before tying into his more relevant, yet limited, experience. Boldfacing and bullets direct the eye to important information.

STEWART M. WRIGHT

(555) 330-0000 ● swright@email.com ● 2555 Barton Creek Way ● Austin, TX 78735

March 4, 2004

Mr. James Monroe
Recruiter
AAA Recruitng
555 Jefferson Street, Suite 300
Dallas, TX 75555

Dear Mr. Monroe:

Are your clients seeking a ***talented consultative and technical sales professional*** with a solid track record of multimillion-dollar sales contributions? If so, you will want to review the enclosed résumé.

As my résumé indicates, my background demonstrates over seven years of achievments using field sales, marketing, and account-management skills in highly competitive markets. As a current Regional Sales Manager, my territory accountability is $25 million, and I am on target to exceed my personal sales quota of $13.5 million.

A few benefits I have to offer your clients:

- **Consistent history of exceeding multimillion-dollar sales quotas as both individual producer and leader of field sales teams.**

- **A competitive edge by using excellent interpersonal, relationship-building, and solution-sales skills for both internal and external customers.**

- **Understanding and comprehensive knowledge of technical services and products to gain a strategic sales advantage. Assimilate new market data and make significant sales contributions with minimal start-up time.**

Although I excel in my current position, I am interested in using my ***highly marketable sales and management skills, knowledge, and abilities*** in new areas of industry services and products.

The opportunity to provide you with more details of my qualifications would be greatly appreciated. I will call you on Wednesday, June 30th, to schedule a convenient time to meet.

Thank you for your consideration of our potentially beneficial relationship. I look forward to meeting with you soon.

Sincerely,

Stewart M. Wright

Enclosure: résumé

228

Account Manager. *Karen D. Wrigley, Austin, Texas*

This letter was sent to a recruiter. The letter shows how the applicant may be useful to the recruiter's clients. Boldfacing emphasizes the applicant's credentials as being "highly marketable."

DAVID MARCEL

February 24, 2004

Hiring Agent, Title
Company Name
Address

Dear Hiring Manager:

Your posting for a [position title] caught my attention as it seems an ideal match for my experience and talents. As a top-notch sales professional with a well-established record of accomplishment, I believe I am someone who can be an asset to your company. With proven expertise in the areas of new business development, client retention, and business expansion, and a passion for achieving goals, I would like to explore the possibility of putting my experience to work for you.

As you can see from my résumé, my background includes more than 11 years of experience in sales and account management. During my career, I have consistently performed at the highest levels and have been recognized for many achievements. In my current position as an account executive, I source and sell directory advertising to commercial clients. With $2 million in annual sales to my credit, my performance ranks in the top 5% statewide. My success in generating new business is striking and I have brought on many major new contracts. One of these, an advertising deal that has brought in more than $80,000 for two years running, stands as one of the largest sales in company history. In short, I am someone who has the know-how to drive sales and grow revenues.

Key to my success, I am able to build an easy rapport with prospective clients and am quick to identify their needs, positioning me to effectively market solutions that work. Persistent and detail-oriented, you will also find that I am also skilled at negotiating and closing deals. With thorough follow-through, I have earned the appreciation of satisfied clients who have rewarded me with repeat sales over the years. These skills and traits have served me well in the past, allowing me to make significant contributions to bottom-line revenues. With a solid record of accomplishment behind me, I am confident I can do the same for you.

I would enjoy the opportunity to discuss your needs and how I might be able to meet them. Please feel free to contact me at the address and phone number listed below to arrange a meeting. I look forward to hearing from you soon.

Thank you for your consideration.

Sincerely,

David Marcel

Enclosure

0000 WAVERLY COURT ▪ HILLSDALE, NJ 22222
(333) 333-3333 HOME ▪ (444) 444-4444 CELL ▪ dmarcel@aol.com

229

Account Manager. *Carol A. Altomare, Three Bridges, New Jersey*

Expertise, experience and achievements, worker traits and skills, interest in an interview, and thanks are the topics of this letter. A small font allows much information and still provides plenty of white space.

SHEILA BEST 555-555-5555

sheilabest@email.com
0000 Rabbit Road, Birmingham, AL 35210

January 21, 2004

Chairman, Search Committee
Birmingham Chamber of Commerce
106 N. Starline
Birmingham, AL 35210

Dear Chairman:

With strong family roots in Birmingham County and 10 years of broad-based Chamber experience, I feel my qualifications make me an ideal candidate for the president position with the Birmingham Chamber.

Born and raised in Mountain Brook and a graduate of Central High School, I know the Birmingham community very well. As Senior Vice President of the Mountain Brook Chamber of Commerce, I have full P&L responsibility for a $1.6 million budget encompassing production and sales, membership, and operations. While Vice President of Publications and Directory, I directed a staff of 11 in successfully meeting or exceeding annual financial objectives for five consecutive years.

My chamber experience includes…

➤ implementation of innovative programs and benefits to expand and retain membership;

➤ sales and production of the only chamber-produced directory in the United States;

➤ documented success in establishing long-term, mutually beneficial and profitable corporate liaisons and alliances; and

➤ the establishment of a network of contacts to maintain the strong community tie.

I would appreciate the opportunity to discuss in more detail how my experience might benefit the Birmingham Chamber and will give you a call early next week to make sure you have received my résumé and to answer any questions you may have. I look forward to speaking with you.

Sincerely,

Sheila Best

Enclosure

230

President, Chamber of Commerce. *Cindy Kraft, Valrico, Florida*

Knowledge of an area and promotional abilities are two key requirements for a chamber of commerce leader. The second paragraph and the bulleted items show the applicant's suitability.

Bob Madden
1645 Franklin Avenue
Phoenix, AZ 99999
(555) 555-5555

April 16, 2004

Frank Armstrong
Search Committee Chair
Sun Devil Athletic Association, Inc.
Arizona State University
1910 University Drive
Tempe, AZ 99999

Dear Mr. Armstrong,

I am writing to express my interest in the Assistant Director position with the Sun Devil Athletic Association, Incorporated. I offer a distinguished record of achievements in directing process improvements and designing action plans to achieve organizational goals.

Your organization has been highly recommended to me by Robert Franklin. He has appreciated your friendship over the years and has advised me to forward my résumé. I am accustomed to a fast-paced environment where deadlines are priority and handling multiple jobs simultaneously is the norm. I enjoy a challenge and work hard to attain my goals, and I believe that if I had the opportunity to interview with you, it would be apparent that my skills are far-reaching.

I believe the combination of my education and business experience offers me the unique opportunity to make a positive contribution to your organization. My skills and experience include the following:

- Extensive background in all areas of staff management, budget development, strategic planning, public relations, and marketing
- Excellent communication skills
- Demonstrated ability to approach management from a broad base of management experience in a number of areas, particularly the development and implementation of new programs
- Career experience complemented by a Bachelor's degree in Marketing

Although the accompanying résumé illustrates my strengths well, I am certain of my abilities to make a significant contribution early on and that a personal interview would better demonstrate how I could meet the needs of the Sun Devil Athletic Association. I look forward to the opportunity of discussing in person how my expertise could best fit your needs. In the interim, thank you for your consideration, attention, and forthcoming response.

Sincerely,

Bob Madden

Enclosure

231

Assistant Director, Athletic Association. *Denette Jones, Boise, Idaho*

The opening paragraph indicates the targeted position, and the second paragraph begins with a referral to build rapport with the reader. Bullets point to significant skills and experience.

DAVID SMITH
12000 Jefferson Avenue, Newport News, VA 23606
Home: 555-555-5555 ■ Mobile: 000-000-0000 ■ DSmith@leader.com

STRATEGIC MANAGER ■ SENIOR BUSINESS DEVELOPER ■ MARKETING TEAM LEADER

January 30, 2004

E. Ransom, CEO
Newport News Life
One Chesapeake Way
Newport News, VA 23606

Hello, my name is David Smith.

I specialize in bringing strategic vision, integrity, and energized team leadership to growth companies that are looking for high-impact results.

I've spent the past 20 years leading a wide range of growth organizations and projects. Now I'm looking for the next opportunity to join a committed, enthusiastic, and creative team environment that wants proven senior leaders and repeatable results.

If I work for your company, you can count on me to excel at driving new revenue sources and exceeding sales projections. My thorough understanding of direct marketing principles and consumer "hot buttons" will directly drive quantitative results. You will get a leader who wants the responsibility to develop passionate, motivated, and powerful teams that embrace change, while seeding the next generation of business leaders for your company. You can expect formalized programs in "new idea" creation and implementation, to ensure that business development is a dynamic, ongoing process. You will also gain an unmatched commitment to people, both inside your business and outside with your valuable customers.

My résumé is attached for your consideration. I would love to meet with you to discuss my fit with your company and any needs or goals that I can help you meet.

If you take the time to meet with me, I guarantee you will walk away from our meeting with at least one great idea for your business—whether or not we end up working together! I will call you next week to schedule a meeting.

Sincerely,

David Smith

Enclosure: Résumé

232

Senior Business Developer. *Helen Oliff, Reston, Virginia*

The target company wanted a match with its existing leadership team. The writer embedded a "vision statement" to demonstrate the applicant's leadership philosophy and management style.

CHRIS PRENTICE

000 Cranberry Street
Salt Lake City, UT 84117

Email: cprentice@hotmail.com

Mobile: (555) 555-5555
Residence: (000) 000-5511

5 February 2004

Mr. Fred Hall
Director of Sales & Marketing
TechIT Inc.
4024 South 2100 Street
Salt Lake City, UT 84117

Re: Senior Business Development Manager

Dear Mr. Hall:

As I read your advertisement, it becomes evident that the candidate you seek needs proficiency in many areas. A clear resolve for quality, revenue growth, and profits, coupled with continuous improvement and firm leadership, will be essential to ride the turbulence of the market as we enter these troubled times.

At the same time, consultation, communication, and teamwork will underpin trust, cooperation, and the development of a shared vision, so that your company's long-term growth can be achieved.

In short, the market today is not for the faint-hearted, yet the current crop of challenges to the IT industry are not insurmountable if an individual with my experience, capability, and tenacity takes on the role.

Commercially, I am the seasoned manager you seek. I have extensive national experience in introducing products to market and winning prominence against established competitors. I have built distribution networks, fought hard-won battles to win market share and brand acceptance, and demonstrated the type of maturity that can win consensus in the most highly charged of atmospheres.

Team-focused, I am a strong proponent of the power of people, believing in the "all hands on deck" philosophy to achieve common goals.

Fresh from my last assignment as the Director of New Business for a provider of information systems to the SME market, I have a renewed sense of confidence toward tackling new challenges.

Naturally, I would be delighted to meet with you to review your needs in detail, and I have enclosed a copy of my résumé to provide a basis for future discussions. I will call you in the next couple of days to see if our schedules can permit a brief meeting.

I look forward to speaking with you soon.

Sincerely,

Chris Prentice

233

Senior Business Development Manager. *Gayle Howard, Chirnside Park, Melbourne, Australia*

Eight short paragraphs quicken the reading tempo of this letter and make it seem shorter than it is. Five of the paragraphs are only one sentence. The impression is that this person does not waste time.

CONRAD JAMES

122 Pine Bluff Circle • Manlius, New York 13105 • 555-555-5555 • conniej@yahoo.com

March 26, 2004

Mr. Claude Closer
Vice President for Sales & Marketing
Sunshine Industries, Inc.
1234 Seminole Boulevard
Orlando, Florida 33333

Dear Mr. Closer:

Capitalizing on close to six years of experience in sales and management roles with customer-oriented organizations, I am seeking an opportunity in a corporate setting where my capabilities can further your business objectives, while offering career development opportunities. With this goal in mind, I have enclosed for your consideration a résumé outlining my experience.

Some key points you may find relevant to a sales, marketing, and/or management trainee role with your firm include

- *Selling capital equipment to business and government accounts, including developing long-term, consultative relationships with customers.*

- *Supporting sales operations by developing specifications, responding to competitive bid requests, and managing a variety of vendor-relations functions.*

- *Managing capital projects, including $500K and $750K renovations of restaurant facilities, as well as the assembly/fabrication of custom equipment for municipal highway departments.*

- *Providing leadership to groups of up to 24 customer service employees in retail and hospitality business environments, including recruiting and training team members.*

I am convinced that my skills can contribute to your ongoing business success, and that my professional development can significantly benefit from joining a leading organization such as yours. I would enjoy speaking with you in person about potential opportunities and ways that I can address your needs. I will be visiting Orlando the week of May 21st and would be pleased to meet with you during that time. Please contact me to arrange an initial interview.

Thank you for your time and consideration. I look forward to talking with you soon.

Sincerely,

Conrad James

Enclosure

234

Corporate Sales/Management Position. *Arnold G. Boldt, Rochester, New York*

This candidate had management experience in retailing and the hospitality industry. He wanted to transition to a corporate environment. The writer played up large capital projects and business sales.

THOMAS LEONE CORDEIRO
000 Eighth Avenue West
Manhattan, NY 77777
(000) 333-9999

February 6, 2004

Rodney Spurrier, Director of Human Resources
Avery Missile Design Systems, Inc.
000 Washington Highway, Suite 000
New London, CT 00000

Dear Mr. Spurrier:

I am writing to you in response to your need for a Sales Manager, as advertised in *The New York Times*, February 6, 2004. I fully believe my qualifications will meet or exceed your ideal candidate standards.

With 17 successful years of experience in business sales, management, and customer service to my credit, I welcome the opportunity to discuss my qualifications for this opening in sales management with Avery Missile Design Systems. My positions as sales manager and supervisor have shown positive results in vastly increased sales volumes through reorganizing and rebuilding of staff, instituting powerful incentive programs, and implementing improved marketing procedures.

Experienced in—and undaunted by—challenging work environments, I am capable of assuming concurrent tasking responsibilities while effectively managing a staff with $6M in annual sales volume. Additionally, during my seven years in customer service—the last five as supervisor—I have become adept at dealing with client concerns, resulting in higher sales figures and improved customer satisfaction.

My training, experience, and rapid learning curve in using computers and various applications are borne out in my employment environments during my entire career. My technical background includes positions in operations support, software technical services, software manufacturing, programming, and technical writing. I hope you agree with me that this knowledge strengthens my candidacy for any sales management position requiring fast-paced storage and retrieval of information.

I would appreciate your contacting me to make an appointment at your earliest convenience to review my qualifications for this position, or another for which you may find me suitable. If I do not hear from you by February 15, I will contact your office to request an appointment suitable to your schedule.

Thank you for your consideration of my application for the position of Sales Manager with your firm.

Sincerely,

Thomas Leone Cordeiro

Enclosure: résumé

235

Sales Manager. *Edward Turilli, North Kingstown, Rhode Island*

The applicant, in all paragraphs, confidently proves his strong experience in sales management. His intention to request an appointment if not contacted by a certain date shows his proactive manner.

KATHY CHISHOLM
555 Maynard Street, Providence, Rhode Island 01976, (555) 555-2645

SalesFinders, Inc.
453 Ashland Court, Suite 285
Providence, RI 01976

I am writing to you for help in locating a new job in sales. Your name was in a directory of recruiters.

Currently I am employed as an Assistant National Accounts Manager for Revlon Corporation. My account responsibility is for CVS Pharmacy drugstores, located in Woonsocket, RI. CVS is Revlon's #4 account.

I've been in Providence for almost five years now—and I love it! I want to stay in New England but want to work in an organization where I can better use my creativity and skills to build a top-notch sales department. I'd like to do that as a Regional Manager.

My experience is broad in all areas of sales. Through my development of promotional campaigns and business analysis, I also have marketing experience. People enjoy working with me because of my fun, outgoing personality.

My attached resume and summary sheet describe what I am seeking in my next career move. My current compensation is over $70K, with a base salary of $65K and a 10% bonus.

I would be happy to answer any questions or provide any clarification you may need. Thank you for your consideration as you review your clients' requests for new employees.

Sincerely,

Kathy Chisholm

Attachments

236

Regional Manager. *Gail Frank, Tampa, Florida*

Because this letter was sent to a sales recruiter, the writer used a cartoon and an informal font for the applicant's name to make the letter stand out from all the others recruiters get.

JOHN CORBIN
0000 Monroe Avenue
Cleveland, Ohio 00000
(555) 555-55555
corbin@cox.net

Dear _____:

Could I help you as a sales management executive or general manager?

I have created strong sales and marketing organizations, driving forward consistent revenue growth through the following areas of expertise:

strategic sales planning and management
team building, training and development
identifying and capitalizing on market opportunities
building and managing multichannel distribution networks
developing and managing key account relationships
consultative selling, negotiating and closing skills

At Harmon Company, I designed and implemented sales strategies that **generated a pipeline of more than $45 million** in the first 5 months of employment. At Technology Systems, I rebuilt a new sales team in just 4 months and **grew sales from $2.5 million to $7.5 million** in the first year. At the Benton Company, I delivered **38% cumulative sales growth** over a 3-year period and developed an effective multidistribution network producing more than 40% of overall revenue.

If you have the need, I am confident that I can accomplish profitable results for your company. Regarding salary requirements, I understand that flexibility is important in this market and am willing to discuss your organization's target salary range for an executive with my experience.

May we talk?

Sincerely,

John Corbin

237

Sales Executive/General Manager. *Louise Garver, Enfield, Connecticut*

This sales executive had lost his position in a merger, and this letter helped him gain multiple interviews that led to offers. Highlighting items with boldface, italic, and center-justification is effective.

ADAM JULIENE

123 Glen Street • Denver, CO 00000 • 555.555.5555 • adjul@msnaol.com

January 30, 2004

John Jones
Sales Manager
StorageTek Corporation
1 Tape Drive
Louisville, CO 00000

Dear Mr. Jones:

In today's intensely competitive marketplace, efficient and effective sales operations are critical to a company's success. The ultimate success of any sales operation requires a manager who can develop, implement, and optimize sales processes designed to achieve strategic corporate goals by enabling and empowering the sales teams.

My strengths lie in building quality processes that get the job done and building consensus within cross-functional teams. My track record as outlined in the enclosed résumé demonstrates that I can

- Streamline existing processes and design new processes aligned with corporate infrastructure and existing organizations.
- Build a shared vision and consensus between cross-functional organizations and vested parties.
- Develop business models, market and sales strategies, policies, and organizational structure.
- Clarify and strengthen the organization's core values and principles to facilitate growth, profitability, and employee performance and satisfaction.

I attribute my success to my ability to assume leadership and turn around underperforming organizations by developing/sharing best practices that increase quality, effectiveness, and productivity. Equally important is my talent for developing effective cross-functional relationships. You will find that I am very skilled at developing sound action plans, as well as administering and following through on those plans. I strive to build and maintain a principle-centered environment that preserves the company's core values while stimulating growth and profitability.

I am eager to make an immediate and enduring contribution to StorageTek. I welcome the opportunity to explore my potential contributions.

Thank you for your consideration; I look forward to speaking with you soon.

Sincerely,

Adam Juliene

Enclosure: Résumé

238

Sales Manager. *Roberta F. Gamza, Louisville, Colorado*

The applicant was pursuing an opportunity at a well-respected local employer but did not have any contacts in the organization. Bulleted abilities and a paragraph on skills make the person stand out.

TERRA A. CARR

0000 Tomahawk Road • Shawnee Mission, Kansas 66802
Residence: 555-555-5555 • Wireless: 000-000-0000
Email: terracarr@email.com

CONFIDENTIAL

Your confidentiality and consideration of the accompanying information is requested.

CAREER OVERVIEW

Building corporate value is my expertise… value measured in aggressive strategic marketing in existing and new market sectors. Whether challenged to launch the start-up of a new business unit or product or to introduce innovative marketing programs for repositioning or branding purposes, I have achieved results.

My strengths lie in my ability to conceive and implement the strategic marketing plans to identify new market opportunities, initiate product and service introductions, and negotiate strategic alliances to drive domestic and global market expansion and revenue/profit growth. My challenge has been to expand and strengthen market presence through the introduction of a diversified portfolio of new business development, advertising, and public relations initiatives. I have instilled a sense of entrepreneurial vision and creativity to drive forward innovative strategies to win competitive positioning and accelerated revenue growth.

Although enjoying my current position, *I am exploring opportunities as a senior marketing executive with a progressive organization active in international expansion* where I may continue to provide strong and decisive marketing leadership. I would welcome a personal interview to discuss how my qualifications would benefit your organization. Thank you for your consideration.

Cordially,

Terra A. Carr

Enclosure

239

Senior Marketing Executive. *Gina Taylor, Kansas City, Missouri*

This individual wanted to relocate to the West Coast. Italic draws attention to the centered heading and statement requesting confidentiality. Italic in the last paragraph makes the position evident.

PAUL D. LEWIS

555 Clare Street • Melville, New York 44444 • (333) 222-4444 • salespro@soldout.net

Date

Name
Company
Address

Dear Name:

     Success is broadly founded in hands-on leadership with a firm belief in performance ownership and accountability. With a career track in senior sales management positions with System-Tel, Virtual-Communication, and Global Wireless, my well-honed consultative sales style and drive to succeed have proven effective in building and sustaining C-level relationships and revenue gains across highly competitive vertical markets.

     Perhaps your organization is seeking to recruit a sales executive with these talents to develop and lead its sales organization to success in the face of emerging competition and uncertain economical climates. If this is the case, you will want to consider me as a viable candidate. But first, let me briefly highlight my 13-year sales career with the aforementioned leading organizations to give you a better idea of who I am and the value I would bring to the appropriate executive sales position.

- Over-quota Annual Sales Track Record with System-Tel

  | 2004 | **173%** | 2002 | **142%** | 1999 | **129%** | 1997 | **120%** |
  | 2003 | **166%** | 2001 | **135%** | 1998 | **131%** | 1996 | **133%** |

- Develop and execute sales solution strategies for mid-tier and large-scale corporations.
- Train, coach, mentor, and lead more than 30 top-gun sales professionals.
- Cultivate alliance relationships with industry partners.
- Conceptual, technical knowledge of enterprise-wide, technology-based software solutions.

I realize you must be inundated with résumés—some good, some not—and find it increasingly difficult to decide on top talent. As such, I strongly encourage a meeting—either in person or preliminarily by telephone following your review of my accompanying résumé, to discuss how I can contribute to the growth of your organization's bottom line.

Please note that my total compensation has been in the low six-figure range. However, I am open to a high-five compensation package that includes incentives or bonus opportunities. Thank you in advance for your time and consideration. I look forward to meeting with you soon.

     Sincerely,

     Paul D. Lewis

240

Sales Executive. *Ann Baehr, Brentwood, New York*

The applicant was a sales executive looking for a senior sales management position. His success at sales is a recurrent theme in the first two paragraphs. Boldfacing of percentages highlights growth.

ERIC J. MANSON
Cascade Towers, 0000 76 Avenue, Bloomington MN 55555
Cell / Voice Mail 555 555 5555 • Home 555 555 5555 • E-mail: ejmn@concord.net

February 2, 2004

Mr. Roberto Oltone
Telecommunications Department
Superior Networks
82 Jason Street
Kansas City, Missouri 55555

MARKETING AND SALES MANAGEMENT

Dear Mr. Oltone:

I am most interested in the position advertised recently in the *Sun-Times* and have accordingly attached a professional resume for your review.

With more than 20 years of executive-level experience in marketing electronics and communication equipment and service, I've negotiated numerous contracts; achieved solid revenue growth; and bought, sold, and merged companies. My major strengths fall into the following arenas:

- ❑ Marketing and Sales
- ❑ Business Development
- ❑ Finance
- ❑ Training and Development
- ❑ Management and Leadership

Personal skills enhance my expertise in marketing management. I am known for having tenacity, a tremendous work ethic, an aggressive solution-oriented focus, and a team-oriented manner. My aversion to micromanaging has generated loyalty from others, as has the ability to listen to suggestions and concerns of customers, managers, and staff. With an intuitive nature and vision for the future, problem solving and decision making come easy to me.

I will be calling your office to determine your interview schedule for this position, and look forward to discussing the company's needs and in what ways I might contribute to those plans. Please let me know if you need further information before then.

Sincerely,

Eric J. Manson

241

Marketing and Sales Manager. *Beverley Drake, Rochester, Minnesota*

In this response to a newspaper ad, shadowed square bullets point to major strengths. The third paragraph tells about the applicant's managerial abilities, people skills, and additional strengths.

Lisa A. Santos

555 Victoria Avenue
Augusta, Ontario A1A 1A1
lisasantos@email.com
Home: 555.666.9999
Cell: 555.999.7777

March 3, 2004

Terrance Flaherty, CEO
Consultronix
345 Pine Valley Road, Suite 4460
Augusta, Ontario
B2C 3D4

<u>Re: Director of Marketing</u>

Dear Mr. Flaherty,

I love a challenge!

Whether leading the marketing and promotional initiatives for the Canadian arm of one of the world's largest management consulting firms, spearheading the corporate development efforts of a $25 million fundraising campaign to fight polio, or coordinating high-profile executive luncheons and promotional events with the "who's who" of Canadian business, I approach each challenge with the same "get it done" attitude.

It is exactly this determination—combined with exceptional skills in marketing, promotions, business development, and executive relationship management—that has enabled my successes to date, and that in turn I can offer to your firm. From what I have read in the industry journals of your plans to enter new technology and telecom markets, you need someone who can step in now and create a singular market presence—and with the IT-Com Conference coming to Augusta this September, it needs to be done quickly.

In short, as my attached resume attests, here's what I can offer you:

- **Expertise in creating high corporate visibility and brand recognition**—proven ability to create the appropriate marketing vehicle or event, secure widespread media attention, and stimulate excitement around a product or service

- **A creative mind for promotional opportunities and marketing campaigns**—solid track record for conceiving and organizing high-profile executive luncheons, industry roundtables, and special events

- **Exceptional market research and analysis skills**—critical for appropriate market segmentation and targeted marketing/promotional campaigns

- **Strong project management and leadership capabilities**—organized, focused, and able to pull teams together around a common goal

Please feel free to contact me at your earliest convenience to arrange a personal meeting, and I would be glad to discuss why I'm the person for the job. I already have a number of ideas that should interest you.

I thank you for your consideration and look forward to speaking with you soon.

Sincerely,

Lisa A. Santos

Encl. Résumé

242

Director of Marketing. *Ross Macpherson, Whitby, Ontario, Canada*

The unique first paragraph grabs the reader's attention. Bullets and boldfacing highlight what the applicant can do for the company. This letter stood above the rest; in the end she got the job.

Available for relocation to the Dallas area   C O N F I D E N T I A L

Lily Duart   1200 Westie Circle, Montgomery, Alabama 00000
✆ [000] 000-0000 (Home) — [000] 000-5555 (Office) — [000] 555-5555 (fax) — 001@scratch.com

Monday, 15 March, 2004

Mr. Norman French, CEO
Carley Products, Inc.
625 Express Highway
Building 333
Dallas, Texas, 00000

Dear Mr. French,

In a few seconds, you are going to see a half dozen capabilities I would like to put
under Carley's control, followed by three indicators that reflect my success as a Director
of Sales and Marketing in nationwide competition. Finally, I thought you deserved to
see a half dozen documented contributions to the bottom line. But the story behind the
results is as important as the numbers themselves.

I believe that most people—even your sales and marketing staff—can probably do
much more than they think they can. And I believe the personal rewards they earn at
those new levels will keep them producing at very high rates. I found my philosophy
works wonders, regardless of the product being sold or the market being worked, or the
competitors' actions. Now that I've reached near the top in one industry, I'm ready for
the fun of applying what I've learned in new fields.

It all starts with building mutual, beneficial relationships. Therefore, let me suggest this:
May we talk soon so that I can learn more about Carley's special needs? I'll call in a few
days to find a time when our schedules align.

Sincerely,

Lily Duart

Encl.: Résumé

C O N F I D E N T I A L

243

Director of Sales and Marketing. *Don Orlando, Montgomery, Alabama*

The applicant had very strong ideas about her philosophy of sales and marketing. By setting
these out boldly, the writer appealed to companies that shared the applicant's outlook.

AVAILABLE FOR RELOCATION

Alex McLean

0000 Duart Drive   Montgomery, Alabama 00000   topdog0000@west.com   000.000.0000

Thursday, April 8, 2004

Ms. Laura Worth
Sales Manager
Blue Sky, Inc.
1227 Amelia Island Parkway
Suite 200
Jacksonville, Florida 00000

Dear Ms. Worth:

For years, I've been making sales happen in the immediate future. But there's another reason why I have met or exceeded significantly rising sales goals every year for the last decade: I now generate add-on sales for products I championed from an idea to reduce an inventory. Results? I built my district from scratch and led us from $0 sales to $75M in sales annually.

My company obviously likes what I do. And maybe it's because I love sales so much that now, frankly, I am bored. That's why I am "testing the waters" with this application.

Because I thrive on anticipating requirements, I was thinking about Blue Sky's needs as I considered the form of my résumé. Gone are the tiring recitations of job titles and responsibilities. In their places are a half dozen examples of contributions measured in millions of dollars.

As you read, I hope some central ideas stand out clearly. First, I make it my business to get competitive intelligence faster than our competitors. Second, I make it my business to know my customers' operations almost as well as they do. Third, I make it my business to lead our customers to chose us through clear and compelling evidence that they think is their own good idea.

If Blue Sky can use someone with my track record, I'd like to explore how I can meet your specific sales needs. May I call in a few days to arrange a time to do that?

Sincerely,

Alex McLean

Encl.: Résumé

244

District Salesperson. *Don Orlando, Montgomery, Alabama*

The goal of this letter was to show that the applicant sold at many levels and used what he learned in the market to help his company beat the competition. Note the strong next-to-last paragraph.

TERRY NARBOW
0000 Jasmine Drive
Agoura Hills, California 91301
(555) 555-5555 (000) 000-0000
tnarbow@aol.com

January 23, 2004

M&R Associates
23457 Abelia Road
Calabasas, California 91304

Attention: Ms. Carolyn Hatten

Dear Ms. Hatten:

Achieving sales and marketing success in today's competitive marketplace requires a creative and strategic thinker who has the ability to establish profitable relationships, accelerate revenue growth, and maintain value-added service.

The company I left in 2000 was quite healthy, but despite record sales and profitability, there were few challenges on the horizon. I could have drawn a fine salary while serving secure accounts, but I was motivated to seek greater challenges. So I resigned in order to complete my B.A. in Business with an emphasis in Marketing as quickly as possible since this was my new chosen path.

Let me assure you, however, that I can make a compelling presentation of my candidacy whether I am selected for a position or not. My background encompasses research, development of categories of questions, creation of forms, merchandising, and displays. My innate ability to know what to ask allows for finding the most efficient way to improve procedures. Whatever the task—research, brand management/recognition, sales—it is my constant focus until completed.

Highlights that may be of particular interest include the following:

- Integration of diverse business practices, systems, and infrastructures to create top-performing organizations.
- Success in leveraging advanced technologies with core business operations.
- Cross-functional expertise in sales, new business development, and general management.
- Introduction of innovative marketing, business development, and promotional strategies that accelerated growth within existing business units and delivered revenues beyond projections.
- Realignment and expansion of third-party distribution network, capturing 20% revenue growth and strengthening competitive market position.

I understand that I may not be able to enter the marketing or brand field at a managerial level. All I am asking for is an introduction to one of your clients. Communication skills are one of my strengths (I continually take public speaking courses at various colleges), and I possess the will to succeed.

At this point in my career, I am interested in exploring new opportunities where my creative drive and energy can be further utilized and where I can continue to grow professionally.

Thank you for your consideration.

Sincerely,

Terry Narbow

Enclosure

245

Sales and Marketing Position. *Myriam-Rose Kohn, Valencia, California*

The opening paragraph is a miniprofile, and the second paragraph indicates the value this applicant placed on a bachelor's degree and career growth. Bullets point to areas of experience and success.

Rachel Fehren
name@hotmail.com

Current Address:
0000 Clinton Ave., Lubbock, TX 00000
(806) 000-0000

Permanent Address:
00000 Red Dr., Houston, TX 00000
(713) 000-0000

January 30, 2004

Human Resources Department
Office Max
1111 Durango Street
Houston, TX 00000

Dear Human Resources Representative:

It was with great interest and enthusiasm that I read your advertisement for a Marketing Assistant, as my background and abilities match your requirements for this position. Please allow me to explain briefly how my combination of sales, marketing, and customer service knowledge/experience can contribute to your organization's growth and success.

I will be receiving my B.B.A. degree in Marketing in August of this year; therefore, I have focused the majority of my professional development on marketing studies. However, my work history consists mainly of sales and customer-service positions. I see this as a strength because sales, marketing, and customer service are linked through their many similarities; they all share a common focus on consumer patterns, customer needs fulfillment, and business growth as the ultimate goal.

As a member of your team, I could use my knowledge of marketing and business-development strategies, ability to increase sales, and skills in customer satisfaction/retention to contribute to your organization's growth and success. Additionally, I can add value to your operations through my willingness to put forth an extra effort in all activities and perform tasks beyond those that fall under my job requirements. My former and current supervisors will attest that I am a dependable employee whom they trust implicitly.

My résumé is enclosed to provide you with additional details concerning my background. Thank you for your time and consideration. I look forward to speaking with you.

Respectfully,

Rachel Fehren

Enclosure

246

Marketing Assistant. *Daniel J. Dorotik, Jr., Lubbock, Texas*

This candidate explains well the connections between her college major in marketing and work experience in customer service. She views both marketing and customer service as her skill areas.

SYLVIA PHELPS

7 Moss Lane • Bedford, NJ 55555 • (666) 777-7777 • sphelps@yahoo.com

January 22, 2004

Hiring Agent, Title
Company Name
Address

Dear Hiring Manager:

Perhaps you are seeking a promising, hardworking recent college graduate with a background in marketing and sales for a position within your company. As a creative, energetic individual with excellent communications skills and a pleasant, accommodating manner, I believe I offer the right combination of skills to be just that person.

As you can see from my enclosed résumé, I recently graduated from Midwest University with a Bachelor's degree in Marketing. I totally enjoy my current position as a sales assistant, where I am well liked by my manager and readily given the opportunity to learn and grow. However, I plan to move to Connecticut in the near future and hope to find an equally rewarding position in my new location.

While attending college, I worked in a variety of positions in marketing, sales and administration. In all of these positions, I quickly earned a reputation as a professional, conscientious worker with excellent customer-relations skills. In addition, I am known as someone who is driven to get things done.

Among my other strengths, I have good research skills and solid marketing and advertising instincts. As a fast learner with a large capacity for growth and development, I am confident that, with these skills and traits to offer, I will prove to be an asset to your company.

I would be pleased to have the opportunity to discuss future employment and look forward to speaking with you soon. Feel free to contact me at the address and phone number listed above.

Thank you for your consideration.

Sincerely,

Sylvia Phelps

Enclosure

247

Sales and Marketing Position. *Carol A. Altomare, Three Bridges, New Jersey*

This recent graduate was working in her first postcollege job and wanted to relocate. Notice how each paragraph is positive and upbeat. It is hard to imagine an employer not contacting her for an interview.

SAMUEL KRAMER

555 East End Street, Deer Park, New York 11729 • (555) 555-5555 • Salesman@topproducer.net

Dear Human Resources Administrator:

Perhaps your company is seeking to recruit the talent of someone who can grasp complex concepts, roll with the punches, and contribute to the success of a product's performance. If this is the case, then please accept the accompanying résumé for your review and consideration for a position in which these strengths and diverse experience will be of value.

During my Internship as a Sales and Marketing Associate with Claire Rose, I effectively managed broad areas of the sales and marketing process from building and maintaining key accounts to product promotions. With a background in office management and field sales, I bring an ability to view situations from multiple perspectives and to maximize opportunities. As an effective problem solver, I see my role as one of cutting through red tape and confusion by providing clarity and practical business solutions for the company I represent and its clients.

Creatively, I enjoy brainstorming about innovative ideas that take into consideration demographics, target markets, advertising strategies, and shifts in the economy that have a direct impact on consumer buying trends and the influences that drive those changes. With these combined abilities, I am confident that I would make a significant contribution to the continued success of your company.

Although the accompanying résumé illustrates my background well, I feel that a personal interview would better demonstrate my knowledge and abilities. Therefore, I would appreciate an opportunity to interview with you at a convenient time. Thank you for your review and consideration. I look forward to hearing from you soon.

Sincerely,

Samuel Kramer

248

Sales and Marketing Position. *Ann Baehr, Brentwood, New York*

Phrases such as "complex concepts," "multiple perspectives," and "innovative ideas" point to uncommon thoughtfulness and suggest that this applicant will bring valuable insight to a company.

Gene W. Mandren
19 S.E. Weldrum Avenue • Everett, Washington 99999

555-555-5555 *cell*   *home* 555-555-5555

April 14, 2004

Attn: Human Resources
Shelconney Products, Inc.
P.O. Box 421
Everett, WA 99999

Dear Name:

I have taken the opportunity to enclose a copy of my résumé in application for the position you have advertised under **Sales** in *The Guard*. You will note from my résumé that I have cultivated an outstanding background in sales over the last few years. I have managed million-dollar accounts and have been highly successful in developing strong relationships.

Over the past six years, while I was at General Steel (a nonretail business), I developed accounts from cold calls to ongoing repeat-customer relationships with high-profile customers. I am professional and meet people well. You will find me to be highly disciplined and adaptable with the ability to tenaciously and tactfully "court" customers to their satisfaction, ultimately giving me and my company excellent success. I learn quickly, thoroughly enjoy a challenge, am self-motivated with strong common sense, and do enjoy making money. I work well as a team member as well as independently.

It appears from your advertisement that your requirements and my qualifications may be a close match. I would like the opportunity to meet with you personally where we can discuss how we may further benefit each other. You may reach me easiest at my cell number, 555-555-5555. Thank you for your time in reviewing my résumé, and I look forward to your call.

Sincerely,

Gene W. Mandren

Enclosure

249

Sales Position. *Rosie Bixel, Portland, Oregon*

Two successful activities (development and management) directed to two targets (accounts and customer relationships) are of continuing interest, making this candidate appealing to a company.

JENNIFER M. GADSEN

(555) 555-5555 ◉ jgadsen@email.com ◉ 133 Hillsborough Circle ◉ Auburn, AL 36830

February 21, 2004

SmithKline Beecham
P.O. Box 8454
Rocky Mount, NC 27804-1454

Reference: Ad Code RF3355

Dear Hiring Authority:

As a bachelor of science graduate with more than seven years of proven ability in outside and territory sales, I am eager to apply my ambition, sales experience, and skills to conquer new challenges. My résumé is enclosed for your review and consideration.

A few benefits I offer SmithKline Beecham:

- ◉ **A verifiable track record of successfully building and expanding sales territories from the ground up.**
- ◉ **Highly organized, with a tenacious work ethic, demonstrated by a history of creating and managing a profitable business to finance 100% of tuition concurrently as a full-time college student.**
- ◉ **Effective communicator with strong interpersonal skills and experience interfacing with doctors of veterinary medicine, business owners, and a wide variety of professionals and personalities.**
- ◉ **A sincere desire to provide the highest level of customer service possible while attaining individual, team, and company profitability goals.**

Excelling in today's marketplace requires focus, energy, initiative, creativity, and sales ability—all of which I have demonstrated in my previous work history. The opportunity to discuss how we can mutually benefit from my proven skills, traits, and entrepreneurial talents would be greatly appreciated.

I look forward to speaking with you soon.

Sincerely,

Jennifer M. Gadsen

Enclosure: résumé

250

Sales Position. *Karen D. Wrigley, Austin, Texas*

The applicant wanted to transition to a sales position from an unrelated position. Because the target company valued candidates with a science background, the letter indicates first her B.S. degree.

Norman Baker

00000 Eastland Street
Tulsa, Oklahoma 00000
(000) 000-0000

Attn: Human Resources Department

Attached is my résumé for your review and consideration for employment; I would like to use my talents and expertise in the areas of **sales and/or management**.

After earning my BSBA degree from OSU in 1985, I immediately began a career in sales. Years later, I was approached by the owner of a family business and asked to join forces with him to assist in his growing construction business. This proved to be a successful endeavor, and I am proud of my contributions to the expansion of this company. Unfortunately, with growing concerns about the economy, downsizing became inevitable; thus, I am exploring employment opportunities that will utilize my experience, skills, and knowledge.

As an outgoing, enthusiastic person who easily develops good relationships, sales is an area in which I excel. My sincerity, in addition to a good sense of humor, contributes to my "approachable" demeanor. Because I am technically inclined and a quick study, I am able to comprehend the intricacies of company products and pass along this knowledge in a clear, concise manner to my clients. Being detail-oriented and organized is beneficial in record keeping and scheduling business calls.

I would like to bring these attributes to your organization and assist you in meeting future goals. A personal interview would be appreciated; please contact me at the telephone number listed in my letterhead to schedule a time for us to meet.

Thank you for your interest. I look forward to your reply.

Sincerely,

Norman Baker

251

Sales Position. *Sally Altman, Tulsa, Oklahoma*

The second paragraph is a brief career summary that explains why the applicant is searching for a new position. The third paragraph indicates his worker traits, skill areas, and technical orientation.

Raymond K. Barker

000 S.E. Hemlock Street • George, Washington 99999

555-555-5555 *cell*   *home* 555-555-5555

January 23, 2004

Genesis Network Corporation
1111 NE Third Street
George, Washington 99999

Dear Hiring Professional:

Success in sales and relationship building can be measured by *results*. Over the years, I've delivered significant and measurable bottom-line benefits and have been continuously rewarded with satisfied customers, strong profits, and impressed management.

As you will note from my enclosed résumé, my career has been well balanced among sales, financial project management, and marketing. I've been an innovator, devising and executing new ideas, creative concepts, and original approaches that have led to positive results and top sales closures.

My record demonstrates my ability to contribute to a company's success and profitability. My résumé only highlights my experience. I would appreciate the opportunity to discuss in detail my qualifications with you. My skills appear to match closely what your company is requesting. You may call me at either number listed above to set up a time to meet so that we can further explore where my abilities may blend with your company's needs.

Thank you for taking the time to review my information, and I look forward to meeting you personally.

Sincerely,

Raymond K. Barker

252

Sales and Marketing Position. *Rosie Bixel, Portland, Oregon*

This letter's three main paragraphs show that the candidate is results-oriented in sales and relationship building. The second paragraph indicates a balance among three related activities.

Carlos C. Serito
555 Main Street
Parker, IL 00000
555-555-5555
ccs321@aol.com

March 15, 2004

Mr. James Cohen
Vice President, Sales and Marketing
Technology Division
XYZ Solutions, Inc.
555 Corporate Street
New York, NY 00000

Dear Mr. Cohen:

At the suggestion of Julia Corrado, I have enclosed my résumé for your review. My consistent success in creating and establishing profitable sales and marketing strategies for business technology consulting would be an asset to XYZ Solutions. I understand that one of your priorities for this year is to improve the sales results in the Chicago market, and I would appreciate the opportunity to talk with you about how my Chicago experience can help you achieve that goal.

The primary focus of my experience has been in successful turnarounds of weak or unprofitable territories and product lines. I enjoy the prospect of researching problem areas and developing the relationships and resources needed. In my search I am targeting companies that would benefit from my ability to . . .

- Identify market opportunities in the Midwest and develop new territories for intangible services.
- Build and maintain relationships with corporate and institutional clients, from Fortune 50 to small- and medium-sized businesses.
- Consistently exceed sales quotas, winning sales and sales management competitions; establish effective business plans and budgets; and control expenses.
- Provide in-depth knowledge acquired in a variety of business environments.

You can reach me at the phone number or e-mail listed above. I look forward to discussing the challenges you face in 2004 and beyond. Thank you for your time and attention.

Sincerely,

[signature]

Résumé enclosed

253

Sales and Marketing Position. *Christine L. Dennison, Lincolnshire, Illinois*

This applicant with managerial experience was not looking explicitly for a managerial position but wanted to make use of his Chicago experience to help a company develop its Chicago market.

CAROLYN SMART

223 Friendly Village Court ◆ Salt Lake City, UT 84112
555.555.5555 ◆ Cell: 000.000.0000

Dear Selection Committee:

Not many individuals would possess the fortitude, maturity and energy level necessary to launch a successful production company while still in high school. Well, I did just that; as you review the enclosed resume, I believe you'll be impressed with all I've done since.

My background contains a progressive record of employment in the entertainment and interactive gaming industry, culminating in my most recent role as the Cofounder/Vice President of International Game Developers Cooperative. **I've played a key role in reinforcing the organization's overall performance,** creating strategic marketing campaigns that have resulted in national recognition and have driven a keen amount of interest to the gaming industry and student capabilities here at the University.

In addition to my current role, **I've gained a reputation over the past 6 years for my ability to conceptualize and lead projects through successful conclusion,** perform as both a leader and an essential team player, build strong relationships with respected gaming industry and entertainment leaders and develop savvy marketing / promotional programs that have consistently produced *VERY* strong and measurable results. Additionally, I am well versed in a variety of production-management functions, skilled in team leadership and enjoy playing a role in the success of both individual and corporate efforts.

I offer you a record of **visionary idea generation and problem-solving techniques** that have produced sustainable and impressive results for my employers. I am versatile and possess the unique "Gen-X" perspective and hands-on business expertise necessary for creating profitable marketing strategies within today's age-driven entertainment industry. **I offer a high degree of integrity and professionalism** and believe my proven history of successful entrepreneurial drive and ability to learn from established industry leaders would be an asset in any production, video gaming or marketing-driven setting.

Though you may find that a four-page resume is unusual for someone so young, it is certainly *still* not enough to convey the depth of the knowledge, experience, professionalism and enthusiasm that I will immediately infuse into your organization! I would appreciate the opportunity to meet with you personally to discuss more specifically what I might do for your company.

Thank you for your time, and I really look forward to hearing from you soon to discuss the opportunities afforded by your organization.

Best regards,

Carolyn Smart

254

Marketing Position. *Kim Little, Victor, New York*

The challenge of this letter was to show that a university student, successfully active in business since high school, had already attained uncommon levels of professionalism and marketing expertise.

0000 Marley Avenue, Denver, CO 00000
(000) 000-0000

Deirdre Janovic

bandaide@waycool.com

January 4, 2004

Mr. Brian Paxton
Chief Engineer
Niteglo Productions
900 Blackrock Turnpike
Denver, CO 00000

Dear Mr. Paxton:

I know that you are busy and must receive hundreds of unsolicited resumes from hopeful communications majors looking for work in the music recording industry. To be honest with you, I'm no exception. But before you discard or file away my request, I'd appreciate your attention for just a moment so that I can tell you a little about myself.

First of all, I have an immense, profound love for popular music, whether it be rock, rap or R&B. Since the age of 7, I've been reading liner notes and have amassed quite a thorough knowledge of who's who in the recording business. It's love such as this that breeds dedication. Despite the tremendous competition that I'm up against, nothing will discourage me from pursuing my dreams of a career in the music industry. This is my calling!

Briefly, I offer

- ◆ Boundless creative energy with an imaginative way of dealing with problems.
- ◆ Articulate verbal skills and the ability to deliver messages with impact.
- ◆ Personal assertiveness, especially in face-to-face or phone contact with high-profile clients.
- ◆ A strong sensitivity to the needs of others, enabling the development of solid business relationships.
- ◆ Excellent planning, organizing and numerical skills, as well as a familiarity with computers.

Some examples of my abilities are illustrated in the enclosed resume. Up to now, my work experience has been limited, but my high degree of motivation has been recognized by my employers, who have quickly promoted me to positions of increased responsibility.

My enthusiasm and potential are there, waiting to be unleashed and molded as you see fit. Ultimately, my goal is a position as an artist relations or marketing rep, but all I want at this point is to get my foot in the door of an organization associated with the music recording industry. It doesn't matter if I'm assigned to the mailroom or some other clerical area. Salary is also not my primary concern. I would even be interested in an unpaid internship if it presented an opportunity to learn the industry from the ground up.

If any situations exist where you think I could be of value, or if you have any suggestions as to others with whom it might be beneficial to speak, I'd like to hear from you. I'm looking forward to the chance of meeting with you to discuss these possibilities. Thank you in advance for your time and consideration.

Sincerely,

Deirdre Janovic

Enclosure: Resume

255

Marketing Representative, Music Industry. *Melanie Noonan, West Paterson, New Jersey*

This communications major was looking for an entry-level position in the music recording industry. With little work experience, she was willing to be an unpaid intern just to get her foot in the door.

WESLEY L. KRAMER
0000 East 90th Boulevard
Springfield, Illinois 00000
(777) 888-9999

January 7, 2004

Michael D. Sumono
CEO/President
ABC Company
0000 Broadway
Springfield, IL 00000

Dear Mr. Sumono:

I am your competitor's worst nightmare.

Right now, they are hoping that you will *not* hire me as a sales representative for your company—they *know* what damage I can do to their bottom lines.

Since acquiring my BA in Communications, I have worked in outside sales for office systems companies and currently for a national manufacturer of robotic products. In each job, I have far exceeded established quotas, earning top sales awards and accolades from upper management for these achievements.

How? I love sales … I love to succeed. And because I do, I am motivated to learn all I can about the product, what competitors are selling, what market trends are indicating, and what the individual client wants. Listening intently and taking careful note of a client's surroundings have brought great rewards when it comes to negotiating a sale. Persistence and determination are my credo; I want to be the best rep they've ever worked with.

I am looking for a dynamic company that offers a good product line, favorable work environment, advancement opportunities, and fair compensation for results produced. You may be that company, and I may be the sales talent you need—someone capable of "scaring" your competition.

So, let's find out.

Please contact me at the above number to schedule a convenient time to meet.

Thank you for your consideration—

Wesley L. Kramer

Encl.

256

Sales Representative. *Sally Altman, Tulsa, Oklahoma*

The centered, italic, underlined, unconventional first sentence captures interest immediately. The first three paragraphs support the assertion. The end of the fourth paragraph echoes the unique claim.

Jayne Smyth
101 Main Street
Friendship, CT 06000
555-555-5555
JSmyth@123.zzz

February 10, 2004

Hallmark Cards, Inc.
ATTN: Human Resources Director
P.O. 100000001
Kansas City, MO 64141

Re: Positions for **Sales Professionals**

Dear Human Resources Director:

When you care enough to send the very best...send me!

The opportunity to represent Hallmark Cards, the perennial industry leader, would be a dream come true. Because I share your philosophy that only my best is good enough to offer, I have consistently been a top-producing sales representative for my current employer, constantly exceeding sales quotas and earning recognition from clients, peers and supervisors. Accomplishments have included the following:

☐ Among 50 sales representatives, rank in the top three for the past two years, supporting the achievement of departmental sales goals averaging $500,000 per month.
☐ Regularly produce 30% or more over daily sales goals.
☐ Selected to manage key national accounts.
☐ Commended by peers for providing sales assistance/support with accounts in a competitive environment.
☐ Chosen to mentor new hires.

I offer you solid sales experience, a strong customer focus and effective leadership skills, in combination with an "only the best will do" work ethic. I eagerly anticipate the opportunity to discuss your goals for your new territory and the ways in which I might help Hallmark achieve and exceed them. Thank you for considering my qualifications.

Sincerely,

Jayne Smyth

Enclosure

257

Sales Representative. *Debra O'Reilly*

The targeted company required outside sales experience, which the applicant lacked. The letter emphasized her sales success and good match for the company. Within a week, she got the job.

Janice A. Worthington

0000 E. Ogden Avenue
Naperville, Illinois 06060

000-000-0000
jaw@internetservice.com

March 19, 2004

Ms. Betsy White
Manager
BEW Corporation
555 Main Street
Chicago, Illinois 60606

Dear Ms. White:

This letter is in response to your advertisement for the position of Sales Representative. Having developed strong business skills in sales and marketing, I am currently pursuing a new challenge with an organization such as yours. Please review the enclosed resume, which provides an overview of my career-related experiences and accomplishments.

You are seeking an individual with strong prospecting and cold-calling experience. For the past three years, I have been recognized for turning 85% of my cold calls into customers. I have grown existing business more than 25% in the past 18 months. I have in-depth industry knowledge and pride myself on my ability to develop loyal business relationships with decision makers at all levels of an organization. My strengths include learning and applying selling methodologies, financial analysis, and accurate reporting. All of these skills are transferable to any industry or environment.

If you are currently seeking an individual with a "can-do" attitude who is focused on developing new business, increasing sales, achieving corporate goals, and exceeding customer expectations, we should meet. I would welcome the opportunity to discuss how I could become a contributing member of your sales and marketing team. Please contact me at 000-000-0000.

Sincerely,

Janice A. Worthington

Enclosure

258

Sales Representative. *Patricia Chapman, Naperville, Illinois*

In this response to an ad, the writer plays up the applicant's experience and achievements. The second paragraph indicates strengths, transferable skills, and achievements in percentages.

Mr. Holstein:

** Closing $1 million in directory advertising within only three
months

** Setting new company records for both highest sales
in one day and highest new business sales

** Experience in direct field sales to federal and state
government counsel and state universities

The above are just a few of the reasons I am the ideal candidate for this position.

For more information on my ten-year history as a consistent,
overachieving outside sales representative, please review
the attached resume.

I look forward to speaking with you soon.

Sincerely,

Clay T. Bishop
(512) 917-5555 (cell)
(512) 419-5555 (residence)

259

Sales Representative. *Karen D. Wrigley, Austin, Texas*

The applicant sent this e-mail text (.txt) message to a recruiter who was expecting it. The brevity
of the message was fitting for this particular recipient, who valued concise communications.

Sandy Wexler
777 Vantage Drive, Chalfont, Pennsylvania 19333
Home (666) 888–9999 • Mobile (666) 666–5555

February 22, 2004

Bader Associates
3 Wadsworth Drive
Buckingham, PA 19222

Dear Hiring Manager:

Success in sales is about people, persistence, and performance!

As a sales representative with proven skills and strong sales accomplishments, I am confident my qualifications and experience will be of interest to you. Characteristics that have contributed to my success are...

- Meticulous attention to customer service and follow-up.
- Energy, enthusiasm, and motivation.
- Excellent planning, time-management, and organizational skills.
- Ability to perform effectively in a fast-paced atmosphere.

The enclosed resume summarizes more than 17 years of experience in both business and consumer environments. In each of my previous positions I have quickly attained sales results and established a loyal customer base. I am very proficient in all stages of the sales process—from the cold call to a signature on the contract. The process begins with building rapport with my clients and continues by delivering the extra effort necessary to achieve the goals of all concerned...a "win-win" situation.

My selling skills are complemented by equally strong creative abilities. I am able to work with people to generate ideas that work. My goal is to become a key contributor on your professional sales team and help you meet your overall objectives in any way I can.

Although secure in my present position, I am interested in a more challenging opportunity. It will be a pleasure to meet with you in a confidential interview to discuss my credentials in detail. I am available for a personal interview at your earliest convenience. Please feel free to contact me at either telephone number listed above.

Thank you for your consideration.

Sincerely,

Sandy Wexler

Enclosure

260

Sales Representative. *Karen Conway, Media, Pennsylvania*

This letter, calling for confidentiality, is for a person who is successful in her current position but wants a change for a more challenging opportunity. The whole letter displays her confidence.

C O N F I D E N T I A L   Job #100-12   *Ready to relocate*

Robert Savage

000 Martin Terrace   Starkley, Alabama 00000   robert_savage@zipx.com   ☎ 334.555.5555

Monday February 16, 2004

Ms. Laura Worth
District Sales Manager
TopLine Pharmaceuticals, Inc.
500 Northridge Parkway
Suite 400
Montgomery, Alabama 36100

Dear Ms. Worth:

I would like to join the TopLine Pharmaceuticals team as your newest pharmaceutical sales representative. To give you confidence that I am the right person to interview, this letter anticipates your needs in the following areas:

Your likely requirements:	My capabilities:
❏ **Strong sales experience.**	❏ Proven record in closing the most difficult kind of "sales": persuading all my customers to give up their property at a reasonable price and avoid costly legal battles.
❏ Ability to **master steep learning curves** in new fields.	❏ Three years of handling rapidly increasing responsibility with absolutely no formalized training.
❏ Dedication to **reach tough goals independently.**	❏ Embarked upon a personal, professional development program to learn about your industry from pharmaceutical reps, professional organizations, and trade magazines.

My résumé has the details. It may not look like others you have seen. I thought you deserved a good deal more than the usual unsupported summary of "professional qualifications," standard job titles, and unfamiliar responsibilities. In their places are a half dozen profit-building capabilities I am ready to offer now, backed up by selected examples of performance.

If my approach and track record appeals to TopLine, I'd like to hear about your specific sales requirements. May I call in a few days to arrange a time to do just that?

Sincerely,

Robert Savage

Encl.: Résumé

C O N F I D E N T I A L

261

Pharmaceutical Sales Representative. *Don Orlando, Montgomery, Alabama*

This applicant never had the word "sales" in any of his job titles. To compensate, the writer introduced a table that matched the individual's abilities with likely corporate needs.

TINA B. STEWART

5555 55th Street ▪ Lakeview, Texas 79000 ▪ *(555) 555-5555*

April 12, 2004

TROY PHARMACEUTICALS
5555 Magnum Street
Ft. Cloud, Mississippi 55555

Re: West Texas Pharmaceutical Sales Specialist, Code SPMDT

Dear Human Resources Coordinator:

I am committed to improved patient care, a quality that characterizes value to medical professionals. As an *established pharmaceutical sales representative* covering West Texas and Eastern New Mexico territories, I offer *beneficial industry knowledge* from *six years of experience.* It would be an honor to represent TROY, a highly regarded pharmaceutical company whose mission to enhance and preserve quality of life coincides so closely with mine.

The enclosed résumé reflects a *match between my credentials and your requirements for a pharmaceutical sales specialist.* A qualification summary follows:

JOB REQUIREMENTS	PERSONAL QUALIFICATIONS
Five years of sales experience, preferably pharmaceutical	▪ *Six years of proven success* in pharmaceutical / medical sales industry. ▪ *Established rapport with 200+ West Texas physicians* specializing in a spectrum of healthcare disciplines.
Bachelor's degree	▪ *Bachelor of science* in political science with minor in public relations.
Project and account management experience	▪ Exclusively *acquired six-figure surgical center account,* orchestrated *total equipment installation,* and *troubleshot logistical problems.* ▪ Employ *continuous customer contact, needs assessment, and strategic planning* to manage and grow 180+ accounts.
Sales / persuasion skills	▪ Consistently rank in *top 10% of regional sales* representatives for exceeding 100% of annual sales goals. ▪ Use *scientific / consultative sales approach* to gain customer acceptance of products and services.
Communication and presentation skills	▪ Relate to physicians through *lighthearted yet authoritative communication style* to create enjoyable sales environment. ▪ Incorporate analogies, illustrations, sales / detail aids, and humor into presentations and training seminars to *engage audiences, retain interest, and improve comprehension.*

Given a *preestablished client network, technical knowledge, and personal values,* I am confident I would well serve TROY PHARMACEUTICALS' goals and objectives. I hope to *share business development ideas* during a personal interview and will contact your office within the week to schedule an appointment at your convenience. In the meantime, thank you for your consideration.

Sincerely,

Tina B. Stewart

Enclosure: Résumé

262

Pharmaceutical Sales Specialist. *Edie Rische, Lubbock, Texas*

In going beyond the resume, this Job Requirements… Personal Qualifications format focuses on the candidate's relevant strengths. The style is simple because the individual's achievements speak for themselves.

SANDRA A. PEACE, D.C.
10000 Pleasant Drive, Asheville, NC 28888
Home: (704) 555-1212   *Cell:* (704) 444-7777
sap@mindspring.com

February 1, 2004

Pfizer Inc.
555 Medical Drive
Bldg. 2, Suite 200
Careret, NJ 08000

Re: *The Richmond Times Dispatch* advertisement, October 28, 2004: Pharmaceutical Sales (Code K007)

If there were a recurring theme in my life, it would have to be "Nothing is certain but change." Of course, not everyone may see this as a driving force, but for me it has always served as a great motivator.

In my opinion, success boils down to three things:

- Establishing structured goals and creating/implementing a master plan to achieve those goals
- Developing the skills, knowledge and expertise—in short, the tools—to be successful
- Providing top-quality service to customers

As you will see from my enclosed resume, this strategy has also served me well in business development over the last 12 years. For example, after working as a medical laboratory technician for eight years, I changed career paths—investing four years of professional and academic training to become a chiropractic physician. As a self-starting, focused professional, I achieved this goal, eventually establishing my own practice, which I operated quite profitably for more than eight years. Last year, I sold the practice (at a profit) and moved to Asheville (from Charlotte), where I have managed (very hands-on) a satellite office of another physician.

During the business development phase of my practice—which I always treated as a business—I sought additional training in sales and marketing, receiving ideas and inspiration from the best "gurus" in the business, such as Jay Conrad Levinson (*Guerilla Marketing*); Jay Abraham (*How to Get from Where You Are to Where You Want to Be*); Chet Holmes (*The Seven Steps to Every Sale* and *The 10 Follow-up Steps for Bonding with Clients*); Kenneth Blanchard (*The One-Minute Manager* and *The Heart of a Leader*); Napoleon Hill (*Think and Grow Rich*); and Dale Carnegie (*How to Win Friends and Influence People*), among many others. With Holmes, Abraham and Levinson, I participated in a 90-minute, monthly interactive seminar. I implemented these ideas in my practice, applying sales and marketing strategies to grow the business.

My point in telling you all of this is twofold: (1) to provide some substantive evidence of self-motivation and (2) to demonstrate, as my resume attests, personal sales, marketing and business success. Seeking professional growth, and no stranger to change, I now want to change the course of my life once again.

What do I want to do now? Apply my sales, marketing and business development, relationship-building and medical experience to a career in pharmaceutical sales. I have extensive medical knowledge, an understanding of the physician's mind-set and a desire to succeed.

I would welcome an opportunity to speak with you regarding this—or another related—position with Pfizer, and would appreciate your time and consideration of my qualifications. May we talk?

Sincerely,

Sharon A. Wright

263

Pharmaceutical Sales Representative. *Doug Morrison, Charlotte, North Carolina*

After four years of chiropractic school and eight years in private practice, this applicant wanted to become a sales rep for a pharmaceutical company. This letter shows her personality and motivation.

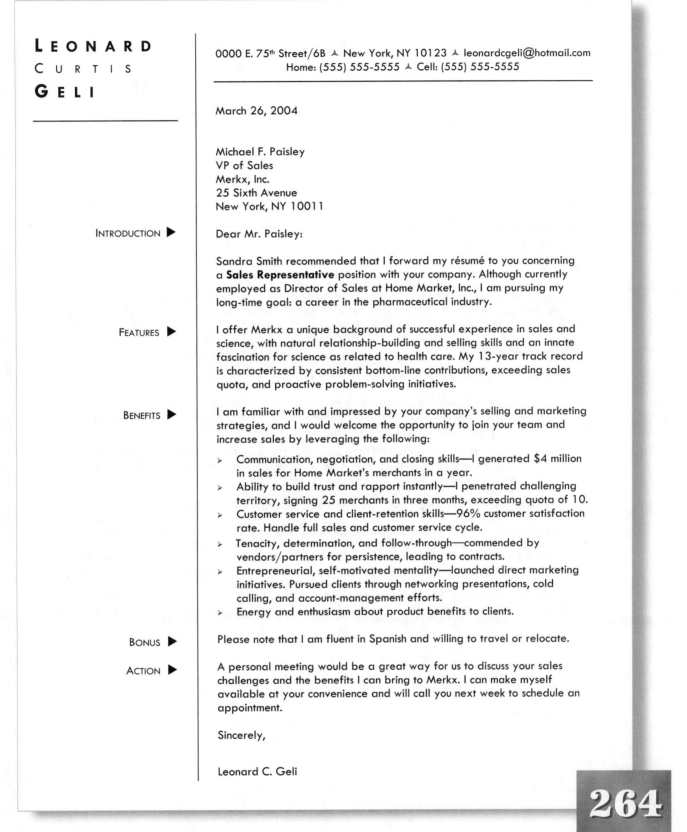

LEONARD
CURTIS
GELI

0000 E. 75th Street/6B ⊼ New York, NY 10123 ⊼ leonardcgeli@hotmail.com
Home: (555) 555-5555 ⊼ Cell: (555) 555-5555

March 26, 2004

Michael F. Paisley
VP of Sales
Merkx, Inc.
25 Sixth Avenue
New York, NY 10011

INTRODUCTION ▶   Dear Mr. Paisley:

Sandra Smith recommended that I forward my résumé to you concerning a **Sales Representative** position with your company. Although currently employed as Director of Sales at Home Market, Inc., I am pursuing my long-time goal: a career in the pharmaceutical industry.

FEATURES ▶   I offer Merkx a unique background of successful experience in sales and science, with natural relationship-building and selling skills and an innate fascination for science as related to health care. My 13-year track record is characterized by consistent bottom-line contributions, exceeding sales quota, and proactive problem-solving initiatives.

BENEFITS ▶   I am familiar with and impressed by your company's selling and marketing strategies, and I would welcome the opportunity to join your team and increase sales by leveraging the following:

➤ Communication, negotiation, and closing skills—I generated $4 million in sales for Home Market's merchants in a year.
➤ Ability to build trust and rapport instantly—I penetrated challenging territory, signing 25 merchants in three months, exceeding quota of 10.
➤ Customer service and client-retention skills—96% customer satisfaction rate. Handle full sales and customer service cycle.
➤ Tenacity, determination, and follow-through—commended by vendors/partners for persistence, leading to contracts.
➤ Entrepreneurial, self-motivated mentality—launched direct marketing initiatives. Pursued clients through networking presentations, cold calling, and account-management efforts.
➤ Energy and enthusiasm about product benefits to clients.

BONUS ▶   Please note that I am fluent in Spanish and willing to travel or relocate.

ACTION ▶   A personal meeting would be a great way for us to discuss your sales challenges and the benefits I can bring to Merkx. I can make myself available at your convenience and will call you next week to schedule an appointment.

Sincerely,

Leonard C. Geli

264

Pharmaceutical Sales Representative. *Ilona Vanderwoude, Riverdale, New York*

With a background in science teaching, premed coursework, and sales, this applicant wanted to go into pharmaceutical sales. The unique headings with bullets match the applicant's aggressiveness.

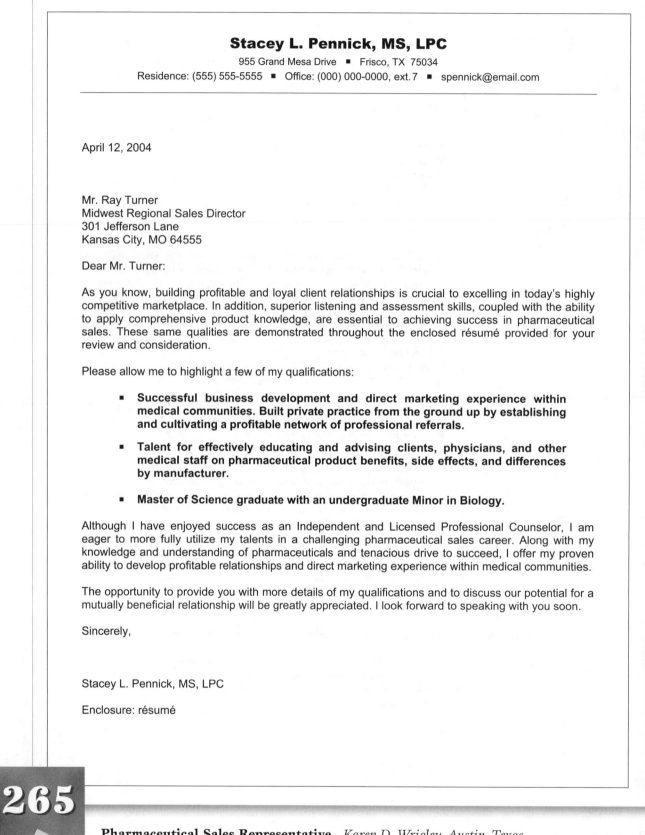

Stacey L. Pennick, MS, LPC

955 Grand Mesa Drive ▪ Frisco, TX 75034
Residence: (555) 555-5555 ▪ Office: (000) 000-0000, ext. 7 ▪ spennick@email.com

April 12, 2004

Mr. Ray Turner
Midwest Regional Sales Director
301 Jefferson Lane
Kansas City, MO 64555

Dear Mr. Turner:

As you know, building profitable and loyal client relationships is crucial to excelling in today's highly competitive marketplace. In addition, superior listening and assessment skills, coupled with the ability to apply comprehensive product knowledge, are essential to achieving success in pharmaceutical sales. These same qualities are demonstrated throughout the enclosed résumé provided for your review and consideration.

Please allow me to highlight a few of my qualifications:

- **Successful business development and direct marketing experience within medical communities. Built private practice from the ground up by establishing and cultivating a profitable network of professional referrals.**

- **Talent for effectively educating and advising clients, physicians, and other medical staff on pharmaceutical product benefits, side effects, and differences by manufacturer.**

- **Master of Science graduate with an undergraduate Minor in Biology.**

Although I have enjoyed success as an Independent and Licensed Professional Counselor, I am eager to more fully utilize my talents in a challenging pharmaceutical sales career. Along with my knowledge and understanding of pharmaceuticals and tenacious drive to succeed, I offer my proven ability to develop profitable relationships and direct marketing experience within medical communities.

The opportunity to provide you with more details of my qualifications and to discuss our potential for a mutually beneficial relationship will be greatly appreciated. I look forward to speaking with you soon.

Sincerely,

Stacey L. Pennick, MS, LPC

Enclosure: résumé

265

Pharmaceutical Sales Representative. *Karen D. Wrigley, Austin, Texas*

The letter emphasizes the applicant's sales-related skills gained in private practice and highlights her knowledge of pharmaceutical products, direct medical-industry experience, and related education.

Agnes Smith-Bucci

95 Huling Lane
Providence, RI 02222

(555) 555-5555
E-mail: sbucci2@aol.com
Cell: (000) 000-0000

March 7, 2004

Mr. Arthur Spellman, Sr.
888 Harris Avenue South
Newport, RI 00000

Dear Mr. Spellman:

Please accept this letter and my application for a pharmaceutical sales position with Pfizer, Inc. I appreciate your invitation to contact you for your assistance in my attempt to receive an interview for employment. If hired, I firmly believe that I will make a solid contribution to Pfizer as a salesperson.

As you may know, my extensive employment experience with sales negotiations in travel and real estate, coupled with an excellent education and training in becoming a Licensed Practical Nurse, provide me with ideal credentials for a position in sales of pharmaceuticals. In addition, my LPN training has served to refocus my own professional objective toward sales in this important, rapidly expanding, and fascinating arena of the health field.

Perceptive to the needs of clients and resolute in securing all potential sales, I have built a solid reputation with employers and customers for being trustworthy, dependable, and dedicated in my responsibilities. I am a proven self-starter willing to take on significant responsibilities, as I have worked competently on independent projects and as a contributing team member.

I genuinely look forward to discussing my qualifications with a Pfizer representative for a position in pharmaceutical sales. I would appreciate a company representative contacting me at my home number, e-mail, or cell phone to set up an interview and an opportunity to tour the facility. If I do not hear from Pfizer by April 7, I will contact their human resources office to request an appointment.

Thank you kindly for your offer to assist me in my application for employment at Pfizer.

Sincerely,

Agnes Smith-Bucci, LPN

Enclosures: résumé / application

266

Pharmaceutical Sales Representative. *Edward Turilli, North Kingstown, Rhode Island*

The applicant coupled her LPN status with her sales experience to break into pharmaceutical sales. The letter stresses her independent work—an excellent foundation for salespeople on the road.

Richard A. Gonzales

0000 Clinton Avenue ▪ Houston, TX 00000 ▪ (281) 000-0000 ▪ name@yahoo.com

January 30, 2004

Human Resources Department
Pfizer Pharmaceuticals
1111 Grant Drive
Houston, TX 00000

RE: Position as Pharmaceutical Sales Representative

Dear Staffing Representative:

I am submitting my résumé in application for the position of Pharmaceutical Sales Representative. I believe I am the ideal candidate for your consideration, not only because my qualifications match your requirements, but also because my strong network of contacts in the local/regional health care industry and ability to build strong relationships will enable me to increase sales growth and market share for your company.

My combination of healthcare experience, pharmaceutical product knowledge, and relationship selling skills has provided me the opportunity to deliver substantial revenue gains for the ABC Medical Center in Houston and develop solid, sustainable relationships with a broad cross-section of healthcare professionals throughout the Greater Houston area. Accomplishments that may be of interest to you include the following:

- I spearheaded a revenue increase of **$600,000** within the first month and **$7.6 million** in my first year as Director of the Cardiac Cath Lab at the ABC Medical Center.
- I created a new computer program that ensured proper matches between physician and lab billing, producing significant savings and demonstrating my ability to pinpoint opportunities for profit growth.
- I maintained an excellent record in pharmaceutical purchasing, serving as the sole point of contact for pharmaceutical sales representatives and playing a pivotal role in physician decisions.

My résumé is enclosed to provide you with specific details concerning my qualifications and accomplishments, but perhaps a personal interview would more fully reveal my ability to contribute to your market share growth. I look forward to the possibility of such a meeting.

Thank you for your time and consideration. Please do not hesitate to contact me if I can answer any questions.

Sincerely,

Richard A. Gonzales

Enclosure

267

Pharmaceutical Sales Representative. *Daniel J. Dorotik, Jr., Lubbock, Texas*

The writer emphasizes specific accomplishments for this applicant, who was seeking to transition to a new position within the same industry. Boldfacing highlights key quantified achievements.

Donald T. Jones

0000 Harvey Penick Drive ▪ Round Rock, TX 78664

Residence: (512) 828-5555 ▪ djones@email.com

April 23, 2004

Mr. Bill Roush
Vice President Global Sales
Medimax Solutions, Inc.
333 Royal Gate Way
Chicago, IL 60604

Dear Mr. Roush:

As you know, in today's economic climate gaining competitive market share is more challenging than ever before. During the past five years, I have consistently generated 30% to 50% market share growth and exceeded annual revenue projections by as much as $5 million. One recent sales achievement was receiving the Top Sales Representative of the Year Award (outperforming 500 Sales Representatives company wide) with a multibillion-dollar company.

Proven ability to drive significant growth in market share, revenues, and profits is what I will bring to Medimax. The enclosed résumé will provide you with additional highlights of my achievements.

A few benefits I offer Medimax:

- **Demonstrated ability to deliver optimal performance in all aspects of complex sales cycles and negotiations by identifying and implementing process improvement opportunities.**

- **Competent representation of highly technical critical care products and solutions. Comprehensive knowledge of medical institutions and spheres of influence gained through more than 10 years of direct industry experience.**

- **Established loyal and profitable relationships with key industry contacts.**

While I have enjoyed success with my current employer, Accu-Heart Technology Systems, I am now highly motivated to seek new challenges with a strong industry leader such as Medimax Solutions, Inc. The opportunity to meet with you personally, to discuss how I can contribute to Medimax, will be greatly appreciated. Please expect my call next Thursday to arrange a convenient date and time for us to meet.

I look forward to speaking with you soon.

Sincerely,

Donald T. Jones

Enclosure: résumé

268

Sales Representative. *Karen D. Wrigley, Austin, Texas*

To position this applicant as a sure bet to the prospective employer, the writer lists the applicant's recent impressive accomplishments in the first paragraph. Bullets point to additional benefits.

TRICIA PARKERSON

P.O. Box 66
Collegeville, PA 99999

tparkerson@dotresume.com

Residence: 555-555-5555
Cellular: 000-000-0002

April 26, 2004

Mr. Edward J. Pinter
Senior Sales Representative
MedMark Pharmaceuticals, Inc.
999 West Valley Road
Norristown, PA 99999

Dear Mr. Pinter:

Thank you for taking the time to talk with me about sales positions at MedMark Pharmaceuticals, following Dr. Nathan's referral.

As a sales professional for 15 years, I have achieved substantial success in driving revenue growth and expanding business in the competitive security industry. My talent for building long-term relationships has been key to my success. For example, I garnered accounts with major corporations, such as Sears, largely through referrals, and created a national distributors' network through contacts that I developed and nurtured.

I firmly believe that I could achieve the same results—or better—for MedMark. Over the past several years I have developed a passion for the medical field, which is at the heart of my decision to transition my qualifications into pharmaceutical sales. I have already established strong relationships with a number of medical practitioners, learned some of the ins and outs of the medical system, and thoroughly researched several drugs, resulting in a new appreciation for their role in people's lives and in the clinical setting.

Dr. Nathan and several other physicians I know agree that I have what it takes to make an impact in the pharmaceutical field. The enclosed résumé will give you an idea of what I could do for MedMark.

I would like to meet with you to discuss the contribution I can make as part of your sales team. I will call you within the next several days to schedule an interview.

Thank you in advance for your consideration. I look forward to speaking with you again soon.

Sincerely,

Tricia Parkerson

Enclosure

269

Pharmaceutical Sales Representative. *Jan Holliday, Harleysville, Pennsylvania*

The letter starts with a thank-you for a phone conversation that was the result of a referral. Then the letter describes elements of the candidate's sales experience that would be of interest to the reader.

Chris L. Patterson

0000 Stonegate Crossing • Murfreesboro, TN 37128
Mobile: 000-000-0000 • Residence: 555-555-5555 • E–mail: cpatterson@email.com

January 10, 2004

Medtronic USA, Inc.
Cardiac Surgery Sales and Marketing Division
333 Sweetwater Circle, Building R
San Francisco, CA 94115

RE: Requisition 33555

Dear Hiring Authority:

In response to your posting for the position of **Valve Sales Representative in the San Antonio market,** I am forwarding my résumé for your review and consideration. As the résumé indicates, my education, experience, and demonstrated abilities uniquely qualify me for this position.

Addressing the specific major requirements listed for this position:

Medtronic Requires:	I Offer:
Bachelor's degree in Biological Science or Business.	Bachelor of Science in Chemistry, Biology Minor, and concentrated studies in human anatomy and physiology.
Three years of medical sales experience in a hospital environment.	Hospital / Medical environment experience working directly with doctors and patients on issues related to care and treatment. Successfully negotiated positive resolutions by using excellent persuasive and interpersonal skills, nearly doubling patient-satisfaction ratings.
Demonstrated success in previous employment, indicating high level of performance.	Proven ability as a high sales performer as demonstrated by a history of tripling company expectations for daily contract closings. Received numerous awards as a top performer in recruiting.

Although I have enjoyed success with my current employer, I am interested in using my education and proven sales ability more fully to drive successful financial rewards for a medical industry leader such as Medtronic, as well as for myself. Presently, I reside in Tennessee; however, I am more than willing to relocate to the San Antonio market (an area I am very familiar with and travel to every year).

The opportunity to meet with you personally to discuss the possibility of a mutually beneficial relationship will be greatly appreciated. Please feel free to contact me on my mobile phone (000-000-0000) at any time. I look forward to speaking and meeting with you soon.

Sincerely,

Chris L. Patterson

Attachment: résumé

270

Valve Sales Representative. *Karen D. Wrigley, Austin, Texas*

The applicant wanted to move from an unrelated industry to the posted position. The writer used columns to show how the applicant's experience matched the company's requirements.

Charles A. Robertson
Regional Sales Manager
Norton & Company
charles_robertson@norton.com

Dear Mr. Robertson:

Your posting for a College Sales Representative in Western and Central New York is of great interest to me. My résumé is attached in Word format for your review.

I have a diverse background, both academically and through employment. In 2001, I earned a Master's in Library Science and have held related positions since 1999. Currently I am Special Services Consultant for 18 public libraries and nine other libraries housed in correctional facilities. Additionally, I hold a BA in Psychology (Magna cum Laude) and have more than 10 years of experience with developmentally disabled adults as a program manager, teacher and residential supervisor. I believe that my professional experience parallels the sales/client relationship in that I seek out, identify and meet the needs of those I serve.

My passions for reading, lifelong learning and computer technology were motivators to return to the classroom for my Master's degree. I possess an intrinsic ability to set and meet both personal and professional goals, evident in pursuit of both degrees while raising a family.

My well-honed interpersonal, organization and communication abilities will also be valuable as a College Sales Representative. I offer Norton enthusiasm, a high comfort factor with the targeted market and the skill and desire necessary to achieve and succeed.

It would be a pleasure to discuss your College Sales Representative opening and my background in greater detail. You may reach me at 555-555-5555 or through e-mail at k_emory@myemail.com.

Thank you for your time and consideration.

Kelly Emory

271

College Sales Representative. *Salome A. Farraro, Mount Morris, New York*

This text-only letter was an e-mail submission. The applicant wanted a position closer to her children. She hoped that her diverse background and strong interpersonal abilities would earn an interview.

Michael J. Remmick

0000 West Pantano Road ◆ Willcox, AZ 84567
555-555-5555 ◆ mickrem@juno.net

January 23, 2004

Mr. Jason P. Peters, Sales Manager
Alliance Products
670 East Third Place
Sierra Vista, AZ 46755

Dear Mr. Peters:

A high-performing sales organization is essential to your company's continued growth and success. As you increase your sales team, you don't want to take chances. You need professionals with track records and experience that prove they have what it takes to be successful. I am a person with a portfolio of proven success who is interested in securing an outside sales position with your company.

As you will see in the enclosed résumé, I have excelled in the tour industry as a Tour Director for more than 15 years. At this point, I suspect you are wondering how my skills and abilities would transfer into "selling" for you. The bottom line is that, as a Tour Director, I was responsible for new product development, managing all aspects of the tour, ensuring that the participants (accounts) were 100% satisfied, and obtaining repeat and referral business. As we both know, this is all part of the sales process.

Through a professional, respectful, and thorough approach and a real talent for developing strong relationships, I contributed to the foundation for *current* and *future* business growth. I would like to do the same for you.

Since it is difficult to get one's personality and enthusiasm on paper, I would welcome the opportunity to begin a dialogue focusing on how I would bring added value and sales to your company. I will take the initiative to contact you next week to schedule a meeting at a mutually convenient time. Thank you for your consideration, and I look forward to speaking with you.

Sincerely,

Michael J. Remmick

Enclosure

272

Sales Representative. *Kay Bourne, Tucson, Arizona*

The applicant was changing his career focus from the tour industry to sales. The letter plays up the individual's success, excellent record, transferable skills, people skills, and interest in an interview.

WILLIAM H. HARRINGTON

1888 Shangri-La Drive · Pleasantville, NC 28888
Home: (555) 555-5555   *Fax:* (000) 000-0000
E-mail: willym@argus.net

March 27, 2004

James L. Starnes
President
Leathercraft Furniture
3030 Haywood Road
Hickory Grove, NC 28601

Dear Mr. Starnes:

I grew up in the furniture business. My grandfather was an executive with Drexel Heritage; my father, a board member of several firms. In spite of my early background, I swore I'd *never* get into the furniture business. But I did. And in the 15 years since I entered the industry (initially as a salesman for Simmons U.S.A. and for the past 14 years as a sales representative for Hickory House), I've discovered that selling quality products excites me. Furniture is simply in my blood!

I think you will know from your own experience that it takes years to develop and cultivate extensive contacts, understand the complexities of fabric applications, and become creative in developing marketing strategies.

This is how I fit in: I have just established a sales company, representing leather and fabrics, in North and South Carolina. I am knowledgeable of the residential side of the business, but to expand my outreach I plan to pursue contract opportunities and alternative distribution routes, including auto manufacturers and the garment industry.

I really want to be of help to you—by representing your line in the Carolinas or other areas in the Southeast. I'll call on present and prospective users to tell them about new and existing products. I can provide expert advice without prejudice. It's my job to do just that.

To illustrate my point, let me tell you the story about the firm that installed a large piece of machinery, but after it was set up, no one could start it. Experts were called in from near and far, each fiddling and adjusting, but to no avail. Finally, as a last resort, the company president called a two-for-cent mechanic (or so they thought). In he strolled with his small sledgehammer and walked over to the machine. He studied the unit for several moments, and then set his eyes on one spot. He struck three blows with the hammer and, much to the surprise of the onlookers, off she went!

    "Just how much do we owe you?" asked the president.
    "One thousand three dollars," replied the mechanic.
    "What's the thousand three dollars for?" asked the president.
    "Three dollars for three blows, and a thousand for knowing where to hit," the mechanic retorted.

So, in the long run, if a fellow knows his business, it's easy; if not, it's too bad for him <u>and</u> his customer. With 15 years of experience, I know "where to hit" when it comes to marketing and selling furniture and fabric. You are taking no chances when you let me help you.

I am enclosing a résumé and list of references. If you think you may be interested in talking about a mutually beneficial relationship, please call me today at (555) 555-5555.

Sincerely,

William H. Harrington

273

Sales Representative. *Doug Morrison, Charlotte, North Carolina*

A sales rep for 15 years, this applicant wanted to strike out on his own. He formed his own company to represent a manufacturer. The letter conveys his knowledge. (Be sure to read the story in the fifth paragraph.)

Keith F. Broden

1655 Cordillera Drive ～ Round Rock, TX 78681

Residence: (555) 555-5555 ～ Mobile: (000) 000-0000 ～ Email: kbroden@email.com

March 25, 2004

Mr. Ben B. Hathaway
Vice President of Sales
Bonita Bay Group
333 New Horizon Lane
Orlando, FL 33333

Dear Mr. Hathaway:

Our mutual business acquaintance, Randy Shehan of Volente Realty, recommended I contact you directly based on his belief that I am a strong candidate for sales opportunities with Bonita Bay Group. Randy also stated that someone with my relative professional background and record of accomplishments would be a good match for your company. *As a current, successful, builder sales agent, I offer Bonita Bay:*

～ **Proven ability to effectively represent builders in marketing residential properties** (from groundbreaking through builder closeout), demonstrated by a solid history of multimillion-dollar sales performances.

～ **Self-motivated and achievement-driven individual** with a unique ability to duplicate success within diverse marketplaces. Talent for establishing and building loyal internal and external customer relationships with a broad range of personality types.

～ **Committed to providing the highest level of customer service possible** while maintaining company, team, and personal profitability.

As the enclosed résumé will indicate, my current employer, Milburn Homes (Division of DR Horton Homes) has provided me with great opportunities to achieve professional success. However, I am now seeking new opportunities for my builder agent experience, knowledge, and skills (while accepting new challenges) with an industry leader such as Bonita Bay Group.

In addition, although my wife and I have enjoyed living in Austin, TX, these past few years, we plan to move closer to family by relocating to the East Coast (preferably to Florida). After researching Bonita Bay Group, I discovered the company's lifestyle, values, philosophies, and priorities are in line with my own. It is exciting to learn about a company with such a strong commitment to balancing customer satisfaction and environmental responsibility.

During the week of Monday, April 11, thru Friday, April 15, I will be in your area and would greatly appreciate the opportunity to meet with you personally to discuss the possibility of our mutually beneficial relationship. I will contact you early next week to arrange for a convenient time and date to meet. Please feel free to contact me on my mobile phone (000-000-0000) anytime.

I look forward to speaking and meeting with you soon!

Sincerely,

Keith F. Broden

Enclosure: *résumé*

274

Real Estate Sales Position. *Karen D. Wrigley, Austin, Texas*

The applicant used a networking connection as an introduction to the decision maker in the targeted company. The letter explains why the applicant wanted to move to Florida and join the company.

RONALD SMITH

1234 Eaton Road   (555) 555-1234
Akron, OH 12345   RSmith@email.com

February 9, 2004

Mr. Timothy Barber
ABC Home Products Division
1234 Box Road
Cleveland, OH 12345

Dear Mr. Barber:

I am writing to express my interest in obtaining the Consumer Market Researcher position at ABC Home Products, posted on the Marketing Association Web site. I believe that I am qualified for this position for several reasons.

My Master's degree is in Consumer Psychology, which emphasizes the behavior of consumers and concepts involving satisfaction, motivation and decision-making processes. An advanced degree in Psychology has provided me with valuable insight and skills in research and design. I am confident in my ability to analyze and quantify human behavior. In addition, I have gained applied experience in assessing behavior and cognitive learning processes through my roles as a Personnel Analyst, Consultant and Teacher. My combination of knowledge, skills and abilities should be extremely beneficial in a position involving product design and consumer market research strategies.

In addition, I possess strong analytical and creative thinking skills. I have a deep interest in human behavior and consumerism and am always looking for new opportunities to explore the ways in which individuals think and behave. My interpersonal and communication skills frequently prove constructive in portraying concepts and viewpoints to others in an innovative and effective manner.

ABC Home Products is a leader in product innovation and employee development, and I would appreciate the opportunity to be a part of the ABC environment. I look forward to hearing from you regarding this exciting opportunity.

Sincerely,

Ronald Smith

275

Consumer Market Researcher. *Tara G. Papp, Mogadore, Ohio*

The second paragraph explains why the applicant believes that he is the right person for the posted position. His graduate degree in Consumer Psychology and applied experience give him an edge.

J. T. TAYLOR   AUTOMOTIVE INDUSTRY PROFESSIONAL

jttaylor@comcast.net **::** 248.969.9933 work **::** 555.555.5555 cell **::** 000.000.0000 home
00000 Meridian, Novi, Michigan 48375

STRATEGIC PLANNING / PROJECT MANAGEMENT / BUSINESS DEVELOPMENT

[Date]

Dear Mr./or Ms. [Last Name]:

As a recent MBA graduate from the University of Michigan, I am pleased to submit my resume for consideration for the position of Marketing Analyst. I think you will find my background, education, motivation, and leadership skills to fit the job description remarkably well and to ultimately be profitable to your organization's marketing function.

Currently I work in a technical area relying heavily on my refined analytical skill. However, as evident in my pursuit of an MBA with a concentration in Marketing and Economics, I am refocusing my career path to encompass more of my creative and macro/planning skills as well. I am looking forward to utilizing my industry and product knowledge together with my strategic thinking abilities and my capability to integrate many different perspectives—always keeping a keen sense of client needs. In addition, my strong organizational, planning, and multitasking skills and team-development experience further qualify me for this position.

I am confident in my skill set because I continue to enhance and prove it. In addition, I am driven by challenges, enjoy learning new things, and can quickly adapt to new environments. Areas of my experience and competency include the following:

Market Research / Forecasting: When pursuing my MBA, I continually led the marketing research function for project groups. In addition, I formed a group of entrepreneurial-minded students aspiring to start local businesses. I serve as the volunteer Marketing Consultant, conducting consumer and trend analyses and competitor benchmarking to identify business opportunities.

Strategic Planning / Analysis: For Anglin Design Associates, I analyzed social and economic factors forecasting short- and long-term prospects for community land developments, as well as assessed segmented user needs and proposed site-planning alternatives. I developed ideas and provided pro-forma projections for contract projects, including commercial and residential green-space development.

Product Knowledge / Design: With three years of experience involved in the automotive product development process, I have acquired a wealth of industry, product, and design knowledge from preliminary design through to prototype and production.

Project Management / Negotiation: I cofounded an award-winning commercial design and planning division of a major company, established key client networks, negotiated favorable contracts, and led a cross-functional team to ensure smooth project execution. This included management of numerous urban space planning projects that required my expertise in conceptual design, detailed construction implementation, estimating, marketing, and final sales presentations.

Thank you for your time in meeting with me and reviewing my credentials. If you need further information, please do not hesitate to contact me. I look forward to hearing from you shortly.

Sincerely,

J. T. Taylor

276

Marketing Analyst. *Jennifer N. Ayres, Clarkston, Michigan*

This professional within a large organization was steered on a path different from the one she wanted to follow. She pursued an MBA to redirect her path from the technical realm to marketing.

Monique Almondry

134 Mt. Veil Avenue	Chicago, Illinois 99999	555-555-5555

April 1, 2004

Hiring Professional
Gap, Inc.
Chicago, Illinois
Fax # 555-555-5555

I appreciate this opportunity to apply for the Assistant Buyer position you have available at Gap, Inc. Enclosed is a copy of my résumé for your review.

As you will note, I have recently been working as an Assistant Buyer in Jefferson, Illinois, where I had the privilege of working in-depth with the 2002 Olympic vendors and strategizing to merchandise top-selling trends. This was, indeed, an exciting adventure. I thoroughly enjoy working together with others to produce a winning outcome. I have strong analytical skills with a keen sense for upcoming design and fashion. With the experience of working in the background in office management and the processing of paperwork required to operate a successful fashion business, I have gained invaluable knowledge about attractive layouts, store design, and the complete process of the fashion industry.

You will find I work well with others and am a strong motivator. I also work efficiently with business planning and predicting trends. I am professional and look forward to developing a long-term career in the fashion and design industry.

I would like to meet with you personally to discuss further where your requirements and my qualifications may blend. You may reach me at 555-555-5555 to set up an interview time. Thank you for your time. I look forward to meeting with you soon.

Sincerely,

Monique Almondry

277

Assistant Buyer. *Rosie Bixel, Portland, Oregon*

The second paragraph summarizes the applicant's relevant experience, interest in working with vendors and identifying fashion trends, analytical skills, and knowledge of the fashion industry.

James Bader

00000 Stone River Drive ▪ Houston, TX 00000 ▪ name@hotmail.com
residence: (713) 000-0000 ▪ mobile: (281) 000-0000

February 14, 2004

Steve Johnson, Program Director
The Home Depot
5515 1-59
Houston, TX 00000

Dear Mr. Johnson:

It is with great interest and enthusiasm that I am submitting my résumé in application for The Home Depot Store Leadership Program. As the current industry leader in home improvement products and services with more than $45 billion in annual revenues (**ranked #9 in *Fortune's* Global Most Admired Companies** list), The Home Depot has certainly established itself as a company poised for even greater success in the future, and I feel that my skills and abilities make me a worthy candidate for the Associate position within this program.

Throughout my career in marketing and HR management, I have maintained a consistent record of meeting and exceeding goals for business growth, organizational leadership, and service delivery. Allow me to briefly call your attention to some of my accomplishments:

> ➢ Initiated recruiting process for start-up operations that led to the hiring of **150** customer service representatives in **two months,** despite the fact that I had no prior experience as an HR Manager.

> ➢ Selected as my company's representative for the **Leadership Houston** program based on my leadership potential, gaining valuable knowledge and insight into team building and leadership.

> ➢ Increased **Alumni and Family Relations network and support** for the University of Houston through special events coordination, training of volunteer networks, and marketing campaigns.

In an August 2001 article from CBS.MarketWatch.com, Home Depot CEO Robert Nardell emphasized that "…in this environment you can't wait for the customer," and I agree that a proactive, results-oriented approach to business growth is the key to success and profitability in the current market. That The Home Depot has continued to succeed and expand despite the struggling economy further attests to its staying power as a leader in the field, and I am confident that I would contribute to The Home Depot's growth and success in a future position.

My résumé is enclosed to provide additional details concerning my background and achievements, but I am certain that a personal interview would more fully reveal my capabilities and desire to join The Home Depot team. Thank you, Mr. Johnson, for your time and consideration of my candidacy.

Sincerely,

James Bader

Enclosure

278

Retail Manager. *Daniel J. Dorotik, Jr., Lubbock, Texas*

For this ad response, the applicant has done his research and mentions company information and a quotation from the CEO. The goal is admission to a leadership program rather than a specific job.

Lisa A. Guerrero

1111 Martin Lane ▪ Philadelphia, PA 00000 ▪ (000) 000-0000 ▪ name@yahoo.com

Barnes & Noble College Bookstores
3434 Smith Street
Philadelphia, PA 00000

RE: Position as General Merchandise Manager, Job ID 000-000

Dear Human Resources Representative:

It was with great interest that I learned about your opening for a General Merchandise Manager, as my qualifications match your requirements for this position. I am confident I can contribute to the success of Barnes & Noble College Bookstores; therefore, please accept my résumé in application for this position and allow me to explain briefly how I meet your requirements and how I can add value to your organization.

As I read your company's advertisement, I noted several connections between what you seek and my background:

Your Requirements:	My Qualifications:
▪ College degree preferred	▪ Bachelor of Arts degree from Temple University
▪ Strong commitment to customer service	▪ Exceeded service delivery goals as Customer Care Manager for Verizon Wireless
▪ 3 years of retail management experience	▪ 4 years as Senior Assistant Manager for retail outlet Shoppers Galore
▪ Team-leadership skills	▪ As manager with Verizon, led team to improved QA scores and 3× sales increase within 3 months of hire
▪ Excellent communication skills	▪ Superb communicator with customers, team members, and upper management
▪ Flexibility is required	▪ Worked varying hours and weekend shifts frequently as manager with Shoppers

Beyond my qualifications, what I can contribute most significantly to your company's future success is my ability to develop great relationships. Whether resolving a customer concern, addressing an issue with upper management, or mentoring a fellow team member, I consistently use a "positive communication" approach that leads to resolved problems and happy customers. In addition, my dedication and work ethic are strong, as my former supervisors will readily verify.

Thank you for your time and review of my qualifications. Please do not hesitate to contact me if you have any questions, and I wish you the best in your candidate search for this position.

Sincerely,

Lisa A. Guerrero

Enclosure

279

General Merchandise Manager. *Daniel J. Dorotik, Jr., Lubbock, Texas*

In this ad response, the writer links the job seeker's qualifications to company requirements line by line. Bullets in both columns help the reader read matching items from column to column.

Kendall Rose Coleman

76 Columbia Street
Poughkeepsie, NY 12601
555.555.5555

000 West 57th Street, Apt. E
New York, NY 10021
000.000.0000

January 27, 2004

Ms. Grace Amere, Fashion Director
Paisley Park Designs
123 Prince Street
New York, NY 10025

Dear Ms. Amere:

Please accept this letter of introduction and enclosed résumé for consideration for a merchandising position within your firm. As a graduate of F.I.T. (Fashion Institute of Technology) with a B.B.A. in Fashion Marketing, my training is current, and I have a solid understanding of textiles and apparel in the global economy.

My academics have been supplemented with real-world experience through F.I.T.'s internship program, which provides advanced experience through employment. Working in various capacities throughout college helped develop my business competency and enhanced my knowledge of contemporary processes, fashion concepts and merchandising strategy. As an intern, I demonstrated a strong commitment to appropriate business practices and excelled at creative plans and trend analysis.

Throughout college, I consistently demonstrated initiative and disciplined work habits. In addition to earning my degree and internship participation, I worked full-time with major retail chains in order to pay for school. Working full-time while being a full-time student in New York City sharpened my time-management skills. It also contributed to my understanding of the commercial impact of decisions as well as my awareness of the importance of positive customer relations.

With exposure to various retail markets and experience in the development of marketing/merchandising strategies, I feel that my ability to provide vision and access new ideas is abundant. This, combined with my powerful work ethic, will enable me to make immediate contributions toward your company's goals.

Thank you in advance for your time and attention. I look forward to hearing from you.

Sincerely,

Kendall Rose Coleman

Enclosure

280

Merchandising Position.   *Kristin M. Coleman, Poughkeepsie, New York*

Unlike many recent graduates without much work experience, this applicant worked full time in major retail chains to pay for school. The letter makes much of this relevant full-time experience.

Jenny Johansen
0000 S.E. Highway 313, Unit F-7 • Deschutes, Oregon 99999
Email: jjjj3953@aol.com   555-555-5555   *Tel* 555-555-5555

April 9, 2002

Gene Reserve
Store Manager
Starbucks
1900 S.E. Miller Road
Deschutes, Oregon 99999

Dear Gene:

Your name has been given to me as one who could introduce me to your District Manager. I would like the opportunity to apply for a position as **Store Manager** for a Starbucks store. I've taken the liberty to enclose a copy of my résumé. Please feel free to pass this letter and my résumé on to your District Manager.

As you will note, I have spent 12 years working in the fast-food industry. I am now eager to transfer to working for Starbucks. This is an area that has fascinated me over the last few years, and I am now ready for a change. I have experience managing a crew, empowering them to be the best they can be, and providing excellent customer service for McDonald's. I have created a strong cash flow for the stores I have been involved with by making sure the customer is well taken care of, monitoring inventory and maintaining control of labor costs. The successful daily operations have also been an important portion of my duties, as well as the implementation and maintenance of all company policies.

Your requirements for a **Store Manager** appear to match my qualifications very closely. I am highly "service" focused and understand the inner workings, financial requirements, and team spirit required to operate a successful store. My résumé only briefly describes my skills. I would appreciate the opportunity to meet with your District Manager directly to further discuss where my qualifications and Starbucks requirements may blend. Please have your District Manager give me a call at her earliest convenience to set up a time when we may meet.

Thank you for your time and assistance.

Sincerely,

Jenny Johansen

281

Store Manager. *Rosie Bixel, Portland, Oregon*

In this networking letter, the applicant asks the reader to pass the letter and a resume on to the hiring manager. The second paragraph tells of relevant experience; the third indicates strengths.

AMY MOU

IIT Research Institute • Life Sciences Operation
10 West 35th Street • Chicago, IL 60616
W: 555-555-5555 • H: 000-000-0000
amy_mou@iitri.org

April 10, 2004

Professor Doron Lancet
Bioinformatics Unit
Department of Molecular Genetics
The Weizmann Institute of Science
Rehovot 76100, Israel

Dear Professor Lancet:

Last August, I had the distinct pleasure of working with you as one of many assistants involved in the GeneCards project. While recently browsing the international GeneCards Web site, I was thrilled to find out that a full-time bioinformatics scientist position will be added to the GeneCards team, commencing this September. My credentials, rigorous scientific approach, and first-rate analytical and problem-solving skills equip me to offer the necessary qualifications mix you require to be a member of the cutting-edge GeneCards team.

Enclosed for your review, my résumé chronicles 15 years of experience as a research scientist in a laboratory environment. My expertise, bioinformatics science, includes a background in microbiology, computational and molecular biology, and toxicology. In January 2001, I was one of the first scientists in the world to earn the Certified Bioinformatics Specialist credential. A fully qualified Oracle Database Administrator, C++ programmer, and biostatistical programs user, I currently supervise the genetic toxicology lab at IIT Research Institute in Chicago.

My résumé is a good summary, but I feel that it is during a personal interview that my potential to be a meaningful addition to your team would be fully demonstrated. I'm scheduled to be in Israel this coming August to again participate in the GeneCards project. This would be a perfect opportunity for you to personally observe me in action and schedule a formal interview.

I will call you in two weeks, during regular business hours, of course, to see about arranging a meeting at your convenience while I'm there. Should you prefer to call me before then, I can be reached at the any of above-listed phone numbers.

Thank you for your time and consideration. I look forward to meeting you once again.

Very truly yours,

Amy Mou

282

Bioinformatics Scientist. *Nick V. Marino, Bishop, Texas*

The applicant knew the reader as the hiring authority and reminded him of their acquaintance and her qualifications based on experience, certification, and rare skills. She clearly requests an interview.

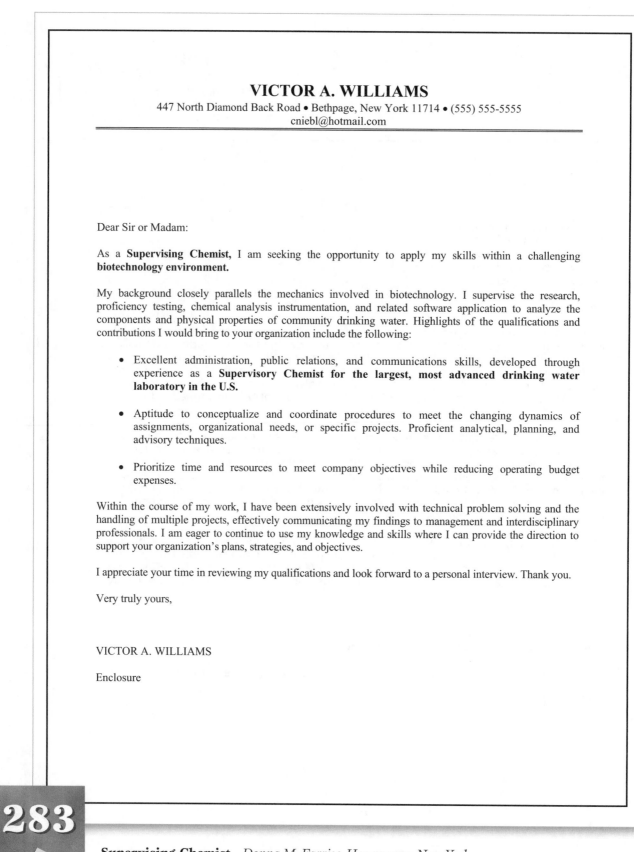

VICTOR A. WILLIAMS

447 North Diamond Back Road • Bethpage, New York 11714 • (555) 555-5555
cniebl@hotmail.com

Dear Sir or Madam:

As a **Supervising Chemist,** I am seeking the opportunity to apply my skills within a challenging **biotechnology environment.**

My background closely parallels the mechanics involved in biotechnology. I supervise the research, proficiency testing, chemical analysis instrumentation, and related software application to analyze the components and physical properties of community drinking water. Highlights of the qualifications and contributions I would bring to your organization include the following:

- Excellent administration, public relations, and communications skills, developed through experience as a **Supervisory Chemist for the largest, most advanced drinking water laboratory in the U.S.**

- Aptitude to conceptualize and coordinate procedures to meet the changing dynamics of assignments, organizational needs, or specific projects. Proficient analytical, planning, and advisory techniques.

- Prioritize time and resources to meet company objectives while reducing operating budget expenses.

Within the course of my work, I have been extensively involved with technical problem solving and the handling of multiple projects, effectively communicating my findings to management and interdisciplinary professionals. I am eager to continue to use my knowledge and skills where I can provide the direction to support your organization's plans, strategies, and objectives.

I appreciate your time in reviewing my qualifications and look forward to a personal interview. Thank you.

Very truly yours,

VICTOR A. WILLIAMS

Enclosure

283

Supervising Chemist. *Donna M. Farrise, Hauppauge, New York*

This letter uses boldface to call attention to the most important information about the applicant: his name at the top, his occupation, his targeted field of activity, and his current position.

TAMMY D. MILLER
17 Old Willets Path
Hauppauge, New York 11788
(555) 555-5555
tammydmiller@yahoo.com

Dear Sir or Madam:

I have recently relocated to New York with the intention of pursuing a position in the field of *scientific research.* My goal is to obtain an opportunity within a **Biotech/Bioengineering company.** I genuinely desire to be an integral part of a team research effort and the clinical trial process. Highlights of my academic achievement and employment experience include the following:

> - **Exceptional Academic Record…B.S. in Microbiology** with a concentration in **Molecular Biology…**consistently maintained superior grades with *honors in Virology, Immunology, Advanced Bacteriology, and Microbial Genetics.*

> - **Analytical and Organizational Skills…**practical employment allowed me to demonstrate my **strength in data research, analysis, and documentation.**

> - **Strong Project Management Skills…**with extensive experience working as a Structured Finance Coordinator, Center Director, Area Supervisor, and R.O.T.C. Cadet. I have been **involved in the planning, data research, written communication, and public service** that resulted in significant accomplishments in leadership, organization, and self-discipline.

> - **Communication and Public Relations Skills…**in each of my positions, I have dealt cooperatively with the general public, colleagues, and superiors. My skills at interpersonal relations and cross-cultural communications are considerable.

Throughout my academic background and employment history, I have consistently driven myself to meet challenges and achieve goals. It is within this type of challenging and results-oriented environment that I thrive.

I would appreciate the opportunity to meet and further share with you my qualifications and enthusiasm for joining your company research team.

Sincerely,

TAMMY D. MILLER

Enclosure

284

Researcher. *Donna M. Farrise, Hauppauge, New York*

In this letter the writer of Cover Letter 283 shows the same technique of using boldface to direct attention to key information. Bold italic is an additional attention-getting enhancement to show the field and honors.

JOHN H. CLARKE, LCPC

0000 N. Buffalo Grove Road
Arlington Heights, Illinois 60004
Telephone: (555) 555-5555

April 8, 2004

James Morgenstern, Ph.D.
Director of Adult Services
Alexian Brothers Northwest Mental Health Center
1606 Colonial Parkway
Palatine, Illinois 60067

Dear Dr. Morgenstern:

I am a Licensed Clinical Professional Counselor and a Master of Arts–Psychology graduate from UIC and am presently conducting a search for a position in an accredited mental health agency or psychotherapy practice. Please review the attached curriculum vitae as it may relate to potential opportunities that might exist within your organization.

My CV indicates that I have 10+ years of experience working in the business world prior to my enrollment at UIC, as well as my current position as a Psychotherapist and previous counseling internship. In my business career, I interacted with many different personality types and developed a keen interest in general psychological issues of adults. I frequently dealt with difficult customers and felt limited in my ability to assist them beyond the boundaries of my employers' products or services. I finally concluded that I could best serve people if I had more knowledge of human behavior, which is why I chose to enter the field of professional psychology. Since your agency provides services for adult populations, I feel that my current experience, academic coursework and business background represent a good fit.

I would welcome the opportunity to further discuss my educational and professional background in relation to the needs of your agency's clientele. Please feel free to contact me at your earliest convenience. Thank you for your time and consideration.

Sincerely,

John H. Clarke, LCPC

Curriculum Vitae enclosed.

285

Licensed Clinical Professional Counselor. *Joellyn Wittenstein-Schwerdlin, Elk Grove Village, Illinois*

This candidate mentions to potential employers how he transitioned from the business world to the status of Licensed Clinical Professional Counselor (LCPC) while working his way through school.

ROY NASH

4900 Boulevard, Carson City, NV 00000   (000) 000-0000

January 15, 2004

Ms. Sadie Brown, M.S.W.
Director
Hope Rehabilitation Center
860 Truckee River Parkway
Reno, NV 00000

Dear Ms. Brown:

As a follow-up to a recent phone conversation with your associate, I learned that there may be opportunities for employment within your organization, and I am writing to express my interest. I have not only a clear understanding of the problems leading to addictive behavior but also the prerequisite education to work in alcohol and drug counseling. I sincerely want to help others who are experiencing the same horrors I went through as an alcoholic and cocaine addict. My ultimate goal is to become a Certified Alcohol and Drug Counselor, for which I need to accumulate 6,000 hours of practical experience under the direction of certified counselors.

Currently, I am a counselor assistant at Straight and Narrow, a psycho-social rehabilitative agency, where I have begun to develop my professional and clinical skills through work with groups of substance abusers in recovery. I am considered by others to be self-determined, enthusiastic, and reliable, with the ability to adjust well in a new environment.

My resume is enclosed for your review. If your rehabilitative staff requirements allow for continued training with a certified counselor, I would like to learn more about the opportunity. I will be calling you within a week to determine your interest and perhaps arrange for a time when we can meet.

Very truly yours,

Roy Nash

Enclosure

286

Alcohol and Drug Counselor (in Training). *Melanie Noonan, West Paterson, New Jersey*

As a follow-up to a recent phone call, this letter expresses interest in a possible position and tells of the applicant's relevant experience and current extensive work for certification. See Resume 21 (page 383).

JASMINE HIGHLANDER

555 Harrison Avenue   Brentwood, NY 55555   (333) 444-5555   advocate@4campuslife.net

Date

Name
Company
Address

Dear Name:

The accompanying resume is presented for your review and consideration for the position of Assistant Director of College Housing. To further illustrate my qualifications, the following outlines the scope of my experience as it pertains to this position's specific requirements.

Your requirements	My qualifications
• Bachelor's degree, or	• Master's degree in Clinical Counseling.
• Four years of experience in lieu of degree.	• Eight years of combined experience in residence hall administration and counseling capacities.
• Promote and develop educational programming and maintain extensive budget.	• Plan, develop, and implement educational programs, and manage an operational budget.
• Administration of three to five residence halls housing approximately 1,000 students.	• Administration of residence halls housing up to 500 students.
• Supervise, develop, and evaluate three to five full-time residence hall directors.	• Supervise, develop, and evaluate 26 Resident Advisors with direct responsibility for four RAs and a Head Resident Advisor (HRA).
• Develop departmental policies and procedures, manage area office including billing, occupancy, and facilities records.	• Direct all aspects of front desk management and facilities maintenance operations.
• Assist in the development and leadership of departmental committees, and serve as manager for student conduct cases.	• Held a one-year position as Vice President of Committees for the Student Government with the State University of New York.

Thank you for your review and consideration. I look forward to speaking with you soon.

Sincerely,

Jasmine Highlander

287

Assistant Director of College Housing. *Ann Baehr, Brentwood, New York*

A two-column format is useful for showing how an applicant's qualifications match a company's requirements. This letter shows further that some of the qualifications can exceed requirements.

ANNA M. SANCHEZ

123 Fort Avenue • Anywhere, Michigan 55555 • (555) 555-0000 • Cellular (555) 888-2222

February 8, 2004

John Gomez, Director
Family Community Center
555 Main Street
Anywhere, Michigan 55555

Dear Mr. Gomez,

After serving the Family Community Center for more than 17 years, I have had the opportunity to grow in my profession as an office assistant while helping others in time of need. It gives me pleasure to know I am able to provide much-needed assistance to individuals who turn to our center for support.

My experience has allowed me to work with a large number of adults and children from different ethnic backgrounds, providing assistance to individuals assigned to community service, as well as the elderly. I speak and read Spanish fluently, which is a must because our center serves a great number of Hispanics in the local area.

At this time, I feel my experience and commitment to the Family Community Center has positioned me to take on increased responsibilities. My objective is to secure the Direct Assistance Coordinator position upon its availability, and I welcome the opportunity to discuss my qualifications further. I have enclosed my resume to give you a brief review of my background and experience.

I will follow up with you next week to answer any questions you may have regarding my application. If you would like to speak sooner, please contact me anytime. Thank you in advance for your consideration.

Regards,

Anna M. Sanchez

Enclosure

288

Direct Assistance Coordinator. *Maria E. Hebda, Trenton, Michigan*

This future position was the person's goal after 17 years of service to the organization. She believed that she could take on additional responsibilities and built a case for being considered seriously.

Heather C. Bjorn

999-B Stetson Boulevard
Cranston, SC 55555
(111) 222–3333
heatherb@earthlink.com

March 16, 2004

Ms. Rebecca Phipps, Director of Human Resources
South Carolina State Department of Social Services
1111 Baltimore Street, 2nd Floor
Cranston, SC 55555

Dear Ms. Phipps:

Please accept this letter of application for employment in the South Carolina Social Services
Division for Children and Their Families. My education, training, and experience have built a
solid, relevant foundation for employment in this division, as I believe my current enclosed
résumé proves.

Working with children in multicultural and diverse socioeconomic strata is a challenge in which I
am eager to engage as a professional social worker. Although I am content and qualified to
continue in my current position with the Easter Seals–SC, Cranston ARC, I feel that my greater
strength and enthusiasm lie in assisting youth, as evidenced in my volunteer work with the
Children's Crusade. Developing and promoting proper independent living skills is a goal and
dream of mine that I shall pursue until I am in such a position to assist youngsters during their
crucial, formative time of cultural and behavioral development.

If you feel that my credentials, along with my genuine enthusiasm to work with children, are
sufficient to meet your criteria for employment in this field, please contact me when an opening
occurs. I can be reached at heatherb@earthlink.com or (111) 222-3333 during the day or evening.
I look forward eagerly to meeting with you to discuss my professional qualifications.

Thank you for your time in consideration of my application.

Sincerely,

Heather C. Bjorn

Enclosure: résumé

289

Social Services Counselor. *Edward Turilli, North Kingstown, Rhode Island*

The challenge of this letter was to prove to the recruiter that the applicant, having performed
well for Easter Seals in social services, would thrive in a career directly assisting needy, disadvantaged youth.

EVELYN MORRIS
0000 Summit Drive • Englewood, NJ 00000 • (555) 555-5555 • Morris30@aol.com

January 6, 2004

Mr. Suzanne Reynolds
Director, Social Services
Borrin Correctional Institution
2299 Central Avenue
Englewood, NJ 00000

Dear Ms. Reynolds:

Becoming a social worker has been a lifelong dream of mine, and I have taken the first step toward fulfilling this dream. In May, I will graduate with a bachelor's degree. As part of my educational training, I am seeking an internship at the Borrin Correctional Institution to further develop my clinical social work skills while applying my training to benefit others.

Currently, I am completing a clinical internship at the Borrin Families in Crisis Center. This experience has not only taught me valuable lessons about human life, but has also reinforced my interest in employment in a correctional environment following graduation. My future plans include pursuing a master's degree in clinical social work.

Complementing my education in social work are both employment and volunteer experiences that relate to my career interests while adding to my skill development in this profession. Such experiences over the past several years have included employment as a medical assistant at a physician practice, providing support services to families of children with cancer at a community hospital and volunteering at a crisis-counseling center. In addition, my professors and supervisor at the Borrin Families in Crisis Center have frequently commented on my natural aptitude for a career in social work.

Highly self-motivated with an energetic style, I am eager to learn new skills and enhance my education while contributing to your organization. My strengths also include communications, maturity and the ability to relate effectively with individuals at all levels and cultural backgrounds as demonstrated throughout my prior career in business.

I look forward to discussing an internship opportunity at your institution and appreciate your consideration.

Sincerely,

Evelyn Morris

290

Social Worker. *Louise Garver, Enfield, Connecticut*

This prospective graduate was seeking an internship at a correctional facility to develop her clinical social work skills. The letter indicates her experience and strengths. She secured the internship.

Marie C. Bedford

0000 West 81st Avenue
St. Louis, MO 00000

home: (000) 000-0000
name@msn.com

January 15, 2004

Human Resources Department
United Way
155 Toulouse Street
St. Louis, MO 00000

Dear Human Resources Representative:

It was with great interest that I read your advertisement for the position of Program Manager. I believe that my qualifications and experience match your requirements, and I am confident that I can add to your continued success and growth.

My 10 years of experience as a Director of Social Services, Care Plan Coordinator, Case Manager, and Social Worker have provided me the opportunity to build a strong track record of success in program leadership, service delivery, and community relations development. Thus, I could benefit your firm's sales growth in several ways:

- I have met and exceeded objectives in providing the highest level of service for patients in facilities ranging from **120** to **176** beds, earning the respect and trust of residents and family members;
- I have demonstrated the ability to maintain **100%** compliance with state and federal regulations, with personal commendations from state auditors and several "zero violations" scores on state audits;
- I keep up-to-date about changes and developments in all aspects of the human/social services industry, and my current plans include re-obtaining my **LSW** license;
- I am a results-driven program management and community relations professional who builds strong networks and develops win-win relationships with program participants, team members, and community leaders.

My positive attitude and dedication to both personal and professional growth are traits I held when I initially entered into the field of social services, and they remain an integral part of my work ethic today. You can be assured that I will demonstrate an uncompromising focus on service delivery, quality assurance, and the achievement of organizational objectives and goals as a member of your team.

My résumé is enclosed to provide you with additional details concerning my background and qualifications. I will contact you within the week to follow up on this inquiry; perhaps we could arrange a meeting to discuss how I could contribute to your organization.

Thank you for your time and consideration. Please do not hesitate to contact me if I can answer any questions.

Sincerely,

Marie C. Bedford

Enclosure

291

United Way Program Manager. *Daniel J. Dorotik, Jr., Lubbock, Texas*

The writer called this a "resume letter" because it has specific details and bulleted statements. Specific numbers illustrate accomplishments. Boldfacing calls attention to the numbers and the applicant's LSW license.

FRANKLIN HARRIS

84 Park Boulevard • East Syracuse NY 13900
555/555-5555 • fharris@myemail.com

February 10, 2004

Reverend Henry Richmond
President
Onondaga County Coalition of Churches
PO Box 857
Syracuse NY 13909

RE: Projects Coordinator

Dear Reverend Richmond:

Your posting from the *Syracuse Daily News* is of great interest to me. In the next month, I will be retiring from the State of New York and am seeking a challenging, rewarding and flexible opportunity. My résumé is enclosed for your review.

Project and program coordination and management have been a staple of my career with the state, beginning in Social Services (Foster Care and Child Protection Services) and concluding in the Division of Parole. Beyond tenure in these departments, I have been an instructor, trainer and curriculum developer … director of two nonprofit organizations … and the designer and first coordinator of a public school's home/school program. Contributing to my community has always been important, and notable current involvement includes President of the East Syracuse–Minoa Central School Board, Uniform Instructor for the Sea Cadets and Councilman for the Town of East Syracuse.

Educational credentials earned include a BS in Criminal Science with graduate studies in Social Work as well as Psychology. I am a Certified Peace Officer in line with my Parole Division experience. I have completed diverse professional development as well as training necessary to serve responsibly in several volunteer capacities.

In addition to my well-honed interpersonal and communication skills, positive attitude and dedication, my familiarity with your service area and established contacts in it would be beneficial. I am very comfortable having accountability for an organization's effective use of its resources and am confident in my ability to contribute positively as your Projects Coordinator.

It would be a pleasure to discuss this opportunity with you in greater detail, and I invite you to contact me at 555-5555 or through email at fharris@myemail.com. I look forward to talking with you soon.

Thank you for your time and consideration.

Sincerely,

Franklin Harris

292

Projects Coordinator. *Salome A. Farraro, Mount Morris, New York*

Retiring from the New York State Division of Parole, this individual applied for the Projects Coordinator position. This letter, together with his resume, helped him get an interview and an offer.

Carmen M. Kennedy

carmkenn@hotmail.com

642 Riverview Drive ▼ Parkersburg, WV 26000 ▼ 304.224.0000

April 2, 2004

Kristi Vanderpool
PO Box 1278
Vienna, WV 26111

Dear Ms. Vanderpool:

To inspire and enable all young people, especially those from disadvantaged circumstances, to realize their full potential as productive, responsible and caring citizens.

The mission of the Boys & Girls Clubs of America is something that I strongly believe in. That is why I read with great interest your recent ad in the St. Mary's Oracle for a Teen Outreach Coordinator with the Boys and Girls Clubs of Wirt County. As a native of Wirt County with a lifelong desire to work with children and excellent leadership skills, I believe I have much to offer in this capacity.

A music education major at Marietta College, I prepared for a future career of educating children. I've spent more than 100 hours in the classroom working with, teaching and observing students and have realized that this is where I want to focus my career working to prepare the youth of today for tomorrow's world. In addition, I have been actively involved in various youth activities throughout my life. It would be an honor for me to be able to contribute to the Boys & Girls Clubs' mission of providing

- *A safe place to learn and grow.*

- *Ongoing relationships with caring adult professionals.*

- *Life-enhancing programs and character-development experiences.*

- *Hope and opportunity.*

An interview would allow me to share my qualifications in greater detail and learn more about this exciting opportunity. I will call you next week to follow up. Thank you for your time and consideration. I look forward to speaking with you soon.

Sincerely,

Carmen M. Kennedy

Enclosure

293

Teen Outreach Coordinator. *Melissa L. Kasler, Athens, Ohio*

The writer used information from the mission statements of the Boys & Girls Clubs of America to convey this applicant's dedication. She was called for an interview immediately and given the job.

George Lease
3333 Falcon Drive • Fairfield, ND 99999
555-555-5555

Date

Name
Company
Address

Dear Hiring Professional:

In response to your recent advertisement, I've enclosed a copy of my résumé. I have recently moved to the Northwest from Texas, where I owned an automotive repair shop. I still have quite a bit of equipment but am not interested in owning or starting a business again.

I have very strong diagnostic and repair skills with the belief that no job is too difficult. While building a strong business, I developed the reputation of complete honesty with the ability to perform accurate and lasting repairs. I also had a strong reputation among the dealers, with them often calling me for advice. My work was honored by a company that provided rebuilt motors by warranting any motor supplied by them that I installed. As you can see, I developed a positive and strong business reputation for high quality and honest work. I would like to assist another company in their success by providing top-notch technician work for them.

The position you have available appears to be one that matches my skills very closely. I would like the opportunity to meet with you personally where we may further discuss your requirements and my abilities. You may contact me at 555-555-5555 to set up a mutually convenient time. Thank you for taking the time to review my résumé, and I look forward to your call.

Sincerely,

George Lease

Enclosure

294

Automotive Repair Position. *Rosie Bixel, Portland, Oregon*

Having moved to a new location, this applicant wanted only to work for another firm. The task of the letter is to convey the impressive reputation he had earned as the owner of a repair shop.

00000 Spring Road
Columbus, Ohio 99999
444-444-4444
brianpetra@resume.com

Brian T. Petra

DATE

CONTACT NAME
ORGANIZATION
ADDRESS
CITY, STATE ZIP

Dear CONTACT NAME:

Are you currently seeking an **NC Machine Repair Mechanic** with more than 15 years of experience in testing, troubleshooting, repairing, and making design improvements to automated equipment? If so, I would like to apply for the position.

As you will note on my attached resume, I have more than 500 hours of formal and hands-on training in hydraulics, lasers, numerical control procedures, and computer skills. In addition, I would bring the following to your team:

- Pursue work with energy, drive, and a strong accomplishment orientation
- Efficiently develop and implement plans to accomplish goals
- Focus on achieving positive, concrete results
- Understand how to get things done and achieve objectives while working with cross-organizational teams
- Possess excellent communication skills

Given the opportunity, I can make an immediate contribution to your company and would appreciate the opportunity to meet with you to discuss your requirements. I will call your office next week, or I can be reached at 444-444-4444 to schedule an appointment. Thank you for your consideration.

Sincerely,

Brian T. Petra

Enclosure: Resume

295

NC Machine Repair Mechanic. *Diana Ramirez, Seatac, Washington*

This applicant, having expertise with automated equipment and numerical control procedures, was looking for specialized work. Bullets point to worker traits valued by most employers.

Elizabeth Denton

1814 Taylor Drive ~ North Brunswick, NJ 08902
(555) 555-5555 (H) ~ (000) 000-0000 (C) ~ E-mail: lizdent3@msn.com

Date

Name
Company
Address

RE: Maintenance Mechanic

Dear Sir/Madam:

As a professional **Facilities** and **Maintenance Mechanic,** I understand that success depends on several factors. These include timely upkeep of machinery maintenance and repair, supervision of maintenance programs, and monitoring outside contractors. My extensive hands-on experience as a mechanic has allowed me to ensure timely completion of projects and adherence to corporate safety requirements.

Throughout my career I have been promoted and have acquired increasing responsibilities within every position. In my latest position as a Mechanic for Heinz Foods, I had the reputation for excellent machinery knowledge and a keen attention to detail.

Heinz Foods is downsizing the plant in Edison, NJ, and I have accepted a voluntary separation package from the company. I would like to continue my career with a new company offering me new challenges.

Thank you for your consideration. I possess excellent hands-on knowledge as well as supervisory expertise, and I look forward to meeting with you personally so that we may discuss how I may make a positive contribution to your team.

Very truly yours,

Elizabeth Denton

Enclosure

296

Maintenance Mechanic. *Beverley and Mitchell I. Baskin, Marlboro, New Jersey*

This applicant had been downsized and was looking for a new, challenging position in which she could use her skills as a mechanic. These are mentioned in the first paragraph. See Resume 22 (page 384).

Ralph Forte
43–74 Belt Parkway
Brooklyn, NY 00000

Home: (000) 000-0000

Cell: (000) 000-0000

January 11, 2004

New York Post
P.O. Box 4498
New York, NY 00000

Dear Hiring Manager:

In your ad in last Sunday's *Post,* you stated that you needed an experienced elevator mechanic. As you will see when you read my resume, I believe I have the necessary skills and qualifications to excel at this job.

For most of my career, I have been involved in all aspects of elevator installation and maintenance. I have a thorough understanding of all of the requirements necessary for a successful job, and my organizational ability allows me to complete my assignments well within the acceptable time frame.

My present position entails the coordination of equipment and its component parts according to client specifications as outlined on blueprints. I take pride that my work always has passed rigid inspections.

As I am accustomed to preparing logs and reports, paperwork would be no problem. I am considered a good communicator, using this ability to train other personnel and make recommendations to owners/managers to increase efficiency at the installation sites where I have worked. The frequent travel you describe in your ad would not interfere with my personal obligations.

If this position is still available, I would like the opportunity to talk with you in person and discuss how my skills would benefit your company. You may contact me on my cell phone during the workday or at home after 4:30 p.m.

Sincerely,

Ralph Forte

297

Elevator Mechanic. *Melanie Noonan, West Paterson, New Jersey*

This response to an ad indicates that the experienced applicant is able to perform all aspects of elevator installation and maintenance, including all of the necessary paperwork.

Eric P. Stanley

48 Marine View Drive
Federal Way, WA 99999
(555) 555-5555
ericstanley@resume.net

April 11, 2004

XYZ Company
ATTN: George Jones
VIA FAX: (444) 444-4444

To Whom It May Concern:

I was introduced to your company by subcontractor John Peterson, who was contracted to do work at the Ellensburg, Washington, wind farm project. I assisted him in standing three met towers and reinforcing existing shoring on the remaining towers. This is where I met Ken Roberts, Mike Henly, and other employees of XYZ. After further observation of XYZ through our correspondence and the Internet, I was very intrigued by the work XYZ does and the direction the company is headed toward providing an environmentally clean power solution. I wish to express my interest in obtaining full-time employment with XYZ.

As you can see by my résumé, I would bring a diverse knowledge of the tools and equipment necessary to perform the job. With my strong customer service skills, sales background, and attention to detail, I can be counted on to produce the high-quality work the job demands. My previous work history has taught me the importance of adhering to deadlines and financial guidelines set by the company. I have experienced, firsthand, the inner workings of enXco and found the work to be physically challenging and personally satisfying. I feel that my work history has prepared me for the professionalism and hard work ethic your company requires.

I look forward to the possibility of working with XYZ. I would like to express my willingness to work flexible hours and travel for projects as needed. I thank you for your time and consideration in this matter and will be in contact with your office to set up a meeting at a convenient time.

Sincerely,

Eric P. Stanley

Enc.: Résumé

298

Wind-Power Technology Position. *Diana Ramirez, Seatac, Washington*

The opening paragraph indicates a referral who introduced the applicant to employees of a company. The applicant's research led to his interest in that company as a possible employer.

TOM NEWTON

0000 Whitewood Court • North Brunswick, New Jersey 08902 • 555.555.5555

QUALITY ASSURANCE PROFESSIONAL
QUALITY CONTROL ~ LABORATORY TECHNICIAN

Date

Name
Company
Address

Re: Quality Assurance Position

Dear Sir or Madam:

Enclosed is my resume for your review. I am confident that my long-term chemical/food experience with various types of manufacturing processes would serve as an asset to your company.

I have 5 years of experience working as a **Quality Assurance Technician** at Northeast Foods, where I performed analytical checks and quality assurance procedures for food and beverage products.

I am considered a quick learner with high concentration skills. In addition, I feel that my interpersonal skills, honesty, and rapport with fellow employees will benefit the company.

Other skills that I have gained though my employment are weighing and blending of batch ingredients according to formula, as well as inventory control. I have always been known for my accuracy and hardworking attitude.

Thank you for your consideration. I look forward to speaking with you personally so that we may discuss my qualifications in greater detail.

Sincerely yours,

Tom Newton

Enclosure

299

Quality Assurance Technician. *Beverley and Mitchell I. Baskin, Marlboro, New Jersey*

The applicant was looking for another quality assurance position. Five brief paragraphs tell of his experience, activities, people skills, on-the-job skills, and interest in an interview. See Resume 23 (page 386).

41 Grayson Way, Indianapolis IN 55555
(555) 555-5555

January 23, 2004

Mrs. Penelope Jackson
Human Resource Manager
Duncan Electric & Gas Company
Corner of Stapleton and Merryman Avenues
Knoxville, Tennessee 55555

Position Desired: ELECTRICAL LINEMAN

Dear Mrs. Jackson:

Since graduating from Mercy County Technical College two years ago, I have worked in the electrical field on a number of emergency and routine projects, including assignments abroad. This experience involves installation, repair and maintenance of transmission and distribution lines and transformers.

Prior experience involves supervising, coordinating and working with considerable responsibility. I believe that many of the personal and work qualities I offer are ones that employers value and have difficulty finding:

Dependability	Flexibility	High Attendance
Work Ethic and Integrity	Dedication	Commitment to Quality and Accuracy

In a global environment that often requires working alongside people with varying temperaments and from various cultures, I'm especially proud to be able to work effectively and efficiently with all kinds of people. My ability to communicate well with others and to promote team efforts are excellent, and I'm always willing to lend a hand when needed. Leadership experience has taught me patience, diplomacy and tolerance.

I will be calling your office to check on interview scheduling for this position, and I look forward to the opportunity to meet with you to discuss details. If you need additional information, please contact me at the above phone number.

Sincerely,

Larry Duvall

Enclosure: Resume

300

Electrical Lineman. *Beverley Drake, Rochester, Minnesota*

The applicant indicates in turn his experience, worker traits as transferable skills, people skills, and interest in an interview. His transferable worker traits stand out clearly in three columns.

SANDRA BACHUS, CPP

55 Pinehurst Road
Augusta, Ontario A1A 1A1
(555) 666-9999 • bachus@email.com

February 5, 2004

Pauline Ho
Senior Human Resources Manager
SciTech Pharmaceuticals
2345 Industry Circle
Pinehurst, Ontario
B2C 3D4

<u>**Re: Senior Component Technician**</u>

Dear Mrs. Ho,

"Sandra is considered an expert in her field...and continues to be the 'go-to' person."

With more than 10 years of experience overseeing packaging specifications, artwork, and production for some of the world's largest pharmaceutical firms, I have developed exhaustive expertise in all aspects of the industry—from technical specifications to quality control, production engineering, artwork, labelling, and distribution.

As the current Senior Component Development Specialist with ABC Packaging Inc., I coordinate 20–30 concurrent packaging projects at any given time for the full range of OTC and prescription products. I am very excited at the prospect of joining your team as your new Senior Component Technician as I am now anxious to apply my expertise to new and more challenging scenarios. The qualifications that distinguish me include the following:

✓ **Certified Packaging Professional** (recertified 2003) and **PAC Alumni certification** (2001)

✓ Exhaustive technical knowledge of **packaging components, processes, equipment, and tooling capabilities**

✓ Reputation for identifying opportunities to **improve processes, maximize efficiencies, and reduce costs** based on engineering and production requirements

✓ Skilled in **managing all artwork and creative processes**—familiar with a wide variety of printing processes and alternatives (flexography, gravure, etc.), further encouraging ability to produce top quality every time

✓ Excellent **communication and client/vendor relations** skills, internally and externally

If you are interested in speaking to a highly motivated and skilled professional with a reputation for excellence and continuous improvement, then I would welcome the opportunity to meet to discuss this opportunity in person.

I look forward to meeting with you and thank you for your consideration.

Sincerely,

Sandra Bachus

Encl.

301

Senior Component Technician. *Ross Macpherson, Whitby, Ontario, Canada*

The page border, thick horizontal line, opening testimonial, and bulleted qualifications in bold-face helped this candidate stand head and shoulders above other applicants with more traditional letters.

ALEXIS M. SMITH
0000 Archway Drive ▪ Charlotte, North Carolina 28888 ▪ (555) 555-5555

April 5, 2004

www.alltel.com/careers

ATTN: Placement Professional

Someone once said, "There are no great companies, just the people who work for them." Sounds as if the person who said this was referring to an organization—like Alltel—that espouses the philosophy of cooperative teamwork.

Your advertisement in *The Charlotte Observer* (April 4) for a Coordinator–Number Administrator certainly seems to describe such an environment, with an opportunity that rewards team performance.

If so, I'd like to become a member!

Throughout my experience with AT&T, I was given opportunities to contribute to resolving customer problems, provide administrative and technical support, and coordinate processes—through both in-house and field staff, as well as customers. Based on my training in the telecommunications industry, I know how to troubleshoot, monitor, and coordinate line problems. I worked in the Technical Department in the Business Center.

Following retirement from AT&T two years ago, I have continued to upgrade my skills, including advanced training in Word, Access, Excel, PowerPoint, and Windows, among others.

I'm confident that I could contribute effectively to the Alltel team. May we schedule a time to discuss our mutual goals?

Thank you for your consideration.

Sincerely,

Alexis M. Smith

302

Coordinator–Number Administrator. *Doug Morrison, Charlotte, North Carolina*

After 30 years of work, this applicant had "retired." Having energy and youthful vigor, however, she wanted to work for a new team—something that she had always been good at and liked doing.

Dear Hiring Manager:

For as long as I can remember, I have had a talent for keeping things well organized and operating efficiently. Post-it-Notes, schedules, databases, and Excel spreadsheets are a part of my everyday life. I bring order to clutter and structure to chaos. If you feel that these skills and talents would prove to be advantageous to the Macy's West Visitors Center, then I would like to schedule a time for us to meet.

In addition to strong organizational skills, I offer you:

    + more than five years of experience in the travel, hospitality, and tourism industry

    + strong computer skills with a knack for Internet research and database creation and management

    + a solid work ethic and a commitment to giving whatever it takes to get a job done, right and on time

My professional office skills and strengths are complemented by a positive, can-do attitude, excellent listening skills, and a sense of humor. I have built an extensive network in Las Vegas and have assembled a diverse blend of personal and professional references to attest to my abilities.

I hope you will see what a valuable addition I would make to your team of professionals and phone me. I can be reached at 555.555.5555 or 555.555.0000. Thank you for your consideration.

Sincerely,

Kathryn R. Hill

303

Travel Industry Professional. *Norine Dagliano, Hagerstown, Maryland*

This letter was e-mailed in response to a job posted on the employer's Web site. The letter, a brief overview of the candidate's skills, got an immediate reply. An interview occurred the next day.

Karrie MacNeal

0000 West Union Street ▼ Athens, Ohio 45701 ▼ 555.555.5555 ▼ kmacneal@msn.com

February 12, 2004

Ms. Susan Andrews
Human Resources Manager
Flyaway Travel Agency
229 South First Street
Athens, Ohio 45701

Dear Ms. Andrews:

It was with great interest that I read your recent ad in the *Athens Messenger* for a Travel Consultant, and I would like to be considered a serious candidate for this position. My resume is enclosed for your review and consideration.

Simply stated, travel has been my passion for more than 15 years! Even though my educational and career paths have taken me in a different direction up to this point, I have recently decided to follow my heart and pursue a career in the travel industry. Because of my desire to work in travel, I enrolled in the Travel Associate Training Program through Career Quest and will complete it next month.

Throughout my career I have utilized an ability to communicate effectively, both orally and in writing, with people from all walks of life. My counseling skills enable me to identify and respond appropriately to client needs. In addition, the time I spent as a Customer Service Manager allowed me to develop and enhance skills in sales, public speaking, event planning and database management skills that I believe would also be invaluable in your Travel Consultant position.

With a passion for travel, successful career experience in sales and current industry training, I am confident I would be an asset to your travel agency. Feel free to contact me to set up an interview or to answer any questions you may have regarding my background and experience. I look forward to speaking with you soon.

Sincerely,

Karrie MacNeal

Enclosure

304

Travel Consultant. *Melissa L. Kasler, Athens, Ohio*

The applicant had a strong travel background and wanted to transition from customer-service counseling to travel consulting. The writer focused on travel-related activities and transferable skills.

DESMOND MASSEY

000 Augusta Court • Pinehurst, Ontario A1A 1A1
(555) 666-7777 • dmassey@email.com

March 12, 2004

Pinehurst Transit Commission
Human Resources Department
Placement Services
1111 Batterley Street
Pinehurst, Ontario
A1A 1A1

Re: Operator / Driver Positions

Dear Human Resources Manager,

Put simply, I love to drive—and with more than 600,000 safe miles of large-vehicle driving experience, a conscientious and safety-minded driving style, and years of experience providing the highest levels of customer service, I believe I can offer you both the skills and experience you are looking for in a PTC Operator/Driver.

I have been fortunate. My unique career has afforded me the opportunity to drive and transport loads throughout Canada and the U.S. in a variety of vehicles, including 18- and 30-wheel trailers. While most of my positions were in operations and customer service, these frequent driving opportunities represented an aspect of the job that I thoroughly enjoyed, and as I now find myself seeking a career change, I am finally in the position to pursue a long-standing desire to drive for a living.

I encourage you to review the attached résumé detailing my qualifications, highlights of which include

- ✓ **Extensive large-vehicle driving experience—CDL License, Class A with Trailer and Air Brake endorsements**
- ✓ **Outstanding customer service skills from 11+ years in sales and account management—personable, friendly, and professional**
- ✓ **Able to work flexible work schedules and nonstandard shifts**

I would welcome the opportunity to meet and discuss in person the value I could add as a PTC Operator/Driver. I am very enthusiastic about this opportunity and am confident that I have the right combination of skills and experience to exceed your expectations.

Thank you for your consideration, and I look forward to hearing from you soon.

Sincerely,

Desmond Massey

Encl.

305

Operator/Driver. *Ross Macpherson, Whitby, Ontario, Canada*

After 15 years in a family business, this candidate wanted to turn his passion for driving into a full-time career. The letter conveyed his love for driving and his qualifications, making him stand out.

Lawrence Blake

0000 Franklin Avenue • Boise, ID 99999 • (555) 555–5555

March 2, 2004

Monty Cramer
Executive Director of Facilities Administration
University of Idaho
0000 University Drive
Boise, Idaho 99999

Dear Mr. Cramer,

Please accept this letter as application for the Parking and Transportation Services Director position currently available with your organization. My resume is attached for your review and consideration, and I believe you will find me well qualified.

Detailed on my résumé is a solid background in the transportation industry, with more than 10 years of experience. In this capacity, I have developed an expertise in service improvement, operations management, and customer service. I am confident that my experience in these areas will prove to be an asset to the University of Idaho.

Additionally, I am familiar with short- and long-range planning for public transportation. I am known for effectively identifying and resolving problems before they affect related areas, personnel, or customers.

I am certain of my abilities to make a significant contribution early on and believe that a personal interview would better demonstrate how I would be of value to the University of Idaho. I look forward to the opportunity of discussing in person how my expertise could best fit your needs and contribute to your organization's continued success. In the interim, thank you for your consideration, attention, and forthcoming response.

Sincere regards,

Lawrence Blake

Enclosure

306

Parking and Transportation Services Director. *Denette Jones, Boise, Idaho*

The second and third paragraphs indicate how the applicant is qualified for the position indicated in the first paragraph. The letter refers especially to his experience, expertise, and problem-solving skills.

SHARON KINGREY, CTC

000 Williamson Drive   Home (555) 000-0000
Hendersonville, TN 00000   Office (555) 000-0000

May 1, 2004

Robert T. Alden
President
Global Travel Adventures
2100 West End Avenue, Suite 920
Nashville, TN 00000

Re: Director of Corporate Travel

Dear Mr. Alden,

A slowing economy and rising gas prices are among the recent headlines that are affecting U.S. travelers and their summer travel plans. Corporate travelers, too, are sensitive to economic fluctuations and may need to adjust their business schedules to reflect the "belt tightening" imposed by many companies. According to Dr. Stephen Gooden, senior vice president of research for the Travel Industry Association of America, "The challenge lies with the industry to package the travel product to stimulate demand."

As a Certified Travel Counselor with 18 years of industry experience, I am accustomed to working with both corporate and leisure travelers to plan and coordinate their unique travel needs. I have established myself as a top producer and been highly successful in cultivating repeat business into long-standing, loyal customers. As a manager, I have identified and capitalized on key marketing opportunities and, through persistence and leadership by example, built highly productive, cohesive sales teams. By participating in ongoing educational workshops and seminars, I have kept current on the ever-changing needs of today's travel-savvy consumer.

Given my professional background and personal travel experiences, I feel uniquely qualified to meet your needs for a Director of Corporate Travel. I believe that the combination of my management experience, sales and customer service capabilities, and thorough understanding of the travel industry will help boost your bottom line. I will call you Thursday morning concerning any questions we both may have and to discuss a personal meeting. Thank you for your time, and I look forward to speaking with you.

Sincerely,

Sharon Kingrey

Enclosure

307

Director of Corporate Travel. *Carolyn S. Braden, Hendersonville, Tennessee*

This applicant had a background in both travel sales and management. She wanted a management position with a major agency. The first paragraph indicates her knowledge of economic issues.

TIM CARLETON
5 Ninth Avenue ▸ Winona MN 55555
Cell Phone 555 • 555 • 5555
E-mail timcarl@chosen.com

January 5, 2004

David Sherrill, Regional Director
Mississippi Express
P.O. Box 555
Wabasha, MN 55555

Dear Mr. Sherrill:

I appreciate the time you spent with me yesterday discussing the sales position in the Rochester area and would like to reiterate my interest in the position. Enclosed is a resume reflecting my work history and philosophy.

A manager's and a company's success in the workplace is measured in many ways: from productivity of workers ▸ results from managers ▸ job satisfaction ▸ low employee turnover ▸ quality of work, products and services ▸ accountability ▸ respect toward self, company and customers. A rewarding work environment is one in which employees and managers can expand their knowledge, skills and contributions. When an atmosphere of self-pride and company pride prevails, everyone wins—worker, company and customer. Attitudes mean a lot and reflect greatly on the mental image customers carry with them after the sale.

My record has been a good one. I've been able to motivate myself, as well as others, and to generate trust, respect and win-win results. Stability and accomplishment mark my career, as does ongoing learning. The Internet has opened such possibilities that knowledge is limited only by time and interest in using the Net as a tool for research of industry growth and direction, overall business trends, labor statistics, tax changes and sales and marketing ideas.

While interviews and references are the preferred methods of learning more about candidates, at least a sketch of past accomplishments can help in forming a mental image of the person. You will see that general business skills complement the people skills—which is my greatest strength and interest. I truly enjoy working with others and have been exploring possibilities in which my biggest contributions can be not only helping a company meet its goals, but also creating an avenue in which I'm enriching in some way the lives of others or the world we leave behind. Social responsibility is a high priority.

I look forward to hearing from you further to discuss the company's direction, needs and concerns. In the next few days, I will contact you to determine your plans for filling this position and to see if you have questions or need additional information.

Sincerely,

Tim Carleton

Enclosure: Resume

308

Thank-You Letter. *Beverley Drake, Rochester, Minnesota*

After an interview without a resume, the applicant uses this thank-you letter to impress the reader further. The second paragraph expresses the applicant's views on success and a winning work environment.

KEVIN STERLING

000 Third Avenue/3W • New York, NY 10017 • Tel: 555-555-5555 • Fax: 555-555-5555 • kevin_sterling@msn.com

January 10, 2004

Mr. John Green
15 Green Street
New York, NY 10011

Dear Mr. Green:

It has been a while since we spoke at your company's fundraising event last winter.

As you may know, I have been helping a number of organizations with significant challenges as part of their executive team after successfully selling my company, Media XYZ, Inc., in 2003.

Now that the time has come to move on, I was wondering if you could help me identify contacts that I can approach at Fortune 500 technology ventures, where I can combine my technological and general management skills to provide strong, decisive, hands-on leadership, preferably to an operations, professional services, or consulting division. I currently reside in New York City but am open to relocation.

My success with my own company (integrated marketing, servicing Fortune 100 and e-commerce clients) and my consulting projects, as well as during prior employment, lies in my ability to quickly generate results. Never satisfied with the status quo, I developed a keen eye for identifying and capitalizing on market opportunities and am adept at swiftly responding to market changes and customer demands. Even though my track record goes back only ten years, I have demonstrated achievements in

- Managing businesses to turn around performance and achieve full potential
- Analyzing and controlling all aspects of multisite operations to reduce costs and improve profits
- Negotiating favorable domestic and international deals, acquisitions and strategic alliances, and partnerships
- Combining expertise in strategic/tactical marketing and business development
- Creating and introducing cutting-edge technologies and procedures
- Training, motivating, and directing 140+ personnel to improve individual and group effectiveness

Because I value your experience and perspective, I have taken the liberty of enclosing a résumé to assist you in evaluating appropriate contacts and suggestions. I would greatly appreciate any ideas, recommendations, or referrals you could offer. Rest assured that I would happily do the same for you if the situation ever arises. I will call you next week to follow up.

Sincerely,

Kevin Sterling

Enclosure

309

Networking Letter. *Ilona Vanderwoude, Riverdale, New York*

This networking letter was for an ex-entrepreneur reentering the workforce. The writer is upfront about his entrepreneurship instead of masking it with titles such as *president* or *managing partner.*

JOHN P. Citizen
10501 E. Ogden Avenue
Chicago, Illinois 60603
000-000-0000

February 5, 2004

Mr. Samuel Jackson
Kincaid Company
595 E. Ogden Avenue
Suite 780
Naperville, Illinois 60563

Dear Mr. Jackson:

Please accept this letter as written acceptance of your offer of employment dated February 1, 2004. Enclosed are both copies of the signed Employment Agreement per the request of Ms. Jamie Brown.

As we agreed, I will be available to start employment on February 21, 2004. Prior to my start date, please contact me at 555-555-5555 to discuss additional details.

I look forward to a long and mutually rewarding business relationship with Kincaid Company.

Sincerely,

John P. Citizen

Enclosures

310

Acceptance Letter. *Patricia Chapman, Naperville, Illinois*

This is an example of an offer-acceptance letter. Important details are date of acceptance, enclosed signed copies of an Employment Agreement (if any), an employment start date, and contact info.

3

P·A·R·T

Best Resume Tips

Best Resume
Tips at a Glance

Best Resume Tips

In a passive job search, you rely on your resume to do most of the work for you. An eye-catching resume that stands out above all the others may be your best shot at getting noticed by a prospective employer. If your resume is only average and looks like most of the others in the pile, the chances are great that you won't be noticed and called for an interview. If you want to be singled out because of your resume, it should be somewhere between spectacular and award-winning.

In an active job search, however, your resume complements your efforts at being known to a prospective employer *before* that person receives it. For this reason, you can rely less on your resume for getting someone's attention. Nevertheless, your resume has an important role in an active job search that may include the following activities:

- Talking to relatives, friends, and other acquaintances to meet people who can hire you before a job is available

- Creating phone scripts to speak with the person who is most likely to hire someone with your background and skills

- Using a schedule to keep track of your appointments and callbacks

- Working at least 25 hours a week to search for a job

When you are this active in searching for a job, the quality of your resume confirms the quality of your efforts to get to know the person who might hire you, as well as your worth to the company whose workforce you want to join. An eye-catching resume makes it easier for you to sell yourself directly to a prospective employer. If your resume is mediocre or conspicuously flawed, it will work against you and may undo all of your good efforts in searching for a job.

The following list offers ideas for making resumes visually impressive. Many of the ideas are for making resumes pleasing to the eye; other ideas are for eliminating common writing mistakes and stylistic weaknesses.

Some of these ideas can be used with any equipment, from a manual typewriter to a computer with desktop publishing software. Other ideas make sense only if you have a computer system with word processing or desktop publishing. Even if you don't have a computer, take some time to read all of the ideas. Then, if you decide to use the services of a professional resume writer, you will be better informed about what the writer can do for you in producing your resume.

Best Resume-Writing Strategies

1. **Although many resume books say that you should spell out the name of the state in your address at the top of the resume, consider using the postal abbreviation instead.** The reason is simple: it's an address. Anyone wanting to contact you by mail will probably refer to your name and address on the resume. If they appear there as they should on an envelope, the writer can simply copy the information you supply. If you spell out the name of your state in full, the writer will have to "translate" the name of the state to its postal abbreviation.

   Not everyone knows all the postal abbreviations, and some abbreviations are easily confused. For example, those for Alabama (AL), Alaska (AK), American Samoa (AS), Arizona (AZ), and Arkansas (AR) are easy to mix up. You can prevent confusion and delay simply by using the correct postal abbreviation.

   If you decide to use postal abbreviations in addresses, make certain that you do not add a period after the abbreviations. This applies also to postal abbreviations in the addresses of references, if you provide them.

   Consider, however, not using the state postal abbreviation when you are indicating only the city and state (not the mailing address) of a school you attended or a business where you worked. In these cases, it makes sense to write out the name of the state in full.

2. **Adopt a sensible form for phone numbers in the contact information and then use that form consistently.** Do this in your resume and in all of the documents you use in your job search. Some forms for phone numbers make more sense than others. Compare the following forms:

123-4567	This form is best for a resume circulated locally, within a region where all the phone numbers have the same area code.
(222) 123-4567	This form is best for a resume circulated in areas with different area codes.
222-123-4567	This form suggests that the area code should be dialed in all cases. But that may not be necessary for prospective employers whose area code is 222. Avoid this form.
222/123-4567	This form is illogical and should be avoided also. The slash can mean an alternate option, as in ON/OFF. In a phone number, this meaning of a slash makes little sense.
1 (222) 123-4567	This form is long, and the digit *1* isn't necessary. Almost everyone will know that 1 should be used before the area code to dial a long-distance number.
222.123.4567	This form is becoming popular, particularly with designers.

   Note: For resumes directed to prospective employers outside the United States, be sure to include the correct international prefixes in all phone numbers so that you and your references can be reached easily by phone.

3. **Whether your resume begins with an Objective statement or a Professional Goal, make it focused, developed, or unique so that it grabs the reader's attention.** See the Objective statement in Resume 22. If your opening statement fails to do this, the reader might discard the resume without reading further. Whatever opening you use, it is your first opportunity to sell yourself.

4. **If you can sell yourself better with some other kind of section, consider omitting an Objective statement and putting a Summary of Qualifications, a Profile, or an Areas of Expertise section just after the contact information.** See Resumes 3, 4, 5, 7, 8, 11, and 15.

5. **A Professional Highlights section placed early in the resume helps to feature important information.** See Resume 15.

6. **Displaying your qualifications, areas of expertise, skills, or strengths in columns makes them easy to alter if your target job or target industry changes.** See Resumes 16, 22, and 23.

7. **Spend considerable time determining how to present your skills.** You can present them in various ways, such as Office Skills (Resume 3), Areas of Expertise (Resume 8), Competencies (Resume 10), Technical Summary (Resume 11), Computer Skills (Resume 14), Professional Highlights (Resume 15), Career Highlights (Resume 20), Relevant Qualifications (Resume 21), Summary of Qualifications (Resume 22), and Professional Strengths (Resume 23).

8. **In the Experience section or elsewhere, state accomplishments, not just duties or responsibilities.** The reader often already knows duties and responsibilities for a given position. Accomplishments, however, can be attention-getting. The reader probably considers life too short to be bored by lists of duties and responsibilities in a stack of resumes. See Resumes 3, 17, and 18.

9. **In the Experience section and for each position held, consider explaining responsibilities in a paragraph and using bullets to point to achievements, contributions, or awards.** See Resumes 1, 17, and 18.

10. **When you indicate achievements, consider quantifying them (Resumes 1, 3, 10, and 17) or providing a separate heading for them (Resume 19).**

11. **When skills, abilities, qualifications, or responsibilities are varied, group them according to categories for easier comprehension.** See Resumes 17 and 19.

12. **Include information that explains lesser-known companies.** See Resume 10.

13. **Group positions to avoid repetition in a description of duties.** See Resume 5.

Best Resume Design and Layout Tips

14. **Use quality paper correctly.** If you use quality watermarked paper for your resume, be sure to use the right side of the paper. To know which side is the right side, hold a blank sheet of paper up to a light source. If you can see a watermark and "read" it, the right side of the paper is facing you. This is the surface for typing or printing. If the watermark is unreadable or if any characters look backward, you are looking at the "underside" of a sheet of paper—the side that should be left blank.

15. **Use adequate "white space."** A sheet of white paper with no words on it is impossible to read. Likewise, a sheet of white paper with words all over it is impossible to read. The goal is to have a comfortable mix of white space and words. If your resume has too many words and not enough white space, the resume looks cluttered. If it has too much white space and too few words, the resume looks skimpy and unimportant. Make certain that adequate white space exists between the main sections. For resumes with a satisfying amount of white space, see Resumes 3, 6, 8, 15, 20, 21, and 22. For resumes with adequate white space even with a small font size, see Resume 2. For white space accomplished through center-alignment, see Resume 14.

16. **Margins in resumes for executives, managers, and other administrators tend to be narrower than margins in other resumes.** See Resume 16. Narrower margins are often used in connection with smaller type to get more information on a one- or two-page resume.

17. **Be consistent in your use of line spacing.** How you handle line spacing can tell the reader how good you are at details and how consistent you are in your use of them. If, near the beginning of your resume, you insert two line spaces (two hard returns in a word-processing program) between two main sections, be sure to put two line spaces between main sections throughout the resume.

18. **Be consistent in your use of horizontal spacing.** If you usually put two character spaces after a period at the end of a sentence, make certain that you use two spaces consistently. The same is true for colons. If you put two spaces after colons, do so consistently.

    Note that an em dash—a dash the width of the letter *m*—does not require spaces before or after it. No space should go between the *P* and *O* of P.O. Box. Only one space is needed between the postal abbreviation of a state and the ZIP code. You should insert a space between the first and second initials of a person's name, as in I. M. Jobseeker (not I.M. Jobseeker). These conventions have become widely adopted in English and business communications. If, however, you use other conventions, be sure to be consistent. In resumes, as in grammar, consistency is more important than conformity.

19. **Make certain that characters, lines, and images contrast well with the paper.** The quality of "ink" depends on the device used to type or print your resume. For a test, send yourself a copy of your resume and see how it makes the trip through the mail. If you use an inkjet or laser printer, check that the characters are sharp and clean, without ink smudges or traces of extra toner. Mail yourself a laser-printed envelope to make sure that it looks good after a trip through the mail. A cover letter with a flaking address does not make a good impression.

20. **Use vertical alignment in stacked text.** Resumes usually contain tabbed or indented text. Make certain that this "stacked" material is aligned vertically. Misalignment can ruin the appearance of a well-written resume. Try to set tabs or indents that control this text throughout a resume instead of having a mix of tab stops in different sections. If you use a word processor, make certain that you understand the difference between tabbed text and indented text, as in the following examples:

   Tabbed text: This text was tabbed over one tab stop before the writer started to write the sentence.

   Indented text: This text was indented once before the writer started to write the sentence.

   Note: In a number of word-processing programs, the Indent command is useful for ensuring the correct vertical alignment of proportionally spaced, stacked text. After you use the Indent command, lines of wrapped text are vertically aligned automatically until you terminate the command by pressing Enter.

21. **For the vertical alignment of dates, try left- or right-aligning the dates.** This technique is especially useful in chronological resumes and combination resumes. For several examples of right-aligned dates, look at Resumes 2, 4, 6, and 7.

22. **Use as many pages as you need for portraying your qualifications adequately to a specific interviewer for a particular job.** Try to limit your resume to one page or two pages, but set the upper limit at four pages. No rule about the number of pages makes sense in all cases. The determining factors are a person's qualifications and experiences, the requirements of the job, and the interests and pet peeves of the interviewer. If you know that an interviewer refuses to look at a resume longer than a page, that says it all. You need to deliver a one-page resume if you want to get past the first gate.

   More important than the question of how many pages is the issue of complete pages. A full page sends a better message than a partial page (which says "not enough to fill"). Therefore, one full page is better than 1.25 pages, and two full pages are better than 1.75 pages.

23. **When you have letters of recommendation, use quotations from them as testimonials.** Devoting some space (or even a full column) to the positive opinions of "external authorities" helps make a resume convincing as well as impressive. When placed effectively, such quotations can build respect, add credibility, and personalize a resume. See Resume 4.

24. **Unless you enlist the services of a professional printer or skilled desktop publisher, resist the temptation to use full justification for text.** The price that you pay for a straight right margin is uneven word spacing. Words may appear too close together on some lines and too spread out on others. Although the resume might look like typeset text, you lose readability. Professional resume writers sometimes use full justification effectively for variety.

25. **If you can choose a typeface for your resume, use a serif font for greater readability.** Serif fonts have little lines extending from the tops, bottoms, and ends of the characters. These fonts tend to be easier to read than sans serif (without serif) fonts, especially in low-light conditions. Compare the following font examples:

Serif	Sans Serif
Baskerville	Avant Garde
Courier	Futura
Times New Roman	Helvetica

Words such as *minimum* and *abilities,* which have several consecutive thin letters, are more readable in a serif font than in a sans serif font.

26. **If possible, avoid using monospaced fonts, such as Courier, in which the width of each character is the same.** For example, in a monospaced font the space for the letter *i* is as wide as the space for the letter *m*. Therefore, in Courier type *iiiii* is as wide as *mmmmm*. Courier was a standard of business communications during the 1960s and 1970s. Because of its widespread use, it is now considered "common." It also takes up a lot of space, so you can't pack as much information on a page with Courier type as you can with a proportionally spaced type such as Times New Roman.

27. **Think twice before using all uppercase letters in parts of your resume.** A common misconception is that uppercase letters are easier to read than lowercase letters. Actually, the ascenders and descenders of lowercase letters make them more distinguishable from each other and therefore more recognizable than uppercase letters. For a test, look at a string of uppercase letters and throw them gradually out of focus by squinting. The uppercase letters become a blur sooner than lowercase letters. Professional resume writers, however, may use uppercase letters effectively for emphasis and variety.

28. **Think twice about underlining some words in your resume.** Underlining defeats the purpose of serifs at the bottom of characters by blending with the serifs. In trying to emphasize words, you lose some visual clarity. This is especially true if you use underlining with uppercase letters in centered or side headings.

29. **If you have access to many fonts through word processing or desktop publishing, beware of becoming "font happy" and turning your resume into a font circus.** Frequent font changes *can* distract **the reader,** AND SO CAN GAUDY DISPLAY TYPE such as this.

30. **To make your resume stand out, consider using a nonstandard format or an unconventional display font in the contact information or in the headings.** See Resumes 2, 12, and 16. What is usually fitting for resumes for some prospective jobs, however, is not always the most appropriate resume strategy for executive positions. Try to match the style of your resume to the target company's "corporate image" if it has one.

31. **Be aware of the value differences of black type.** Some typefaces are light; others are dark. Notice the following lines:

A quick brown fox jumps over the lazy dog.

A quick brown fox jumps over the lazy dog.

Most typefaces fall somewhere between these two. With the variables of height, width, thickness, serifs, angles, curves, spacing, ink color, ink density, boldfacing, and typewriter double-striking, type offers an infinite range of values from light to dark. Try to make your resume more visually interesting by offering stronger contrasts between light type and dark type. Browse through the Exhibit of Resumes at the end of this section and notice the differences in light and dark type.

32. **Use italic characters carefully.** Whenever possible, use italic rather than underlining as an enhancement when you need to call attention to a word or phrase. You might consider using italic for duties or achievements. Think twice, however, about using italic throughout your resume. The reason is that italic (slanted) characters are less readable than normal (vertical) characters. The reader might have to hold the resume at an angle to make an all-italic resume more readable. Such a maneuver can be irritating. Even so, "all italic" may be just the thing to make a particular resume stand out.

33. **Use boldfacing to make different job titles more evident.** See Resumes 4, 8, 10, and 12.

34. **For getting attention, make headings white on black if you use software that has this capability.** Resume 20 displays the candidate's initials as white letters in a dark box.

35. **If you use word processing or desktop publishing and have a suitable printer, use special characters to enhance the look of your resume.** For example, use enhanced quotation marks (" and ") instead of their typewriter equivalents (" and "). Use an em dash (—) instead of two hyphens (--) for a dash. To separate dates, try using an en dash (a dash the width of the letter *n*) instead of a hyphen, as in 2003–2004. If you use "to" rather than an en dash between dates in a range (as in 2002 to 2004), use "to" consistently. Whenever you use an em dash or an en dash, avoid a space before and after the dash.

36. **To call attention to an item in a list, use a bullet (•) or a box (■) rather than a hyphen (-).** Browse through the sample resumes and notice how bullets are used effectively as attention getters.

37. **For variety, try using bullets of a different style, such as diamond (♦) bullets, rather than the usual round or square bullets.** Examples with diamonds are Resumes 7 and 11. For other kinds of bullets, see Resumes 1 (shadowed squares), 5 (filled squares), 7 and 8 (decorative arrow tips), 9 (unfilled circles), 10 (filled squares), and 12 (decorative).

38. **Make a bullet a little smaller than the lowercase letters after it.** Disregard any ascenders or descenders on the letters. Compare the following bullet sizes:

 • Too small   ● Too large   • Better   •Just right

39. **If possible, visually coordinate the resume and the cover letter with the same font, line enhancement, border, or graphic to catch the reader's attention.** See Resume 3 and Cover Letter 16, Resume 8 and Cover Letter 86, Resume 12 and Cover Letter 148, Resume 21 and Cover Letter 286, and Resume 22 and Cover Letter 296.

40. **Use a horizontal line or a combination of lines to separate your contact information from the rest of the resume.** See Resumes 6, 8, 12, and 15. Resume 2 uses a series of small, filled squares to simulate a horizontal line.

41. **Use horizontal lines or bars to separate the different sections of the resume and thus make them visible at a glance.** See Resumes 11 and 14. Resume 16 contains shaded bars to distinguish the headings.

42. **For variety in dividing sections of your resume or in presenting contact information, use partial horizontal lines that extend from the end of a short line of left-aligned text to the right margin.** See Resume 16. Note that Resume 8 has partial lines that extend from the centered occupation to *both* the left and right margins.

43. **To avoid a cramped one-page resume that has small print, narrow margins, and reduced line spacing, consider using a two-page resume instead.** (Those who insist on one-page resumes will not agree with this tip.)

44. **Use thicker horizontal lines to call attention to a section of the resume.** See Resume 1.

45. **Use vertical lines or bars to spice up your resume.** See Resumes 4 and 5.

46. **Use various kinds of boxes (single line, shadowed, or decorative) to make a page visually more interesting.** See Resumes 4 and 9.

47. **Use a page border to make a page visually more interesting.** See Resume 3. Resume 5 contains a partial page border for visual interest.

48. **Use centered headings to make them easy to read down a page.** See Resumes 9, 13, 14, 15, and 23.

49. **Consider using hanging indentation of section headings to make them stand out.** See Resumes 12 and 21.

50. **Near the top of the first page but below the contact information, place a list of keywords that can easily be scanned for storage in an online resume database.** See Resumes 1, 13, 16, and 20.

Best Resume-Writing Style Tips

51. **Check that words or phrases in lists are parallel.** For example, notice the bulleted items in the Relevant Experience section of Resume 1. All the entries contain verbs in the past tense.

52. **Use capital letters correctly.** Resumes usually contain many of the following:

    Names of people, companies, organizations, government agencies, awards, and prizes

    Titles of job positions and publications

    References to academic fields (such as chemistry, English, and mathematics)

    Geographic regions (such as the Midwest, the East, the state of California, Oregon State, and northern Florida)

Because of such words, resumes are minefields for the misuse of uppercase letters. When you don't know whether a word should have an initial capital letter, don't guess. Consult a dictionary, a handbook on style, or some other authoritative source, such as an official Web site. Often a reference librarian can provide the information you need. If so, you are only a phone call away from an accurate answer. Use headline style in headings. That is, capitalize the first letter of the first word, the last word, and all main words. Use lowercase letters for the first letter of articles (*a, an, the*), conjunctions (*and, but, or, nor, for, yet, so*), and prepositions of four or fewer letters (*at, by, on, into,* and so on). Capitalize, however, the first letter of prepositions of five or more letters (*among, across,* and so on). If you use "small caps" as a font enhancement (Format, Font, Small caps in Microsoft Word), create the heading in upper- and lowercase letters and select the heading before you apply the Small caps option.

53. **Check that you have used capital letters and hyphens correctly in computer terms.** If you want to show in a Computer Experience section that you have used certain hardware and software, you may give the opposite impression if you don't use uppercase letters and hyphens correctly. Note the correct use of capitals and hyphens in the following names of hardware, software, and computer companies:

LaserJet	Hewlett-Packard	Photoshop
PageMaker	QuarkXPress	PostScript
Sound Blaster	Microsoft Word	PhotoSmart

The reason that many computer product names have an internal uppercase letter is for the sake of a trademark. A word with unusual spelling or capitalization is trademarkable. When you use the correct forms of these words, you are honoring trademarks and registered trademarks and showing that you are in the know.

54. **Use all uppercase letters for most acronyms.** An *acronym* is a pronounceable word usually formed from the initial letters of the words in a compound term, or sometimes from multiple letters in those words. Note the following examples:

COBOL	COmmon Business-Oriented Language
ERISA	Employee Retirement Income Security Act
FORTRAN	FORmula TRANslator

An acronym such as *radar* (*ra*dio *d*etecting *a*nd *r*anging) has become so common that it is no longer all uppercase. If you think a reader may not know the meaning of an acronym, use the full term.

55. **Be aware that you may need to use a period with some abbreviations.** An *abbreviation* is a word shortened by removing the latter part of the word or by deleting some letters within the word. Here are some examples:

adj. for adjective	*amt.* for amount
adv. for adverb	*dept.* for department

Usually, you can't pronounce an abbreviation as a word. Sometimes, however, an abbreviation is a set of uppercase letters (without periods) that you can pronounce as letters. AFL-CIO, CBS, NFL, and YMCA are examples.

56. **Be sure to spell every word correctly.** A resume with just one misspelling is not impressive and may undermine all the hours you spent putting it together. Worse than that, one misspelling may be what the reader is looking for to screen you out, particularly if you are applying for a position that requires accuracy with words. If you calculate the salary you don't get *times* the number of years you might have worked for that company, that's an expensive misspelling!

    You may be able to catch most misspellings with the spelling checker of your word processor. Be wary of spelling checkers, however. They can detect a misspelled word but cannot detect when you have inadvertently used a wrong word (*to* for *too*, for example). Be wary also of letting someone else check your resume. If the other person is not a good speller, you may not get any real help. The best authority is a good, *current* dictionary.

57. **For words that have more than one correct spelling, use the preferred form.** This form is the one that appears first in a dictionary. For example, if you see the entry **trav·el·ing** *or* **trav·el·ling**, the first form (with one *l*) is the preferred spelling. If you make it a practice to use the preferred spelling, you will build consistency in your resumes and cover letters.

58. **Avoid British spellings.** These slip into American usage through books and online articles published in Great Britain. Note the following words:

British Spelling	American Spelling
acknowledgement	acknowledgment
centre	center
judgement	judgment
towards	toward

59. **Avoid hyphenating words with such prefixes as** *co-, micro-, mid-, mini-, multi-, non-, pre-, re-,* **and** *sub-.* Many people think that words with these prefixes should have a hyphen after the prefix, but most of these words should not. The following words are spelled correctly:

coauthor	microcomputer	minicomputer
coworker	midpoint	multicultural
cowriter	midway	multilevel
nondisclosure	prearrange	reenter
nonfunctional	prequalify	subdirectory

    Note: If you look in a dictionary for a word with a prefix and can't find the word, look for the prefix itself in the dictionary. You might find there a small-print listing of a number of words that have the prefix.

60. **Be aware that compounds (combinations of words) present special problems for hyphenation.** Writers' handbooks and books on style do not always agree on how compounds should be hyphenated. Many compounds are evolving from *open* compounds (two different words) to *hyphenated* compounds (two words joined by a hyphen) to *closed* compounds (one word). In different dictionaries, you can therefore find the words *copy editor, copy-editor,* and *copyeditor.* No wonder the issue is confusing! Most style books do agree, however, that when some compounds appear as an adjective before a noun, the

compound should be hyphenated. When the same compound appears after a noun, hyphenation is unnecessary. Compare the following two sentences:

> I scheduled well-attended conferences.

> The conferences I scheduled were well attended.

For detailed information about hyphenation, see a recent edition of *The Chicago Manual of Style* (the 15th edition is now current). You should be able to find a copy at a local library.

61. **Be sure to hyphenate so-called *permanent* hyphenated compounds.** Usually, you can find these by looking them up in a dictionary. You can spot them easily because they have a "long hyphen" (–) for visibility in the dictionary. Hyphenate these words (with a standard hyphen) wherever they appear, before or after a noun. Here are some examples:

all-important	self-employed
day-to-day	step-by-step
full-blown	time-consuming

Note: The *Chicago Manual of Style*, 15th Edition, now recommends that these hyphenated compounds should no longer be considered permanent but should be without a hyphen (or hyphens) when they appear after a noun (see Tip 60).

62. **Use the correct form for certain verbs and nouns combined with prepositions.** You may need to consult a dictionary for correct spelling and hyphenation. Compare the following examples:

start up	(verb)
start-up	(noun)
start-up	(adj.)
startup	(noun, computer and Internet industry)
startup	(adj., computer and Internet industry)

63. **Avoid using shortcut words, such as abbreviations like *thru* or foreign words like *via*.** Spell out *through* and use *by* for *via*.

64. **Use the right words.** The issue here is correct *usage*, which often means the choice of the right word or phrase from a group of two or more possibilities. The following words and phrases are often used incorrectly:

alternate (adj.)	Refers to an option used every other time. OFF is the alternate option to ON in an ON/OFF switch.
alternative	Refers to an option that can be used at any time. If cake and pie are alternative desserts for dinner, you can have cake three days in a row if you like. The common mistake is to use *alternate* when the correct word is *alternative*.
center around	A common illogical expression. Draw a circle and then try to draw its center around it. You can't. Use *center in* or *center on* as logical alternatives to *center around*.

For information about the correct *usage* of words, consult a usage dictionary or the usage section of a writer's handbook, such as Strunk and White's *Elements of Style*.

65.   **Use numbers consistently.** Numbers are often used inconsistently with text. Should you present a number as a numeral or spell out the number as a word? One approach is to spell out numbers *one* through *nine* but present numbers 10 and above as numerals. Different approaches are taught in different schools, colleges, and universities. Use the approach you have learned, but be consistent.

66.   **Use (or don't use) the serial comma consistently.** How should you punctuate a series of three or more items? If, for example, you say in your resume that you increased sales by 100 percent, opened two new territories, and trained four new salespersons, the comma before *and* is called the *serial comma*. It is commonly omitted in newspapers, magazine articles, advertisements, and business documents, but it is often used for precision in technical documents or for stylistic reasons in academic text, particularly in the Humanities.

67.   **Use semicolons correctly.** Semicolons are useful because they help to distinguish visually the items in a series when the items themselves contain commas. Suppose you have the following entry in your resume:

> Increased sales by 100 percent, opened two new territories, which were in the Midwest, trained four new salespersons, who were from Georgia, and increased sales by 250 percent.

The extra commas (before *which* and *who*) throw the main items of the series out of focus. By separating the main items with semicolons, you can bring them back into focus:

> Increased sales by 100 percent; opened two new territories, which were in the Midwest; trained four new salespersons, who were from Georgia; and increased sales by 250 percent.

Use this kind of high-rise punctuation even if just one item in the series has an internal comma.

68.   **Use dashes correctly.** One of the purposes of a dash (an em dash, or long dash) is to introduce a comment or afterthought about preceding information. A colon *anticipates* something to follow, but a dash *looks back* to something already said. Two dashes are sometimes used before and after a related but nonessential remark—such as this—within a sentence. In this case, the dashes are like parentheses, but more formal.

69.   **Use apostrophes correctly.** They indicate possession (Tom's, Betty's), the omission of letters in contractions (can't, don't), and some plurals (x's and o's), but they can be tricky with words ending in *s*, possessive plurals, and plural forms of capital letters and numbers. For review or guidance, consult a style guide or a section on style in a dictionary.

70.   **Know the difference between *its* and *it's*.** The form *its'* does not exist in English, so you need to know only how *it's* differs from *its*. The possessive form *its* is like *his* and *her* and has no apostrophe. The form *it's* is a contraction of *it is*. The trap is to think that *it's* is a possessive form.

Exhibit of Resumes

This part of the book contains an Exhibit of 23 resumes that accompanied cover letters in the first part of the book. Cross-references let you know readily which cover letter accompanied a particular resume so that you can view the two documents as a package.

Resume writers commonly distinguish between chronological resumes and functional (or skills) resumes. A *chronological resume* is a photo—a snapshot history of what you did and when you did it. A *functional resume* is a painting—an interpretive sketch of what you can do for a future employer. A third kind of resume, known as a *combination resume,* is a mix of recalled history and self-assessment. Besides recollecting "the facts," a combination resume contains self-interpretation and is therefore more like dramatic history than news coverage. A chronological resume and a functional resume are not always that different; often, all that is needed for a functional resume to qualify as a combination resume is the inclusion of dates for some of the positions held.

Instead of making 200 copies of a resume and sending the same document to different prospective employers, you should consider tailoring each resume to a specific job target. Creating multiple versions of a resume may seem difficult, but it is easy to do if you have (or have access to) a personal computer and a laser printer or some other kind of printer that can produce quality output. You will also need word-processing capability. Remember that most professional resume writers have the hardware and software, and they can make your resume look like those in the Exhibit. A local fast-print shop can make your resume look good, but you will probably not get there the kind of advice and service that a professional resume writer provides.

James M. Olson

9803 Clinton Avenue ▪ Houston, TX 77068
(281) 000-0000 ▪ name@msn.com

ACCOUNTANT

Detail-focused, highly ethical accounting professional with a BBA in Accounting and work experience demonstrating consistent achievement of organizational and fiscal objectives and goals. Able to pinpoint discrepancies and errors to prevent continuing and potentially unnecessary cost expenditures. Willing to accept responsibilities beyond immediate job duties and take on special projects at management request. Proficient in Excel, Access, other MS programs, J.D. Edwards, and proprietary software. *Knowledge and skill areas include*

- Audits & Financial Statements
- Accounts Receivable/Payable
- Financial Reconciliations
- General Ledger Accounting
- Record/Systems Automation
- Financial Research Projects
- Strategic & Financial Analysis
- Audit Review Procedures
- Teamwork & Communication

Education

TEXAS UNIVERSITY, Houston, TX
Bachelor of Business Administration (BBA) in Accounting, 2000

Accounting G.P.A.: 3.5/Member, Beta Alpha Psi—for Honors Accounting, Finance, and IT students

Relevant Experience

Accountant, CITY OF NAME, Anywhere, TX   2001–Present

Fully responsible for several core accounting functions within municipality of 200,000 residents, including preparing financial statements and monthly reports/reconciliations, analyzing expense reports, integrating technology to facilitate accounting tasks, and completing special research projects as needed. Assigned significant role in managing finances of WTMPA, organizing large bodies of financial data, and preparing all financial statements for 2001 and 2002 audits. *Selected Accomplishments:*

- ❑ **Records Analysis & Error Identification**—Researched, identified, and helped resolve several large discrepancies in receivables and payables, all favorable to City of Name:
  - *$100,000 in A/R account for City of Name's power purchases;*
  - *$20,000 underpayment for A/R in General Fund Account;*
  - *$10,000 excess in A/P for Internal Service funds.*
- ❑ **Policy Development**—Played key role in development of new travel policy, with projected elimination of problems previously stalling productivity of accounting and internal audit functions.
- ❑ **Financial Analysis**—Compiled analysis of franchise fees subsequently used by Assistant City Manager in evaluating potential effects of pending legislation.
- ❑ **Audit Review Compliance**—Prepared cash-flow and financial statements for external auditors on 13 Internal Service and 10 Special Revenue funds, with zero notes from auditors on review documents.
- ❑ **Teamwork & Collaboration**—Coordinated project with legal division that revived dormant accounts and ensured proper disposition. Worked with Chief Accountant to construct new reporting model.
- ❑ **Technology Improvement**—Changed automatic accounting instruction table in J.D. Edwards system, leading to correction of multiple unnecessary entries and subsequent cost/time savings.

Collection Agent, CITYBANK, Irving, TX   1997–2001

Trained new employees on account software; prepared detailed financial/customer reports for management.

Manager, TANNING SALON, Irving, TX   1996–1997

Managed A/P, A/R, payroll, and other financial functions in addition to general management activities.

Combination. *Daniel J. Dorotik, Jr., Lubbock, Texas*

The area of interest is the Accountant information below the person's name and above the Education section. The horizontal lines work together as a top-and-bottom frame for the area.

THOMAS DORAN   555 555-5555

EDUCATION

BA in Advertising; Minor in Marketing ACADEMIA UNIVERSITY, Camary, Texas   *Fall 2004*
17 hours Spanish

FOREIGN EXCHANGE PROGRAMS

THE CENTER FOR BILINGUAL MULTICULTURAL STUDIES, Citalynda, Zapata, Mexico   *Spring 2003*
Studied Spanish six hours a day, five days a week. Lived with Mexican family and other foreign students, and
traveled throughout Mexico learning foreign culture and economics.
- **Volunteered for Niños de la Calle.**

HUSTER HASS SCHOOL, Don Hogg, Holland   *Fall 2002*
Studied international marketing and management and organizational management for six months. Also studied
Dutch law. Lived in dorm environment and traveled throughout Europe learning foreign culture. Helped organize
school functions and give new-student orientations.

RELEVANT PROJECTS

ADVERTISING COALITION 2003 NATIONAL STUDENT COMPETITION
Selected out of 21 members to serve on creative team of three members. Created a four-year integrated marketing
communications plan book for auto dealership, manufacturer of products for the transportation industry. Researched
and analyzed industry; wrote creative brief; designed Web page and magazine ads; and targeted portfolio to financial
opinion leaders, stock and shareholders, employees, and customers.
- **Won second place at nationals.**

CAMPAIGN BOOK FOR STATE LOTTERY COMMISSION
One of a group of five compiling proposals for awareness campaign for state lottery. Six-member group created 13
advertisements to be presented to lottery commissioner.

WORK EXPERIENCE

Wait Staff, HOME COOKIN' CORNER, Bullnose and Camary, Texas   *2002–Present*
Provided standard wait-staff services and balanced out cash and tips each day. Transferred from full-time summer
job in Bullnose to part-time position in Camary.
- **Requested by regular customers.**

Director, WeeCare After-School Program, WEECARE, Camary, Texas   *2000–2002*
Oversaw five staff members who coordinated activities for 80 children ages 5–12. Handled discipline issues with
both staff and participants and dealt with collection issues. Facilitated complete program organization and facility
readiness.
- **Asked to return to director's position after study abroad.**

Full-time Daycare Counselor, WEECARE, Bullnose, Texas   *Summer 2000*
Organized arts and crafts and play activities for children and created projects. Interfaced with parents and handled
issues. Acted as mentor to children.

ACTIVITIES

- Member, State Advertising Federation   *2003*
- Member and Social Chair, Kuptta Kai Fraternity   *2000–Present*
- Volunteer, Challenged Veterans Store   *1999*
- Volunteer, Heart Saving Association   *1998*

5555 55ᵗʰ Street ▪ Camary, Texas 55555 ▪ tdoran@yahoo.com

2

Combination. *Edith A. Rische, Lubbock, Texas*

This student had relevant experience both abroad and in academic competition. His goal was
foreign advertising, so foreign language and exchange programs are highlighted.

Angela Granato

1234 Pinewood Street
Charleston, SC 00000

(000) 000-0000
agranato@fastmail.com

PROFILE

Customer service professional, skilled in problem solving and responsive to needs of clients, coworkers and management. Poised, resourceful and adaptable to any office environment. Organizational ability to handle multiple priorities and meet deadline schedules. Attentive to detail, with sharp awareness of omissions/ inaccuracies, and prompt to take corrective action. A self-starter and quick study, eager to assume increasing levels of responsibility.

OFFICE SKILLS

Professional phone manner; data entry and word processing; updating/ maintenance of files and records; composition of routine correspondence.

EMPLOYMENT HISTORY

CUSTOMER SERVICE REPRESENTATIVE
Liberty Insurance Corporation, Charleston, SC (1999–2004)

Hired as data entry operator and advanced to customer service position in less than a year. Took over problem desk, which had been inadequately handled by 2 previous employees. Worked closely with underwriters, answering client inquiries by phone or mail. Analyzed complex situations affecting insurance coverage. Recognized opportunities to increase sales and advised clients when coverage was lacking in specific policy areas.

> *Key Accomplishments:* During major restructuring of company resulting in 70% staff reduction, assumed more than triple the normal account responsibility, from 450 to more than 1,500, while still in training. Simultaneously studied for insurance licensing course; passed exam on first try, with score of 95.

APPLICATIONS SCREENER
Marshall & Reiner Insurance Agency, Charlotte, NC (1997–1999)
(Applications processing center for Mutual Surety Corporation)

Screened homeowners' new lines of business applications, verifying coverage against individual state regulations. Filled in whenever needed for switchboard, typing and clerical assignments.

HOMEMAKER/CHILD CARE RESPONSIBILITIES (1990–1997)

CENSUS TAKER
U.S. Census Bureau, Charleston, SC (1990)

Visited individuals who had not filled out census forms properly. Worked in a multiethnic territory, overcoming language barriers and mistrust. Clarified discrepancies and ensured accuracy and completeness of reported information.

SUBROGATION CLERK
Royal Guard Insurance Company, Middleton, SC (1988–1990)

Started as receptionist and promoted shortly thereafter to handle various clerical assignments in Subrogation Department. Prepared paperwork for file with arbitration board. Kept subrogation ledgers up-to-date for auditors' review.

EDUCATION

Carolina State University—65 credits in Business Administration (1986–1988)

American Insurance Academy—Completed 12-week basic course in Property and Casualty, Insurance Law, and Health Insurance (2000)

3

Combination. *Melanie Noonan, West Paterson, New Jersey*

Bold side headings make it easy to see at a glance the resume's main sections. Italic helps the reader spot employers, schools, and the Key Accomplishments paragraph. See Cover Letter 16 (page 48).

DAVID E. JOHNSON

2345 Mountainview Court
La Crosse, Wisconsin 55555
Home: (608) 652-9090 / Office (608) 383-5252

PROFILE

Dynamic and results-oriented teaching professional with superior interpersonal communication skills and 12+ years of experience in training, coaching, and motivating. Demonstrated capabilities in the following areas:

- Classroom Management
- Curriculum Development
- Parental Participation
- Instructional Materials
- Special Events Management
- Consultative & Group Instruction

TEACHING EXPERIENCE

LA CROSSE SCHOOL DISTRICT—WISCONSIN   1999 to Pres.
Substitute Teacher (Grades 1–8)
Taught a varied curriculum at 8 elementary schools within the district. Specifically requested by faculty to fill in and remembered by students for interesting and creative teaching methods. Experience in team teaching and adapting curriculum for special-needs students.

LA CROSSE EAST HIGH SCHOOL—WISCONSIN   1985 to 1986
Substitute Teacher & Asst. Coach (Grades 9–12)
Taught in all classrooms and served as Assistant Cross-Country and Track Coach for Varsity and JV teams.

LA CRESCENT SCHOOL DISTRICT—MINNESOTA   1983 to 1985
Substitute Teacher (Grades K–12)
Prepared lesson plans and developed units for physical education curriculum.

BUSINESS MANAGEMENT EXPERIENCE

GOLDMAN FOODS—LA CROSSE, WISCONSIN   1996 to Pres.
Store Director   1985 to 1995
Recruited to turn around unprofitable grocery store. Developed "back to basics" approach and built a team environment among 57 employees. Created an effective action plan, delegated responsibilities, and delivered sales growth of 8%, labor reductions of 1½%, and substantial increases in customer counts (+500/week).

EDUCATION

MARQUETTE UNIVERSITY—MILWAUKEE, WISCONSIN   1983
B.S. Education—Physical Education Major (4-year athletic scholarship)

CERTIFICATIONS

Wisconsin 43 Substitute (current)
Wisconsin 530 Physical Education (current)

INTERESTS

Distance running, softball, and soccer.

"Mr. Johnson is an excellent role model for students and they do enjoy his classes. He has excellent people skills and his prior background as a manager of people for a food store has helped sharpen his people skills. Your school will be obtaining an excellent instructor who has unlimited potential for the field of teaching."

Joan White,
Interim Principal,
La Crosse East
Middle School

"Mr. Dave Johnson has taught in the area of physical education [and] demonstrated a knowledge and sincere desire [for] working with students at this level. They respect him even though the position of substitute teacher can be rather difficult. [He] has demonstrated an ability to effectively carry out lesson plans and handle discipline, in whatever unit he has been asked to instruct, with professional assurance."

Bill M. Wolfe,
P.E. Dept. Chair,
La Crosse East
Middle School

4

Combination. *Michele J. Haffner, Glendale, Wisconsin*

The applicant was transitioning to teaching after many years as a successful business manager. Strong testimonials offset a lack of teaching experience other than substitute teaching.

GEORGE CRANDALL, EIT

0000 Smith Avenue
Houston, TX 79000

Home: (000) 000-0000
name@lycos.com

Career Profile

ENVIRONMENTAL ENGINEER-IN-TRAINING

- Focused, analytical professional with strong engineering educational background complemented by work experience involving field research and evaluation projects.
- Able to balance creative thinking with logical design ideas; enjoy opportunities to develop solutions that address challenging environmental problems.
- Work effectively in both self-managed and team-based projects; maintain high ethical and quality standards, professional demeanor, and cooperative attitude.
- Use hands-on, detail-oriented approach in completing projects and assignments.

Knowledge & Skill Areas:

*Field Research • Report Writing • Experimental Design & Methods • Project Planning
Quality Assurance Standards • Research & Development • Environmental Hazards
Systems Analysis • Regulatory & Safety Compliance • Engineering Documentation
Environmental Sample Analysis • Risk Assessment • Client/Customer Communications*

Education

Masters of Environmental Engineering, 2002 / GPA: 3.75
Bachelors of Environmental Engineering, 2000 / GPA: 3.30
University, Houston, TX

Selected Upper-Level Coursework:

- Design of Air Pollution Systems
- Solid & Hazardous Waste Treatment
- Environmental Impact Analysis
- Environmental Systems Design
- Design of Wastewater Treatment Plants
- Groundwater Contaminant Transport
- Geoethnical Practices for Waste Disposal
- Environmental Law & Policies

Project Highlights:

- **"Best Bench Scale Demonstration Award"**—Worked with group of 6 students to plan, develop, and present winning bench scale model (addressing water quality issues) at 2 design competitions, 1999 & 2000, at the Waste Energy Research Consortium.
- **"Design of Wastewater Treatment Plants"**—Played key role in design project for treatment plant based on quality assurance and regulatory compliance factors. Delivered well-received presentation to Masters-level class upon completion.
- **"Environmental Impact Statement"**—Developed proposal-oriented report detailing most effective, environmentally sound strategies for controlling brushes within region.

Work Experience

Research Associate, 2002–Present
Research Assistant & Laboratory Technician, 1998–2001
Research Assistant, Summer 2001 (Texas National Environmental & Engineering Lab)
University, Houston, TX (1998–Present)

Conduct research, sample collection and analysis, experimental design, and explosives evaluations using high-performance liquid chromatography, and perform other related activities in positions involving field studies and frequent travel to various counties within East Texas region. Report directly to Laboratory Manager; additionally responsible for daily maintenance of weather stations.

- **Bioremediation of Explosives in Vadose Zone**—Conduct explosives contamination studies and evaluations for government agency Pantex to recommend strategies for remediation projects with highest potential for success.
- **Overall Work Performance**—Put forth consistent effort in meeting and exceeding job requirements; worked overtime hours and maintained full-time class schedule throughout employment. Recognized for intelligent, thorough work habits.

Activities

Society of Environmental Professionals—Member, 3 years; Secretary, 1 year
Civil Engineering Honor Society—Chi Epsilon

5

Combination. *Daniel J. Dorotik, Jr., Lubbock, Texas*

Including information about school-related projects is a way to offset a recent graduate's lack of much work experience. See, for example, Project Highlights in the Education section.

SEAN L. STEEPER

17 Woodcliff Road
Westboro, MA 01581

Home: 333-333-3333
slsteeper@hotmail.com

INDUSTRIAL ENGINEER
New Product Design • *Manufacturing Process Redesign* • *Project Management*

EDUCATION

University of Massachusetts ~ Amherst, MA
B.S. Industrial Engineering ~ Graduated with Honors ~ May 2003

RELEVANT COURSEWORK

Engineering Design • Systems Engineering • Computer Integrated Manufacturing • Production Systems
Production Engineering • Operations Research • Oral and Visual Communications
Industrial Psychology • Ergonomics • Quality Management

ACADEMIC PROJECTS

- Researched and recommended alternative methods for coating coronary stents for a leading manufacturer of cardiovascular products. Designed and manufactured prototype for spray-coating each stent, as opposed to the current practice of dipping them, which resulted in a 25% reduction in defects.
- Designed a facility and assembly-line layout to optimize production for an electronics products company.
- Generated a comprehensive Safety and Development Plan for a medical devices company.
- Created an ergonomically efficient material-handling trolley.

ENGINEERING EXPERIENCE

ABC Cardiovascular, Amherst, MA   5/02–10/02
Industrial Engineer, Co–op

- Designed, developed, and implemented a unique device for facilitating the movement of coronary stent and catheter products from one workstation to another, resulting in a 20% decrease in scrapped product.
- Revised and simplified the Standard Operating Procedure for a label-printing machine that included detailed, easy-to-follow troubleshooting procedures and digital photographs.
- Analyzed production reports associated with a crimping machine and successfully identified one product that was consistently more prone to defects than others. Recommended machine adjustments to alleviate defects.
- Optimized floor space by rearranging and redesigning four production cells within a tightly constricted space.
- Member of a team to prepare for a critical FDA audit. Ensured machines were fully validated and safety guards were properly and securely in place.

ADDITIONAL EXPERIENCE

Albright Roofing and Painting, Framingham, MA   9/03–Present
Construction Laborer—Contribute to roofing and home painting projects.

Dunmore Plastering, Southboro, MA   Summers 01 and 03
Plasters Foreman—Organized and monitored building materials and inventory levels.

Independently Employed, Amherst, MA   1/99–5/01
Agricultural Contractor—Performed agricultural contract work for farmers.

6

Combination. *Jeanne Knight, Melrose, Massachusetts*

"The focus on Education, Relevant Coursework, Academic Projects, and Engineering Experience nicely positions this new graduate for a full-time position as an Industrial Engineer"—resume writer's note.

Eileen Gonzales

00 Michalis Court
West Islip, New York 11795

Home Phone (555) 555-5555
E-mail: name@aol.com

PROFILE

Accounts Payable professional offering extensive education, superb communication skills and commitment to excellence that will enable a meaningful contribution to a dynamic, growth-oriented company.

➢ Financial/Managerial Accounting
➢ Advanced/Multinational Financial Management
➢ Corporate Finance/Money and Banking
➢ Information Systems/Budgeting/Forecasting
➢ Financial Planning/Asset Management

➢ Systems/Application Development Creation
➢ Quality Control/Customer Services
➢ Security Analysis and Portfolio Management
➢ Financial Management of Business Enterprise
➢ Business/Operations Management

SUMMARY OF HIGHLIGHTS/QUALIFICATIONS

◆ Comprehensive knowledge of financial and administrative operations. Organized and efficient, able to plan ahead with an eye for potential problems, skilled at implementing solutions to ensure maximum effectiveness of plans as well as a strong initiative in decision making and assumption of responsibilities.

◆ Articulate communicator with a flair for creative procedures in operational management, strategic planning and problem-solving skills.

EDUCATION

1998–2002 **PENNSYLVANIA STATE UNIVERSITY,** Pennsylvania
B.S. in Business Finance pending December 2002—Gold Key Honor Society Member 2000–2002

INTERNSHIPS

First Data Corporation F.D.C., Melville, New York *Summer 2002*
Gained valuable experience directing a wide variety of diverse functions, setting priorities and implementing decisions to achieve immediate and long-term goals. Supported efforts in enhancing production output, product quality and cost savings.
▪ Collected, analyzed and updated invoices/developed reports through MS Access, ensuring validity of invoices.
▪ Maintained project management initiation database and exported reports utilizing Excel for distribution.

Expanets, New York, New York *Summer 2001*
Played a key role meeting objectives while presenting a high level of self-motivation, creativity and initiative to achieve results while demonstrating an innate ability to work well in high-pressure, fast-paced environments.
▪ Effectively maintained relationships with existing customer base while developing new accounts by enhancing company image and awareness of products. Improved overall standards and expanded services executing PowerPoint presentations and reports for clients. Coordinated/scheduled meetings.

RELATED EXPERIENCE

Access Temporary Agency, Melville, New York *1998–2000*
Held temporary office positions during summer and school vacations. Organized, planned and executed various procedures collaborating with upper-level managers to obtain greater efficiency throughout office. Provided customer service and mediated grievances.
▪ Audited expense reports for validity in a manufacturing company; encoded expense items to be posted to general ledger and ensured entries were updated to the company's MIS system. Provided management through weekly MIS reporting.

Action Store Fronts, West Islip, New York *1997–1998*
Assistant Office Manager—aided in the coordination of office services, personnel and budget preparation and kept official records. Functioned as staff support providing various administrative and clerical services.
▪ Typed/edited business proposals; organized and maintained database. Answered calls and took messages.

COMPUTER SKILLS

➢ MS Word, Excel, Access, PowerPoint; desktop publishing; Lotus 1-2-3

CLUBS AND ORGANIZATIONS

◆ Blue Band Silk Line Member, 2002
◆ Student Government Association, 1996–2000—*Acting Secretary*
◆ Student Union Board, 1998–1999

◆ Future Business Leaders of America, 1995–1998—*Captain all four years, leading to college team, 1999*
◆ *Softball 1989–1996/Dance 1998–2000*

VOLUNTEER EXPERIENCES

➢ March of Dimes
➢ Triathlon

➢ Habitat for Humanity
➢ Dance Marathon

References available on request.

Combination. *Deborah Ann Ramos, Staten Island, New York*

The two-column format for the Profile section is flexible. The lists of bulleted items can be altered (tailored) for each targeted company. Bold italic makes the names of workplaces visible. See Cover Letter 69 (page 102).

35–12 Cottonboll Drive
Selma, AL 00000

Yasheika Ojimobi

Banquet Management Specialist

yasheika@partytime.com

Phone: (000) 000-0000
Pager: (000) 000-0000

Areas of Expertise

- Hands-on management in any service area
- Experience with start-up establishments
- Daily opening and closing responsibilities
- Supplier selection/negotiation
- Purchasing of food and paper products

- Inventory maintenance
- Food quality and sanitation issues
- Service staffing and supervision
- Portion/waste/cost control
- Payroll and budgeting

Personal and Professional Qualifications

- Commitment to superior customer service
- Excellent attendance record throughout employment
- Resourceful in dealing with food or staff shortages

- Attentive to special dietary needs
- Maintain high morale and low turnover
- Time management/multitasking ability

Employment

Assistant Banquet Manager
ROYAL INN AND CONFERENCE CENTER, Selma, AL   1990 to Present
A 144-room hotel with professional conference facilities, which include 15 meeting rooms, a grand ballroom with capacity for up to 400, and private meeting and banquet space for up to 250; total banquet seating for 750.

- Report to both banquet manager and general hotel manager. Ensure that all details are attended to in the proper setup for weddings, banquets, meetings, and special events.
- Supervise and schedule staff to service 2–6 daily meetings and 2–3 ongoing banquets evenings and weekends.
- Coordinate bar and kitchen operations, expediting the smooth running of banquet and meeting functions.
- Make arrangements for audio/visual requirements for business meetings.
- Act as the manager on call for problems in other areas of the hotel in absence of regular managers. In this capacity, respond to guest dissatisfaction issues; also intervene in crisis situations that could affect safety and comfort of the guests.
- Take charge of catering functions for hotel employee social events twice a year (average attendance of 350), as well as food/snack service for administrative meetings and recognition luncheons.
- Received Hospitality Award in 1998 for exemplary work to produce happy customers.

Banquet Server
ACE TEMPORARY AGENCY, Selma, AL   1989–1990
- Involved in all phases of service at banquets and private parties contracted through this company.
- Was frequently requested at Royal Inn whenever additional staff was required, then hired permanently.

Counter Person and Back-of-House Worker
ANNIE'S DINER, Selma, AL   1987–1989
- Gained practical experience in every area of running a food-service business.

Education

INTERNATIONAL CORRESPONDENCE SCHOOLS, Scranton, PA
- Certificate course in Hotel Restaurant Management   1990

ROYAL INN CAREER DEVELOPMENT PROGRAM
- Core Skills in Food Service Management   1992
- Food Service Sanitation Certification   1993
- Introduction to Computers   1994

8

Combination. *Melanie Noonan, West Paterson, New Jersey*

As was true for the Profile section in the preceding resume, the two-column lists of bulleted items are easily altered to tailor the resume to each targeted company. See Cover Letter 86 (page 120).

MARIANNE L. PERRAULT

900 East Shelter Road
Oldetown, Rhode Island 09999

Fax: (401) 555-6666
E-mail: marip@foxx.net
Phone: (401) 333-8877

QUALIFICATIONS

➢ Proven ability to train, schedule, supervise, and effectively manage 60 employees preparing 1,000 airline passenger meals per day.
➢ Competent leader with extensive experience in prioritizing, delegating, and controlling work flow in municipal government and high-volume private-industry work environments.
➢ Proficient in effectively organizing, handling, and monitoring a wide variety of tasks.
➢ Comfortable with operating Microsoft Office 2000, Windows ME, Corel, and Internet research on PC and Macintosh platforms.

EXPERIENCE

Food-Air Associates, Inc., Providence, RI
Vice President and Pricing Administrator for family-owned business, 1994–present
  o Manage accounts payable/receivable for very profitable, high-volume airline catering kitchen serving American, USAirways, United, Northwest, Southwest, and Delta Air Lines.
  o Review and analyze monthly P&L statement generated by accounting firm.
  o Establish costs of goods and services; audit and reconcile inventory.
  o Negotiate contract terms with major airline clients.
  o Hire, train, schedule, and manage up to 60 employees.
  o Design and implement quality-assurance measures to maintain high standards and consistent business retention to clients serving a total of 1,000 passenger meals per day.

Oldetown Police, Oldetown, RI
Administrative Assistant to the Chief of Police (part-time), 1992–1994
  o Researched, prepared, and wrote grants for municipal benefit.
  o Assisted in assembling data for annual police budget submissions to town council.
  o Provided accurate, courteous responses to inquiries on police matters of a sensitive nature.

EDUCATION

John Phelps University, Newport, RI
  o Master of Science in Business Administration, 1994

Rhode Island University, Providence, RI
  o Bachelor of Science in Finance, 1992
  o Cecelia H. Belknap Scholar: GPA over 3.85 (four years)

VOLUNTEER

Providence Chamber of Commerce; Oldetown Animal League; Providence GRO-Business Associates; Air-Transportation League; R.I. Fraternal Order of Police.

– EXCELLENT REFERENCES FURNISHED UPON REQUEST –

9

Combination. *Edward Turilli, North Kingstown, Rhode Island*

The two boxes make this resume different from most others. The hollow bullets also are not common. Boldfacing and italic make the name, headings, workplaces, jobs, and universities stand out.

Joseph D. Morten

167 Helman Lane • Bridgewater, New Jersey 08807
908.555.5555 (H) • 908.444.4444 (Fax) • jMorten439@aol.com

HUMAN RESOURCES / CORPORATE TRAINING
Supervision ~ Business Management ~ Employee Relations ~ Coaching

Energetic, reliable and adaptable professional with a solid understanding of human resources, business operations and various corporate environments. Proven abilities in creatively identifying methods for improving staff productivity and organizational behavior. Recognized for ability to introduce innovative management techniques into a multicultural workforce.

Results-oriented professional with excellent communication and interpersonal skills. Accurately perform challenging tasks with precision and attention to detail. Excel at organizing and setting up new procedures, troubleshooting and taking adverse situations and making them positive.

Competencies Include

- Human Resources Management
- Operations Management
- Teambuilding/Leadership
- Organizational & Project Management

- Training & Development
- Staffing Requirements
- Problem Resolution
- Employee Scheduling

Professional Experience

Waste Removal, *Plainfield, NJ (August 1997–September 2002)*
CFA Administrator
Waste Removal is the nation's largest full-service waste removal / disposal company
- Maintained and monitored multiple databases for the more than 120 pieces of equipment in the trucking company inventory.
- Generated accurate reports of budgets, repair costs, and personnel scheduling.
- Dramatically improved maintenance shop productivity through close budget monitoring.
- Served as a key link between management and mechanics, utilizing excellent interpersonal and communications skills. Acknowledged for improving the overall flow of information throughout the organization.
- Initiated, planned and managed the implementation of high-turn inventory-management systems and procedures. The new inventory system was credited with improving the operation of a very high-volume parts operation.
- Assumed a leadership role in the company by completely reorganizing the physical inventory process to ensure greater accuracy and system integrity.
- Managed the successful integration of two new parts operations, turning a possible negative situation into a very positive one.

Easy Video Entertainment, *Colonia, NJ (March 1994–August 1997)*
Store Manager
Retail video rental and sales chain with more than 600 outlets and 5,000 employees worldwide
- Managed all daily store operations including a staff of 5 employees. Responsible for recruitment, hiring, firing, training and scheduling of all staff members.
- Ability to train and motivate staff to maximize productivity and to control costs with hands-on management and close monitoring of store budgets.
- Attained a 25% increase in sales over a 12-month period, leading all 45 stores in the district. The store ranked 40th in overall sales volume of the 600 stores in the company.
- Maintained a consistent Top 20 ranking for sales of high-profit coupon books.
- Used excellent leadership, team-building and communication skills to develop subordinates and encourage cooperation and responsibility. Ensured compliance with corporate HR programs.
- Developed and implemented creative and aggressive promotional techniques that resulted in the store consistently exceeding its sales goals.

Education

BA ~ Psychology, *FAIRLEIGH DICKINSON UNIVERSITY, Madison, NJ*

10

Combination. *Beverley and Mitchell I. Baskin, Marlboro, New Jersey*

The tilde (~), used to separate fields of activity in the profile, is echoed in the Education section at the bottom of the page. Each workplace in boldface is "explained" by a statement in italic.

RICHARD LEVINSON

0000 Preston Avenue ◆ Houston, TX 77000 ◆ (281) 000-0000 ◆ myname@aol.com

Career Target: Software Programmer / Software Engineer

PROFILE

Talented software programmer with BBA degree, strong educational background in programming, and experience using cutting-edge development tools. Articulate and professional communication skills, including formal presentations and technical documentation. Productive in both team-based and self-managed projects; dedicated to maintaining up-to-date industry knowledge and IT skills.

Knowledge & Skill Areas:

- Software Development Lifecycle
- Object-Oriented Programming
- Problem Analysis & Resolution
- Web Site Design & Development

- Requirements Gathering & Analysis
- Technical & End User Documentation
- Software Testing & Troubleshooting
- Project Teamwork & Communications

TECHNICAL SUMMARY

Languages:	Java, C, C++, JSP, ASP, Rational, HTML, SQL, Unified Process
Operating Systems:	Linux, Windows XP/2000/9x
Object-Oriented Design:	UML, Design Patterns

EDUCATION

TEXAS UNIVERSITY, Houston, TX
Bachelor of Business Administration in Computer Science, 2002

- ◆ Earned place on President's List for 3 semesters (4.0 GPA)
- ◆ Member, Golden Key National Honor Society & Honors Fraternity
- ◆ Selected for listing in *Who's Who Among Students in American Universities and Colleges*

Relevant Coursework:

- Software Engineering
- Project Management
- Database Design

- Systems Engineering
- Differential Equations
- Classical / Modern Physics

- Calculus I, II, III
- Logic Circuits
- Systems Analysis

Project Highlights:

- ◆ **Software Engineering**—Served as Design Team Leader and member of Programming group for semester-long project involving development of software for actual implementation within Texas University Recreation Center. Determined requirements, created "look and feel" for user interface, and maintained explicit written documentation.

- ◆ **Systems Engineering**—Teamed with group of 4 in conceptualizing and designing client-server application to interconnect POS and inventory systems for retail outlet, delivering class presentation that highlighted specifications and projected $2 million in cost savings.

COMMUNITY COLLEGE, Houston, Texas
- ◆ 3.96 GPA / Concentration in Computer Science coursework

EXPERIENCE

DATAFRAME CONCEPTS, L.L.C., Houston, TX   2000–Present
Software Developer

- ◆ Worked with small team of developers to brainstorm and implement ideas for shipping/receiving software, representing leading-edge concept within transportation industry.

- ◆ Planned and initiated redesign of existing standalone application, utilizing object-oriented design/programming and Java in creating thin-client GUI for new distributed system.

- ◆ Collaborated with marketing director in strategies to further business growth, including Web site enhancement that drove 65% increase in visitor interest for product offering.

* References and additional information will gladly be provided upon request.

11

Combination. *Daniel J. Dorotik, Jr., Lubbock, Texas*

The applicant had limited work experience, so the writer emphasized skills and education. To de-emphasize experience, the writer put the Experience section at the bottom of the resume.

Danielle Quinones

danielleq@homenet.com

Current Residence:	**After June 1, 2004:**
515 Abernathy Court	70 Turtleback Trail
Richland, NJ 00000	San Jose, CA 00000
(000) 000-0000	(000) 000-0000

Seeking position as Administrative Assistant in a busy law firm that requires a self-starter with exceptional organizational ability

Skills

- ❖ Computer literacy using Microsoft Word, including legal document applications.
- ❖ Proficiency with machine dictation/transcription and other office technology.
- ❖ Meticulous in the setup and maintenance of complex legal files, with associated correspondence and billing detail.
- ❖ Efficient in managing a diary system to meet all scheduled commitments.
- ❖ Extensive experience in personal injury litigation (including subrogation), with exposure also to real estate, medical malpractice, construction, environmental and matrimonial cases.

Relevant Experience

Feinberg, Radcliffe, Cullen & Martini, LLP, Newark, NJ   *1999–Present*

Legal Administrative Assistant for law firm employing 14 attorneys and 50 support staff.
- ❖ Hired in floater position for two summers and during college breaks. Self-trained in all aspects of legal secretarial responsibilities, demonstrating strong dedication and interest in the operations of a law office.
- ❖ In 2001, promoted to full-time position for an associate involved with defense for insurance companies and claimants.
- ❖ Manage a heavy volume of files, with more than 100 cases open simultaneously; 20–30 of these are nonroutine subrogation matters.
- ❖ After minimal instruction, entrusted with the preparation of all details of motions, including signing authority attesting to completion of documents.
- ❖ Anticipate and fulfill lawyers' needs so that all deadlines are met, thereby protecting the firm from incurring costly penalties.

Other Experience

Banner Shoe Stores, Corporate Office, North Orange, NJ   *1996–1999*

Aide to Purchasing Assistant (part-time during school months)
- ❖ Handled all secretarial and clerical duties for the Purchasing Department.
- ❖ Responded promptly to calls from 150 stores nationwide for supplies and services needed to properly run their operations.

Education

Creighton Hill University, North Orange, NJ   *1996–1999*
- ❖ Completed 3 years toward B.A. in Psychology
- ❖ Member, Beta Tau Sorority; Alumni Relations Chairperson
- ❖ Financed 30% of educational expenses through part-time employment

Combination. *Melanie Noonan, West Paterson, New Jersey*

An unusual font ties together visually the person's name and side headings. Distinctive bullets help to draw the eye down the page. Boldfacing makes the occupations stand out. See Cover Letter 148 (page 182).

PATRICIA JUHASZ

555 Riddle Avenue • Smithtown, NY 55555 • (888) 999-0000 • Pjuhasz@telcomm.net

Legal Assistant/Paralegal Assistant

Experienced Legal Assistant with excellent office management and client-attorney relation skills seeking an entry-level Paralegal Assistant position where a working knowledge of legal terminology, general law, and legal proceedings, and continuing education in Paralegal Studies will be utilized and expanded. Bring experience working within a Legal Department/Collection Agency environment in the following select areas:

Civil Litigation…Collections…Settlements…Affidavits…Skip Tracing…Attorney Sourcing & Selection
Bankruptcies…Judgments…Liens…Summons & Complaint…Estate Searches…Statute of Limitations

PROFESSIONAL EXPERIENCE

Legal Assistant, Legal Recoveries, Inc., Lake Grove, NY   1998–present

Joined this Collection Agency's legal department at a time of unit-wide staffing changes. Responsible for managing a high volume of civil litigation case files for major accounts that partially included Century Detection, Credit Union of New York, AB Bank National Association, and St. Mary's Hospital.

- Collaborate extensively with internal departments including collections, medical billing, finance, production, special projects, and clerical to obtain, verify, and process documentation pertaining to the status of more than 50 weekly referred collections cases forwarded to the legal department.
- Carefully source and select nationally based bonded attorneys utilizing the *American Lawyers Quarterly, Commercial Bar Directory, National Directory List,* and *Columbia Directory List;* determine the appropriate choice upon obtainment and review of résumés, copies of insurance policies, and court filing fees.
- Perform estate searches and integrate traditional investigative methods and the DAKCS database system to gather account histories and case-sensitive documentation for attorneys, including
  debtors and guarantors, credit bureau reports, court affidavits, judgments, skip-tracing records, bankruptcy notices, banking statements, proof of statute of limitations, proof of assets, and trial letters.
- Maintain communications with attorneys and clients from point of referral/discovery to trial phase to facilitate and expedite case settlements that historically award clients a minimum of 80% in recovered funds.

EDUCATION

Bachelor of Science in Paralegal Studies, 1998
ST. JOSEPH'S COLLEGE, Brentwood, NY

COMPUTER SKILLS

Windows 2000; WordPerfect and Microsoft Word; DAKCS

EARLIER WORK HISTORY

Administrative Assistant, State Insurance, Patchogue, NY	1997–1998
Office Support Assistant, Financial Association of America, Inc., Islip, NY	1995–1997
Appointment Coordinator, Phlebotomy Services, Huntington, NY	1991–1996
Senior Office Support Assistant, AB National Bank, Hicksville, NY	1986–1991

Professional References Provided on Request

13

Combination. *Ann Baehr, Brentwood, New York*

The focus is on the applicant's most relevant experience. Earlier experience is put near the bottom. Keywords are used to indicate areas of expertise at the end of the profile. The page border is shadowed.

JENNIFER GONZALES

334–30 Kissena Blvd., Flushing, NY 55555 • (555) 222-7777 • JGonzales@lawandorder.net

Seeking a position in the field of

Law Enforcement

CITY——STATE——FEDERAL——PRIVATE

➤ Highly motivated, energetic law enforcement student with strong work ethic and professional goals.
➤ Bring five years of experience in office support and retail sales positions while attending college full time.
➤ Bilingual with an articulate fluency in English and Spanish; personable, easygoing communication style.
➤ Meet challenges head on; work well in stressful situations and fast-paced settings.
➤ Analytical with a lot of common sense, intuitive instincts, and ability to think outside of the box.
➤ Maintain excellent research, organization, time-management, and problem-assessment/resolution skills.

Education

Bachelor of Arts, Forensic Psychology—expected August 2004
John Jay College of Criminal Justice, New York, NY
Honors Candidate: Psi Chi Chapter National Honor Society in Psychology

Academically trained in criminalistics and psychology:

Select Courses: Analysis of Criminal Behavior, Concepts of Forensic Science, Abnormal Psychology,
Physical Fitness in Law Enforcement, Criminal Law, Group Dynamics
Select Projects: Crime Scene Observation, Forensic Study of Microscopic Fibers, Fingerprint Analysis

Work Experience

Receptionist, Volvoville, Massapequa, NY	4/98–Present
Payroll Clerk, People's Alliance Federal Credit Union, Hauppauge, NY	4/00–7/00
Sales Associate, Annie Sez, East Northport, NY	2/98–6/98
Senior Sales Associate, Rainbow Shops, Commack/Bay Shore, NY	9/97–2/98

• Provide front-desk representation, clerical support, and customer service for Volvo and subsidiary, Land Rover, directing customer traffic with a proven ability to maintain open lines of communication.

• Managed more than 50 business payroll accounts utilizing cross-trained experience in teller and payroll services.

• Prepared and uploaded weekly exempt/non-exempt payroll data into network system for clients to download.

• Completed mandatory training that included a film study on a mock robbery to learn observation techniques.

• Held increasingly responsible sales positions, achieving recognition for over-quota floor sales and cashier management skills, and manager-requests to return during school breaks based on performance and reliability.

• Provided excellence in customer service while assisting in all areas of inventory and display merchandising.

Computer Skills

Windows XP/Me; Microsoft Word, LexisNexis, PsychInfo, Criminal Justice Abstracts,
InfoTrak Health, Sociological Abstracts, Internet research

14

Combination. *Ann Baehr, Brentwood, New York*

Making explicit four areas of interest—city, state, federal, and private—below the Law Enforcement heading reduced the risk that this graduate would be limited to just one area of interest in her job search.

CAROL A. YOUNG

3 TABBY DRIVE • FLEMINGTON, NJ 08822
OFFICE (908) 237-1883 • FAX (908) 237-2069 • CAA@WORLDCLASSRESUMES.COM

Credentialed résumé writer with a demonstrated commitment to providing superior products and top-notch service

SUMMARY OF QUALIFICATIONS

Independent, self-motivated, and conscientious professional with strong customer focus. Excellent writing skills with extensive experience developing marketing materials, customer communications, and job search documents. Able to draw on diverse experience to understand client needs and develop effective, targeted résumés.

PROFESSIONAL HIGHLIGHTS

- Opened résumé business, coordinating all aspects of start-up, including creating and producing all business communications materials: brochures, business cards, flyers, and the company's Web site.
- Established proven record of accomplishment in writing winning résumés and other job search documents.
- With background that spans the fields of research, development, manufacturing, marketing, technical service, administrative customer service, career development, training, and project management, successfully work with technical, administrative, and executive professionals at all levels.
- Competently draw out key information from clients to effectively market skills and abilities.
- Astute and analytical; always operate with the understanding that knowing and adapting to the audience is the key to effective communication.
- Recognized for leadership and commitment to quality improvement. Strong track record of providing outstanding customer satisfaction.

CERTIFICATION

Certified Professional Résumé Writer, Professional Association of Résumé Writers, 2001

EMPLOYMENT HISTORY

WORLD CLASS RÉSUMÉS, *Owner,* 2000 to Present
RESUME.COM, *Elite Writer,* 2000 to Present
LIBERTY LIFE, *Implementation Consultant,* Voluntary Benefits Group, 1999 to 2000
KAPLAN, *Prep Course Instructor and Tutor,* 1999 to 2001
YORK OIL CORPORATION, *Senior Research Engineer,* Fuels Marketing Support, 1995 to 1999
SPECIALTY CHEMICALS, INC., *Staff Engineer,* Petroleum Catalyst Group, 1990 to 1995

EDUCATION

STATE UNIVERSITY, Master of Education (Counseling Psychology), 1996
CITY COLLEGE, Bachelor of Science (Chemical Engineering), 1990

15

Combination. *Carol A. Altomare, Three Bridges, New Jersey*

Here is the resume writer's own resume. It is included in this Exhibit to give an example of at least one professional resume writer's background. Note her degrees in science and psychology.

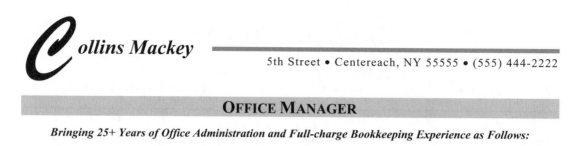

$\mathcal{C}$ollins Mackey

5th Street • Centereach, NY 55555 • (555) 444-2222

OFFICE MANAGER

Bringing 25+ Years of Office Administration and Full-charge Bookkeeping Experience as Follows:

♦ Accounts Payable / Receivable	♦ Expense Control	♦ Human Resources Management
♦ Weekly Payroll	♦ Account Management	♦ Staff Training and Supervision
♦ Credit and Collections	♦ Account Reconciliation	♦ Customer Service / Client Relations
♦ Statement Billings	♦ Month-end Closings	♦ Computerized Processes

PROFESSIONAL EXPERIENCE—*Overview*

Recognized throughout longstanding career for ability to develop, implement, and manage full-charge, computerized bookkeeping functions while overseeing multifaceted office administration procedures

- As Office Manager for August Publications, fully manage company-wide accounting and reporting functions for five subsidiaries, as well as weekly payroll processes for 45 salaried employees.
- Liaison among senior management, employees, and clients to ensure proper lines of communication critical in addressing myriad problems and issues requiring immediate attention and resolve.
- Manage Accounts Payable/Receivable and expense-control procedures, including bank and account reconciliation, cash receipts, disbursements, finance charges, billings, invoicing, purchase order and inventory verification, chargebacks, rebates, and preparation of daily bank deposits.
- Negotiate and enforce collections to recover funds and expedite the clearance on delinquent accounts.
- Collaborate extensively with external auditors, providing in-depth assistance with periodic corporate audits.
- Perform thorough credit analyses, research financial histories, and review account status as a prerequisite to qualifying new accounts, authorizing purchases, and extending/increasing lines of credit of up to $200,000.
- Establish and maintain Human Resources–related employee files reflecting salary increases, deductions, garnishments, benefits, payroll exceptions, and W-2 withholdings, exercising a high level of confidentiality.
- Skilled at interviewing, hiring, training, and evaluating employees in areas of accounting procedures.
- Research account transactions, demonstrating a keen ability to recognize and resolve discrepancies.
- Follow through on timely and accurate month-end closings and financial reporting activities.

WORK CHRONOLOGY

Office Manager,	August Publications, Hauppauge, NY	1996–present
Office Manager,	Quality Insurance, Huntington, NY	1986–1996
Office Manager,	DSG Management Corp., Melville, NY	1983–1985
Controller's Assistant,	Georgia Interiors, Farmingdale, NY	1979–1983
Credit/Collections Supervisor,	EastTel Sales Corp., New York, NY	1978–1979
Accounts Payable/Receivable Clerk,	Syobel Corp., New York, NY	1973–1978

COMPUTER PROFICIENCIES

Windows 2000; MS Word and Excel; WordPerfect; Lotus; Peachtree Accounting

EDUCATION

Bachelor of Arts, Business Management/Accounting, Banes College, 1982

16

Combination. *Ann Baehr, Brentwood, New York*

The writer condenses extensive experience onto one page, using keywords, an Overview section representing many similar positions to avoid repetition, and a compact Work Chronology section.

LAURA D. WENN

899 Lancona Road   (555) 555-5555
Dallas, TX 00000   ldw56@yahoo.com

RETAIL MANAGEMENT PROFESSIONAL

Nine years of retail management experience demonstrating a consistent track record of outstanding sales, merchandising and customer service results. Equally strong qualifications in all areas of fine jewelry department operations: P&L, budgeting, inventory control, training, security and other functions. Effective communicator, leader and problem solver who builds teamwork and possesses the initiative to exceed goals.

EXPERIENCE

LAWRENCE FINE JEWELRY CORPORATION, Seattle, WA (1993–present)
Progressed rapidly from part-time position to manager at several stores, including the following:

Manager—G. Fox, Randolph Mall, Dallas, TX (1999–present)
Manager—G. Fox, Valley Mall, Phoenix, AZ (1995–1999)
Manager—G. Fox, Turner Mall, Tucson, AZ (1994–1995)
Assistant Manager—G. Fox, Forest Mall, San Antonio, TX (1993–1994)

Summary of Responsibilities

Operations Management—Hold profit-and-loss accountability; manage all aspects of day-to-day department performance of stores ranging from $500,000 to $2M in annual sales. Direct sales, inventory control, visual merchandising, housekeeping, security, administration and compliance to company policies/procedures. Managed 2 stores concurrently over 4-month period with highly successful sales results during busy Christmas season.

Staff Supervision & Training—Supervise teams of up to 13 fine-jewelry specialists. Experienced in personnel recruiting, selection, training, developing, scheduling and supervising associates. Motivate staff to achieve performance goals and ensure productive department operations.

Customer Relations & Service—Develop and manage customer relations to maximize service satisfaction, promote goodwill and generate repeat/referral business that contributes to sales growth. Monitor and resolve any service issues.

Selected Achievements

- Increased Randolph store sales from $1.1M to $1.4M (27%) in 2000 and maintained .02% shrink—well below company average of 2.1%.
- Increased percent-to-store sales at Valley Mall from 2.8% to 5.2%, surpassing company average of 2.5%. Grew annual sales at Valley Mall from $.8M in 1995 to $1.1M (37%) in 1996, $1.4M (27%) in 1997, $1.7M (21%) in 1998 and $2M (18%) in 1999.
- Selected by Regional Manager to serve as Training Store Manager for the region; recognized for the ability to recruit quality candidates who have successfully advanced within the company.

Awards

- Earned **Branch Manager of the Year** and **Branch of the Year** awards in 2000 in the Southwest Region.
- Twice named **Manager of the Year** out of 50 stores in 1998 and 1996 in the Southwest Region.
- Winner of 3 sales performance awards in 2000: **Goal Achievers, Best Increase in % to Store** and **Best Event Business. Christmas Contest** winner in 1999, exceeding sales goal by 15%.
- Selected runner up for 3 awards in 2000: **Best in Operations, Best Visual Department** and **Best Buyer Communication.** Ranked #3 in **Christmas Contest** in 2000, exceeding sales goal by 21%.

EDUCATION / PROFESSIONAL DEVELOPMENT

B.A., Retail Management, Valhalla College, Dallas, TX

Completed various company-sponsored training courses in management, personnel recruiting, staff training and development, sales, customer service and related topics.

Combination. *Louise Garver, Enfield, Connecticut*

The applicant was applying for a position with a competitor in Arizona. She had held positions with the same responsibilities at several stores. To eliminate repetition, the writer summarized key duties.

EDWARD J. BROWER

999 Wilson Drive ▪ Dallas, TX 75200 ▪ (972) 555-7777 ▪ ejbrower@email.com

Country Club Management Professional
Proven track record of driving revenues to unprecedented levels

Challenge-driven visionary with comprehensive knowledge of all aspects of country club management, seven years of experience in hospitality industry, and core competencies in

Club Management	*Strategic Marketing*
Member Service & Satisfaction	*Crucial Planning & Execution*
Interdepartmental Communications	*Revenue & Profitability Acceleration*

EDUCATION & PROFESSIONAL DEVELOPMENT

UNIVERSITY OF HOUSTON—Houston, TX
Conrad N. Hilton College of Hotel & Restaurant Management
Bachelor of Science, Hotel and Restaurant Management (1996)

WHARTON COUNTY JUNIOR COLLEGE—Wharton, Texas
Associate of Applied Sciences, Supervisory Management (1993)

CLUB MANAGERS ASSOCIATION OF AMERICA
Pursuing **Certification in Club Management**

RELEVANT EMPLOYMENT CHRONICLE

LOVELY COUNTRY CLUB—Dallas, TX (1996–Present)
Clubhouse Manager/Assistant Manager

Progressed from assistant manager to clubhouse manager and assumed challenge of reconstructing food, beverage, service, housekeeping, maintenance/repair, and security processes for 5,800-sq.-ft. clubhouse, ballroom with 250 capacity, large bar/ lounge, and kitchen. Oversee staff of 25–30 (five directs), all club marketing, budget of $1.3 million, and inventory of $672,000; and placate and ensure satisfaction of 833 membership. **Direct all operations in absence of general manager.**

Selected Accomplishments

- Successfully revamped and revitalized club; developed innovative strategies and processes, which **boosted morale** and **productivity; slashed labor** and **food costs;** and **escalated** annual **revenues** from approximately **$900,000 to $1.3 million.**
- Devised and launched exciting **youth, social,** and **dining** activities, which dramatically enhanced member interest and participation.
- Honored with challenge of organization, planning, and execution of **Annual Eisenhower International Golf Classic,** which resulted in being named **Host Club** for its annual events.
- Recognized as club's **"computer system guru";** troubleshoot and diagnose system malfunctions throughout club.

Positions held while pursuing degree:

Server/Busboy, WILDWOOD HOTEL—Houston, TX (1995–1996)

- **Promoted to server within five months** because of demonstrated commitment to personalized, superior customer service.

Guest Service Agent, GARDEN SUITES HOTEL—Houston, TX (1993–1995)

- **Awarded highest customer service/excellence award** possible by guest nominations while attending front desk.

PROFESSIONAL AFFILIATIONS & HONORS

CLUB MANAGERS ASSOCIATION OF AMERICA (Since 1996)
Chronicled in **"Who's Who Among Students in American Junior Colleges"**
Recipient of Phi Beta Lambda's **"Outstanding Student Award"**
Volunteer Director, House Services—*Gourmet Night* (1995)
Historian/Parliamentarian, Phi Beta Lambda (1991, 1992)

18

Combination. *Ann Klint, Tyler, Texas*

Much center-justified information in this resume creates adequate white space even inside a page border. Boldfacing ampersands and the first letter of certain words in headings is distinctive.

BAXTER A. LEEDS

45 Kaiwan Street   Taipei, Taiwan   555-05050505   bestoys@xix5.net

PROFESSIONAL GOAL

Opportunity in the toy manufacturing industry where experience in creative product development, team leadership, and mass production will contribute to business growth and success in the USA and Asia.

PROFESSIONAL PROFILE

- Successful background in the toy industry with a leading manufacturer in both the USA and Asia.
- Highly creative in design, construction, and production of seasonal, novelty, and licensed products.
- Broad understanding of living and working in Asia; knowledge of customs, beliefs, and culture.
- Dedicated commitment to quality products, expense control, and customer satisfaction.
- Valued by colleagues for work ethic, team leadership, creativity, and open-mindedness.

EXPERIENCE

BESTOYS, INC.—Taipei, Taiwan   **1992–Present**
Creative Director
USA-based toy company with manufacturing operations in Taiwan.

Creative Product Development
- Manage product aesthetic and function during product engineering and development process.
- Conceptualize in 3D with mechanical ability to develop pattern, starting with minimal item definition.
- Strong knowledge of model-building techniques and experience with all relevant materials.
- Collaborate with company's CEO and Asian Division President on product development initiatives.

Management/Team Leadership
- Direct 100-member Taiwan prototype staff in all phases of the prototyping/manufacturing process.
- Independently supervise work, coping with fluctuating work loads while maintaining accuracy to product design without missing deadlines.
- Effective interpersonal skills and a respect for people of all backgrounds and nationalities.
- Communicate via e-mail with USA product management on daily item needs and changes.

Manufacturing for Mass Production/Licensed Products
- Skilled in meeting mass production costs, scheduling, and engineering specifications.
- Work directly with BesToys' Asian engineering staff and production vendor engineering on item construction to meet aesthetic, function, schedule, and item cost.
- Manufacture a vast number of products including boys', girls', spring, seasonal, novelty, and licensed products for vastly successful brand names.
- Effectively complete a large volume of licensed goods for sale/distribution in various world markets.

Key Contributions

- Opened a new prototype facility in Taiwan to meet increased corporate demands, maximize output of sales samples, and reduce prototyping costs.
- Utilize a management style of empowerment, support, and assertiveness in meeting deadlines.
- Monitor and control USA designs built in Taiwan to ensure highest quality standards.

EDUCATION

BFA with Honors
Marketing and Advertising Design—Santa Rosa Fine Arts Academy, Santa Rosa, California, 1992

■■■■■■■

19

Combination. *Billie Ruth Sucher, Urbandale, Iowa*

The applicant brought the writer "vast pages of information about his background." The writer organized and categorized this information into keyword/skills areas to showcase his experience.

Gregg S. Lane

Ph.: (555) 555-5555
Fax: (800) 000-0000

GSL

129 Avenida del Sol, Apt. 136
Northview, CA 99999
www.spirit.com
soul2@gsl.com

Author ▪ *Producer* ▪ *Inspirational Speaker*

FCC Certified Cable Access Producer:

➢ *Well-versed in FCC rules and regulations.*
➢ *Proficient in problem solving, with ability to quickly adapt to the unexpected.*
➢ *Experienced in Preparing Run Sheets ▪ Editing ▪ Writing ▪ Program Planning and Coordinating ▪ Managing Logistics and Personnel ▪ Virtually all aspects of production.*
➢ *Effective communicator who interacts well with people from a wide range of social and cultural backgrounds.*
➢ *Able to tackle issues by producing programs that are relevant, informative, and stimulating.*

CAREER HIGHLIGHTS	▪ **Host, Writer, and Executive Producer—*The Spirited Soul*** Cable Television Broadcast—Weekly 30-minute teaching program applying philosophy and phenomenology to inspire awareness and appreciation for the spiritual presence in our daily lives. *Originally aired 1992–1996; updated and revived Feb 2004.* Multicultural demographic for both programs: Casitas Heights, Westview, Norwood, Thousand Hills, San Lopez, West/South Marina.	2004
	▪ **Host, Writer, and Executive Producer—*The Spirited Soul*** Radio Broadcast Station KTYM—30-minute teaching program with presentations derived from philosophical and spiritual works. Audience demographic: Culturally diverse, encompassing Casitas Heights, Westview, Norwood, Thousand Hills, West Marina.	1992 to 1996
	▪ **Founded Spiritual Essence—A nonprofit outreach program.**	1992
	▪ **Host and Producer—*Computer Awareness*** Cable Television Broadcast—Weekly 30-minute show that focused on desktop publishing and related technology. Featured guests who were experts in the field.	1992

EDUCATION	▪ State University—Loma Pointe, CA
	   – *Bachelor of Arts in Communications Studies—2001*
	     Emphasis on Speech and Broadcast Communications, Rhetoric, Advanced Phenomenology
	   – Enrolled in Master's Program—Communications Studies major
	
	 ▪ Central College—Central City, CA
	   – *Broadcasting—1990*	

PROFESSIONAL AFFILIATIONS	Member—Elite Communications Association Member—Nationwide Communication Association	
PUBLICATIONS	Lane, Gregg S.: *Heritage Unveiled,* Second Edition. Lane Pub. Co. 210 p. Copyright 1993. Lane, Gregg S.: *Modern Predictions.* Jolie Enterprises. 54 p. Copyright 1990. Lane, Gregg S.: *Heritage Unveiled.* Lane Pub. Co. 144 p. Copyright 1972.	

20

Combination. *Gail Taylor, Torrance, California*

The bold script type for the applicant's name and roles captures attention first. The gray box and gray horizontal line are almost as eye-catching. Next, special tip bullets direct the reader's eyes down the page.

ROY NASH
◆ 4900 Boulevard, Carson City, NV 00000 ◆ (000) 000-0000

FOCUS
To acquire field experience necessary to become an alcohol and drug rehabilitation counselor.

RELEVANT QUALIFICATIONS

➢ Former alcohol and drug abuser now in recovery, having completed a rigorous rehabilitation program without any recidivism for more than 3 years.
➢ Avid supporter of others experiencing the nightmare of addiction; keenly sensitive to their feelings and needs to enable joining with clients in early stages of interaction.
➢ Confident facilitator; relate comfortably with diverse cultural and socio-economic populations in didactic sessions with groups of from 12 to more than 40.
➢ Observant of clients' behaviors, with documentation of improvements or lack thereof, to assist authorities in planning appropriate actions upon their release from the 28-day program.

EDUCATION

St. Jude's College, Reno, NV
➢ Graduate of the Recovery Assistance Program Training (RAPT), 2002.
➢ Completed 270 educational hours toward CADC certification. Curriculum included Addiction and Its Effects, The Recovery Process, Family Counseling, Individual Counseling, and Group Counseling.

➢ Passed written exam given by the International Certification Reciprocating Consortium (ICRC), 2002.

PROFESSIONAL EXPERIENCE

Counselor-in-Training at Straight and Narrow, a psycho-social 12-step rehabilitative agency in Carson City, NV (2002 to present).
➢ Conduct 1½-hour didactic sessions to groups that include mentally ill chemical abusers (MICA), focusing on their recovery.
➢ Assist with the new client intake process, assessing and prioritizing service requirements.
➢ Orient prospective clients to the rehabilitative setting and the programs available to them.
➢ Facilitate the adjustment of introductory groups daily, providing them with support and encouragement to stay with the program.
➢ Schedule clients for art therapy and daily recreation and coordinate their other activities.
➢ Ease clients' transition into didactic sessions by introducing deep-breathing and relaxation techniques as a part of daily meditation preliminaries.

PREVIOUS EMPLOYMENT

Bartender, Happy Days Bar & Grill, Reno, NV (1991-2001)
Server, Bartolucci's Ristorante, Reno, NV (1989-1991)

VOLUNTEER ACTIVITIES

➢ Initiated support group in Carson City for parents of drug-addicted/alcohol-dependent children and adolescents, working closely with the police department and D.A.R.E. program.

Combination. *Melanie Noonan, West Paterson, New Jersey*

As in Resume 12, a strong font ties together the person's name and side headings. Distinctive bullets draw the eye down the page. Boldfacing makes the occupations stand out. See Cover Letter 286 (page 321).

Elizabeth Denton

1814 Taylor Drive ~ North Brunswick, NJ 08902
(732) 821-7227 (H) ~ (732) 406-1927 (C) ~ E-mail: lizdent3@msn.com

Objective

To continue my career as a Maintenance Professional using my experience in various facets of manufacturing operations.

Summary of Qualifications

Broad-based responsibilities in the following areas:

- Project Management
- Maintenance Supervision
- Budget Management
- Problem Solving
- Electrical Maintenance
- Hydraulic Maintenance
- Quality Assurance Technician
- Chemical Batch Control
- Forklift Maintenance

Profile

Strengths include excellent communications with all levels of personnel...known as a results-oriented professional with attention to detail and accuracy.

Enjoy performing multiple tasks/projects while keeping an eye on bottom-line profits for the company.

Experience

HEINZ FOODS, Edison, NJ   **1995–2003**

Mechanic   **1997–2003**

- Performed preventive maintenance and repair of equipment and facility grounds for this food and beverage manufacturing operation with 7 manufacturing lines.
- Responsible for machine ownership during product changes, including maintenance and process adjustments.
- Recommended process machinery improvement projects of all sizes, some in excess of $1 million.
- Familiarity with conveyors, bottle cleaners, labelers, packers, palletizers, and filling machines.
- Led the team to eliminate iodine spray on fillers during sterilization.
- Thorough knowledge of mechanical, electrical, hydraulic, and plumbing systems for process equipment as well as for the building and grounds.

Maintenance Group Leader   **1995–1997**

- Extensive knowledge of the processes and equipment in the food, beverage, bottling, and packaging industry.
- Served as a forklift technician and driver on a computerized forklift.
- Performed quality assurance procedures on batches during the mixing and bottling process.
- Thorough knowledge of procedures and techniques used for shipping and receiving, and materials handling.

Continued

22

Combination. *Beverley and Mitchell I. Baskin, Marlboro, New Jersey*

A double-line page border ties together visually the two pages of this resume. Left-aligned, bold side headings make the main sections evident throughout. In the Summary of Qualifications, the three-column list of bulleted responsibility areas is useful for tailoring the

Elizabeth Denton

Page 2

NORTH BRUNSWICK TOWNSHIP, North Brunswick, NJ   **1989–1994**

School Bus Driver
- Responsible for driving children that were handicapped or had other special needs.

RIDER STUDENT TRANSPORTATION, New Brunswick, NJ   **1988–1989**

School Bus Driver
- Responsible for driving children to and from school along routine routes.

METROPOLITAN LIMOUSINE, East Brunswick, NJ   **1983–1988**

Owner
- Managed all internal functions of the company, including hiring drivers, dispatching drivers to jobs, billing, and ensuring that the vehicles were maintained properly.

Computers

Knowledge of Microsoft Word and Excel, Lotus 1-2-3, e-mail, and the Internet.

Special Training/Licenses

CDL Class B with passenger endorsement

Boat Operators License

Forklift License

PMMI Basic Hydraulic and Pneumatic Components

PMMI Basic Mechanical Components

PMMI Basic Electrical Components

Community Service

Coached North Brunswick Youth Soccer team to 8 consecutive winning seasons.

Hobbies include woodworking, crafting, gardening, and computers.

resume to different job targets. That is, you can easily replace one or more items in the list with new items of particular interest to a different employer without altering the resume's formatting. See Cover Letter 296 (page 331).

TOM NEWTON

1511 Whitewood Court • North Brunswick, New Jersey 08902 • 732.297.8846

QUALITY ASSURANCE PROFESSIONAL
QUALITY CONTROL ~ LABORATORY TECHNICIAN

Top-performing manufacturing professional with an outstanding reputation for enforcing stringent safety and quality protocols. Acknowledged as an expert troubleshooter, able to visualize desired outcomes, design strategic action plans, and follow through during the manufacturing process.

Professional strengths include

- Equipment Calibration
- Lab Solutions Preparation
- Manufacturing Processes
- Troubleshooting/Problem Solving
- Leadership/Supervision

- Analytical Skills
- Juice Batch-Making
- Productivity Improvements
- Production Processes & Standards
- Quality Improvement/Assurance

- Precision Measurements
- Product Analysis/Inspection
- Micro Plating
- RTCIS Product Releases
- Chemical Operations

BUSINESS EXPERIENCE

NORTHEAST FOODS, Dayton, NJ   1997–2003
Quality Assurance Technician
- Monitored and analyzed quality control for food and beverage manufacturing operation.
- Extensive knowledge of quality control issues and processes for juice-making production.
- Conducted laboratory experiments and preventative maintenance work.
- Selected, weighed, and blended ingredients according to formula for the batch-making of a juice drink.
- Performed analytical checks and quality assurance processes for food and beverage products.
- Implemented new ideas and techniques, resulting in improved quality control methodologies and procedures.
- Knowledge of *BOC/GMP* and safe operating practices within the manufacturing environment.
- Utilized *Micro Plating* expertise with micro-bacterial samples to develop new processes for quality assurance.
- Calibrated analytical and laboratory technical equipment such as refractometers, viscometers, balances, and autoclaves.
- Utilized strong troubleshooting and analytical skills to improve the production processes.
- Instituted laboratory solutions for manufacturing processes; utilized packaging equipment knowledge to improve operational functionality.

NATIONAL DISTRIBUTION CENTERS, Dayton, NJ   1991–1997
Building Maintenance Technician
- Responsible for daily maintenance and upkeep of warehouse equipment, the facility, and the building grounds. Performed painting and repairs, and ensured the security of the warehouse.
- Assisted the operational people with inventory control.

EDUCATION
AA ~ Chemistry ~ Middlesex County College ~ Edison, NJ

23

Combination. *Beverley and Mitchell I. Baskin, Marlboro, New Jersey*

Horizontal lines separate visually the main sections, which have centered headings. As in the preceding resume, the three-column bulleted list is easily tailored to different job targets. See Cover Letter 299 (page 334).

List of Contributors

List of Contributors

The following professional writers contributed the cover letters and resumes in this book. To include here the names of these writers and information about their business is to acknowledge with appreciation their voluntary submissions and their insights about the cover letters and resumes. Cover letter and resume numbers after a writer's contact information are the *numbers of the writer's cover letters and resumes* included in the Gallery, not page numbers.

Australia
New South Wales
Sydney

Jennifer Rushton
Keraijen
Level 14, 309 Kent St.
Sydney, NSW, 2000 Australia
Phone: 61 2 9994 8050
Fax: 61 2 4571 1971
E-mail: info@keraijen.com.au
Web site: www.keraijen.com.au
Member: CMI, PRWRA
Certification: CRW
Cover letter: 163

Queensland
Victoria Point West

Beverley Neil
d'Scriptive Words
P.O. Box 3281
Victoria Point West, QLD, 4165 Australia
Phone: 61 7 3206 9622
Fax: 61 7 3206 9633
E-mail: d_scriptive@powerup.com.au
Member: AORCP, PRWRA, QWC
Certification: CRW
Cover letter: 22

Victoria
Hallam

Annemarie Cross
Advanced Employment Concepts/AEC Office
  Services
P.O. Box 91
Hallam, Victoria, 3803 Australia
Phone: 61 3 9708 6930
E-mail: success@aresumewriter.net
Web site: www.aresumewriter.net
Member: CMI, PARW/CC, PRWRA
Certification: CEIP, CPRW, CRW, CCM,
  CECC
Cover letters: 59, 189

Melbourne

Gayle Howard
Top Margin Résumés Online
P.O. Box 74
Chirnside Park, Melbourne, 3116, Australia
Phone: 61 3 9726 6694
Fax: 61 3 9726 5316
E-mail: getinterviews@topmargin.com
Web site: www.topmargin.com
Member: CMI, PARW/CC, PRWRA, ASA
Certification: CPRW, CRW, CCM, CERW
Cover letters: 106, 233

Canada
Ontario
Toronto

Howard Earle Halpern
Résu-Card
167 Pannahill Rd.
Toronto, Ontario
Canada M3H 4N6
Toll-free: (877) 866-5454
E-mail: halpern@sympatico.ca
Web site: www.NoBlock.com
Member: PARW/CC
Certification: CPRW
Cover letter: 17

Whitby

Ross Macpherson
Career Quest
131 Kirby Crescent
Whitby, Ontario
Canada L1N 7C7
Phone: (905) 438-8548
Toll-free: (877) 426-8548
Fax: (905) 438-4096
E-mail:
  ross@yourcareerquest.com
Web site:
  www.yourcareerquest.com
Member: CMI, PARW/CC, ACPI
Certification: MA, CPRW, CJST,
  CEIP, JCTC
Cover letters: 3, 15, 134, 162,
  178, 210, 242, 301, 305

United States

Debra O'Reilly
A First Impression
Phone: (860) 583-7500
Toll-free: (800) 340-5570
Fax: (860) 585-9611
E-mail:
  debra@resumewriter.com
Web site:
  www.resumewriter.com
Member: PARW/CC, CMI,
  NRWA
Certification: CPRW, JCTC,
  CEIP, IJCTC, FRWC
Cover letter: 257

Alabama
Montgomery

Don Orlando
The McLean Group
640 S. McDonough St.
Montgomery, AL 36104
Phone: (334) 264-2020
Fax: (334) 264-9227
E-mail:
  yourcareercoach@aol.com
Member: CMI, PARW/CC,
  Phoenix Career Group
Certification: MBA, CPRW,
  JCTC, CCM, CCMC
Cover letters: 21, 24, 63, 100,
  116, 146, 170, 199, 243, 244,
  261

Arizona
Tucson

Kathryn Bourne
CareerConnections
5210 E. Pima St., Ste. 130
Tucson, AZ 85712
Phone: (520) 323-2964
Fax: (520) 795-3575
E-mail: CCmentor@aol.com
Web site:
  www.bestfitresumes.com
Member: CMI, PARW/CC
Certification: CPRW, JCTC,
  CEIP
Cover letters: 11, 103, 142, 272

California
Campbell

Georgia Adamson
A Successful Career / Adept
Business Services
180 W. Rincon Ave.
Campbell, CA 95008-2824
Phone: (408) 866-6859
Fax: (408) 866-8915
E-mail: success@
  ablueribbonresume.com
Web site: www.
  ABlueRibbonResume.com
Member: CMI, NRWA,
  PARW/CC
Certification: CCMC, CCM,
  CEIP, CPRW, JCTC
Cover letter: 126

Los Angeles

Alyssa Pera
Legal Authority
617 S. Olive St., Ste. 1210
Los Angeles, CA 90014
Toll-free: (800) 283-3860
Fax: (213) 895-7306
E-mail:
  alyssa@legalauthority.com
Web site:
  www.legalauthority.com
Member: PARW/CC
Certification: CPRW
Cover letters: 151, 152, 153,
  154, 156

Vivian VanLier
Advantage Resume & Career
Services
6701 Murietta Ave.
Los Angeles, CA 91405
Phone: (818) 994-6655
Fax: (818) 994-6620
E-mail: vvanlier@aol.com
Web site:
  www.CuttingEdgeResumes.com
Member: CMI, NRWA,
  PARW/CC
Certification: CPRW, JCTC,
  CEIP, CCMC
Cover letters: 122, 209

Torrance

Gail Taylor
Hire Power Résumé Services
21213-B Hawthorne Blvd. #5224
Torrance, CA 90503
Phone: (310) 793-4122
Fax: (310) 793-7481
E-mail: hirepwr@yahoo.com
Web site:
  www.call4hirepower.com
Member: CMI, NRWA,
  PARW/CC
Certification: CEIP, CPRW
Resume: 20

Valencia

Myriam-Rose Kohn
JEDA Enterprises
27201 Tourney Rd., Ste. 201
Valencia, CA 91355-1857
Phone: (661) 253-0801
Toll-free: (800) 600-JEDA
Fax: (661) 253-0744
E-mail: myriam-rose
   @jedaenterprises.com
Web site:
   www.jedaenterprises.com
Member: CMI, NRWA,
   PARW/CC
Certification: CPRW, CEIP,
   IJCTC, CCM, CCMC
Cover letters: 35, 77, 167, 245

Colorado

Aurora

Michele Angello
Corbel Communications
19866 E. Dickenson Pl.
Aurora, CO 80013
Phone: (303) 537-3592
Fax: (303) 537-3542
E-mail: corbelcomm1@aol.com
Web site: www.corbelonline.com
Member: PARW/CC
Certification: CPRW
Cover letter: 181

Louisville

Roberta F. Gamza
Career Ink
Louisville, CO 80027
Phone: (303) 955-3065
Fax: (303) 955-3065
E-mail: roberta@careerink.com
Web site: www.careerink.com
Member: CMI, NRWA,
   PARW/CC, PRWRA
Certification: CEIP, JCTC, CJST
Cover letters: 5, 111, 129, 238

Connecticut

Enfield

Louise Garver
Career Directions, LLC
115 Elm St., Ste. 203
Enfield, CT 06082
Phone: (860) 623-9476
Toll-free: (888) 222-3731
Fax: (860) 623-9473
E-mail: careerpro@cox.net
Web site:
   www.resumeimpact.com
Member: CMI, NRWA,
   PARW/CC, ACA, NCDA,
   ACPI, CPADN
Certification: MA, JCTC, CMP,
   CPRW, MCDP, CEIP
Cover letters: 18, 32, 45, 67, 79,
   80, 105, 166, 175, 208, 237,
   290
Resume: 17

Florida

Pompano Beach

Cathy Childs
133 N. Pompano Beach Blvd.,
   #310
Pompano Beach, FL 33062
Phone: (352) 223-0354
E-mail: hitchy-koo@juno.com
Member: PARW/CC
Certification: CPRW
Cover letters: 64, 200

Tampa

Gail Frank
Frankly Speaking: Resumes That
   Work!
10409 Greendale Dr.
Tampa, FL 33626
Phone: (813) 926-1353
Fax: (813) 926-1092
E-mail:
   gailfrank@post.harvard.edu
Web site:
   www.callfranklyspeaking.com
Member: PARW/CC, NRWA,
   PRWRA, CMI, SHRM, ASTD
Certification: NCRW, CPRW,
   JCTC, CEIP, MA
Cover letters: 58, 81, 82, 184,
   187, 190, 212, 236

Valrico

Cindy Kraft
Executive Essentials
P.O. Box 336
Valrico, FL 33595
Phone: (813) 655-0658
Fax: (813) 354-3483
E-mail: careermaster
   @exec-essentials.com
Web site:
   www.exec-essentials.com
Member: CMI, Coachville, IACC,
   AACC
Certification: CCMC, CCM,
   JCTC, CPRW
Cover letters: 1, 62, 73, 230

Georgia

Macon

Lea J. Clark
Lea Clark & Associates
4521 Dorset Dr.
Macon, GA 31206
Phone: (478) 781-4107
Fax: (478) 781-6960
E-mail: lclark352001@cox.net
Member: PRWRA, Who's Who
   in Executives and Professionals
Certification: CRW, BIT
Cover letters: 28, 143

Idaho

Boise

Denette D. Jones
Jones Career Specialties
4702 Gage St.
Boise, ID 83706
Phone: (208) 331-0561
Fax: (208) 361-0122
E-mail: ddjones
   @jonescareerspecialties.com
Web site:
   www.jonescareerspecialties.com
Member: CMI, NRWA, PRWRA
Cover letters: 84, 118, 174, 193,
   202, 231, 306

Illinois

Elk Grove Village

Joellyn Wittenstein-Schwerdlin
A-1 Quality Résumés & Career
* Services*
1819 Oriole Dr.
Elk Grove Village, IL 60007
Phone: (847) 285-1145
Fax: (847) 285-1838
E-mail: joellyn@interaccess.com
Web site:
  www.prwra.com/a-1resumes
Member: CMI, PRWRA
Certification: JCTC, CPRW
Cover letter: 285

Lincolnshire

Christine L. Dennison
Dennison Career Services
Lincolnshire, IL 60069
Phone: (847) 405-9775
E-mail: chris
  @thejobsearchcoach.com
Web site:
  www.thejobsearchcoach.com
Member: PARW/CC, Greater
  Lincolnshire Chamber of
  Commerce
Certification: CPC
Cover letters: 83, 253

Naperville

Patricia Chapman
CareerPro-Naperville, Inc.
520 E. Ogden Ave., Ste. 3
Naperville, IL 60563
Phone: (630) 983-8882
Fax: (630) 983-9021
E-mail: pat@career2day.com
Web site: www.career2day.com
Member: CMI, PRWRA, NAFE
Certification: CRW
Cover letters: 123, 225, 258, 310

Schaumburg

Steven Provenzano
A-Advanced Résumé Service, Inc.
* and ECS: Executive Career*
* Services, Inc.*
850 E. Higgins Rd., #125-Y
Schaumburg, IL 60173-4788
Phone: (630) 289-1999
Fax: (630) 582-1105
E-mail:
  ADVRESUMES@aol.com
Web site: TopSecretResumes.com
Member: PARW/CC
Certification: CPRW
Cover letter: 127

Waukegan

Eva Locke
Workforce Development
415 Washington St., Ste. 104
Waukegan, IL 60085
Phone: (847) 249-2200, ext. 110
Fax: (847) 249-2214
E-mail: elocke@co.lake.il.us
Web site:
  www.co.lake.il.us/workforce
Member: PRWRA
Cover letters: 91, 138

Iowa

Urbandale

Billie Ruth Sucher
Billie Sucher & Associates
7177 Hickman Rd., Ste. 10
Urbandale, IA 50322
Phone: (515) 276-0061
Fax: (515) 334-8076
E-mail: betwnjobs@aol.com
Member: CMI, SHRM
Certification: M.S., CTMS, CTSB
Resume: 19

Maryland

Hagerstown

Norine Dagliano
ekm Inspirations
14 N. Potomac St., Ste. 200
Hagerstown, MD 21740
Phone: (301) 766-2032
Fax: (301) 745-5700
E-mail: ndagliano@yahoo.com
Web site:
  www.ekminspirations.com
Member: CMI, PARW/CC
Certification: CPRW
Cover letters: 25, 26, 182, 303

Upper Marlboro

Daree Allen-Woodard
Woodard Communication &
* Design*
P.O. Box 475
Upper Marlboro, MD 20773-
  0475
Phone: (301) 213-6303
Fax: (301) 952-8857
E-mail: dareemark@netscape.net
Web site:
  www.WoodardCommDesign.com
Member: NRWA
Cover letter: 219

Massachusetts

Concord

Jean Cummings
A Resume For Today
123 Minot Rd.
Concord, MA 01742
Phone: (978) 371-9266
Toll-free: (800) 324-1699
Fax: (978) 964-0529
E-mail:
  jc@AResumeForToday.com
Web site:
  www.AResumeForToday.com
Member: CMI, PARW/CC
Certification: M.A.T., CPRW,
  CEIP
Cover letter: 147

Melrose

Jeanne Knight
Career and Job Search Coach
P.O. Box 828
Melrose, MA 02176
Phone: (617) 968-7747
E-mail: jeanne@careerdesigns.biz
Web site: www.careerdesigns.biz
Member: CMI, NRWA
Certification: JCTC
Resume: 6

Needham

Wendy Gelberg
Advantage Resumes
21 Hawthorn Ave.
Needham, MA 02492
Phone: (781) 444-0778
Fax: (781) 444-2778
E-mail: wgelberg@aol.com
Member: NRWA, CMI, Career
  Planning & Adult Development
  Network
Certification: CPRW, IJCTC
Cover letter: 97

Michigan
Clarkston

Jennifer Nell Ayres
Nell Resources
P.O. Box 2
Clarkston, MI 48347
Phone: (248) 969-9933
Fax: (248) 969-9935
E-mail:
    jennifer@nellresources.com
Web site:
    www.nellresources.com
Member: CMI, PRWRA
Cover letter: 276

Flint

Janet L. Beckstrom
Word Crafter
1717 Montclair Ave.
Flint, MI 48503-2074
Phone: (810) 232-9257
Toll-free: (800) 351-9818
Fax: (810) 232-9257
E-mail:
    wordcrafter@voyager.net
Member: CMI, PARW/CC
Certification: CPRW
Cover letters: 8, 13, 38, 46, 68,
    78, 194, 197, 215, 223

Trenton

Maria E. Hebda
Career Solutions, LLC
Trenton, MI 48183
Phone: (734) 676-9170
Fax: (734) 676-9487
E-mail:
    mhebda@writingresumes.com
Web site:
    www.WritingResumes.com
Member: PARW/CC, CMI,
    NRWA, PRWRA
Certification: CCMC, CPRW
Cover letters: 27, 74, 176, 288

Minnesota
Rochester

Beverley Drake
*CareerVision Resume & Job
    Search Systems*
1816 Baihly Hills Dr. SW
Rochester, MN 55902
Phone: (507) 252-9825
Fax: (507) 252-1559
E-mail: bdcprw@aol.com
Member: CMI, PARW/CC
Certification: CEIP, IJCTC,
    CPRW, CPC
Cover letters: 87, 90, 109, 112,
    137, 241, 300, 308

Missouri
Kansas City

Gina Taylor
A-1 Advantage Career Services
1111 W. 77th Terrace
Kansas City, MO 64114
Phone: (816) 523-9100 and
    (913) 341-5500
Fax: (816) 523-6566
E-mail:
    ginaresume@sbcglobal.net
Web site:
    www.excitingresumes.com and
    www.ginataylor.com
Member: CMI, PARW/CC
Certification: CPRW, MRW
Cover letters: 6, 164, 239

New Jersey
Edison

Patricia Traina-Duckers
The Resume Writer
P.O. Box 595
Edison, NJ 08818-0595
Phone: (732) 239-8533
Fax: (732) 906-5636
E-mail:
    sales@theresumewriter.com
Web site:
    www.theresumewriter.com
Member: CMI, PRWRA, NRWA,
    PARW/CC
Certification: CPRW, CRW, CEIP
Cover letter: 217

Flemington Area

Carol A. Altomare
World Class Résumés
P.O. Box 483
Three Bridges, NJ 08887-0483
Phone: (908) 237-1883
Fax: (908) 237-2069
E-mail:
    caa@worldclassresumes.com
Web site:
    www.worldclassresumes.com
Member: PARW/CC
Certification: CPRW
Cover letters: 2, 14, 19, 34, 37,
    39, 40, 54, 66, 70, 99, 101,
    124, 133, 135, 150, 158, 159,
    179, 186, 201, 203, 218, 229,
    247
Resume: 15

Iselin

See Marlboro.

Mahwah

Igor Shpudejko
Career Focus
23 Parsons Ct.
Mahwah, NJ 07430
Phone: (201) 825-2865
Fax: (201) 825-7711
E-mail: Ishpudejko@aol.com
Web site:
    www.CareerInFocus.com
Member: CMI, PARW/CC
Certification: CPRW, JCTC,
    MBA, BSIE
Cover letters: 4, 72, 131

Marlboro

Beverley and Mitchell I. Baskin
BBCS Counseling Services
6 Alberta Dr.
Marlboro, NJ 07746
    Also at Iselin, NJ, and
    Princeton, NJ
Toll-free: (800) 300-4079
Fax: (732) 972-8846
E-mail: bbcs@att.net and
    info@bbcscounseling.com
Web sites:
    www.baskincareer.com and
    www.job-research.com
Member: NRWA, NCDA,
    NECA, MACCA, AMHCA
Certification: Ed.S, MA, LPC,
    NCCC, MCC, CPRW
Cover letters: 108, 132, 155,
    296, 299
Resumes: 10, 22, 23

Princeton

See Marlboro.

West Paterson

Melanie Noonan
Peripheral Pro, LLC
560 Lackawanna Ave.
West Paterson, NJ 07424
Phone: (973) 785-3011
Fax: (973) 256-6285
E-mail: PeriPro1@aol.com
Member: NRWA, PARW/CC
Certification: CPS
Cover letters: 16, 86, 148, 157,
    207, 255, 286, 297
Resumes: 3, 8, 12, 21

New York

Altamont

John Femia
Custom Résumé & Writing Service
1690 Township Rd.
Altamont, NY 12009
Phone: (518) 872-1305
Fax: (518) 872-1305
E-mail: customresume1@aol.com
Member: PARW/CC
Certification: CPRW
Cover letters: 43, 71, 76, 171,
    191

Brentwood

Ann Baehr
Best Resumes
122 Sheridan St.
Brentwood, NY 11717
Phone: (631) 435-1879
Fax: (631) 977-2821
E-mail:
    resumesbest@earthlink.net
Web site:
    www.e-bestresumes.com
Member: CMI, NRWA,
    PARW/CC
Certification: CPRW
Cover letters: 60, 113, 114, 149,
    195, 240, 248, 287
Resumes: 13, 14, 16

Hauppauge

Donna M. Farrise
Dynamic Resumes of Long Island,
    Inc.
300 Motor Pkwy., Ste. 200
Hauppauge, NY 11788
Phone: (631) 951-4120
Toll-free: (800) 528-6796 and
    (800) 951-5191
Fax: (631) 952-1817
E-mail:
    donna@dynamicresumes.com
Web site:
    www.dynamicresumes.com
Member: CMI, NRWA,
    PARW/CC
Certification: JCTC
Cover letters: 96, 115, 145, 283,
    284

Hicksville

Deanna Verbouwens
Ace in the Hole Resume Writing &
    Career Services
14 Mitchell Ct.
Hicksville, NY 11801
Phone: (516) 942-5986
E-mail: verbouwens@yahoo.com
    and info@aceinthehole.net
Web site: www.aceinthehole.net
Member: PARW/CC
Cover letters: 12, 44

Medford

Deborah Wile Dib
Advantage Resumes of New York
Executive Power Coach
77 Buffalo Ave.
Medford, NY 11763
Phone: (631) 475-8513
Fax: (501) 421-7790
E-mail: deborah.dib
    @advantageresumes.com
Web sites:
    www.advantageresumes.com
    and
    www.executivepowercoach.com
Member: CMI, NRWA,
    PARW/CC, PRWRA, NAFE
Certification: CCM, CCMC,
    NCRW, CPRW, CEIP, JCTC
Cover letter: 160

Mount Morris

Salome A. Farraro
Careers TOO
3123 Moyer Rd.
Mount Morris, NY 14510
Phone: (585) 658-2480
Toll-free: (877) 436-9378
Fax: (585) 658-2480
E-mail:
    sfarraro@careers-too.com and
    srttoo@frontiernet.net
Web site: www.careers-too.com
Member: PARW/CC
Certification: CPRW
Cover letters: 94, 271, 292

Poughkeepsie

Kristin M. Coleman
Custom Career Services
44 Hillcrest Dr.
Poughkeepsie, NY 12603
Phone: (845) 452-8274
Fax: (845) 452-7789
E-mail:
    kristincoleman44@yahoo.com
Member: CMI
Cover letters: 50, 85, 206, 280

Riverdale

Ilona Vanderwoude
Career Branches
P.O. Box 330
Riverdale, NY 10471
Phone: (718) 884-2213
Fax: (646) 349-2218
E-mail:
    ilona@careerbranches.com
Web site:
    www.CareerBranches.com
Member: CMI, PRWRA,
    Coachville
Certification: CCMC, CPRW,
    CJST, CEIP
Cover letters: 198, 264, 309

Rochester

Arnold G. Boldt
Arnold-Smith Associates
625 Panorama Trail, Bldg. One,
    Ste. 120C
Rochester, NY 14625
Phone: (585) 383-0350
Fax: (585) 387-0516
E-mail: Arnie@ResumeSOS.com
Web site: www.ResumeSOS.com
Member: CMI, PARW/CC,
    NRWA, PRWRA
Certification: CPRW, JCTC
Cover letters: 144, 211, 234

Smithtown

Linda Matias
CareerStrides
34 E. Main St., #276
Smithtown, NY 11787
Phone: (631) 382-2425
Fax: (631) 382-2425
E-mail: linda@careerstrides.com
Web site:
   www.careerstrides.com
Member: CMI, NRWA
Certification: CEIP, JCTC
Cover letter: 51

Staten Island

Deborah Ann Ramos
Aerobi's Computerized Typing
   Service
446 Pelton Ave.
Staten Island, NY 10310-2132
Phone: (718) 815-4638
Fax: (718) 815-2431
E-mail: aerobi@aol.com
Web site:
   aerobisresumeservices.com
Member: NRWA, PARW/CC
Certification: CPRW
Cover letters: 69, 95
Resume: 7

Victor

Kim Little
Fast Track Resumes
1281 Courtney Dr.
Victor, NY 14564
Phone: (585) 742-2467
Toll-free: (877) 263-7581
Fax: (585) 742-1907
E-mail:
   info@fast-trackresumes.com
Web site:
   www.fast-trackresumes.com
Member: CMI, PARW/CC
Certification: JCTC
Cover letter: 254

North Carolina
Charlotte

Doug Morrison
Career Power
2915 Providence Rd., Ste. 250-B
Charlotte, NC 28211
Phone: (704) 365-0773
Fax: (704) 365-3411
E-mail: dmpwresume@aol.com
Web site:
   www.careerpowerresume.com
Member: CMI, PARW/CC,
   PRWRA
Certification: CPRW
Cover letters: 7, 98, 120, 263,
   273, 302

Ohio
Athens

Melissa L. Kasler
Résumé Impressions
540 W. Union St., Ste. D
Athens, OH 45701
Phone: (740) 592-3993
Toll-free: (800) 516-0334
Fax: (740) 592-1352
E-mail: resume@frognet.net
Web site:
   www.resumeimpressions.com
Member: CMI, PARW/CC
Certification: CPRW
Cover letters: 49, 56, 293, 304

Findlay

Sharon Pierce-Williams, M.Ed.
The Résumé.Doc
609 Lincolnshire Lane
Findlay, OH 45840
Phone: (419) 422-0228
Fax: (419) 425-1185
E-mail:
   Sharon@TheResumeDoc.com
Web site:
   www.TheResumeDoc.com
Member: CMI, PARW/CC,
   Findlay-Hancock County
   Chamber of Commerce
Certification: M.Ed., CPRW
Cover letter: 36

Huber Heights

Teena Rose
Résumé to Referral
7211 Taylorsville Rd., Office
   208
Huber Heights, OH 45424
Phone: (937) 236-1360
Fax: (937) 236-1351
E-mail:
   admin@resumetoreferral.com
Web site:
   www.resumebycprw.com
Member: PARW/CC, CMI
Certification: CPRW, CEIP, CCM
Cover letter: 140

Mogadore

Tara G. Papp
Accomplished Résumés
1196 Waterloo Rd.
Mogadore, OH 44260
Phone: (330) 628-0073
Fax: (330) 628-0073
E-mail: tgpapp@aol.com
Web site: www.
   accomplishedresumes.com
Member: NRWA, PARW/CC,
   SHRM, SIOP
Certification: CPRW
Cover letters: 42, 55, 117, 275

Oklahoma
Tulsa

Sally Altman
Career Résumés
5321 S. Sheridan, Ste. 13
Tulsa, OK 74145-7509
Phone: (918) 663-4200
Fax: (918) 663-4202
E-mail:
   sally@careerresumesOK.com
Web site: careerresumesOK.com
Member: PARW/CC
Certification: CPRW
Cover letters: 89, 177, 180, 196,
   220, 251, 256

Oregon

Portland

Rosie Bixel
A Personal Scribe
4800 SW Macadam Ave., Ste. 105
Portland, OR 97239
Phone: (503) 254-8682
Fax: (503) 255-3012
E-mail: aps@bhhgroup.com
Web site: www. bhhgroup.com/resume.asp
Member: NRWA
Cover letters: 20, 75, 188, 216, 224, 249, 252, 277, 281, 294

Jennifer Rydell
Simplify Your Life Career Services
6327-C SW Capitol Hwy. PMB 243
Portland, OR 97239-1937
Phone: (503) 977-1955
Fax: (503) 245-4212
E-mail: jennifer @simplifyyourliferesumes.com
Web site: www. simplifyyourliferesumes.com
Member: CMI, NRWA, PARW/CC
Certification: CPRW, NCRW, CCM
Cover letters: 33, 57, 130, 192

Pennsylvania

Harleysville

Jan Holliday
Arbridge Communications
Harleysville, PA 19438
Phone: (215) 513-7420
Toll-free: (866) 513-7420
E-mail: info@arbridge.com
Web site: www.arbridge.com
Member: NRWA, CMI, IWA
Certification: MA, NCRW, Certified Webmaster
Cover letters: 9, 23, 204, 269

Media

Karen Conway
Premier Resumes
1008 N. Providence Rd.
Media, PA 19063
Phone: (610) 566-8422
Toll-free: (866) 241-5300
Fax: (610) 566-3047
E-mail: premresume@aol.com
Member: PARW/CC
Certification: CPRW, CEIP
Cover letters: 48, 53, 104, 107, 161, 205, 260

Rhode Island

Newport Area

Edward A. Turilli
Director, Career Development Center
Salve Regina University
Anthem Résumé and Career Services (ARCS)
918 Lafayette Rd.
North Kingstown, RI 02852
Phone: (401) 268-3020
Fax: (401) 341-2994
E-mail: turillie@salve.edu
Web site: www. salve.edu/office_careerdev
Member: CMI, PARW/CC, NCDA, NACE, RICC
Certification: MA
Cover letters: 47, 52, 88, 92, 93, 214, 221, 235, 266, 289
Resume: 9

Tennessee

Hendersonville

Carolyn S. Braden
Braden Résumé Solutions
108 La Plaza Dr.
Hendersonville, TN 37075
Phone: (615) 822-3317
Fax: (615) 826-9611
E-mail: bradenresume @comcast.net
Member: CMI, PARW/CC
Certification: CPRW
Cover letter: 307

Texas

Austin

Karen Wrigley
AMW Career & Résumé Services
Austin, TX
Phone: (512) 246-7423
Toll-free: (800) 880-7088
Fax: (512) 246-7433
Mobile: (512) 630-4250
E-mail: kwrigley@amwresumes.com
Web site: www.amwresumes.com
Member: CMI
Certification: CPRW, CJCTC
Cover letters: 213, 227, 228, 250, 259, 265, 268, 270, 274

Bishop

Nick V. Marino
Outcome Résumés and Career
710 Aurora Dr.
Bishop, TX 78343
Phone (631) 584-3121
Toll-free: (866) 899-6509
Fax: (270) 837-3852
E-mail: outcomerez@earthlink.net and outcomeresumes@stx.rr.com
Web site: www.outcomeresumes.com and www. federalresumeservice.com
Member: CMI, PARW/CC, PRWRA, AJST, CPADN
Certification: CPRW, CRW, CEIP, CFCM, CFRW/C, CFJST
Cover letters: 61, 65, 119, 282

Lubbock

Daniel J. Dorotik, Jr.
100PercentResumes
9803 Clinton Ave.
Lubbock, TX 79424
Phone: (806) 783-9900
Fax: (214) 722-1510
E-mail: dan@100percentresumes.com
Web site: www.100percentresumes.com
Member: NRWA, PARW/CC
Certification: NCRW
Cover letters: 41, 102, 128, 139, 141, 165, 169, 172, 183, 222, 226, 246, 267, 278, 279, 291
Resumes: 1, 5, 11

Edith A. Rische
Write Away Resume
5908 73rd St.
Lubbock, TX 79424-1920
Phone: (806) 798-0881
Fax: (806) 798-3213
E-mail: erische@door.net
Web site:
   www.writeawayresume.com
Member: NRWA
Certification: NCRW, JCTC
Cover letters: 121, 262
Resume: 2

Tyler

Ann Klint
Ann's Professional Résumé Service
2130 Kennebunk Lane
Tyler, TX 75703-0301
Phone: (903) 509-8333
Fax: (734) 448-1962
E-mail: Resumes-Ann@tyler.net
   and ann_klint@hotmail.com
Member: NRWA
Cover letter: 110
Resume: 18

Victoria

MeLisa Rogers
Ultimate Career
270 Live Oak Lane
Victoria, TX 77905
Phone: (361) 575-6100
Toll-free: (866) 573-7863
Fax: (361) 574-8830
E-mail:
   success@ultimatecareer.biz
Web site:
   www.ultimatecareer.biz
Member: PARW/CC, SHRM,
   ASTD
Certification: M.S. HRD, CPRW
Cover letters: 29, 30, 125, 185

Virginia
Reston

Helen Oliff
Principal
Turning Point
2307 Freetown Ct., #12C
Reston, VA 20191
Phone: (703) 716-0077
Fax: (703) 995-0706
E-mail:
   helen@turningpointnow.com
Web site:
   www.turningpointnow.com
Member: CMI, PARW/CC
Certification: CPRW, CFRWC,
   ECI
Cover letters: 136, 232

Washington
Bellingham

Janice M. Shepherd
Write On Career Keys
Top of Alabama Hill
Bellingham, WA 98226-4260
Phone: (360) 738-7958
Fax: (360) 738-1189
E-mail: Janice@
   WriteOnCareerKeys.com
Web site:
   www.WriteOnCareerKeys.com
Member: CMI, PARW/CC
Certification: CPRW, JCTC, CEIP
Cover letter: 168

Seatac

Diana Ramirez, RC
Ramirez Consulting Group
2604 S. 208th St.
Seatac, WA 98198
Phone: (206) 870-7366
Mobile: (253) 332-5521
E-mail:
   ramirezconsulting@yahoo.com
Web site:
   www.ramirezconsulting.us
Member: NRWA, NCDA,
   NWWA
Certification: Licensed
   Counselor, State of Washington
   SHRM, Human Resources
   Management
Cover letters: 10, 31, 295, 298

Seattle

Alice Hanson
Aim Resumes
P.O. Box 75054
Seattle, WA 98175-0054
Phone: (206) 527-3100
Fax: (206) 527-3101
E-mail: alice@aimresumes.com
Web site: www.aimresumes.com
Member: CMI, NRWA,
   PARW/CC, PSCDA, NRWA
Certification: CPRW
Cover letter: 173

Wisconsin
Glendale

Michele J. Haffner
Advanced Résumé Services
1314 W. Paradise Ct.
Glendale, WI 53209
Toll-free: (877) 247-1677
Fax: (414) 247-1808
E-mail:
   info@resumeservices.com
Web site:
   www.resumeservices.com
Member: PARW, Coachville
Certification: CPRW, JCTC
Resume: 4

Professional Organizations, Certifications, and Finding a Resume Writer or Career Coach

The following sections contain contact information for various career-related organizations and certification programs.

Resume Writers' Organizations

To contact the resume writers' organizations, see the following information:

Career Masters Institute
119 Old Stable Rd.
Lynchburg, VA 24503
Phone: (434) 386-3100
Fax: (434) 386-3200
E-mail: wendyenelow@cminstitute.com
Web site: www.cminstitute.com

National Résumé Writers' Association
P.O. Box 184
Nesconset, NY 11767
Phone: (888) NRWA-444
E-mail: AdminManager@nrwaweb.com
Web site: www.nrwaweb.com

Professional Association of Résumé Writers and Career Coaches
1388 Brightwaters Blvd., NE
St. Petersburg, FL 33704
Phone: (800) 822-7279
Fax: (727) 894-1277
E-mail: PARWCCHQ@aol.com
Web site: www.parw.com

Professional Résumé Writing and Research Association
1106 Coolidge Blvd.
Lafayette, LA 70503
Phone: (800) 225-8688
E-mail: laurie@prwra.com
Web site: www.prwra.com

Federal Job Search and Resumes

For information on the certification programs for Certified Federal Job Search Trainer (CFJST) or Certified Federal Resume Writer & Coach (CFRWC), contact the following:

Ten Steps to a Federal Job™
The Resume Place, Inc.
89 Mellor Ave.
Baltimore, MD 21228
Phone: (410) 744-4324
Fax: (410) 744-0112
E-mail: kathryn@resume-place.com
Web site: www.resume-place.com or www.tensteps.com

Finding a Resume Writer or Career Coach

For additional online resources regarding certified career professionals, visit the following Web sites:

www.CertifiedResumeWriters.com
www.CertifiedCareerCoaches.com

Occupation Index

Note: The following entries are, in most cases, target positions for the job seekers. (If the target position is not stated clearly, the current or most recent position is listed here.) The numbers are cover letter numbers in the Gallery, not page numbers.

Resumes Index

Note: The following occupations represent the current or most recent position of the job seekers. The numbers are resume numbers in the Exhibit of Resumes, not page numbers.

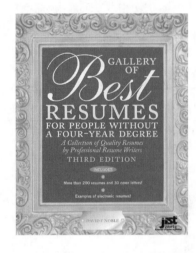

APR - - 2009

pert Resumes for
Teachers and Educators

Wendy S. Enelow and Louise M. Kursmark

Professional resume writers share their step-by-step resume writing secrets, as well as samples of real job-getting resumes. This gallery of more than 180 pages of carefully selected sample resumes is targeted to helping you land the top teaching and training jobs: Early Childhood Educators, Elementary Educators, Secondary-School Educators, Specialty Teachers, Educational Support Professionals, University Educators, Educational Administrators, and Corporate Training and Development Professionals.

ISBN 1-56370-799-3 / Order Code LP-J7993 / **$16.95**

Expert Resumes for
Computer and Web Jobs

Wendy S. Enelow and Louise M. Kursmark

Contains more than 180 pages of sample resumes targeted to high-tech jobs—from entry-level to executive! Professional resume writers share their secrets and sample resumes for landing today's fastest-growing, highest-paying computer and Web jobs. The authors provide step-by-step writing instructions, techniques for deciding what type of resume to use, and a directory of online job search resources.

ISBN 1-56370-798-5 / Order Code LP-J7985 / **$16.95**

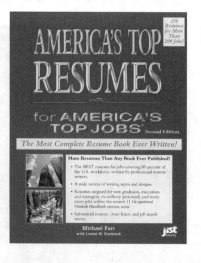

America's Top Resumes
for America's Top Jobs, Second Edition

Michael Farr with Louise M. Kursmark

The only book with sample resumes for all major occupations covering 80 percent of the workforce. Nearly 400 of the best resumes submitted by professional resume writers, grouped by occupation, and annotated by the authors. Includes career planning and job search advice.

ISBN 1-56370-856-6 / Order Code LP-J8566 / **$19.95**